STRESS AND FISH

Edited by

A. D. PICKERING

Freshwater Biological Association
Cumbria, England

1981

ACADEMIC PRESS

A Subsidiary of Harcourt Brace Jovanovich, Publishers

London   New York   Toronto   Sydney   San Francisco

ACADEMIC PRESS INC. (LONDON) LTD
24–28 Oval Road,
London NW1

U.S. Edition published by
ACADEMIC PRESS INC.
111 Fifth Avenue,
New York, New York 10003

British Library Cataloguing in Publication Data

Stress and fish.
  1. Stress (Physiology)
  2. Stress (Psychology)
  I. Pickering, A. D.
  597'.5041'88   QL615

  ISBN 0–12–554550-9

  LCCN: 81–67907

Printed in Great Britain by
J. W. Arrowsmith Ltd, Bristol

Contributors

R. Billard Laboratoire de Physiologie des Poissons, I.N.R.A. 78350 Jouy-en-Josas, France

C. Bry Laboratoire de Physiologie des Poissons, I.N.R.A, 78350 Jouy-en-Josas, France

E. M. Donaldson West Vancouver Laboratory, Resource Services Branch, Department of Fisheries and Oceans, 4160 Marine Drive, West Vancouver, British Columbia, Canada

F. B. Eddy Department of Biological Sciences, Dundee University, Dundee, DD1 4HN, Scotland

J. M. Elliott Freshwater Biological Association, The Ferry House, Far Sawrey, Nr. Ambleside, Cumbria, LA22 0LP, England

A. E. Ellis D.A.F.S. Marine Laboratory, P.O. Box 101, Victoria Road, Aberdeen, AB9 8DB, Scotland

T. C. Fletcher N.E.R.C. Institute of Marine Biochemistry, St. Fittick's Rd., Aberdeen, AB1 3RA, Scotland

C. Gillet Laboratoire de Physiologie des Poissons, I.N.R.A., 78350 Jouy-en-Josas, France

A. S. Grimm Department of Zoology, The Brambell Laboratories, University College of North Wales, Bangor, Gwynedd, LL57 2UW, Wales

G. M. Hughes Research Unit for Comparative Animal Respiration, University of Bristol, Woodland Road, Bristol, BS8 1UG, England

F. Mazeaud Institute Océanographique, 195, Rue Saint-Jacques, 75005 Paris, France

M. M. Mazeaud Institute Océanographique, 195, Rue Saint-Jacques, 75005 Paris, France

D. J. McLeay Aquatic Toxicology Division of Applied Biology, B.C. Research, 3650 Wesbrook Mall, Vancouver, British Columbia, Canada

M. Nikinmaa Department of Zoology, Division of Physiology, University of Helsinki, Arkadiankatu 7, SF-00100 Helsinki 10, Finland

A. D. Pickering Freshwater Biological Association, The Ferry House, Far Sawrey, Nr. Ambleside, Cumbria, LA22 0LP, England

C. B. Schreck Oregon Cooperative Fishery Research Unit, Oregon State University, Corvallis, Oregon 97331, U.S.A.

G. R. Smart Shearwater Fish Farming Limited, Finnarts Bay, Ballantrae, Ayrshire, Scotland

A. Soivio Department of Zoology, Division of Physiology, University of Helsinki, Arkadiankatu 7, SF-00100 Helsinki 10, Finland

G. A. Wedemeyer U.S. Department of the Interior, Fish and Wildlife Service, National Fisheries Research Center, Building 204, Naval Support Activity, Seattle, Washington 98115, U.S.A.

Preface

The problems of stress, in relation to fish and fisheries biology, have received increasing attention during the past decade. Information is scattered throughout the scientific literature but until now there has been no single source of reference to collate this research. With this in mind, the council of the Fisheries Society of the British Isles concluded that an international symposium on the subject would form a suitable vehicle for the exchange and dissemination of such information and bring together, for the first time, those fish biologists, fisheries scientists and managers with an active interest in the problems of stress. The symposium "Stress in Fish" was held at the University of East Anglia, Norwich, England, September 9–12, 1980, and among the participants were 14 invited speakers whose contributions form the basis of this book. The organizers deliberately maintained a broad interpretation of the concept of stress in order to attract participants with different interests and from different backgrounds thereby promoting healthy discussion. The contributors to this book were invited to review specific aspects of the phenomenon of stress and, at the same time, present original research. Consequently this volume not only collates existing information but extends our present knowledge in the form of hitherto unpublished work.

In the first part of the book, emphasis is placed on the endocrinological/physiological responses of fish to stress—without this fundamental information it is difficult to interpret the fish's subsequent performance. Problems of stress are of particular importance in the intensive cultivation of fish and this area is covered in detail by several contributors. Similarly, the harmful influences of man's activities on the aquatic environment and the subsequent responses of fish under such circumstances are well documented. It is inevitable in a book of this type that some degree of overlap of interest will occur and to this end the individual papers have been cross-referenced. This should enable the reader to pursue a subject that may not be the prime consideration of one particular author. The abstracts of the oral and poster papers presented at the Norwich symposium are also included in this volume.

The organization of the symposium and the preparation of this book has involved the cooperation of many people, to all of whom I am extremely grateful. The officers and council of the F.S.B.I. provided the organizational framework and gave their services willingly, when required. I am particularly pleased to acknowledge and thank the other members of the organizing committee: Dr A. S. Grimm (Bangor), Mr R. Lloyd (M.A.F.F.), Dr D. J. Solomon (M.A.F.F. and Meetings Secretary of the F.S.B.I.), Dr D. J. Swift (M.A.F.F.) and Dr G. Shelton (U.E.A.). Dr Solomon, in conjunction with Mr R. Lloyd (U.E.A.), was responsible for the smooth running of the symposium at Norwich and Dr Grimm organized the poster session and edited the abstracts for this volume. The symposium was opened by Mr E. D. Le Cren (F.B.A. and President of the F.S.B.I.) who, together with the chairmen—Prof. J. H. Phillips (Hull), Dr R. Billard (I.N.R.A., France), Dr B. J. Hill (M.A.F.F.), Mr R. Lloyd (M.A.F.F.), Dr E. M. Donaldson (Vancouver), Dr A. S. Grimm (Bangor)—contributed most significantly to the success of the meeting. I am also grateful to the director and staff of the M.A.F.F. Fisheries Laboratory, Lowestoft for inviting the participants to visit their laboratory during the course of the symposium. With regard to the editorial duties involved in the preparation of this book my thanks are due to all the contributors for their splendid cooperation, Dr J. M. Elliott (F.B.A.) for valuable advice, the F.B.A. librarian Mr J. E. M. Horne and his staff for help on numerous occasions and to Mrs J. Hawksford for her efficiency in typing the manuscripts. Finally, I would like to thank my wife, Christine, for her support and encouragement throughout the whole venture.

F.B.A. Windermere
May, 1981

A. D. PICKERING

Contents

    A. S. GRIMM

    Abstracts of the Oral Papers 325
    Abstracts of the Poster Papers 337
    Fish Species Index 355
    Subject Index 359

1. Introduction: the Concept of Biological Stress

A. D. PICKERING

Freshwater Biological Association, Far Sawrey, Nr Ambleside, Cumbria, England

There are few concepts that have evoked as much discussion and disagreement as that of stress when applied to biological systems. Indeed, the problems of loose or inconsistent terminology have prompted some biologists to advocate abolishing the word stress in favour of other, less equivocal terms. Despite these difficulties, the use of biological stress as a rubric to encompass those harmful factors which influence biological systems not only still persists but appears to attract increasing attention. Consequently, I believe that it is more constructive in this introductory chapter to attempt to expose some of the basic reasons for this uncertainty and to consider the relevance of stress in the specific context of fish and fisheries biology.

I TERMINOLOGY

The concept of biological stress has stimulated numerous, formal definitions in the scientific literature, the variety of which bears testimony to the difficulty of establishing a single, comprehensive definition. All definitions of stress, however, share the common premise of a stimulus acting on a biological system and the subsequent reaction of the system. Even at this level there exists a fundamental difference in terminology. Some workers (e.g. Cannon, 1935; Meier, 1972; Leffler, 1978; Ulanowicz, 1978) equate stress with the stimulus whereas others (e.g. Esch *et al.*, 1975; Esch and Hazen, 1978; Lugo, 1978) define stress as the response of the system. Moreover, in the widely accepted work of Professor Hans Selye, stress was originated in terms of the applied stimulus (Selye, 1946) and subsequently redefined as the response of the system, with the stimulus now being termed the stressor (Selye, 1956). For consistency of definition there are certain attractions in maintaining the mechanical analogy by using the word stress to refer to the stimulus. Although strain, the mechanical consequence of stress, was used by Cannon (1935) in his classical paper on homeostasis, it has not been widely adopted to describe the reaction of a biological system to stress.

Because this whole problem is really one of semantics and the relative merits of the different systems of terminology are arguable, no attempt has been made to *impose* a single system of nomenclature on the authors contributing to this book. In this way, it is hoped to present a wide view of the concept of stress as it appears to biologists from different backgrounds. However, it is worthwhile echoing the sentiments of Lazarus (1971) who urged that each scientist, whatever his disciplinary or conceptual bias might be, should take care to specify clearly the manner in which he uses certain stress concepts thereby avoiding "the worst pitfalls of loose terminology". In this respect, contributors have taken care to maintain consistency in their use of terminology within each paper. For the purposes of this introduction, unless otherwise specified, stress will be used to describe a stimulus, the reaction of the system being the stress response.

II MEASUREMENT OF STRESS RESPONSES

The phenomenon of a stimulus and a subsequent reaction is, of course, a basic feature of all biological processes regardless of the level of organization and so the outstanding problem is to distinguish between stress responses and normal adaptive responses. Most workers probably have an intuitive notion of what constitutes a stress response but difficulties arise when attempts are made to define this in precise terms. The majority of definitions refer to stress responses as reactions which deviate, either qualitatively or quantitatively from normality. At first inspection this approach seems to be useful, but its value hinges upon a clear understanding of what constitutes normality. Unfortunately, the concept of normality is probably as elusive as that of stress when it comes to rigorous definition, and one can be drawn into a circular argument in which stress responses are defined as non-normal responses with normality being defined as the unstressed situation. For the present, it is simpler to think of stress responses as extreme forms of a continuous series of adaptive responses.

This lack of a clear, unequivocal distinction between stress and normality has prompted more quantitative approaches to the problem. In general, these fall into two categories—examples of both can be found in this book. The first approach is based upon quantifying the immediate physiological responses of an animal to stress and the second is concerned with measuring long-term changes in the performance capacity of an animal. The classical work on the morphological and physiological responses of animals to stress is undoubtedly that pioneered by Selye (1936, 1946, 1950, 1956), work that originated from an interest in medical physiology. In order to discuss this work it is necessary to use the terminology ultimately adopted by Selye in which stress is defined in terms of the response of the animal with the stimulus being referred to as the stressor. Selye's concept of stress differs from others in that stress is considered to be an essential component of normal metabolism, rather than a deviation from normality. The central feature of this thesis is one of a common response to a wide variety of stressors. The components of this response are collectively known as the General Adaptation Syndrome (GAS) which can be divided on a temporal basis into stages of alarm, resistance and exhaustion. As Selye carefully points out, the totality of responses to a stressor is composed of some reactions which are specific to that particular stimulus and other responses (i.e. stress) which are common reactions to all stressors regardless of their nature. Thus, the GAS is rarely, if ever, present in a pure form and it requires considerable investigation to distinguish the general responses from the specific ones.

However, the validity of a concept of physiological non-specificity has been recently challenged (Mason, 1975a, b) on the grounds that the apparently common response to a wide variety of stimuli does, in fact, represent a specific response to a common feature of all the stimuli—one of emotional arousal or awareness. This psychological component of stress has been demonstrated in fish by Schreck (1981, this volume) who presents evidence to show that elimination of "awareness" reduces the magnitude of the physiological stress response. If the applicability of the GAS to fish is to be validated, it is essential that the considerable effort already made towards a detailed analysis of physiological stress responses is maintained. In this connection, the papers by Donaldson, Eddy, Hughes, Mazeaud and Mazeaud (1981, this volume) examine and review many of the neuroendocrine/physiological responses of fish to stress.

The other approach to quantifying the response of animals to stress is by measuring changes in their performance capacity. The ultimate measure of performance of an individual is based on survival. Brett (1958), in a definition which relates primarily to individual animals, considers stress to be "a state produced by any environmental factor which extends the normal adaptive responses of an animal, or which disturbs the normal functioning to such an extent that the chances of survival are significantly reduced". This definition is useful when referring to individuals but it is not so readily applicable to higher levels of organization (e.g. populations) in which, under certain circumstances, a decrease in the probability of survival of one individual may directly increase the probability of survival of other members of the population by means of reduced, intraspecific competition. Elliott (1981, this volume) examines the effects of thermal stress on fish from a similar viewpoint, using survival as the ultimate measure of success. Other, more specific aspects of performance capacity can also be measured, by monitoring changes in growth rate, for example (Elliott, 1981, this volume; Smart, 1981, this volume) or reproductive success (Billard et al., 1981, this volume) and specific challenge tests, based on the performance capacities of fish in the face of environmental stresses, are reviewed by Wedemeyer and McLeay (1981, this volume).

These two approaches to measuring stress responses should not be mutually exclusive although they have, on occasions, resulted in differences of opinion between workers. It is conventional to classify stress responses as primary (neural and neuro-endocrine responses) and secondary (the physiological consequences of such primary responses), a system used by Mazeaud et al. (1977) and extended by Wedemeyer and McLeay (1981, this volume) to include tertiary responses such as changes in behaviour, decreased growth rate and increased susceptibility to diseases. However, this system should be seen for what it really is—a system of convenience, and it should not disguise the fact that the response of an animal to stress is an integrated response involving aspects at all levels (primary, secondary and tertiary). If stress responses are considered at only one level, considerable difficulties may arise when examining the reactions of fish to certain pollutants or to chronic stresses such as overcrowding. For example, Schreck and Lorz (1978) failed to show any significant effects of cadmium on the plasma cortisol levels of coho salmon, *Oncorhynchus kisutch*, even though the pollutant was present at levels which were ultimately lethal. Thus, if changes in plasma cortisol levels are accepted as valid indicators of stress responses in fish (see Donaldson, 1981, this volume) and part of Selye's GAS, a discrepancy exists between assessment of the response in physiological terms and in terms of the performance capacity (in this case the probability of survival) of the fish. Similarly, ideal compensation in plasma cortisol levels occurs in fish exposed to a chronic crowding stress (Schreck, 1981, this volume) although the performance of the fish in terms of growth, resistance to infection etc. may still be impaired. The short-term endocrinological/physiological responses of fish to stress may, in themselves, reduce the performance capacity of fish but it does not follow that a reduction in performance is always associated with such responses. If stress responses are defined in terms of the performance of a fish, the immediate physiological changes occurring in response to most, but not all, forms of stress may be considered as just one type of stress response, perhaps more closely allied to "fright", which may under certain circumstances reduce the performance capacity of the fish. For a conceptual model of the inter-relationships between stress, the environment and performance capacity the reader is referred to Schreck (1981, this volume).

III RELEVANCE OF STRESS TO FISH AND FISHERIES BIOLOGY

Regardless of its validity, Selye's concept of a General Adaptation Syndrome does highlight an important aspect of many of the primary and secondary responses of an individual to stress—i.e. they are essentially adaptive. It is inevitable, and proper, that much has been written about the deleterious effects of such responses in fish but it is important to bear in mind that these reactions have evolved as adaptive mechanisms which enable the animal to maintain homeostasis in the face of an external force. In simple terms this may be seen as a general shift from anabolism to catabolism thereby allowing the animal to utilize energy reserves not normally available. With fish, a likely behavioural (tertiary) response under these circumstances would be flight from the stress, but under conditions of chronic stress (e.g. those sometimes associated with intensive fish culture) it may not be possible for the animal to escape. In these cases, a stress response will not only be ineffective but may be ultimately deleterious to the state of well-being of the fish. For the purposes of intensive cultivation, attention is now being given to the possibility of accelerating the selection of strains of fish with high thresholds for stress responses (i.e. "domesticated" fish).

Intensive fish cultivation is a striking example of an activity in which stress and stress responses are of immediate economic importance. Acute forms of handling stress, such as those associated with the routine hatchery procedures of grading, transportation and artificial stripping, almost invariably result in marked physiological stress responses with an elevation of plasma catecholamines and corticosteroids (see the contributions by Donaldson, Mazeaud and Mazeaud, and Schreck, 1981, this volume). The secondary changes in osmotic and ionic regulation are well documented (Eddy, 1981, this volume) and this knowledge has led to the important expedient of ameliorating such changes in freshwater fish by using dilute saline solutions when handling or transporting fish, thereby promoting higher survival rates (Hattingh *et al.*, 1975; Long *et al.*, 1977; Kutty *et al.*, 1980). An understanding of the responses of fish to acute, physical stress is also of paramount importance to experimental fish biologists who, often unavoidably, handle fish prior to, or during, their investigations. In these cases, the time courses of such responses are as important as their magnitude, if the investigators are to ascertain the appropriate recovery times before experimentation can proceed. Such practical difficulties are illustrated in the contribution of Soivio and Nikinmaa (1981, this volume) in which the method of taking a blood sample from a fish is shown to significantly influence the degree of swelling of the erythrocytes.

Chronic stresses associated with intensive fish farming include such phenomena as deterioration of water quality (Smart, 1981, this volume) and the less obvious but equally important stresses of social interaction. The very act of rearing fish at unnaturally high stocking densities may exacerbate problems of social dominance, with submissive fish showing enhanced interrenal activity (Schreck, 1981, this volume), reduced growth rate and increased susceptibility to infections. Overcrowding and water quality deterioration may increase the probability of disease by providing environmental conditions favourable to the survival and transmission of pathogens in the water. In addition, stress-induced immunosuppression in the fish may aggravate the situation. As with many other aspects of biology, considerable information has been derived from medical and mammalian sources but progress is now being made in the study of stress, defence mechanisms and diseases in fish (Ellis, 1981, this volume; Fletcher, 1981, this volume).

The pressures of industrial requirements and the recreational demands upon aquatic ecosystems have resulted in biological stress at all levels of organization, not least with respect to fish populations. Important research has been, and is still being, undertaken to determine lethal limits when fish are subjected to deleterious changes in the environment as a direct result of man's activities. However, attention is now being focussed on the sublethal effects of such changes. For example, Elliott (1981, this volume) reviews the sublethal effects of thermal stress on a wide range of freshwater, teleost fish and presents new data for the brown trout, *Salmo trutta*. Similarly, Hughes (1981, this volume) examines the effects of low concentrations of metal pollutants on gill structure and respiratory physiology of the rainbow trout, *Salmo gairdneri*, under normal and hypoxic conditions. This is one of very few investigations which attempt to examine the responses of fish to two or more simultaneous stresses and this is clearly an area for future research. Environmental stresses are rarely present in isolation and experimental investigations of such phenomena are almost certainly complicated by stresses associated with the process of experimentation itself (handling, confinement, anaesthesia, etc.). The effects of environmental stress on populations and ecosystems are outside the scope of this book and the reader is referred to Thorp and Gibbons (1978) for a collection of papers on energy and environmental stress in aquatic ecosystems.

The views expressed in this introductory chapter are, of necessity, personal ones and it would be remarkable indeed, with a subject so difficult to define in precise terms, if they were in complete agreement with those of the other contributors or the reader. However, if this introduction has placed the remaining chapters of this book in context and stimulated the reader to further thought, its basic aim will have been realized.

REFERENCES

Billard, R., Bry, C. and Gillet, C. (1981). Stress, environment and reproduction in teleost fish. In *Stress and Fish* (A. D. Pickering, ed.), pp. 185–208. London and New York: Academic Press.

Brett, J. R. (1958). Implications and assessments of environmental stress. In *Investigations of Fish-power Problems* (P. A. Larkin, ed.), pp. 69–83. H. R. MacMillan Lectures in Fisheries, University of British Columbia.

Cannon, W. B. (1935). Stresses and strains of homeostasis. *Am. J. med. Sci.* **189**, 1–14.

Donaldson, E. M. (1981). The pituitary–interrenal axis as an indicator of stress in fish. In *Stress and Fish* (A. D. Pickering, ed.) pp. 11–47. London and New York: Academic Press.

Eddy, F. B. (1981). Effects of stress on osmotic and ionic regulation in fish. In *Stress and Fish* (A. D. Pickering, ed.), pp. 77–102. London and New York: Academic Press.

Elliott, J. M. (1981). Some aspects of thermal stress on freshwater teleosts. In *Stress and Fish* (A. D. Pickering, ed.) pp. 209–245. London and New York: Academic Press.

Ellis, A. E. (1981). Stress and the modulation of defence mechanisms in fish. In *Stress and Fish* (A. D. Pickering, ed.), pp. 147–169. London and New York: Academic Press.

Esch, G. W. and Hazen, T. C. (1978). Thermal ecology and stress: a case history for red-sore disease in largemouth bass. In *Energy and Environmental Stress in Aquatic Ecosystems* (J. H. Thorp and J. W. Gibbons, eds), pp. 331–363. Technical Information Center, U.S. Department of Energy. CONF-771114.

Esch, G. W., Gibbons, J. W. and Bourque, J. E. (1975). An analysis of the relationship between stress and parasitism. *Am. Midl. Nat.* **93**, 339–353.

Fletcher, T. C. (1981). Non-antibody molecules and the defence mechanisms of fish. In *Stress and Fish* (A. D. Pickering, ed.), pp. 171–183. London and New York: Academic Press.

Hattingh, J., Fourie, F. and van Vuren, J. (1975). The transport of freshwater fish. *J. Fish Biol.* **7**, 447–449.

Hughes, G. M. (1981). Effects of low oxygen and pollution on the respiratory systems of fish. In *Stress and Fish* (A. D. Pickering, ed.), pp. 121–146. London and New York: Academic Press.

Kutty, M. N., Sukumaran, N. and Kasim, H. M. (1980). Influence of temperature and salinity on survival of the freshwater mullet, *Rhinomugil corsula* (Hamilton). *Aquaculture* **20**, 261–274.

Lazarus, R. S. (1971). The concepts of stress and disease. In *Society Stress and Disease. Vol. 1. The Psychosocial Environment and Psychosomatic Diseases* (L. Levi, ed.), pp. 53–58, London: Oxford University Press.

Leffler, J. W. (1978). Ecosystem responses to stress in aquatic microcosms. In *Energy and Environmental Stress in Aquatic Ecosystems* (J. H. Thorp and J. W. Gibbons, eds), pp. 102–119. Technical Information Center, U.S. Department of Energy. CONF-771114.

Long, C. W., McComas, J. R. and Monk, B. H. (1977). Use of salt (NaCl) water to reduce mortality of chinook smolts, *Oncorhynchus tshawytscha*, during handling and hauling. *U.S. Natl. Mar. Fish. Ser. Mar. Fish. Rev.* **39**, 6–9.

Lugo, A. E. (1978). Stress and ecosystems. In *Energy and Environmental Stress in Aquatic Ecosystems* (J. H. Thorp and J. W. Gibbons, eds) pp. 62–101. Technical Information Center, U.S. Department of Energy. CONF-771114.

Mason, J. W. (1975a). A historical view of the stress field. Part I. *J. Human Stress* **1**(1), 6–12.

Mason, J. W. (1975b). A historical view of the stress field. Part II. *J. Human Stress* **1**(2), 22–36.

Mazeaud, M. M. and Mazeaud, F. (1981). Adrenergic responses to stress in fish. In *Stress and Fish* (A. D. Pickering, ed.), pp. 49–75. London and New York: Academic Press.

Mazeaud, M. M., Mazeaud, F. and Donaldson, E. M. (1977). Primary and secondary effects of stress in fish: some new data with a general review. *Trans. Am. Fish. Soc.* **106**, 201–212.

Meier, R. L. (1972). Communications stress. *A. Rev. Ecol. Systemat.* **3**, 289–314.

Schreck, C. B. (1981). Stress and compensation in teleostean fishes: response to social and physical factors. In *Stress and Fish* (A. D. Pickering, ed.), pp. 295–321. London and New York: Academic Press.

Schreck, C. B. and Lorz, H. W. (1978). Stress response of coho salmon (*Oncorhynchus kisutch*) elicited by cadmium and copper and potential use of cortisol as an indicator of stress. *J. Fish. Res. Bd Can.* **35**, 1124–1129.

Selye, H. (1936). A syndrome produced by diverse nocuous agents. *Nature, Lond.* **138**, 32.

Selye, H. (1946). The general adaptation syndrome and the diseases of adaptation. *J. clin. Endocr.* **6**, 117–230.

Selye, H. (1950). Stress and the general adaptation syndrome. *Br. Med. J.* **1**, 1383–1392.

Selye, H. (1956). *The Stress of Life*. New York, Toronto, London: McGraw-Hill Book Co., Inc.

Smart, G. R. (1981). Aspects of water quality producing stress in intensive fish culture. In *Stress and Fish* (A. D. Pickering, ed.), pp. 277–293. London and New York: Academic Press.

Soivio, A. and Nikinmaa, M. (1981). The swelling of erythrocytes in relation to the oxygen affinity of the blood of the rainbow trout, *Salmo gairdneri* Richardson. In *Stress and Fish* (A. D. Pickering, ed.), pp. 103–119. London and New York: Academic Press.

Thorp, J. H. and Gibbons, J. W. (eds) (1978). *Energy and Environmental Stress in Aquatic Ecosystems*. Technical Information Center, U.S. Department of Energy. CONF-771114.

Ulanowicz, R. E. (1978). Modeling environmental stress. In *Energy and Environmental Stress in Aquatic Ecosystems* (J. H. Thorp and J. W. Gibbons, eds), pp.

1–18. Technical Information Center, U.S. Department of Energy. CONF-771114.

Wedemeyer, G. A. and McLeay, D. J. (1981). Methods for determining the tolerance of fishes to environmental stressors. In *Stress and Fish* (A. D. Pickering, ed.) pp. 247–275. London and New York: Academic Press.

2. The Pituitary–interrenal Axis as an Indicator of Stress in Fish

EDWARD M. DONALDSON

West Vancouver Laboratory, Resource Services Branch, Dept. of Fisheries and Oceans, West Vancouver, B.C. Canada

Abstract. The mechanism by which exposure to stress results in an increase in corticosteroid production from the interrenal is described in the context of a review of the pituitary–interrenal axis. Particular emphasis is placed on the salmonid literature. At the pituitary level, topics covered include: the control of ACTH release, the cellular origin and biochemistry of ACTH, changes in ACTH production during stress. At the interrenal level, topics covered include: the cellular origin and biochemistry of the corticosteroids, the effect of ACTH or stress on plasma corticosteroid concentrations, diurnal and seasonal rhythms, changes accompanying sexual maturation, corticosteroid secretion rates. The use of measurement of changes in the pituitary–interrenal axis as indicators of stress in fish is discussed from the point of view of environmental factors such as handling, anaesthetics and crowding and with regard to the effect of pollutants.

I INTRODUCTION

The development of an understanding of the role of stress responses in fish is the key to a better understanding of the problems associated with the intensive culture of fish during all or part of their life cycle. In turn, the key to a better understanding of stress responses in fish lies in developing knowledge of the mechanisms by which external changes (e.g. environmental, handling) and internal changes (e.g. disease state, nutritional imbalance) are detected by the external and internal sensory systems of the fish and result in the primary stress responses. These primary responses or effects have been divided into two categories, increased production of corticosteroids and increased production of catecholamines (Mazeaud *et al.*, 1977). These two primary neuro-endocrine responses bring about a number of biochemical physiological and immunological changes which have been described as the secondary effects (Mazeaud *et al.*, 1977). It is the purpose of this chapter to delineate and characterize the hypothalamic-pituitary interrenal mechanism by which stresses bring about the primary corticosteroid stress response in fish and to provide examples of the use of this primary response to quantify the response of fish, especially salmonids, to stressful situations.

II THE HYPOTHALAMUS

(a) Hypothalamic Control of ACTH Secretion in Fish

The earliest experimental evidence for the control of ACTH secretion by a hypothalamic factor in fish was provided by Sage and Purrot (1969). These workers incubated goldfish, *Carassius auratus*, pituitaries in the presence of a crude goldfish hypothalamic extract and showed an increase in the release of ACTH into the incubation medium. Saline extracts of goldfish hypo-thalamus contained no ACTH activity. Mollies, *Poecilia latipinna*, bearing pituitary autotransplants responded to injection stress with an increase in plasma cortisol concentration suggesting that release of CRF material into the blood stream had occurred (Hawkins *et al.*, 1970). Later Hawkins and Ball (1973) showed that plasma cortisol levels were increased in pituitary autotransplanted mollies after injection of either arginine vasopressin or arginine vasotocin, the latter being a naturally occurring hypothalamic and neurohypophyseal octapeptide in the teleost (Perks, 1969).

Injection of lyophilized, acid extracts of telecephalon or hypothalamus from the long nose sucker, *Catostomus catostomus*, into betamethasone blocked goldfish resulted in significantly increased plasma cortisol levels whereas similar extracts of cerebellum had no effect (Fryer and Peter, 1977a). Similar extracts from goldfish hypothalami and telencephalons also induced the same effect in goldfish (Fryer and Peter, 1977a). As the goldfish used for the assay were not hypophysectomized the results suggest that these extracts contained either CRF or ACTH. However, the former possibility is more likely as Sage and Purrot (1969) were not able to detect ACTH activity in saline extracts of goldfish hypothalamus. Destruction of the nucleus lateral tuberis pars anterior (NLTa) and rostral nucleus lateral tuberis pars posterior (NLTp) in the goldfish by radio frequency lesions resulted in significant suppression of the corticosteroid response to sham-injection, shallow water or thermal stress (Fryer and Peter, 1977b). These findings confirm the earlier observation that electrical stimulation of the basal hypothalamic tissue in the carp, *Cyprinus carpio*, resulted in a significantly increased plasma cortisol concentration (Redgate, 1974) and indicate that the NLT is involved in the control of ACTH and may be the source of CRF in the goldfish. Fryer and Peter (1977b) were also able to show that large lesions of the nucleus preopticus (NPO) depleted neurosecretory material from the neurointermediate lobe of the pituitary and interfered with the corticosteroid stress response. They conclude that the neurohypophyseal octapeptides may have a physiological role in the control of ACTH secretion in the teleost. Destruction of the habenular nuclei in the epithalamus of the goldfish resulted in an enhanced thermal stress response indicating that the epithalamus may be the source of an inhibitory factor which suppresses ACTH secretion or that lesions in this area interrupted neural pathways which suppress ACTH secretion by inhibition of CRF release (Fryer and Peter, 1977b). In a third series of experiments, Fryer and Peter investigated the location of corticosteroid negative feedback inhibition on ACTH secretion in the goldfish. Implantation of cortisol pellets into the NLT or preoptic recess of the third ventricle resulted in a suppression of the corticosteroid stress response after sham-injection while placement of cortisol in the pituitary had no effect (Fryer and Peter, 1977c). These results suggest that a corticosteroid negative feedback acting on the hypothalamus may inhibit the release and/or synthesis of CRF and that feedback in the preoptic-posterior telencephalon region may suppress the activity of the NPO-neurohypophyseal system. Vasotocin and/or isotocin produced by the NPO may have a direct action on ACTH release at the pituitary level, may stimulate CRF release or may potentiate the effect of CRF on ACTH secretion (Fryer and Peter, 1977c).

Recently Fryer and Maler (1980) have used horse radish peroxidase (HRP) to identify putative CRF neurones in the hypothalamus of the goldfish. Systemically injected HRP underwent retrograde transport into nucleus preopticus perikarya. Stress or injection of the steroid hydroxylase inhibitor, metopirone, resulted in an enhanced uptake of HRP into the parvocellular neurones of the NPO but not into the magnocellular neurones. Treatment with metopirone over a period of 5 days resulted in a decrease in the number of neurosecretory granules in most of the parvocellular neurones in the NPO suggesting that those metopirone sensitive parvocellular neurones are CRF neurones (Fryer and Maler, 1980). Current proposals for the hypothalamic control of ACTH in teleosts are illustrated in Fig. 1 (from Peter and Fryer, 1981).

(b) Studies on Corticotropin Releasing Factor

Corticotropin releasing factor (CRF) was the first hypothalamic releasing factor to be demonstrated in the mid 1950s by Saffran and Schally (1955)

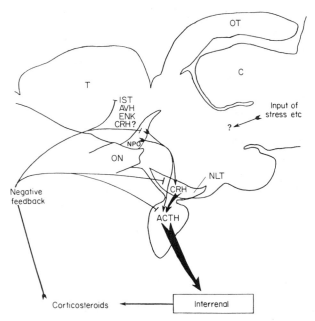

Fig. 1   Diagram illustrating the hypothalamic control of ACTH secretion in teleost. Abbreviations are as follows: NPO, nucleus preopticus; NLT, nucleus lateral tuberis; ON, optic nerve; T, telecephalon; OT, optic tectum; C, cerebellum; CRH, corticotropin releasing hormone; ACTH, adrenocorticotropin; IST, isotocin; AVT, arginine vasotocin; ENK, meta enkephalin (from R. E. Peter and J. N. Fryer (in press)). Endocrine function of the hypothalamus of actinopterygians. In *Fish Neurobiology and Behaviour* (R. E. Davies and R. G. Northcutt (eds) University of Michigan Press, Ann Arbor).

working at the Allan Memorial Institute in Montreal and also by Guillemin and Rosenberg (1955) at Baylor University in Houston. Despite the fact that CRF was the first hypophysiotropic factor to be identified and named (Saffran *et al.*, 1955) its chemical structure still remains a mystery. In fact, as several types of hypothalamic or neurohypophyseal preparations have been shown to have CRF activity there is doubt as to whether there is a single CRF or whether there are several CRFs.

Early studies suggested that lipid extracts of hypothalamic tissue contained CRF activity but de Wied *et al.* (1958) showed that these preparations probably stimulated the secretion of CRF by the hypothalamus rather than acting directly at the pituitary level. In mammals, the posterior pituitary octapeptide vasopressin causes ACTH release in many test systems for CRF detection. However, vasopressin releases ACTH for only a short period *in vitro* from isolated rat anterior pituitary cells while hypothalamic median eminence extract causes a prolonged release of ACTH under the same conditions (Junnila and Sayers, 1977). On the other hand, vasotocin has ACTH releasing characteristics that are similar to those of hypothalamic extracts (Buckingham and Hodges, 1977). It has been suggested that vasopressin may have a CRF function in the acute response to stress while other CRFs may be involved during prolonged stress (Saffran and Schally, 1977).

Studies based on the original CRF (Saffran et al., 1955) have led to the identification of several small peptide CRFs. Two of these have similarities to α MSH, although α MSH does not have CRF activity, and have been referred to as α CRFs (Schally et al., 1962). A third peptide, β CRF, has chemical and physical properties similar to vasopressin and its amino acid sequence has been partially determined based on the acetylated amino terminus of α MSH and a modification of lysine vasopressin (Schally and Bowers, 1964):

Acetyl Ser . Try . CyS Phe His [Asn; Gln] . CyS . [Pro, Val] . Lys . Gly-NH$_2$.
This vasopressin-like CRF has still not been fully characterized.

Recently Schally et al. (1978) have fractionated a large number of pig hypothalami and identified high, intermediate and low molecular weight CRFs. The low molecular weight CRF consisted of catecholamines and a tetradecapeptide which is identical to residues 33–46 of the α chain of porcine haemoglobin and is thus thought to be an artifact. The intermediate molecular weight or small peptide CRF activity consisted of several distinct fractions one or more of which may be physiological CRF (Schally et al., 1978, 1979). The high molecular weight CRF was obtained free of ACTH-like material and is a basic polypeptide which may be pro CRF, the precursor of physiological CRF (Schally et al., 1979). Studies by (Boyd et al., 1978) have shown that the porcine hypothalamus contains large amounts of immunoreactive ACTH and suggest that this would have been a problem in earlier studies utilizing corticosteroid measurement as an end point in CRF assays. They were however, able to identify by chromatography a CRF fraction separate from ACTH.

Chromatographic fractionation of rat stalk median eminence extract using ascorbic acid as an antioxidant followed by bioassay using a perfused rat, isolated anterior pituitary cell column coupled with an ACTH radio-immunoassay revealed three CRF peaks, one in the void volume having low activity, a second non-specific peak and a third major peak of CRF activity (Gillies and Lowry, 1979). This latter CRF peak coincided with the peak of arginine vasopressin (AVP) immunoactivity and cochromatographed with synthetic arginine vasopressin. Recombination of this AVP fraction with the minor CRF area from the void volume resulted in a 3-fold potentiation of CRF activity. Recombination of the first and second peaks resulted in a variable stimulation of CRF activity. Thus, Gillies and Lowry (1979) have shown that the CRF activity of stalk median eminence extract consists of vasopressin CRF plus synergistic factors which have inherent unstable CRF activity. They propose that the vasopressin CRF precursor molecule is synthesized in the supraoptic nucleus or the paraventricular nucleus and packaged into neurosecretory granules which pass by axonal transport through the zona externa of the median eminence to the portal vessels of the mammalian system. Here the ACTH releasing activity of the vasopressin is modulated by the synergistic CRFs which are released during stress. This hypothesis, proposed by Gillies and Lowry (1980), provides a "fail safe mechanism" which permits the modulation of ACTH release in different stress situations plus control of the normal circadian rhythm.

Thus, while it appears that the final verdict is not yet in on the nature of all of the substances which control ACTH release from the pituitary gland, the current evidence favours Selye's contention that multiple factors are involved.

III THE PITUITARY

(a) Identification of ACTH Cells

The localization of the corticotrope cells in teleosts has been the subject of several reviews including those of Ball and Baker (1969), Olivereau (1970) and most recently that of Follenius and Dubois (1980). Coverage here has been restricted to the identification of ACTH producing cells in salmonids. An early study by van Overbeeke and McBride (1967) delineated the tinctorial characteristics of the various cell types in the pituitary of the sockeye salmon, *Oncorhynchus nerka*, during the life cycle but did not directly identify the ACTH cells on a functional basis. Positive identification was achieved in the following year (Fagerlund *et al.*, 1968) in both the above species and in the rainbow trout, *Salmo gairdneri*, using the MacConail's lead haematoxylin stain which is specific for corticotrope cells (Ball and Olivereau, 1966). In this study, metopirone SU4885 was injected into the salmon and trout to inhibit the 11 β hydroxylation of compound S into cortisol. The resultant decrease in circulating cortisol levels resulted in a reduced feedback inhibition of ACTH and a consequent degranulation of the lead-haematoxylin-positive cells of the pars distalis. Furthermore, this pallisade like layer of corticotropes became hypertrophied in the salmon and at higher dosage levels in the trout. In this study, cytoplasmic granules in the cells of the pars intermedia also proved to be lead haematoxylin positive. However, these cells were not affected by metopirone treatment (see section on ACTH biosynthesis and structure).

Injection of dexamethasone ($1 \, \text{mg kg}^{-1}$) into adult sockeye salmon six times over a 75-day period resulted in a reduction in the lead haematoxylin positive granulation of the corticotrope cells (Fagerlund and McBride, 1969). Thus dexamethasone treatment, which had been shown earlier (Donaldson and McBride, 1967) to be an effective feedback inhibitor of interrenal stimulation in trout, appeared to have caused a reduction in the ACTH content of the corticotropes of these sockeye salmon. Dexamethasone treatment did not affect the staining characteristics of the lead haematoxylin positive cells of the pars intermedia.

Other studies on the corticotropin-producing cells of the salmonid rostral pars distalis include those of Nagahama and Yamamoto (1969a) also on the sockeye salmon, Olivereau (1964) on the chinook salmon, *Oncorhynchus tshawytscha*, and chum salmon, *Oncorhynchus keta*, the rainbow trout and Atlantic salmon, *Salmo salar*, Nagahama and Yamamoto (1969b) on the chum salmon, Baker (1963) on *Salmo fario*, and Oguri (1971) on the rainbow trout.

The first report of the use of immunohistochemical techniques to identify the corticotropes in a teleost was that of McKeown and van Overbeeke (1969) on the sockeye salmon. In this study, the ACTH cells were located using antibodies to porcine ACTH and β 1–24 corticotropin. The strongest level of fluorescence was obtained with the antibody to porcine ACTH and this was attributed to the β 1–24 corticopin antibody having a lower titre. No fluorescence was reported in the pars intermedia. Further studies on the use of anti-ACTH to identify corticotropes in another salmonid, the rainbow trout, were conducted by Follenius and Dubois (1976, 1980) and Follenius *et al.* (1978). These workers obtained a strong reaction with β 1-24 ACTH antiserum in the corticotrope cells and were able to show by means of the electron microscope that the immunoreaction was due to fine secretory granules in the cytoplasm. No reaction occurred when the antiserum was treated with 1–24 ACTH and the only cells reacting with the 1-24 ACTH antiserum were those which stained with alcian blue or lead haematoxylin.

The cells of the pars intermedia of the trout also cross react with β 1-24 ACTH antiserum, thus, ACTH or CLIP may be present in these cells but not necessarily secreted (Follenius and Dubois, 1976) (see section on biosynthesis and structure of ACTH). This finding is in agreement with an early study which showed that ACTH-related peptides were produced during *in vitro* incubation of trout pituitaries (Scott and Baker, 1975).

The corticotrope cells of the rostral pars distalis and the pars intermedia cells of the trout have also been shown to give a positive reaction with α endorphin antiserum. The former cells gave the stronger response. The intensity of the reaction in the pars intermedia varied from cell to cell and fish to fish suggesting the possibility of physiological variation (Follenius and

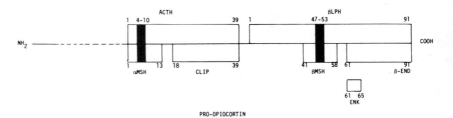

Fig. 2   Diagram illustrating the structural relationships of proopiocortin and its component hormones. The shaded areas represent the heptapeptide sequence common to ACTH, β LPH, α MSH and β MSH. ACTH, adrenocorticotropin; β LPH, β lipotropin; α and β MSH, α and β melanophore stimulating hormone; CLIP, corticotropin-like intermediate-lobe peptide; β END, β endorphin; END, Met enkephalin (modified, with permission, from Kawauchi, 1979).

Dubois, 1978; see Fig. 2 for the relationship between endorphin, β LPH and ACTH). In mammals, α endorphin consists of 16 residues corresponding to β LPH$^{61-76}$ while β endorphin consists of 31 residues corresponding to β LPH$^{61-91}$ (Fig. 2). Immunoreactive β endorphin was recently extracted from the pituitary of the coho salmon, *Oncorhynchus kisutch* (Pezalla *et al.*,1978). As ACTH and endorphin are now believed to originate from the same precursor molecule, proopiocortin, it is possible that endorphin is released during stress at the same time as ACTH (Guilleman *et al.*, 1977) and that it may play a role in decreasing sensitivity to pain during stress.

(b) Extraction and Bioassay of Adrenocorticotropin

The first evidence for adrenocorticotropic activity in extracts of fish pituitary glands was provided by Ito *et al.* (1952) who showed that pituitary preparations from the bonito, *Katsuwonus vagans*, and the tuna, *Thunnus orientalis*, possessed rat adrenal ascorbic depleting activity. Rinfret and Hane (1955) also obtained a positive response in the Sayer's assay for extracts from chum salmon pituitary glands as did Woodhead (1960) in extracts of Arctic cod, *Gadus morhua*, pituitary glands. The cod pituitary extracts were also able to maintain the adrenal weight of hypophysectomized rats. *In vitro* corticosteroidogenesis in mouse adrenal slices was stimulated by addition of material obtained by *in vitro* incubation of unstimulated goldfish pituitary glands (Purrot and Sage, 1967). Extracts of elasmobranch, *Squalus acanthias* and *Raja rhina*, and holocephalan, *Hydrolagus colliei*, pituitary glands were shown to stimulate corticosteroidogenesis in incubates of chicken adrenal tissue (de Roos and de Roos, 1967).

In none of these studies was the putative fish adrenocorticotropin (ACTH) tested to determine whether it would stimulate corticosteroido-genesis in a fish. With this in mind ACTH was purified to the acid acetone powder (AAP) (Donaldson et al., 1968a) and oxycellulose stages from chinook salmon pituitary glands using the methods of Li (1952) and Astwood et al. (1951) respectively. These two preparations were assayed against porcine ACTH using rainbow trout in which endogenous ACTH release had been inhibited by injection of dexamethasone (Donaldson and McBride, 1967). Blood samples were obtained from a caudal vessel one hour after ACTH injection into the dorsal aorta and plasma cortisol was determined using a validated fluorimetric technique (Donaldson et al., 1968b). The trout interrenal proved to be very sensitive to both of the salmonid ACTH preparations and to the porcine ACTH (Fig. 3). The

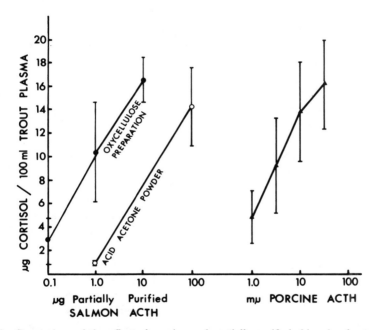

Fig. 3 Comparison of the effect of porcine and partially purified chinook salmon ACTH on plasma cortisol in dexamethasone treated rainbow trout (Donaldson and Dye, 1968, unpublished).

parallel slopes of the dose–response lines for the salmonid and porcine preparations provided some initial evidence for similarity of the cortico-steroidogenic segments of the two corticotropins. Comparison of the par-tially purified *Oncorhynchus* ACTH with porcine ACTH gave a specific activity of 0.17 IU mg^{-1} for the AAP and 4.4 IU mg^{-1} for the oxycellulose preparation (E. M. Donaldson and H. M. Dye, 1968, unpublished). On the basis of the activity of the AAP and a pituitary water content of 84% (Donaldson et al., 1972) these pituitary glands from sexually mature Pacific salmon contained 19 mU ACTH mg^{-1} dry weight. This concentration is similar to the corticotropin content of chum salmon pituitary glands determined by adrenal ascorbic acid depletion in the rat (20 mU mg^{-1}) (Rinfret and Hane, 1955) and higher than that in the cod (3.5 mU mg^{-1}) (Woodhead, 1960). It is of interest to note here that in a recent study on pituitary glands from mature chum salmon, Kawauchi (1979) comments on the relative lack of ACTH compared to MSH and CLIP.

Using the corticosteroid response in dexamethasone-blocked mice, Fontaine-Bertrand et al. (1969) assayed the ACTH content of crude pituitary extracts from the Atlantic salmon and the carp. The salmon extract gave a parallel response while the carp preparation gave a non-parallel response when compared to porcine ACTH. After further purification of the carp ACTH using an oxycellulose technique, a parallel response was obtained. Investigation of the ACTH content of Atlantic salmon pituitaries from parr through smolt to adult gave a range of 18.5 to 58.3 mU ACTH mg^{-1} but revealed no significant differences either during the life cycle or between the sexes (Fontaine-Bertrand et al., 1969). A particularly interesting aspect of this study was the comparison of the ACTH and MSH contents of the different parts of the salmon pituitary gland. In females during the spawning migration, the rostral pars distalis, pars distalis and pars intermedia plus neurohypophysis contained 122, 29.2 and <8 mU ACTH mg^{-1} and 927, 1167 and 9900 U MSH mg^{-1} respectively. These findings confirmed earlier histological studies on the localization of ACTH synthesis in the salmon pituitary gland (Fagerlund et al., 1968) and on the site of MSH synthesis in the trout pituitary (Baker, 1965).

(c) Biosynthesis and Structure of Adrenocorticotropin

Recently, significant advances have been made in elucidating the biosynthesis of adrenocorticotropin in fish and other vertebrates (Baker, 1979). In all gnathostomes, ACTH appears to be derived from a prohormone, proopiocortin, having a molecular weight of approximately 31 000 daltons and containing approximately 260 amino acid residues (Roberts and Herbert, 1977). Proopiocortin (Fig. 2) contains within it the sequences of ACTH; β lipotropin, β LPH; α and β melanophore stimulating hormones, α and β MSHs; corticotropin-like intermediate lobe peptide, CLIP; β endorphin, β END and encephalin, ENK. This prohormone probably evolved by partial gene duplication without separation of the gene products.

The heptapeptide sequence Met-Glu-His-Phe-Arg-Trp-Gly is thus repeated in ACTH, α MSH, β lipotropin and β MSH (Fig. 2) in most vertebrates. However, in two species of dogfish (Love and Pickering, 1974; Bennett *et al.*, 1974) and the chum salmon (Kawauchi, 1979), the sequence is modified in β MSH and presumably also in β lipotropin. The individual hormones are formed by enzymic cleavage from proopiocortin. The two large peptides characterized to date are ACTH and β LPH. It is not yet known whether the smaller hormones are formed from ACTH and β LPH or whether they are produced directly by cleavage of proopiocortin. Biosynthesis of proopiocortin is thought to occur in both the corticotrope cells of the pars distalis and the melanotrope cells of the pars intermedia. However in the corticotropes, ACTH is the end product which is secreted while in the melanotropes, further cleavage results in the production of approximately equimolar quantities of α MSH and CLIP (Scott *et al.*, 1974). The structure of dogfish, *Squalus acanthias*, ACTH (Lowry *et al.*, 1974) and the partial structure of chum salmon ACTH (Kawauchi, 1979; Kawauchi *et al.*, 1980) are compared to the structure of human ACTH (Riniker *et al.*, 1972) in Fig. 4. It is evident that the three ACTH molecules each contain 39 residues, have molecular weights in the region of 4500 daltons and share significant areas of identical amino acid sequence indicating that there have been strong selective pressures exerting a conservative influence on the structure of this molecule which mediates the stress response in all gnathostomes. Studies in higher vertebrates have shown that N-terminal residues 1–24, which are identical in all mammals, are particularly important in the stimulation of corticosteroid biosynthesis. In the 1–24 region, dogfish ACTH differs from mammalian ACTH only in amino acids 13, 15, and 20, while the partial sequence of chum salmon ACTH differs only in position 24 (Fig. 4).

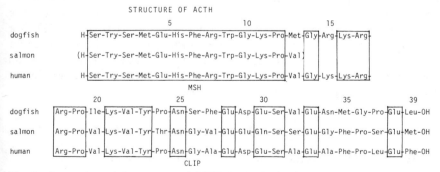

Fig. 4 Comparison of the structure of ACTH in the dogfish (Lowry *et al.*, 1974) and human (Riniker *et al.*, 1972) with partial sequence of ACTH (α MSH and CLIP) from the chum salmon (Kawauchi, 1979). Amino acids common to all three structures have been enclosed.

IV THE INTERRENAL

Studies on the functional morphology and corticosteroidogenic capability of the interrenal and its homolog, the mammalian adrenal cortex, were stimulated over two decades ago by Chester Jones (1957). Research has continued at a significant level since that time and several reviews have been published including those of Chester Jones et al. (1969), Idler and Truscott (1972), Butler (1973), Sandor et al. (1976) and Jorgenson (1976). In the context of this review, the information accumulated to date may be briefly summarized as follows. The teleost interrenal is generally found embedded in the anterior portion of the kidney or head kidney in association with the post-cardinal veins, although variation from this pattern can occur (Nandi, 1962). In the immature or gonadectomized sockeye salmon, the intr renal tissue consists of groups of small, densely-packed cells with slightly basophilic cytoplasm and spherical, chromatin-rich nuclei containing inconspicuous nucleoli. On the other hand, in mature or sex hormone treated sockeye, the cells become hypertrophied, lack cytoplasmic basophilia and may contain small vacuoles. The nuclei also become enlarged and contain conspicuous nucleoli (McBride and van Overbeeke, 1969; van Overbeeke and McBride, 1971). The activity of the interrenal can be assessed histopathologically by measuring the nuclear diameters of the interrenal cells. The mean nuclear diameter increases during chronic stress.

The major corticosteroids which have been identified from teleostean blood plasma are cortisol and cortisone (Idler and Truscott, 1972, for review). Cortisol is believed to be secreted from the interrenal and is normally found in higher concentrations than cortisone. Cortisone is thought to be produced peripherally from cortisol by 11β- hydroxysteroid dehydrogenation (Donaldson and Fagerlund, 1972). In addition to cortisol and cortisone there is evidence for the presence of small amounts of corticosterone, 20β dihydrocortisone and possibly 11-deoxycortisol in the plasma of post-spawned sockeye salmon (Idler and Truscott, 1972). For investigations on the stress response in teleosts it is generally accepted that cortisol is the appropriate corticosteroid to monitor, although the additional measurement of cortisone levels can also be of value for example, during maturation and ageing in the Pacific salmon.

V THE HYPOTHALAMIC-PITUITARY–INTERRENAL AXIS

(a) Evidence for a Pituitary–interrenal Axis in Salmonids

Studies on the pituitary–interrenal axis in salmonids indigenous to the Pacific coast of North America, were initiated by O. H. Robertson and his collaborators. Cortisol was identified as the major corticosteroid in the plasma of the rainbow trout by Hane and Robertson (1959) and Nandi and Bern (1960, 1965) were able to show that cortisol was produced during *in vitro* incubation of head kidney tissue. Earlier Rinfret and Hane (1955) had obtained evidence for the presence of adrenocorticotropin in the pituitary of the chum salmon based on its ascorbic acid depleting activity in the rat. A pituitary extract from chinook salmon (Schmidt *et al.*, 1965) was found to stimulate the atrophied interrenal cells of hypophysectomized *Couesius plumbeus* (van Overbeeke and Ahsan, 1966). Further confirmation of the presence of a pituitary–interrenal axis in salmonids was provided by investigating the effect of hypophysectomy in the rainbow trout (Donaldson and McBride, 1967). In fish examined 3 months after hypophysectomy, the interrenal tissue had undergone considerable atrophy; nuclear and cell diameters were reduced and there was a reduction in cytoplasmic granulation (Table I). Plasma cortisol levels were less than half the sham-operated control values one day after hypophysectomy and declined further over the next two weeks. The lowest values were observed in fish held for 3 months (Table I). When hypophysectomized trout and sham-operated controls were

TABLE I   The Effects of Hypophysectomy on the Interrenal Gland of the Rainbow Trout. Fish were Examined 3 Months after the Operation (from Donaldson and McBride, 1967).

	n	Body weight (g)	Length (cm)	GSI	Cortisol (μg 100 ml^{-1})	Interrenal nuclear diameter (μ)
Intact	2	672·5	35·5	3·62	3·8	5·95
Sham hypox	2	758·0	36·9	2·25	5·7	6·00
Hypox	2	219·0	27·0	0·09	0·85	4·20

stressed by lowering the water level to 2–6 cm for 30 minutes, the control fish responded with a significant increase in plasma cortisol while the cortisol level in hypophysectomized fish showed no significant change (Table II). The removal of the pituitary gland had thus prevented these fish from responding to stress by elevating plasma cortisol. Treatment of sham-operated trout with dexamethasone, a potent synthetic corticosteroid which does not interfere with measurement of cortisol, resulted in a lowering of plasma cortisol to the basal level found in hypophysectomized fish. Treatment of hypophysectomized trout with dexamethasone resulted in no further decline in plasma cortisol (Table II). These data are consistent with the hypothesis that dexamethasone had caused feedback inhibition of ACTH synthesis and/or release. It is significant that the basal cortisol concentrations measured in the dexamethasone-treated and hypophysec- tomized fish were the same, indicating that the feedback inhibition mechanism is capable of virtually shutting down ACTH release from the pituitary gland of the teleost. Later we were able to show that a partially purified preparation of *Oncorhynchus* ACTH was capable of causing a dose related increase in plasma cortisol concentration in dexamethasone suppressed rainbow trout (Fig. 3—E. M. Donaldson and H. M. Dye, 1968, unpublished).

TABLE II The Effects of Stress (Lowering the Water Level to 2–6 cm for 30 min) on the Blood Cortisol Levels of Hypophysectomized, Dexamethasone-blocked and Control Rainbow Trout (from Donald- son and McBride, 1967).

	n	Plasma cortisol ($\mu g\ 100\ ml^{-1}$)	Statistical comparison
Sham hypox	37	$8 \cdot 1 \pm 5 \cdot 8$	
Hypox	19	$1 \cdot 6 \pm 1 \cdot 8$	
Sham hypox + stress	12	$13 \cdot 4 \pm 5 \cdot 7$	
Hypox + stress	4	$2 \cdot 5 \pm 3 \cdot 2$	
Sham hypox + dexamethasone	13	$1 \cdot 6 \pm 1 \cdot 2$	
Hypox + dexamethasone	18	$1 \cdot 9 \pm 1 \cdot 6$	

*$p < 0 \cdot 05$.

The next step in the establishment of the existence of a pituitary– interrenal axis in salmonids was the use of the 11β- hydroxylation inhibitor metopirone (Fagerlund *et al.*, 1968). In rainbow trout, injection of a low dose of metopirone for a short period resulted in an increase in plasma cortisol while injection of metopirone at higher dosages or for a longer period resulted in a decrease in plasma cortisol concentration. These changes in plasma cortisol were accompanied by a dose-related increase in interrenal nuclear diameter and by degranulation of the lead-haematoxylin- positive cells of the pars distalis. Similar results were obtained in the same study when metopirone was injected into gonadectomized sockeye salmon and injection of a repository form of ACTH into the latter species resulted in increased plasma cortisol concentrations and increased interrenal nuclear diameters. Collectively, the data are interpreted as indicating that meto- pirone is toxic, and thus stressful, at low levels while its 11β hydroxylase inhibitory effect predominates at higher dosages. The increase in interrenal nuclear diameter in the metopirone- and ACTH-treated salmon, and the degranulation of the lead haematoxylin-positive corticotropes, show that the interrenal response to metopirone is mediated by ACTH released in the absence of cortisol feedback inhibition (Fagerlund et al., 1968). Recently van Kemenade et al. (1980) have shown that metopirone treatment does in fact lower both the biological and immunoactive ACTH content of the trout pars distalis.

Injection of dexamethasone into adult sockeye salmon resulted in a decrease in the level of granulation in the corticotropes and an inhibition of the increase in interrenal cell activity normally observed during maturation. Cortisol concentrations in the dexamethasone-treated fish were reduced to a low but measurable level and were not further reduced by an increase in the dosage of dexamethasone injected (Fagerlund and McBride, 1969).

The reduction in corticotrope granulation indicates that a feedback inhibition mechanism is operating which appears to reduce the rate of ACTH synthesis while the low level of cortisol still present in the plasma of dexamethasone-treated salmon indicates that the feedback inhibition mechanism is not capable of completely shutting off corticosteroid biosynthesis. Healthy salmon treated with dexamethasone responded to the stress of blood sampling with a slight but non-significant increase in plasma cortisol while control salmon responded to the above stress with a marked increase in plasma cortisol concentration. On the other hand, in three out of eight maturing salmon, which had not received prophylactic treatment to prevent the *Saprolegnia* and other infections which occur in maturing salmon, the normal dose of dexamethasone lowered plasma cortisol but did not prevent the stress response to blood sampling. Subsequently, a higher dose of dexamethasone did inhibit the stress response in a group of four fish. These observations indicate that the normal functioning of the feedback mechanism may be impaired in diseased fish or that the "set point" is altered. It is significant that these same three fish referred to above had elevated resting plasma cortisol concentrations prior to dexamethasone administration.

In a subsequent study, injection of porcine ACTH into dexamethasone treated sockeye salmon was shown to increase plasma cortisol levels (Fagerlund, 1970). In gonadectomized fish, injection of porcine ACTH resulted in a marked increase in plasma levels of both cortisol and cortisone and hypertrophy of the interrenal cells while injection of partially purified salmon gonadotropin had no effect on either of these parameters (Donaldson and McBride, 1974).

(b) Parameters for Measurement of the Activity of the
Hypothalamic-pituitary–Interrenal Axis

Parameters for the detection of a stress response in fish by means of the
hypothalamic-pituitary–interrenal (HPI) axis fall into two distinct categories. The first category includes those parameters which are direct
measurements of the activity of the HPI axis itself while the second category
includes those parameters which change as a result of changes in the axis.
The two categories are referred to as the primary and secondary effects of
stress (Mazeaud et al., 1977). The primary category may be further subdivided into histopathological and biochemical parameters (Fig. 5), while
the secondary effects can be subdivided into biochemical, physiological and
hematological parameters.

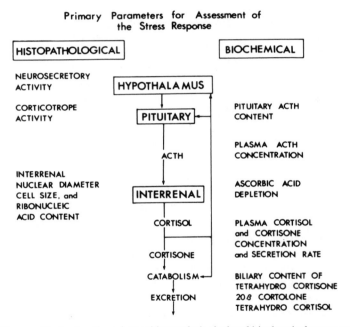

Fig. 5   Diagram illustrating the primary histopathological and biochemical parameters which
may be used for the assessment of the activity of the hypothalamic-pituitary–interrenal axis.

As the hypothalamic control of ACTH production and release is still the
subject of research, the pituitary gland is the highest level in the axis which
can be used at present for the evaluation of the stress response. As indicated
above in the section on the HPI axis, changes can be detected in the activity

of the corticotropes. It is also feasible to measure the level of ACTH stored in the pituitary gland by means of bioassay or radioimmunoassay (RIA). Measurement of the pituitary concentration of ACTH would not however in itself provide a measure of the stress response. Between the evaluation of the activity of the corticotropes and the interrenal the next step is the measurement of plasma ACTH level. Plasma levels have been measured in the goldfish by Singley and Chavin (1975) in response to saline stress and van Kemenade *et al.* (1980) have measured plasma levels of ACTH in the trout during the circannual cycle. In the latter study, the post-spawned fish which had the most active interrenal and corticotrope cells had the lowest plasma ACTH levels. The conclusion drawn was that the plasma ACTH level reflected the annual variation in pituitary ACTH reserve which could be mobilized by the acute stress of sampling. Thus, the use of plasma ACTH as a measure of the stress response would have to take into account the rapidity of the response and the effect of the quantity of ACTH stored in the pituitary.

The interrenal and the corticosteroids which it produces form the most readily used means of assessing the activity of the HPI axis in response to stress. Using histopathological techniques, the degree of interrenal activity can be assessed by measurement of interrenal nuclear diameter or cell size. There are some pitfalls to avoid however, because in the maturing Pacific salmon different groups of interrenal cells show differing levels of activity (van Overbeeke and McBride, 1971) and it is necessary to average a number of measurements from different areas (McBride and van Overbeeke, 1969). Owing to the response time involved, histopathological assessment of interrenal activity is particularly valuable for the assessment of chronic stress such as that caused by crowding or the extended presence of a xenobiotic in the water. Recently the cytophotometric determination of interrenal cellular RNA and interrenal DNA susceptability to Feulgen hydrolysis has been used to evaluate the interrenal response in the brook trout, *Salvelinus fontinalis*, to sublethal acid stress. A biphasic response was observed after 1 and 24 h of exposure (Ashcom *et al.*, 1977). Another measure of interrenal activation is the measurement of ascorbic acid depletion in the anterior kidney. This technique has been used to evaluate the response of rainbow trout and coho salmon to non-specific stress (Wedemeyer, 1969). The assessment of interrenal activity by measurement of plasma cortisol concentration can be used to assess the response of the axis to acute stress or medium term stress in which complete adaptation has not occurred. In the last decade, the techniques for processing numbers of samples for cortisol determination in stress studies (as opposed to the rigorous measurement of small numbers of samples by the double isotope technique) have evolved rapidly from the fluorimetric technique (Donaldson *et al.*, 1968b) through the competitive protein binding technique (Fagerlund, 1970) to the now widely used radioimmunoassay techniques (Hargreaves and Ball, 1977; Peter *et al.*, 1978; McBride *et al.*, 1979; Sangalang *et al.*, 1980). While measurement of the plasma concentration is the most widely used and rapid technique for the assessment of the level of activity of the interrenal in particular and the HPI axis in general it only provides a static measure of cortisol. A further step in the more thorough evaluation of interrenal activity is the determination of the metabolic clearance rate and secretion rate of cortisol and cortisone. This technique has been applied at our laboratory to the investigation of changes in the HPI axis which occur during anadromous migration, sexual maturation and ageing in Pacific salmon (Donaldson and Fagerlund, 1968, 1969, 1970; Fagerlund and Donaldson, 1969, 1970; Donaldson and Dye, 1970), but we have not applied the technique to the investigation of other situations where salmonids are exposed to stresses such as crowding, exposure to pollutants, or at stages in the life cycle prior to anadromous migration. There are also very significant changes in maturing Pacific salmon in the tissue distribution, tissue clearance rate, and rate of interconversion of cortisol and cortisone (Donaldson and Fagerlund, 1972). However, these parameters have not been examined in salmonids exposed to stress.

A further possible means of assessing the activity of the HPI axis is the measurement of corticosteroid catabolites in the bile or urine. The role of the liver in corticosteroid catabolism and the nature of the catabolites present in the bile of rainbow trout have been investigated by Kime (1978) and Truscott (1979) respectively, but measurement of corticosteroid catabolites in the urine appears to have been used only once to evaluate the activity of the HPI axis in salmonids during stress (McKim, 1966).

VI EXAMPLES OF THE USE OF THE HPI AXIS TO EVALUATE THE STRESS RESPONSE IN SALMONIDS

Studies on the use of the HPI axis to measure the response of salmonids to stresses may be divided into three categories: (1) responses to cultural procedures, (2) responses to disease, (3) response to water pollutants. Excluded for the purposes of this review are those studies of the HPI axis in salmonids which relate to natural, life history changes rather than to specific stresses. Also excluded are investigations in which secondary responses were quantified as a measure of the severity of the stress.

(a) Stress Response to Cultural Procedures

In recent years, salmonid culture has developed along two distinct lines, the first being closed system aquaculture where fish are raised intensively from fertilized egg to market size or as broodstock and the second a semi-open system where the salmon or trout are reared intensively for a variable period and are then stocked into rivers, lakes or the ocean. In the second type of culture, a proportion of the fish are caught either by the sport or commercial fishery while another portion return to the hatchery of origin to form the broodstock for the next generation. However, in the case of trout culture facilities, wild broodstock or captive broodstock are often used.

The intensification of salmonid culture and the consequent rearing of fish in man-made environments has resulted in the fish being exposed to a number of stresses which they do not experience at all in the natural environment or do not experience to the same degree. One category of stress occurs as a consequence of the artificial environment itself and can include such factors as temperature, rate of change of temperature, salinity change, stocking density, abrasion, oxygen concentration, free ammonia concentration, pH and water velocity. A second group of potential stresses relates to the artificial diet that is fed to the fish and includes such factors as ration level, protein quality, vitamin concentration, lipid type and quality, mineral level and balance, antinutritional factors, heavy metal and pesticide concentrations. A third group of stresses consists of handling procedures such as capture, anaesthesia, grading, sorting by sex, weighing, measuring, nose tagging, fin clipping and injection. It is evident from the above selection of potential stresses that cultured salmonids may often be subjected to more than one stress at any given time and that some may be acute whereas others are chronic. It is also evident that to date investigators have only scratched the surface in terms of the number of cultural stresses which have been studied. In Table III a number of these investigations have been briefly

TABLE III Examples of the Use of the Primary Response of the HPI Axis to Evaluate Stress Responses in Salmonids to the Stress of Cultural Procedures.

Species	Stress	Parameter	Response	Reference
S. salar	handling	17-hydroxy corticosteroids	+	Leloup-Hatey (1964)
O. tshawytscha	handling	17-hydroxy corticosteroids	+	Hane et al. (1966)
S. gairdneri	shallow water	cortisol	+	Donaldson and McBride (1967)
O. nerka	swimming	cortisol	−	Fagerlund (1967)
	hand net	cortisol	+	
	shallow water	cortisol	+	
	anaesthesia	cortisol	+	
O. nerka	handling and	cortisol	+	Donaldson and
	anaesthesia	cortisol secretion rate	+	Fagerlund (1969)

TABLE III (*continued*)

Species	Stress	Parameter	Response	Reference
O. nerka	handling and anaesthesia	cortisol cortisol secretion rate	+ +	Fagerlund and Donaldson (1969)
O. nerka	anaesthesia and blood sampling	cortisol	+	Fagerlund and McBride (1969)
O. kisutch	cold shock hand net	cortisol cortisol	+ +	Wedemeyer (1969)
S. gairdneri	cold shock hand net shallow water	interrenal ascorbic acid depletion	+ + +	
O. nerka	SW to FW transfer	cortisol cortisol MCR	↓ ↓	Donaldson and Dye (1970)
O. nerka	handling and anaesthesia	cortisol cortisol secretion rate	+ +	Donaldson and Fagerlund (1970)
O. nerka	handling and anaesthesia	cortisone cortisone production rate	+ − + −	Fagerlund and Donaldson (1970)
S. gairdneri	anaesthesia MS 222 benzocaine	interrenal ascorbic acid depletion	+ − −	Wedemeyer (1970)
O. kisutch	cold temperature	cortisol interrenal	+ +	Allan (1971)
S. gairdneri	handling	interrenal ascorbic acid	−	Wedemeyer (1972)
O. kisutch	handling	depletion	−	
S. gairdneri	warm shock	interrenal ascorbic acid	−	Wedemeyer (1973)
O. kisutch	warm shock	depletion	+	
C. lavaretus	capture in net and handling	cortisol	+	Fuller *et al.* (1974, 1976)
S. gairdneri	handling	cortisol	+	Simpson (1975/1976)
S. gairdneri	electroshock	cortisol	+	Schreck *et al.* (1976)
O. tshawytscha	capture in net	cortisol	+	H. M. Dye and E. M. Donaldson (1977 unpublished)
O. kisutch	hypoxia and struggling	cortisol	+	Mazeaud *et al.* (1977)
O. tshawytscha	handling	cortisol	+	Strange *et al.* (1977)
S. clarki	handling warm shock	cortisol	+	Strange *et al.* (1977)
O. tshawytscha	anaesthesia handling	cortisol	+ +	Strange and Schreck 1978
O. tshawytscha	confinement	cortisol	+	Strange *et al.* (1978)
O. tshawytscha	SW transfer	cortisol	+ −	Strange and Schreck (1980)
S. gairdneri	handling confinement stocking	cortisol	+ + +	Barton *et al.* (1980)

summarized and arranged in chronological order. The indices of HPI axis activity which have been used include plasma cortisol concentration, inter-renal histopathology and interrenal ascorbic acid concentration. Recent work at this laboratory using samples provided by G. Haywood and W. C. Clarke has shown that plasma cortisol is elevated in coho salmon presmolts during chronic exposure to ammonia at pH 6·9 (Fig. 6) (E. M. Donaldson,

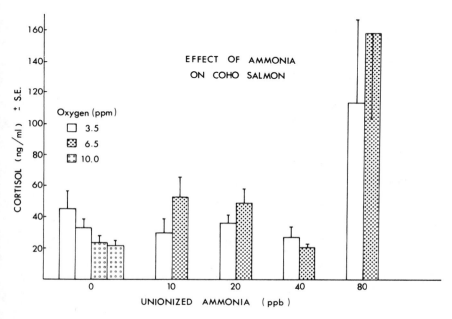

Fig. 6   Effect of chronic exposure to ammonia on plasma cortisol concentration in undisturbed coho salmon at three different oxygen concentrations (E. M. Donaldson, H. M. Dye and G. Haywood, 1980, unpublished).

H. M. Dye and G. Haywood, 1980, unpublished). The data indicate that a relatively low oxygen concentration of 3·5 p.p.m. does not in itself cause a measurable stress response (Fig. 6) although it does reduce growth rate (Haywood *et al.*, in preparation, see also Smart, 1981, this volume). When ammonia is present at 80 p.p.b. the fish in both the 3·5 and 6·5 p.p.m. oxygen groups are stressed. In a second ammonia experiment the fish were handled 2–6 h prior to sampling (Fig. 7). In this study the control concen-trations were elevated but the cortisol concentrations in the salmon exposed to ammonia were even higher.

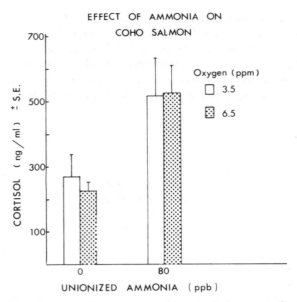

Fig. 7   Effect of chronic exposure to ammonia on plasma cortisol concentration in coho salmon
which had been anaesthetized and handled 2–6 h prior to sampling (E. M. Donaldson, H. M.
Dye and G. Haywood, 1980, unpublished).

Another type of culture stress which has been examined recently is that of
stocking density. The return rate of adult coho salmon to the Capilano
hatchery has been shown to be inversely related to the culture density of the
presmolts during the 15 months in the hatchery prior to release (F. K.
Sandercock and E. T. Stone, 1979, unpublished). In a subsequent study at
this laboratory it has been shown that the interrenal nuclear diameters of
coho smolts raised at the Capilano hatchery were higher in fish raised at
104 600 per Burrows pond than those raised at 56 000 per pond. The
difference (6·82 µm versus 6·10 µm) was significant ($p < 0.05$) in those fish
which comprised the smallest third of the high density group (Fagerlund *et
al.*, 1981). Under different situations, however, other workers have been
unable to demonstrate any relationship between loading density and blood
cortisol levels (see Schreck, 1981, this volume).

A third type of culture stress that we have investigated is the effect of
capture and transport to the hatchery on adult chinook salmon during their
anadromous migration. This experiment was described and plasma
adrenaline values provided in Fig. 4 of Mazeaud *et al.* (1977). Plasma
cortisol values for these same fish are presented in Fig. 8 (H. M. Dye and E.
M. Donaldson, 1976, unpublished). While the plasma catecholamine levels

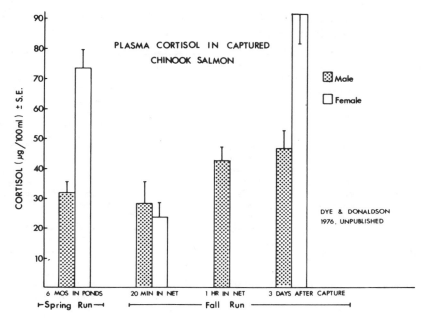

Fig. 8 Effects of capture on plasma cortisol in fall-run chinook salmon from the Puntledge River and comparison with spring-run chinook held for 6 months in ponds (H. M. Dye and E. M. Donaldson, 1976, unpublished).

decreased in the male and female fall run chinook after capture (Mazeaud *et al.*, 1977) the plasma cortisol concentrations in the female chinook were higher 3 days after capture and transfer to the hatchery ponds than 20 minutes after capture. The plasma cortisol level was also high in mature spring chinook which had been in the ponds for 6 months and were sampled at the same time. The high cortisol levels in the female chinook may have been a result of physical confinement in the hatchery ponds and/or been associated with the sexual maturation process.

(b) Stress Response to Disease and Disease Treatments

Salmonids are exposed to disease-related stress in both culture facilities where it may coincide with other stresses such as density or dietary problems and in the natural environment where it may also occur in conjunction with other stresses such as temperature. A number of studies in which the HPI axis has responded during disease have been collated in Table IV. Most of these studies have been concerned, indirectly or directly, with the effect of fungal infections by *Saprolegnia* sp. However, evidence is also available

TABLE IV   Examples of the Use of the Primary Response of the HPI Axis to Evaluate Stress Responses in Salmonids to Disease and Related Factors.

Species	Stress	Parameter	Response	Reference
O. nerka	*Saprolegnia*	cortisol	+	Fagerlund (1967)
O. nerka	*Saprolegnia,* etc.	cortisol cortisol MCR	+ +	Donaldson and Fagerlund (1968)
O. nerka	*Saprolegnia*	cortisol interrenal	+ +	Fagerlund and McBride (1969)
S. gairdneri	endotoxin	cortisol	+	Wedemeyer (1969)
S. gairdneri	formalin	interrenal ascorbic acid	+	Wedemeyer (1971)
O. kisutch	formalin	depletion	+	
S. gairdneri	*Myxobacterium*	cortisol	+	Simpson (1975/1976)
O. nerka	bacterial infection	interrenal cortisol	+ − + −	Williams *et al.* (1977)
S. gairdneri	kanamycin	interrenal cortisol	+ − +	McBride *et al.* (1975) Mazeaud *et al.* (1977)
O. gorbuscha	bacterial kidney disease	cortisol	+	E. M. Donaldson and H. M. Dye (1977, unpublished)
O. kisutch (smolts)	bacterial kidney disease and/or *Cryptobia*	cortisol	+	E. M. Donaldson H. M. Dye, G. A. Hunter and M. L. Skwarok (1980, unpublished)
S. trutta	*Saprolegnia*	cortisol	+	Pickering and Christie (1981)

which indicates an HPI axis response in bacterial disease. Other studies have shown that disease treatment itself including the use of some anaesthetics and antibiotics is stressful Tables III and IV (see also the abstract by Wootten and Williams, 1981, this volume).

In a preliminary study on pink salmon, *Oncorhynchus gorbuscha*, conducted in this laboratory there appears to be a correlation between the severity of bacterial kidney disease and plasma cortisol concentration. In this study, using small numbers of fish, it appears that the infection has to be in an advanced stage before there is a marked change in plasma cortisol (Fig. 9) (E. M. Donaldson and H. M. Dye, 1976, unpublished).

In a recent study, coho smolts from an experimental, semi-natural, rearing channel containing riffles and pools (Mundie and Mounce, 1978) were compared with coho smolts reared at a higher density in a production channel. There was no significant difference between the two groups in plasma cortisol except for a group of moribund diseased fish (B.K.D. and/or *Cryptobia*) at the lower end of the production channel which had significantly higher cortisol concentrations (Fig. 10, E. M. Donaldson, H. M.

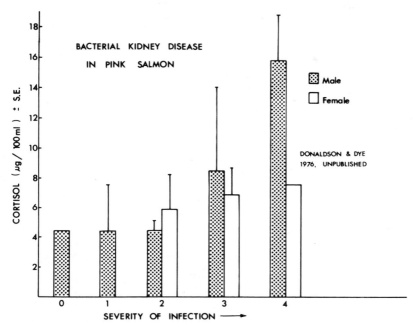

Fig. 9 Effect of bacterial kidney disease on plasma cortisol concentration in pink salmon.
Severity of infection in arbitary units based on inspection of kidney tissue (E. M. Donaldson and
H. M. Dye, 1976, unpublished).

Dye, G. A. Hunter and M. L. Skwarok, 1980, unpublished). It is evident
from the foregoing experiment that plasma cortisol may not be the most
sensitive indicator of HPI axis activity when fish are exposed to mild stress
for an extended period which enables acclimation to occur. This conforms
with the opinion of Schreck (1981, this volume) who argues that ideal
compensation (with respect to blood cortisol levels) may take place in
salmonid fish under conditions of mild, chronic stress, although the performance capacity of the fish may still be impaired. On the other hand,
interrenal histopathology may provide a measure of HPI axis activity in
these circumstances as was evident in the density study at the Capilano
hatchery.

The activity of the HPI axis has been used in the investigation of disease in
salmonids in the natural environment as well as in fish culture facilities.
Prespawning mortality in Horsefly River sockeye salmon was investigated
using both interrenal histopathology and plasma cortisol concentrations
(Williams et al., 1977). Normally, the first group of anadromous migrants
undergoes higher prespawning mortality than the central group of migrants.

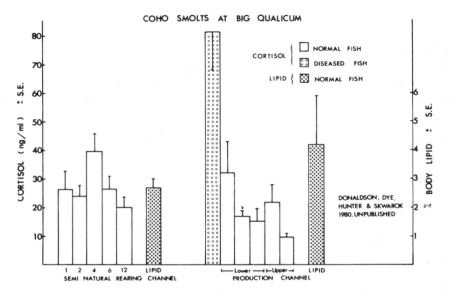

Fig. 10   Plasma cortisol concentration and body lipid content in coho salmon smolts reared in semi-natural and production rearing channels at Big Qualicum River Hatchery. Diseased fish (B.K.D. and/or *Cryptobia*) had a significantly higher mean cortisol concentration. Production fish had a significantly higher lipid content than those in the semi-natural rearing channel, $n = 14$ for cortisol, $n = 5$ for lipid. (E. M. Donaldson, H. M. Dye, G. A. Hunter and M. L. Skwarok, 1980, unpublished).

While differences were observed between the two segments of the run in the activity of the HPI axis using both techniques the interpretation was complicated by the fact that in the year of the investigation the incidence of prespawning mortality was similar in both groups (Williams *et al.*, 1977).

(c) Stress Response to Water Pollutants

Man's activities have had an increasing impact on the natural environment of salmonids and other fish both in fresh water and in coastal, saltwater habitats. Sources of pollution which have the potential to affect water quality for salmonids include sewage and sanitary landfill leachate, eutrophication and consequent chemical weed control measures, pulp mill effluent from the forestry industry, heavy metals from the mining industry and pesticides from the agricultural industry.

A number of research investigations have been conducted which show that many of the above categories of pollutants, when present at an appropriate concentration, induce a stress response in salmonids which can be detected by evaluation of the activity of the HPI axis (Table V). Careful

TABLE V Examples of the Use of the Primary Response of the HPI Axis
to Evaluate Stress Responses in Salmonids to Pollutant Stress.

Species	Stress	Parameter	Response	Reference
S. gairdneri	various	corticosteroid urinary metabolites	+	McKim (1966)
S. gairdneri	chromium	"cortisol"[b]	+	Hill and Fromm (1968)
O. kisutch	kraft pulp mill effluent	interrenal[a]	−	McLeay (1973)
S. gairdneri	endrin	cortisol	+	Grant and Mehrle (1973)
O. nerka	dehydroabietic acid	cortisol cortisone[c]	+ +	Dye and Donaldson (1975)
O. nerka	copper	cortisol cortisone	+ +	Donaldson and Dye (1975)
O. kisutch	coal dust	interrenal	−	Pearce and McBride (1977)
S. gairdneri	2:4-D	interrenal	+	Pearce and McBride (1978)
O. kisutch	copper cadmium	cortisol cortisol	+ −	Schreck and Lorz (1978)
O. kisutch	mercury	cortisol	+	Lorz et al. (1978)
S. gairdneri	landfill leachate	interrenal cortisol	+ +	McBride et al. (1979)
O. nerka	2:4-D	interrenal cortisol	+ +	J. R. McBride, H. M. Dye and E. M. Donaldson (1980, unpublished)
O. kisutch	ammonia	cortisol	+	E. M. Donaldson, H. M. Dye and G. Haywood (1980, unpublished)

[a] Measurement of interrenal nuclear diameter and/or cell size.
[b,c] Measurement of plasma concentration.

examination of the HPI axis response at different concentrations of pollutant can reveal different response modes. A low level of pollutant may cause a slow transitory increase in plasma cortisol concentration followed by a decline to a basal level, indicating that adaptation to the stress has occurred. A moderate concentration of the same pollutant may cause a more rapid and larger perturbation of plasma cortisol again followed by a decline. In these fish however, depending on the actual dose, there may be a secondary rise in plasma cortisol suggesting that the fish have in fact failed to adapt. At high concentrations of pollutant a rapid rise in plasma cortisol may be seen to an elevated level which is often maintained until death ensues. The work conducted in this laboratory on the plasma cortisol response to copper in sockeye salmon illustrates these three categories of response (Donaldson and Dye, 1975).

Our data on copper were confirmed in a subsequent study on coho salmon but a concurrent study on cadmium failed to show a significant effect on plasma cortisol in coho salmon (Schreck and Lorz, 1978). In this study, the earliest sample for plasma cortisol was taken at 6 h and there was some fluctuation in control values. The salmon were reported to be sedated by cadmium and it is possible that this substance causes death without triggering a marked HPI axis response.

Recently we have looked into the effect of sanitary landfill leachate on rainbow trout. This leachate was remarkably toxic and produced a significant response in the HPI axis at concentrations of 5% and 0·5% (Fig. 11). Interestingly, at the lower concentration there was a transitory effect on

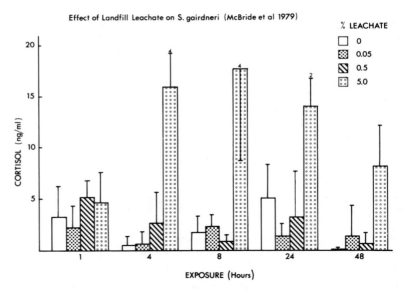

Fig. 11   Effect of sanitary landfill leachate on the plasma cortisol concentration of rainbow trout held in fresh water. $n = 5$ except where indicated on the figure (data derived from McBride et al., 1979).

plasma cortisol after one hour of exposure while the effect on interrenal nuclear diameter at this concentration was only apparent in trout exposed for 7 days (McBride et al., 1979).

Investigation of a form of the herbicide, 2:4-D, which has been used for control of Eurasian milfoil in lakes inhabited by salmonids has shown that it causes a response in the HPI axis in sockeye salmon smolts and fry (J. R. McBride, E. M. Donaldson and H. M. Dye, 1980, unpublished). The response is however, only seen in smolts exposed to a high concentration of the herbicide (Fig. 12).

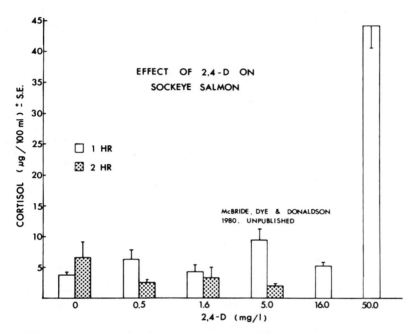

Fig. 12   Effect of the butoxy ethanol ester form of 2:4-D on the plasma concentration of cortisol in sockeye salmon smolts held in fresh water (J. R. McBride, H. M. Dye and E. M. Donaldson, 1980, unpublished).

VII   CONCLUSIONS

Teleosts in general and in the present review, salmonids, in particular, have been shown to have a functional hypothalamic-pituitary–interrenal (HPI) axis which is sensitive and responsive to stresses. The response of the HPI axis to culture procedures, disease, and xenobiotics can in many cases be used to quantify and compare the relative significance of different stresses. The use of the HPI axis may be particularly appropriate where fish are exposed to two or more sublethal stresses simultaneously as the response reflects the integrated effect of the several components.

ACKNOWLEDGEMENTS

I wish to thank my colleagues U. H. M. Fagerlund, J. R. McBride and Helen M. Dye for their collaborative and independent research efforts which have contributed to this paper. I also wish to thank Drs W. C. Clarke, G. Haywood and H. Mundie for permitting the analysis of samples from their experimental fish and Morva, Helen and Michele for able assistance in the preparation of the manuscript.

REFERENCES

Allan, G. D. (1971). Measurement of plasma cortisol and histometry of the inter-renal gland of juvenile pre-smolt coho salmon (*Oncorhynchus kisutch* Walbaum) during cold temperature acclimation. MSc. Thesis, University of British Columbia.

Ashcom, T. L., Markle, J. T., Neff, W. H. and Anthony, A. (1977). Serum cortisol and interrenal ribonucleic acid changes in brook trout subjected to sublethal acid stresses. (Abstract). *Am. Zool.* **17**, 873.

Astwood, E. B., Raben, M. S., Payne, R. W. and Grady, A. B. (1951). Purification of corticotropin with oxycellulose. *J. Am. chem. Soc.* **73**, 2969.

Baker, B. I. (1963). Comportement en culture organotypique des cellules de l'hypophyse de la truite. *C.r. hebd. Séanc. Acad. Sci., Paris* **256**, 3356–3358.

Baker, B. I. (1965). The site of synthesis of the melanophore stimulating hormone in the trout pituitary gland. *J. Endocr.* **32**, 397–398.

Baker, B. I. (1979). The evolution of ACTH, MSH and LPH—structure, function and development. In *Hormones and Evolution* (E. J. W. Barrington, ed.), pp. 643–722. London and New York: Academic Press.

Ball, J. N. and Baker, B. I. (1969). The pituitary gland: anatomy and histophysiology. In *Fish Physiology*, Vol. 2 (W. S. Hoar and D. J. Randall, eds), pp. 1–110. New York and London: Academic Press.

Ball, J. N. and Olivereau, M. (1966). Identification of ACTH cells in the pituitary of two teleosts, *Poecilia latipinna* and *Anguilla anguilla*; correlated changes in the interrenal and in the pars distalis resulting from administration of metopirone (SU 4885). *Gen. comp. Endocr.* **6**, 5–18.

Barton, B. A., Peter, R. E. and Paulencu, C. R. (1980). Plasma cortisol levels in fingerling rainbow trout (*Salmo gairdneri*) at rest and subjected to handling; confinement, transport and stocking. *J. Fish. Res. Bd Can.* **37**, 805–811.

Bennett, H. P., Lowry, P. J., McMartin, C. and Scott, A. P. (1974). Structural studies of α melanocyte-stimulating hormone and a novel β-melanocyte-stimulating hormone from the neurointermediate lobe of the pituitary of the dogfish *Squalus acanthias*. *Biochem. J.* **141**, 439–444.

Boyd, A. E., Sanchez-Franco, F., Spencer, E., Patel, Y. C., Jackson, I. M. D. and Reichlin, S. (1978). Characterization of hypophysiotropic hormones in porcine hypothalamic extracts. *Endocrinology* **103**, 1075–1083.

Buckingham, J. C. and Hodges, J. R. (1977). The use of corticotropin production by adenohypophysial tissue *in vitro* for the detection and estimation of potential corticotrophin releasing factors. *J. Endocr.* **72**, 187–193.

Butler, D. G. (1973). Structure and function of the adrenal gland of fishes. *Am. Zool.* **13**, 839–879.

Chester Jones, I. (1957). *The Adrenal Cortex*. Cambridge University Press. 316pp.

Chester Jones, I., Chan, D. K. O., Henderson, I. W. and Ball, J. N. (1969). The adrenocortical steroids, adrenocorticotropin and the corpuscles of Stannius. In *Fish Physiology*, Vol. 2 (W. S. Hoar and D. J. Randall, eds), pp. 322–376. London and New York: Academic Press.

de Roos, R. and de Roos, C. C. (1967). Presence of corticotropin activity in the pituitary gland of chondrichthyean fish. *Gen. comp. Endocr.* **9**, 267–275.

de Wied, D., Bouman, P. R. and Smelik, P. G. (1958). The effect of a lipid extract from the posterior hypothalamus and of pitressin on the release of ACTH from the pituitary gland. *Endocrinology* **62**, 605–613.

Donaldson, E. M. and Dye, H. M. (1970). Effect of transfer from salt water to fresh water on cortisol dynamics in maturing salmon (*Oncorhynchus nerka*). *Int. Congr. Horm. Steroid, 3rd, Hamburg, 1970. Excerpta Med. Found. Int. Congr. Ser. No.* 210, 236.

Donaldson, E. M. and Dye, H. M. (1975). Corticosteroid concentrations in sockeye salmon (*Oncorhynchus nerka*) exposed to low concentrations of copper. *J. Fish. Res. Bd Can.* **32**, 533–539.

Donaldson, E. M. and Fagerlund, U. H. M. (1968). Changes in the cortisol dynamics of sockeye salmon (*Oncorhynchus nerka*) resulting from sexual maturation. *Gen. comp. Endocr.* **11**, 552–561.

Donaldson, E. M. and Fagerlund, U. H. M. (1969). Cortisol secretion rate in gonadectomized female sockeye salmon (*Oncorhynchus nerka*): effects of estrogen and cortisol treatment. *J. Fish Res. Bd Can.* **26**, 1789–1799.

Donaldson, E. M. and Fagerlund, U. H. M. (1970). Effect of sexual maturation and gonadectomy at sexual maturity on cortisol secretion rate in sockeye salmon (*Oncorhynchus nerka*). *J. Fish. Res. Bd Can.* **27**, 2287–2296.

Donaldson, E. M. and Fagerlund, U. H. M. (1972). Corticosteroid dynamics in Pacific salmon. *Gen. comp. Endocr.* Suppl. **3**, 254–265.

Donaldson, E. M. and McBride, J. R. (1967). The effects of hypophysectomy in the rainbow trout *Salmo gairdneri* (Rich.) with special reference to the pituitary–interrenal axis. *Gen. comp. Endocr.* **9**, 93–101.

Donaldson, E. M. and McBride, J. R. (1974). Effect of ACTH and salmon gonadotropin on interrenal and thyroid activity of gonadectomized adult sockeye salmon (*Oncorhynchus nerka*). *J. Fish. Res. Bd Can.* **31**, 1211–1214.

Donaldson, E. M., Yamazaki, F. and Clarke, W. C. (1968a). Effect of hypophysectomy on plasma osmolarity in goldfish and its reversal by ovine prolactin and a preparation of salmon pituitary "prolactin". *J. Fish. Res. Bd Can.* **25**, 1497–1500.

Donaldson, E. M., Fagerlund, U. H. M. and Schmidt, P. J. (1968b). Fluorimetric method for the determination of cortisol in small quantities of salmonid plasma. *J. Fish. Res. Bd Can.* **27**, 71–79.

Donaldson, E. M., Yamazaki, F., Dye, H. M. and Philleo, W. W. (1972). Preparation of gonadotropin from salmon (*Oncorhynchus tshawytscha*) pituitary glands. *Gen. comp. Endocr.* **18**, 469–481.

Dye, H. M. and Donaldson, E. M. (1974). A preliminary study of corticosteroid stress response in sockeye salmon to a component of kraft pulp mill effluent dehydroabietic acid. *Fish. Mar. Ser. Res. Dev. Tech. Rep. Canada.* No. 461.

Fagerlund, U. H. M. (1967). Plasma cortisol concentration in relation to stress in adult sockeye salmon during the fresh water stage of their life cycle. *Gen. comp. Endocr.* **8**, 197–207.

Fagerlund, U. H. M. (1970). Response to mammalian ACTH of the interrenal tissue of sockeye salmon (*Oncorhynchus nerka*) at various stages of sexual maturation. *J. Fish. Res. Bd Can.* **27**, 1169–1172.

Fagerlund, U. H. M. and Donaldson, E. M. (1969). The effect of androgens on the distribution and secretion of cortisol in gonadectomized male sockeye salmon (*Oncorhynchus nerka*). *Gen. comp. Endocr.* **12**, 438–448.

Fagerlund, U. H. M. and Donaldson, E. M. (1970). Dynamics of cortisone secretion in sockeye salmon (*Oncorhynchus nerka*) during sexual maturation and after gonadectomy. *J. Fish. Res. Bd Can.* **27**, 2323–2331.

Fagerlund, U. H. M. and McBride, J. R. (1969). Suppression by dexamethasone of interrenal activity in adult sockeye salmon (*Oncorhynchus nerka*). *Gen. comp. Endocr.* **12**, 651–657.

Fagerlund, U. H. M., McBride, J. R. and Donaldson, E. M. (1968). Effect of metopirone on pituitary–interrenal function in two teleosts, sockeye salmon (*Oncorhynchus nerka*) and rainbow trout (*Salmo gairdneri*). *J. Fish. Res. Bd Can.* **25**, 1465–1474.

Fagerlund, U. H. M., McBride, J. R. and Stone, E. T. (1981). Stress related effects of hatchery rearing density on coho salmon (*Oncorhynchus kisutch*). *Trans. Am. Fish. Soc.* (in press).

Follenius, E. and Dubois, M. P. (1976). Etude immunocytologique des cellules corticotropes de plusieures espèces de poissons teleosteens: *Gasterosteus aculeatus* L., *Carassius auratus* L., *Lebistes reticulatus* P., *Salmo irideus* Gibb et *Perca fluviatilis* L. *Gen. comp. Endocr.* **28**, 339–349.

Follenius, E. and Dubois, M. P. (1978). Immunocytological detection and localization of a peptide reacting with an α endorphin antiserum in the corticotropic and melanotropic cells of the trout pituitary (*Salmo irideus* Gibb). *Cell Tiss. Res.* **188**, 273–283.

Follenius, E. and Dubois, M. P. (1980). Localization of Anti-ACTH, Anti-MSH, and Anti-α-Endorphin reactive sites in the fish pituitary. In *Synthesis and Release of Adenohypophyseal Hormones* (M. Jutisz and K. W. McKerns, eds), pp. 197–208. New York and London: Plenum Press.

Follenius, E., Doerr-Schott, J. and Dubois, M. P. (1978). Immunocytology of pituitary cells from teleost fishes. *Int. Rev. Cytol.* **54**, 193–223.

Fontaine-Bertrand, E., Daveau-Vautier, M. and Fontaine, Y. A. (1969). Activites corticotrope et melanotrope des extracts hypopysaires de deuse poissons téléostéens (carpe et saumon). Dissociation anatomique de ces deux activités. *J. Physiol., Paris* **61**, 493–506.

Fryer, J. N. and Peter, R. E. (1977a). Hypothalamic control of ACTH secretion in goldfish. I. Corticotrophin releasing factor activity in teleost brain tissue extracts. *Gen. comp. Endocr.* **33**, 196–201.

Fryer, J. N. and Peter, R. E. (1977b). Hypothalamic control of ACTH secretion in goldfish. II. Hypothalamic lesioning studies. *Gen. comp. Endocr.* **33**, 202–214.

Fryer, J. N. and Peter, R. E. (1977c). Hypothalamic control of ACTH secretion in goldfish. III. Hypothalamic cortisol implant studies. *Gen. comp. Endocr.* **33**, 215–225.

Fryer, J. N. and Maler, L. (1980). Identification of putative CRF neurones in the goldfish hypothalamus (Abstract). *The Physiologist* **23**, 145.

Fuller, J. D., Scott, D. B. C. and Fraser, R. (1974). Effect of catching techniques captivity and reproductive cycle on plasma cortisol concentration in powan (*Coregonus lavaretus*) a freshwater teleost from Loch Lomond. (Abstract). *J. Endocr.* **63**(2), 24.

Fuller, J. D., Scott, D. B. C. and Fraser, R. (1976). The reproductive cycle of *Coregonus lavaretus* in Loch Lomond, Scotland in relation to seasonal changes in plasma cortisol concentration. *J. Fish Biol.* **9**(2), 105–117.

Gillies, G. and Lowry, P. J. (1979). The relationship between vasopressin and corticotropin-releasing factor. In *Interaction with the Brain-Pituitary–Adrenocortical System* (M. T. Jones, ed.), pp. 51–61. London and New York: Academic Press.

Grant, B. F. and Mehrle, P. M. (1973). Endrin toxicosis in rainbow trout (*Salmo gairdneri*). *J. Fish Res. Bd Can.* **30**, 31–40.

Guillemin, R. and Rosenberg, B. (1955). Humoral hypothalamic control of anterior pituitary: Study with combined tissue cultures. *Endocrinology* **57**, 599–607.

Guillemin, R., Vargo, T., Rossier, J., Minick, S., Ling, N., Rivier, C., Vale, W. and Bloom, F. (1977). Beta endorphin and ACTH are secreted concomitantly by the pituitary gland. *Science, NY.* **197**, 1367–1369.

Hane, S. and Robertson, O. H. (1959). Changes in plasma 17-hydroxy-corticosteroids accompanying sexual maturation and spawning of the Pacific salmon (*Oncorhynchus tshawytscha*) and rainbow trout (*Salmo gairdneri*). *Proc. Nat. Acad. Sci. U.S.A.* **45**, 886–893.

Hane, S., Robertson, O. H., Wexler, B. C. and Krupp, A. (1966). Adrenocortical response to stress and ACTH in Pacific salmon (*Oncorhynchus tshawytscha*) and steelhead trout (*Salmo gairdneri*) at successive stages in the sexual cycle. *Endocrinology* **78**, 791–800.

Hargreaves, G. and Ball, J. N. (1977). Cortisol in *Poecilia latipinna*; its identification and the validation of methods for its determination in plasmas. *Steroids* **30**, 303–313.

Hawkins, E. F. and Ball, J. N. (1973). Current knowledge of the mechanisms involved in the control of ACTH secretion in teleost fishes. In *Brain-Pituitary–Adrenal Interrelationships*. (A. Brodish and E. S. Redgate, eds), pp. 293–315. Basel: S. Karger.

Hawkins, E. F., Hargreaves, G. and Ball, J. N. (1970). Studies in *in vivo* cortisol secretion and its pituitary control in *Poecilia latipinna* (Teleostei). *J. Endocr.* **48**, lxxiv–lxxv.

Hill, C. W. and Fromm, P. O. (1968). Response of the interrenal gland of rainbow trout (*S. gairdneri*) to stress. *Gen. comp. Endocr.* **11**, 69–77.

Idler, D. R. and Truscott, B. (1972). Corticosteroids in fish. In *Steroids in Non-Mammalian Vertebrates* (D. R. Idler, ed.), pp. 127–252. London and New York: Academic Press.

Ito, Y., Takabatake, E. and Ui, H. (1952). Researches on the fish pituitary. II. Adrenocorticotropic activity of fish pituitary gland. *J. Pharmaceutical Soc. Japan.* **72**, 1029–1033.

Jorgensen, C. B. (1976). Sub-mammalian vertebrate hypothalamic-pituitary adrenal interrelationships. In *General Comparative and Clinical Endocrinology of the Adrenal Cortex, Vol. 1* (I. Chester Jones and I. W. Henderson, eds), pp. 143–206. London and New York: Academic Press.

Junnila, R. D. and Sayers, G. (1977). Differences in the kinetics of ACTH secretion by isolated anterior pituitary cells in response to hypothalamic median eminence (HME) extract, vasopressin, and dibutyryl cyclic AMP (db-c-AMP). *Proc. Endocr. Soc. U.S.A.* **59**, 215.

Kawauchi, H. (1979). Isolation and primary structure of whale and fish pituitary hormones. *J. agric. Chem. Soc. Japan* **53**, R141–R150.

Kawauchi, H., Abe, K. and Takahashi, A. (1980). Corticotropin like intermediate lobe peptide in the salmon pituitary. *Bull. Jap. Soc. scient. Fish.* **46**, 743–747.
Kime, D. E. (1978). The hepatic catabolism of cortisol in teleost fish-adrenal origin of 11-oxotestosterone precursors. *Gen. comp. Endocr.* **35**, 322–328.
Leloup-Hatey, J. (1964). Functionnement de l'interrenal anterieur de deux teleo-steens: le salmon atlantique et l'anguille europeene. *Annls Inst. Oceanogr., Monaco* **42**, 221–338.
Li, C. H. (1952). Recent studies on the problems involved in the preparation, properties and bioassay of adrenocorticotrophic hormone. *Acta endocr.* **10**, 255–296.
Lorz, H. W., Williams, R. H. and Fustish, C. A. (1978). Effects of several metals on smolting of coho salmon *Oncorhynchus kisutch*. *U.S. Environ. Prot. Agency, Environ. Res. Lab., Corvallis*. EPA-600/3-78-090. 85pp.
Love, R. M. and Pickering, B. T. (1974). A β-MSH in the pituitary gland of the spotted dogfish (*Scyliorhinus canicula*): isolation and structure. *Gen. comp. Endocr.* **24**, 398–404.
Lowry, P. J., Bennet, H. P. J., McMartin, C. and Scott, A. P. (1974). The isolation and amino acid sequence of an adrenocorticotrophin from the pars distalis and corticotrophin-like intermediate lobe peptide from the neurointermediate lobe of the pituitary of the dogfish *Squalus acanthias*. *Biochem. J.* **141**, 427–437.
Mazeaud, M. M., Mazeaud, F. and Donaldson, E. M. (1977). Primary and secondary effects of stress in fish: some new data with a general review. *Trans. Am. Fish. Soc.* **106**, 201–212.
McBride, J. R. and van Overbeeke, A. P. (1969). Hypertrophy of the interrenal tissue in sexually maturing sockeye salmon (*Oncorhynchus nerka*) and the effects of gonadectomy. *J. Fish. Res. Bd Can.* **26**, 2975–2985.
McBride, J. R., Donaldson, E. M. and Derksen, G. (1979). Toxicity of landfill leachates to underyearling rainbow trout (*Salmo gairdneri*). *Bull. envir. Contam. Toxicol.* **23**, 806–813.
McBride, J. R., Strasdine, G. and Fagerlund, U. H. M. (1975). Acute toxicity of kanamycin to steelhead trout (*Salmo gairdneri*). *J. Fish. Res. Bd Can.* **32**, 554–558.
McKeown, B. A. and van Overbeeke, A. P. (1969). Immunohistochemical localiza-tion of ACTH and prolactin in the pituitary gland of adult migratory sockeye salmon (*Oncorhynchus nerka*). *J. Fish. Res. Bd Can.* **26**, 1837–1846.
McKim, J. M. (1966). Stress hormone metabolites and their fluctuations in the urine of rainbow trout (*Salmo gairdneri*) under the influence of various sub-lethal stressors. Ph.D. Thesis, University of Michigan.
McLeay, D. J. (1973). Effects of a 12 hr and 25 day exposure of kraft pulp mill effluent on the blood and tissues of juvenile coho salmon (*O. kisutch*). *J. Fish. Res. Bd Can.* **30**, 395–400.
Mundie, J. H. and Mounce, D. E. (1978). Application of stream ecology to raising salmon smolts in high density. *Verh. int. Verein. theor. angew. Limnol.* **20**, 2013–2018.
Nagahama, Y. and Yamamoto, K. (1969a). Fine structure of the glandular cells in the adenohypophysis of the kokanee *Oncorhynchus nerka*. *Bull. Fac. Fish. Hokkaido Univ.* **20**, 159–168.
Nagahama, Y. and Yamamoto, K. (1969b). Morphological studies on the pituitary of the chum salmon, *Oncorhynchus keta*. (1) Fine structure of the adenohypophysis. *Bull. Fac. Fish. Hokkaido Univ.* **20**, 293–301.

Nandi, J. (1962). The structure of the interrenal gland in teleost fishes. *Univ. of Calif. Publs Zool.* **65**, 129–211.

Nandi, J. and Bern, H. A. (1960). Corticosteroid production by interrenal tissue of teleost fishes. *Endocrinology* **66**, 295–303.

Nandi, J. and Bern, H. A. (1965). Chromatography of corticosteroids from teleost fishes. *Gen. comp. Endocr.* **5**, 1–15.

Oguri, M. (1971). A histological study of the ACTH cells in the pituitary glands of freshwater teleosts. *Bull. Jap. Soc. scient. Fish.* **37**, 577–584.

Olivereau, M. (1964). L'hematoxyline au plomb permet -elle l'identification des cellules corticotropes de l'hypophyse des teleosteens? *Z. Zellforsch. mikrosk. Anat.* **63**, 496–505.

Olivereau, M. (1970). Coloration de l'hypophyse avec l'hematoxyline au plomb (H-Pb): données nouvelles chez les teléostéens et comparison avec les resultats obtenus chez d'autres vertebrés. *Acta zool., Stokh.* **51**, 229–249.

Pearce, B. C. and McBride, J. R. (1977). A preliminary study on the occurrence of coal dust in Roberts Bank sediments and the effect of coal dust on selected fauna. *Fish. Mar. Serv. Tech. Rep.* No. PAC/T-77-17.

Pearce, B. C. and McBride, J. R. (1978). A preliminary investigation of the effect of 2,4-dichlorophenoxyacetic acid (butoxy ethanol ester) on juvenile rainbow trout. *Fish. Mar. Serv. Ms. Rep.* No. 1478.

Perks, A. M. (1969). The neurohypophysis. In *Fish Physiology, Vol. 2.* (W. S. Hoar and D. J. Randall, eds) pp 111–205. London and New York: Academic Press.

Peter, R. E. and Fryer, J. N. (1981). Endocrine functions of the hypothalamus of actinopterygians. In *Fish Neurobiology and Behavior* (R. E. Davis and R. G. Northcutt, eds). Ann Arbor: University of Michigan Press, (in press).

Peter, R. E., Hontela, A., Cook, A. F. and Paulencu, C. R. (1978). Daily cycles in serum cortisol levels in the goldfish. Effects of photoperiod, temperature and sexual condition. *Can. J. Zool.* **56**, 2443–2448.

Pezalla, P. D., Clarke, W. C., Lis, M., Seidah, N. G. and Chretien, M. (1978). Immunological characterization of β-lipotropin fragments (endorphin, βMSH and N fragment) from fish pituitaries. *Gen. comp. Endocr.* **34**, 163–168.

Pickering, A. D. and Christie, P. (1981). Changes in the concentrations of plasma cortisol and thyroxine during sexual maturation of the hatchery reared brown trout, *Salmo trutta* L. *Gen. comp. Endocr.* **44**, (in press).

Purrot, R. J. and Sage, M. (1967). *In vitro* assay of ACTH using mouse adrenals. *J. Endocr.* **38**, xvi–xvii.

Redgate, E. S. (1974). Neural control of pituitary adrenal activity in *Cyprinus carpio. Gen. comp. Endocr.* **22**, 35–41.

Rinfret, A. P. and Hane, S. (1955). Presence of ACTH in pituitary gland of Pacific salmon (*O. keta*). *Proc. Soc. exp. Biol. Med.* **90**, 508–510.

Riniker, B., Sieber, P., Rittel, W. and Zuber, H. (1972). Revised amino-acid sequences for porcine and human adrenocorticotrophic hormone. *Nature, Lond.* **235**, 114–115.

Roberts, J. L. and Herbert, E. (1977). Characterization of a common precursor to corticotropin and β-lipotropin; identification of β-lipotropin peptides and their arrangement relative to corticotropin in the precursor synthesized in a cell-free system. *Proc. Nat. Acad. Sci., U.S.A.* **74**, 5300–5304.

Saffran, M. and Schally, A. V. (1955). The release of corticotrophin in anterior pituitary tissue *in vitro. Can. J. Biochem. Physiol.* **33**, 408–415.

Saffran, M. and Schally, A. V. (1977). The status of corticotropin releasing factor (CRF). *Neuroendocrinology* **24**, 359–375.

Saffran, M., Schally, A. V. and Benfey, B. G. (1955). Stimulation of the release of corticotropin from the adenohypophysis by a neurohypophysial factor. *Endocrinology* **57**, 439–444.

Sage, M. and Purrot, R. J. (1969). The control of teleost ACTH cells. *Z. vergl. Physiol.* **63**, 85–90.

Sandor, T., Fazekas, A. G. and Robinson, B. H. (1976). The biosynthesis of corticosteroids throughout the vertebrates. In *General Comparative and Clinical Endocrinology of the Adrenal Cortex, Vol. 1* (I. Chester Jones and I. W. Henderson, eds), pp. 25–142. London and New York: Academic Press.

Sangalang, G. B., Freeman, H. C., Fleming, R. B. and McMenemy, M. (1980). The determination of cortisol in fish plasma by radioimmunoassay. *Gen. comp. Endocr.* **40**, 459–462.

Schally, A. V. and Bowers, C. Y. (1964). Corticotropin-releasing factor and other hypothalamic peptides. *Metabolism* **13**, 1190–1205.

Schally, A. V., Lipscomb, H. S. and Guillemin, R. (1962). Isolation and amino acid sequence of α_2-corticotropin-releasing factor (α_2-CRF) from hog pituitary glands. *Endocrinology* **71**, 164–173.

Schally, A., Coy, D. H. and Meyers, C. A. (1978). Hypothalamic regulatory hormones. *A. Rev. Biochem.* **47**, 89–128.

Schally, A. V., Coy, D. H., Meyers, C. A. and Kastin, A. J. (1979). Hypothalamic peptide hormones: basic and clinical studies. In *Hormonal Proteins and Peptides, Vol. 7* (C. H. Li, ed.), pp. 1–54. London and New York: Academic Press.

Schmidt, P., Mitchell, B. S., Smith, M. and Tsuyuki, H. (1965). Pituitary hormones of the Pacific salmon. 1. Response of gonads in immature trout (*Salmo gairdneri*) to extracts of pituitary glands from adult Pacific salmon (*Oncorhynchus*). *Gen. comp. Endocr.* **5**, 197–206.

Schreck, C. B. (1981). Stress and compensation in teleostean fishes: response to social and physical factors. In *Stress and Fish* (A. D. Pickering, ed.), pp. 295–321. London and New York: Academic Press.

Schreck, C. B. and Lorz, H. W. (1978). Stress response of coho salmon (*Oncorhynchus kisutch*) elicited by cadmium and copper and potential use of cortisol as an indicator of stress. *J. Fish. Res. Bd Can.* **35**, 1124–1129.

Schreck, C. B., Whaley, R. A., Bass, M. L., Maughan, O. E. and Solazzi, M. (1976). Physiological responses of rainbow trout (*Salmo gairdneri*) to electroshock. *J. Fish. Res. Bd Can.* **33**, 76–84.

Scott, A. P. and Baker, B. I. (1975). ACTH production by the pars intermedia of the rainbow trout pituitary. *Gen. comp. Endocr.* **27**, 193–202.

Scott, A. P., Lowry, P. J., Bennett, H. P. J., McMartin, C. and Ratcliffe, J. G. (1974). Purification and characterization of porcine corticotropin-like intermediate lobe peptide. *J. Endocr.* **61**, 369–380.

Simpson, T. H. (1975/76). Endocrine aspects of salmonid culture. *Proc. R. Soc. Edinb.* **B75**, 241–252.

Singley, J. A. and Chavin, W. (1975). The adrenocortical hypophyseal response to saline stress in the goldfish *Carassius auratus*. *Comp. Biochem. Physiol.* **51A**, 749–756.

Strange, R. J. and Schreck, C. B. (1978). Anesthetic and handling stress on survival and cortisol concentration in yearling chinook salmon (*Oncorhynchus tshawytscha*). *J. Fish. Res. Bd Can.* **35**, 345–349.

Strange, R. J. and Schreck, C. B. (1980). Seawater and confinement alters survival and cortisol concentration in juvenile chinook salmon. *Copeia* **1980**, 351–353.

Strange, R. J., Schreck, C. B. and Golden, J. T. (1977). Corticoid stress responses to handling and temperature in salmonids. *Trans. Am. Fish. Soc.* **106**, 213–217.

Strange, R. J., Schreck, C. B. and Ewing, R. D. (1978). Cortisol concentrations in confined juvenile chinook salmon (*Oncorhynchus tshawytscha*). *Trans. Am. Fish. Soc.* **107**, 812–819.

Truscott, B. (1979). Steroid metabolism in fish. Identification of steroid moieties of hydrolyzable conjugates of cortisol in the bile of trout *Salmo gairdneri*. *Gen. comp. Endocr.* **38**, 196–206.

van Kemenade, J. A. M., Goverde, H. J. M. and Lamers, A. P. M. (1980). The adrenocortical tissue and ACTH in the trout, *Salmo gairdneri* ; annual cycles. *Gen. comp. Endocr.* **40**, 346.

van Overbeeke, A. P. and Ahsan, S. N. (1966). ACTH effect of pituitary glands of Pacific salmon demonstrated in the hypophysectomized *Couesious plumbeus*. *Can. J. Zool.* **44**, 969–979.

van Overbeeke, A. P. and McBride, J. R. (1967). The pituitary gland of the sockeye (*Oncorhynchus nerka*) during sexual maturation and spawning. *J. Fish. Res. Bd Can.* **24**, 1791–1810.

van Overbeeke, A. P. and McBride, J. R. (1971). Histological effects of 11-ketotestosterone, 17α-methyltestosterone, estradiol, estradiol cypionate, and cortisol on the interrenal tissue, thyroid gland, and pituitary gland of gonadectomized sockeye salmon (*Oncorhynchus nerka*). *J. Fish Res. Bd Can.* **28**, 477–484.

Wedemeyer, G. (1969). Pituitary activation by bacterial endotoxins in rainbow trout (*Salmo gairdneri*). *J. Bact.* **100**, 532–543.

Wedemeyer, G. (1969). Stress-induced ascorbic acid depletion and cortisol production in two salmonid fishes. *Comp. Biochem. Physiol.* **29**, 1247–1251.

Wedemeyer, G. (1970). Stress of anesthesia with MS222 and benzocaine in rainbow trout (*Salmo gairdneri*). *J. Fish. Res. Bd Can.* **27**, 909–914.

Wedemeyer, G. (1971). The stress of formalin treatments in rainbow trout (*Salmo gairdneri*) and coho salmon (*Oncorhynchus kisutch*). *J. Fish. Res. Bd Can.* **28**, 1899–1904.

Wedemeyer, G. (1972). Some physiological consequences of handling stress in the juvenile coho salmon (*Oncorhynchus kisutch*) and steelhead trout (*Salmo gairdneri*). *J. Fish. Res. Bd Can.* **29**, 1780–1783.

Wedemeyer, G. (1973). Some physiological aspects of sublethal heat stress in the juvenile steelhead trout (*Salmo gairdneri*) and coho salmon (*Oncorhynchus kisutch*). *J. Fish. Res. Bd Can.* **30**, 831–834.

Williams, I. V., Fagerlund, U. H. M., McBride, J. R., Strasdine, G. A., Tsuzuki, H. and Ordal, E. J. (1977). Investigation of prespawning mortality of 1973 Horsefly River sockeye salmon. *Prog. Rep. int. Pacif. Salm. Fish. Comm.* No. **37**, 1–37.

Woodhead, A. D. (1960). The presence of adrenocorticotropic hormone in the pituitary of the arctic cod, *Gadus morhua* L. *J. Endocr.* **21**, 295–301.

Wootten, R. and Williams, H. A. (1981). Some effects of therapeutic treatments with copper sulphate and formalin in rainbow trout, *Salmo gairdneri* Richardson (Abstract). In *Stress and Fish* (A. D. Pickering, ed.), pp. 334–335. London and New York: Academic Press.

3. Adrenergic Responses to Stress in Fish

M. M. MAZEAUD and F. MAZEAUD

Institut Océanographique, 75005 Paris, France

Abstract. In fish there is no equivalent of the mammalian adrenal gland and the chromaffin cells are scattered in different organs depending on the species. The biosynthesis of catecholamines occurs in the chromaffin cells and the inactivation of these molecules is performed by deamination and O-methylation in the liver and kidney before being excreted via the urine. The adrenergic function of fish is very sensitive to stress which inevitably results in an increase of the concentrations of plasma catecholamines. Regardless of the nature of the stress, either adrenaline or noradrenaline may be dominant according to the species. The major features of adrenergic activation are the very high plasma concentrations of catecholamines (10^{-6} M) and the modulation of the discharge in terms of the nature and intensity of the stress. The catecholamine secretion may be mediated by the preganglionic-cholinergic innervation of the chromaffin cells, thereby implicating the nervous system in the adrenergic response.

The adrenergic activation results in secondary effects mainly on the circulation, osmoregulation and energetics. A better understanding of the responses induced by stress allows a more selective evaluation of the fish's impairment and may help to reduce mortality, by alleviating osmoregulatory disturbances during stress, for example.

I INTRODUCTION

In the course of development, growth and reproduction, both captive and wild fish are submitted to stimuli which when present beyond a somewhat arbitrary degree of intensity, become constraints. These constraints resulting from strenuous swimming, capture, handling, confinement, hypoxia or wounds are what we term stress. Thus, for this review stress is used to refer to stimuli which elicit a rather non-specific physiological response, Selye's "general adaptation syndrome" (for further discussion of the concept of stress see Pickering, 1981, this volume).

In fish as well as in other vertebrates, the adaptation syndrome is achieved through modifications of different biological systems. In an earlier review (Mazeaud *et al.*, 1977), a discrimination between the neuro-hormonal changes appearing at the systemic level (referred to as primary effects) and the changes occurring at a more peripheral level as a result of the neuro-hormonal stimulation (referred to as secondary effects) was introduced (Fig. 1).

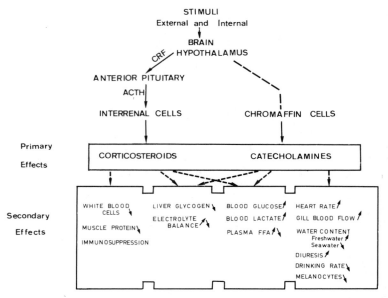

Fig. 1   Scheme incorporating current information on the interrelationship between primary and secondary effects of stress in fish (from Mazeaud *et al.*, 1977, with permission).

Classically, as well as an activation of the pituitary–interrenal axis (see Donaldson, 1981, this volume) another major neuro-hormonal disturbance following stress is reflected by changes in the adrenergic function. This seems to hold true for fish and has received increasing documentation since the early work of Fontaine *et al.* (1963) demonstrated the exceedingly high concentration of catecholamines (CA) in the plasma of fish.

In this paper, we review some data concerning the action of stress on CA metabolism and release into the blood stream and consider the consequences of CA discharge. In this respect, it should be noted that the activation of both interrenal and adrenergic functions in response to stress makes it difficult to distinguish between the secondary effects of corticosteroids and catecholamines. In order to tentatively isolate the adrenergic response, we have concentrated upon those effects which can be mimicked by infusion of CA.

II LOCALIZATION OF CATECHOLAMINES IN FISH

(a) Chromaffin Tissue

Although in fish there is no well defined structure corresponding to the mammalian adrenal medulla, chromaffin cells can be found in several organs which may differ according to the species (see Coupland, 1972, 1979; Holzbauer and Sharman, 1972; Mazeaud, 1972). In cyclostomes, the chromaffin cells are scattered in the walls of the major cardinal veins, in the sinus venosus, and especially among the muscular fibres of the heart; in teleosts, they form small islets lining the walls of the posterior cardinal veins and in some species, are dispersed in the head kidney. In elasmobranchs we see the beginning of organization, with symmetric pairs of small aggregates of chromaffin cells (suprarenal bodies) extending linearly in the body cavity against the kidney, the anterior pair (axillary bodies) being close to the posterior venous sinus and rather well developed in some species (Gannon *et al.*, 1972). Abrahamsson *et al.* (1979) mention that the location of the chromaffin cells of dipnoans seem to be a combination of the different systems observed in the other groups; the cells are found in the anterior part of the left cardinal vein, in the intercostal arteries and in the atrium. Another characteristic of the chromaffin tissue in fish is the lack of close association with interrenal tissue (Oguri, 1960).

These histological results fit very well with the biochemical data (Table I) showing large amounts of CA in the tissues where chromaffin cells are located. At the tissue level, the proportions of adrenaline (A) and noradrenaline (NA) may differ according to the species. A is the major amine found in the heart of a cyclostome, the sea lamprey *Petromyzon marinus* (Mazeaud, 1972), in the head kidney of salmonids (Nakano and Tomlinson, 1967; Mazeaud, 1971), in the cardinal veins of the cod, *Gadus morhua* (Abrahamsson and Nilsson, 1975) while NA is predominant in axillary bodies of elasmobranchs (see Dalmaz and Peyrin, 1978) or in the kidney of the carp, *Cyprinus carpio* (Stabrovski, 1969). In dipnoans, A or NA can each be predominant according to the tissue (Abrahamsson *et al.*, 1979).

(b) Neural Tissue

In addition to the presumed endocrine tissues which show a chromaffin reaction, CA can be detected in various nervous tissues where they serve two

TABLE I The Catecholamine Content of Tissues from Different Fish in Relation to the Phenylethanolamine-N-methyl Transferase (PNMT) Activity.

	Catecholamine contents				
	Adrenaline (A) (μg g^{-1})	Noradrenaline (NA) (μg g^{-1})	A/(A+NA)	PNMT activity (v g^{-1})[a]	Reference
Cyclostomes					
Petromyzon marinus					
whole heart	38·0 ± 11·4	1·5 ± 0·7	0·96	47·8	
atrium	89·0 ± 25·3	3·4 ± 2·1	0·96	69·9 ± 14·9	Mazeaud (1971, 1972)
ventricle	16·7 ± 6·6	0·7 ± 0·4	0·96	34·3 ± 4·9	
Elasmobranchs					
Scyliorhinus canicula					
axillary bodies	4600	5800	0·44	600 (March) 200 (March)	L. Peyrin (unpublished)
Squalus acanthias					
axillary bodies	445 ± 160·8	2139·2 ± 696·2	0·17	104 ± 17·1	Abrahamsson (1979b)
Teleosts					
Salmo gairdneri					
head kidney	19·7 ± 1·9	4·3 ± 0·9	0·81	4·73 ± 0·83	Mazeaud (1972)
Gadus morhua					
head kidney	14·3 ± 2·1	2·3 ± 0·2	0·86	2·8 ± 0·6	
posterior cardinal veins	38·2 ± 5·2	14·3 ± 2·1	0·73	9·4 ± 2·7	Abrahamsson (1979a)
coeliac ganglion	18·8 ± 3·7	3·7 ± 0·5	0·83	4·0 ± 0·8	
Dipnoa					
Protopterus aethiopicus					
heart	4·18 ± 1·10	70·77 ± 17·31	0·06		
intercostal arteries					Abrahamsson *et al.* (1979)
—proximal part	216·2	94·33	0·70		
—distal part	0·33 ± 0·08	0·05 ± 0·03	0·87	32·6 – 117·2	

Values are expressed as mean ± S.D.

different purposes. Firstly, at the peripheral level, they have a direct action on innervated organs and when liberated *in situ* at the nerve endings, may parallel the action of systemic CA. Secondly, in central aminergic fibres, they act as neurotransmitters and contribute to the function of the central nervous system.

(i) *Autonomic nervous system.* This system is very rudimentary in cyclo-stomes (Johnels, 1956) whereas in elasmobranchs a sympathetic chain is organized in the mesonephros area and connects with the spinal nerves by white *rami communicanti* (Young, 1933). In teleosts, the autonomic nervous system is more similar in organization to that of mammals (Young, 1931) with two lateral chains of ganglia, white and grey *rami* and transverse commissures (Burnstock, 1969; Campbell, 1970; Gannon, 1972).

The peripheral innervation is only vagal in the heart of cyclostomes, with a few adrenergic fibres in blood vessels and gut (Rovainen, 1979). The same picture seems to occur in elasmobranchs (see Nilsson *et al.*, 1975). In teleosts, as reviewed by Santer (1977), most arteries, viscera, melanophores and photc phores receive adrenergic innervation (Fig. 2). The heart is under vagal control with a more or less adrenergic innervation depending on the species (Smith, 1978; Holmgren, 1980; Wahlqvist, 1980).

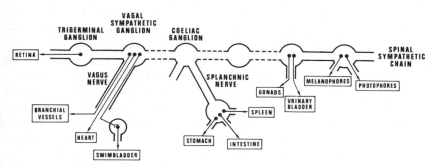

Fig. 2   Schematic representation of peripheral nervous system in a teleost showing the localization and distribution of postganglionic monoaminergic nerves (●——) (from Santer, 1977, with permission).

(ii) *Central catecholaminergic neurones.* As far as is known, in fish central catecholaminergic neurones are mainly related to the hypothalamic area which is very well developed in these vertebrates (see Santer, 1977; Kah *et al.*, 1978; Parent, 1979). Some relationship with the endocrine control of the pituitary has been suggested in elasmobranchs by Urano (1971) and in teleosts (Zambrano, 1975; Olivereau, 1975; Fremberg and Meurling, 1975).

III METABOLISM OF CATECHOLAMINES

(a) Biosynthesis

According to the sequence postulated by Blaschko (1939), the biosynthesis of CA involves hydroxylation of tyrosine into dopa, deamination into dopamine, hydroxylation of dopamine into NA and then methylation into A.

In fish, we have scarce evidence of any regulation affecting the hydroxylation of tyrosine since all we know is that tyrosine hydroxylase is present in the head kidney of the rainbow trout, *Salmo gairdneri* (M. M. Mazeaud, unpublished). The step dopamine–NA has been demonstrated by the activity of dopamine-β-hydroxylase (DβH) in the axillary bodies of an elasmobranch, *Scyliorhinus canicula* (Dalmaz, 1972), in the head kidney of the rainbow trout (M. M. Mazeaud, unpublished), in the cardinal veins of the cod (Jönsson and Nilsson, 1979) and in the chromaffin tissue of a lungfish, *Protopterus aethiopicus* (Abrahamsson *et al.*, 1979).

The biosynthesis of A from NA is catalysed by phenylethanolamine-N-methyl transferase (PNMT). This enzyme is active in cyclostomes, in the heart of lamprey (Mazeaud, 1972); in teleosts, in the head kidney of trout (Mazeaud, 1972), and the head kidney and posterior cardinal vein of cod (Abrahamsson and Nilsson, 1976) and in the intercostal arteries but not in the atrium of the lungfish (Abrahamsson *et al.*, 1979). In several species of elasmobranchs, methylation of NA into A has been demonstrated (Peyrin *et al.*, 1969; Abrahamsson, 1979b). In Table I, we have correlated PNMT activity and CA content in the chromaffin tissue of different species of fish. In mammals, PNMT activity is controlled by corticosteroids (Wurtman and Axelrod, 1966). For this reason, Brandenburger-Brown and Trams (1968) searched for PNMT in the interrenal of several sharks. This organ accumulates radiolabelled NA and shows PNMT activity, reminiscent of the cortex–medulla association found in the adrenal of warm-blooded vertebrates. However, neither hypophysectomy in dogfish (Peyrin and Peres, 1970), nor hydrocortisone injection in rainbow trout (Mazeaud, 1972) modify PNMT activity; moreover, we have noticed the lack of close association between chromaffin cells and interrenal tissue in fish. PNMT is also active in other adrenergic nervous structures such as the coeliac ganglion or splanchnic nerve in the cod (Abrahamsson *et al.*, 1979a).

Besides the Blaschko sequence, another biosynthetic pathway via octopamine (Laduron, 1972) may be hypothesized in fish because octopamine has been found in the heart of the goldfish, *Carassius auratus* (Molinoff and Axelrod, 1972). To what extent CA biosynthesis is responsive to acute or chronic stress remains to be determined.

(b) Turnover

In fish, the circulating CA are picked up by several tissues (Brandenburger-Brown and Trams, 1968; Busacker and Chavin, 1977). If we assume that, in steady state conditions, the plasma CA concentration remains unchanged, we deduce that an amount of CA has been discharged from chromaffin tissue equivalent to that which has been removed. Using radiolabelled A or NA injections and blood sampling via an indwelling catheter in the dorsal aorta, Mazeaud (1979) measured several parameters of CA kinetics in the rainbow trout. Following the injection of ^{14}C-A, the decline of plasma radioactivity corresponds to two semi-log linear regressions from which we deduce the half-life ($t^{1/2} = 65.8$ min) and the distribution space (62% of body weight); for NA, these values are 163 min for $t^{1/2}$ and 42% of body weight for the distribution space. These kinetics are temperature-dependent with a Q_{10} of 2 for A and of 2.85 for NA, these values being close to those found for the carp in preliminary experiments (Mazeaud and Mazeaud, 1965). A similar pattern of plasma radioactivity decline is observed in the cod following an A injection (Ungell and Nilsson, 1979).

If we account for a plasma concentration close to 2×10^{-6} M as is sometimes observed in salmonids during stress, in a 1 kg fish the A discharge during half an hour may be estimated as 0.32×10^{-6} moles, which is approximately the A content of the chromaffin tissue. This raises the question of how the A expenditure during a long-lasting stress can be met; either recycling or increased biosynthesis must be considered.

(c) Catabolism

(i) *Excretion rates.* In fish, nearly the whole of the radioactivity from an injection of labelled CA is found in urine (within 5 days), indicating that the final step of CA excretion occurs via the kidney. No differences were observed between A and NA in this respect. The radioactivity decline is linear in elasmobranchs (62.2% after 24 h) whereas it is faster during the first 48 h in teleosts (Mazeaud and Mazeaud, 1973a). It also seems faster in Atlantic salmon smolts, *Salmo salar,* than in parr, which may be related to the adrenergic tonicity induced by smoltification (Fontaine et al., 1963). In cod, 11.9 to 72.5% of the tracer is recovered in the urine after 24 h (Ungell and Nilsson, 1979). Thus, in fish CA excretion is very rapid and comparable with that of warm-blooded vertebrates (see Mazeaud and Mazeaud, 1973a).

(ii) *Catabolites.* The degradation of CA is performed in essentially the same way in fish as in mammals since deaminated and O-methylated compounds are found either free or conjugated as sulphates or glucuronates. O-methylation is a major pathway (plus eventual deamination) while deamination alone has only a minor importance. In urine, vanillyl mandelic acid (VMA) is preponderant in dogfish, 3-methoxy-4-hydroxyphenyl glycol (MOPEG) in trout (Mazeaud and Mazeaud, 1973b) and metanephrine in cod (Ungell and Nilsson, 1979). As well as occurring in the urine, labelled catabolites have been detected in the kidney of the trout (Mazeaud and Mazeaud, 1973b) and of the elasmobranch, *Gynglymostoma cirratum* (Brandenburger-Brown and Trams, 1968), which confirms the implication of fish kidney in CA degradation.

Monoamine oxidase (MAO) and catechol-O-methyl transferase (COMT) have been detected in many elasmobranch organs (Scheline, 1962; Trams and Brandenburger-Brown, 1967) and also in teleosts (see Mazeaud, 1974), mainly in the kidney for MAO and in the liver for COMT. MAO is also present in significant amounts in the brain of both elasmobranchs and teleosts.

In conclusion, the processes of biosynthesis and inactivation of A and NA are the same in fish as in mammals or birds, with no major innovation taking place in the evolution of vertebrates toward the warm-blooded status.

IV STRESS AND CATECHOLAMINE RELEASE IN FISH

In many species of fish, stress induces an elevation of plasma CA levels as a primary effect (Mazeaud *et al.*, 1977). This elevation occurs within minutes of the onset of stress (Mazeaud, 1971), may last for hours after cessation (Nakano and Tomlinson, 1967) and may exhibit different patterns according to the species and nature of the stress.

(a) Action of Stresses

In cyclostomes, Mazeaud (1969a) reported a 3 min latency for CA discharge in sea lampreys bled under harsh conditions involving struggling and anoxia and a 5-fold increase in plasma A and NA levels after 5 min of forced-swimming. Wound-bearing animals had extremely high CA levels, 20 times the control levels. Similar experiments on the river lamprey, *Lampetra fluviatilis*, led Plisetskaya and Prozoroveskaya (1971) to the same finding. In both species, there is more NA than A in the blood plasma whereas the proportion is reversed in the chromaffin tissue. In the heart, a long-lasting disturbance causes A to increase while NA remains unchanged or decreases.

In elasmobranchs, the first reports on plasma CA (Peyrin *et al.*, 1969; Mazeaud, 1969b) mentioned high concentrations and extreme individual variations which suggests that these animals may be easily stressed. However, Mazeaud (1969b), using nembutal anaesthetization, observed low plasma CA levels in *Scyliorhinus canicula* and, after 30 min anoxia in anaesthetized animals, a high and significant increase in plasma CA (mainly NA). This observation has been confirmed (Fig. 3) on the same species

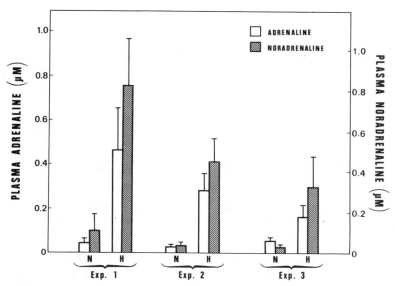

Fig. 3 Effects of hypoxia on plasma catecholamines in elasmobranchs. N: normoxic conditions; H: hypoxic conditions. Exp. 1: in *Scyliorhinus canicula* anaesthetized with nembutal (data from Mazeaud, 1969b). Exp. 2: in *Scyliorhinus canicula* bearing an indwelling cannula (data from Butler *et al.*, 1978). Exp. 3: in *Squalus acanthias* blood-sampled with a syringe (data from Abrahamsson, 1979a). Histograms represent mean values, vertical lines indicate standard deviations.

bearing an indwelling cannula (Butler *et al.*, 1978) and also in *Squalus acanthias* (Abrahamsson, 1979b). Moreover, Butler *et al.* (1979) found that whenever dogfish were submitted to mild hypoxia (P_{O_2} 55 mmHg for 3 days), the only CA to increase slightly was NA while in harsh, anoxic conditions (P_{O_2} 35 mmHg), both A and NA increased very significantly.

In teleosts, early experiments on the carp (Mazeaud, 1964) showed that withdrawal of blood induced a CA discharge after a latency of 15 min. Both forced swimming on a hook and line or anoxia by emersion induced an increase of CA, mainly NA, from 15 to 60 min after the onset of stress, which was confirmed later by Peyraud-Waitzenegger (1978) and Le Bras (1978) on the same species. When the temperature is warmer, carp are more sensitive to stress in terms of CA release (Mazeaud and Mazeaud, 1965; Mazeaud, 1971) as illustrated in Fig. 4. In rainbow trout (Nakano and Tomlinson, 1967), a physical disturbance induced an increase of A, the

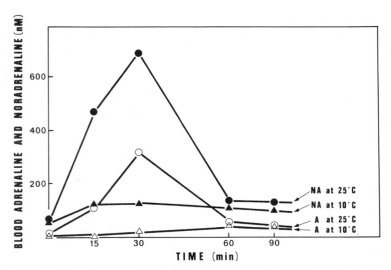

Fig. 4   Effects of anoxia at two different temperatures on circulating catecholamines in a teleost, *Cyprinus carpio* (from Mazeaud, 1971).

predominant amine, after 2 min, of both A and NA after 10 min, with recovery almost completed after 3 h and fully completed after 12–24 h; in the same species, Ristori *et al.* (1979) mention that a mild hypoxia has a weak effect on plasma A and NA.

Several species of Pacific salmon react in a similar manner to the rainbow trout (Mazeaud *et al.*, 1977). Struggling out of the water, transfer from cold to warm water, handling and hauling in net all result in a slight increase of plasma NA and an important, sometimes massive, increase of A within minutes, which returns to resting levels within 3 days (Fig. 5).

In other teleosts, such as the cod (Walhqvist and Nilsson, 1980), the European eel, *Anguilla anguilla* (Peyraud-Waitzenegger, 1978; Le Bras, 1978) and in the lungfish (Abrahamsson *et al.*, 1979), unrest, discomfort or forced swimming also induce plasma CA increases.

At the tissue level, both A and NA increase in the heart of trout after physical disturbance (Nakano and Tomlinson, 1967), no difference being apparent in the head kidney. In carp, a decrease of NA in the liver, heart and head kidney is noticed after 3 h asphyxia (Stabrovski, 1968). If the stress is one of forced swimming, an increase of both catecholamines in the skeletal muscles also occurs.

Besides A and NA, small amounts of dopamine have been found in elasmobranch plasma (Butler *et al.*, 1978, 1979) and axillary bodies (Dalmaz, 1972) and in teleost plasma (Le Bras, 1978; Ristori *et al.*, 1979).

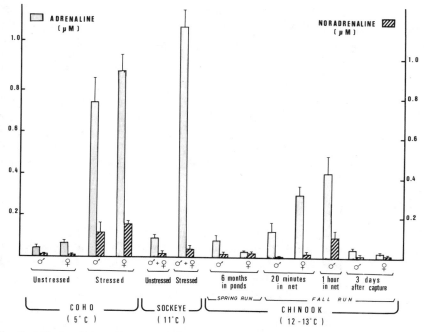

Fig. 5 Effects of struggling out of the water, holding and hauling in a net on plasma catecholamine concentrations in several species of Pacific salmon. Values are means with standard errors (from Mazeaud *et al.*, 1977, with permission).

However during stress, the plasma level does not increase very much in the dogfish (Butler *et al.*, 1978) and does not seem affected in teleosts (Ristori *et al.*, 1979).

In cyclostomes and elasmobranchs as well as in teleosts and dipnoans, various kinds of stresses induce an increase in plasma CA. Both A and NA are implicated in this response, with either being predominant according to the species. In most experimental conditions involving harsh stress, the predominant amine increases by 5- to 20-fold whereas the other increases by only 2- to 5-fold. A major characteristic of the adrenergic response of fish to stress is the extremely high concentration reached in the plasma by the predominant amine. The order of magnitude of this concentration (0.5–1.5×10^{-6} M) is more or less the same in all the lower vertebrate groups reviewed here.

The CA release may be modulated in several ways. Some fish, such as the carp, have been shown to be more responsive in warm water than in cold water (Mazeaud and Mazeaud, 1965; Mazeaud, 1971). The swiftness of the response also depends on the species studied; in cold water (10°C), 5 min after stress there is no difference in blood CA of carp (Mazeaud, 1965) whereas a slight increase may be detected in lampreys (Mazeaud, 1969a) and a tremendous increase in rainbow trout (Nakano and Tomlinson, 1967) and Pacific salmon (Mazeaud et al., 1977). The magnitude of CA release may be directly correlated with increasing intensity and type of stress in both elasmobranchs (moderate hypoxia—Butler et al., 1979) and teleosts (mild hypoxia—Ristori et al., 1979; disturbance—Nakano and Tomlinson, 1967). Moreover, Mazeaud et al. (1977) showed that different stresses caused different degrees of increase in plasma CA levels; 5 min struggling out of the water at 12°C caused a larger increase than holding fish 5 min at 21°C which in turn caused a larger increase than 20 min of capture at 12°C in a seine net.

(b) Resting Levels

The modulation of the adrenergic response in terms of the nature and intensity of stimuli makes it difficult to assess the resting levels of plasma CA in fish. The problem has been approached in different ways by several authors. In cyclostomes, Mazeaud (1969a) reported some plasma resting values of less than $2·5 \times 10^{-10}$ M, while in elasmobranchs, the "resting values" were stabilized at low levels either by nembutal anaesthesia (Mazeaud, 1969b) or by blood-sampling via an indwelling cannula (Butler et al., 1978), the lowest values being 25×10^{-9} M for A and 32×10^{-9} M for NA. In teleosts, some very low resting values ($2·95 \times 10^{-9}$ M for A and $2·30 \times 10^{-9}$ for NA) have been found by Ristori et al. (1979) on rainbow trout kept in small, dark boxes and blood-sampled via an intra-aortic catheter. However, CA assays are being continually developed to give increasing sensitivity and, although different methods may yield somewhat different results (see Bühler et al., 1978), it is anticipated that even lower plasma CA concentrations will be found in fish which are kept unstressed, motionless and deprived of sensory stimulations. Whereas such a situation may parallel that of a lungfish in its cocoon, it seems devoid of biological significance in the majority of fish species.

V CONTROL OF CATECHOLAMINE RELEASE

In cyclostomes, the main CA storage organ, the heart, is devoid of innervation (see Caravita and Coscia, 1966) and moreover seems to be insensitive to acetylcholine (Augustinsson et al., 1956). The CA release may be triggered by P_{O_2} decrease or pH variations, and in ammocoete heart, has been reported to be induced by tyramine (Lignon, 1979).

In elasmobranchs, where the major chromaffin formations are part of the sympathetic chain, the control of CA release through nervous stimulation has been studied in *Squalus acanthias* by Abrahamsson (1979a) who reports that the circulating CA level increases enormously in both control and stressed animals if the dogfish is given a sharp blow to the head just before being bled. Moreover, in perfusion experiments, electric stimulation of the spinal cord causes a marked increase in the outflow of A into the posterior cardinal sinus, which contrasts with the NA increase observed in response to asphyxia. The innervation of the chromaffin cells of elasmobranchs is preganglionic (Gannon, 1972).

In teleosts, the chromaffin cells of the posterior cardinal vein and of the head kidney are richly innervated. In the cod, at the level of the sympathetic ganglion corresponding to the third spinal nerve, some fibres leave the sympathetic chain on the left side and reach the walls of the cardinal veins (Nilsson *et al.*, 1978). These fibres can be electrically stimulated (Abrahamsson and Nilsson, 1978), which results in A and NA release, A dominating as in experiments involving stress. On the other hand, Wahlqvist and Nilsson (1980) severed the first to fourth spinal nerves supplying the cod head kidney. In this case, the CA release induced by a postural stress (applied by lowering the water level in the experimental tank to force the animals on their side, and to struggle to regain their normal posture) was strongly reduced, although not completely abolished. Moreover, perfusion experiments on cod head kidney showed that both acetylcholine and nicotine were able to induce the release of CA in the perfusate. This release is dose-dependent in the range 10^{-9}–10^{-7} M. From these experiments, it can be deduced that in elasmobranchs and teleosts, the activity of chromaffin tissue seems to be under nervous sympathetic control by preganglionic cholinergic fibres.

Another aspect of the interrelations between the nervous activity and systemic CA is the extent to which CA of the adrenergic nerve endings may reach the plasma compartment. Although the presence of both A and NA has been reported in sympathetic neurons of several species of fish (von Euler and Fänge, 1961), there are only scanty indications of their contribution to the general pool of A. The experiments showing the persistence of a small increase of plasma CA induced by stress despite the denervation of the cod head kidney led Wahlqvist and Nilsson (1980) to hypothesize an overflow of A and NA into the plasma from nerve endings.

In a rather different experiment, M. M. Mazeaud (unpublished) investigated the effects of stress on the hypothalamus CA content in rainbow trout. Fish were taken out of the water five times in 48 h; each session lasted 5 min during which the animals were left struggling in hypoxia. Brains were sampled, hypothalami dissected and CA determined by HPLC with electrochemical detection. A significant decrease of hypothalamic NA and dopamine was observed in stressed fish (Fig. 6). However, whereas hypothalamic and plasma CA fluctuate inversely during stress, the passage of CA

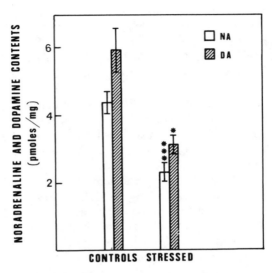

Fig. 6   Effect of stress on catecholamine content in the hypothalamus of a teleost, *Salmo gairdneri*. Stressed fish were left struggling out of water for periods of 5 min—see text for details. Values represent means with standard deviations (M. M. Mazeaud, unpublished).

from brain to plasma remains to be proved. Nevertheless, this possibility cannot be ruled out since Murray *et al.* (1975) in cyclostomes and Peyraud-Waitzenegger (1978) in a teleost, the European eel, observed the passage of CA through the blood–brain barrier. On the other hand, the catabolism of CA *in situ* by rainbow trout brain has already been discussed.

VI CONSEQUENCES OF CATECHOLAMINE RELEASE ON SOME PHYSIOLOGICAL PARAMETERS

The primary response to stress, CA discharge, leads to plasma concentrations of the same order of magnitude (10^{-6} M) as those capable of inducing a physiological response on target organs and it might be assumed that adrenergic fibres have a minor importance in mediating the secondary effects when compared to the role of circulating amines in elasmobranchs (Davies and Rankin, 1973) and in teleosts (Wahlqvist and Nilsson, 1980).

(a) Circulation and Respiration

Catecholamines have positive chronotropic and inotropic actions on the cyclostome heart (see Rovainen, 1979), the *in situ* production of CA by the myocardium having been demonstrated by Lignon (1979).

In elasmobranchs and teleosts, most cardiovascular effects of either stress or CA infusion have been reviewed by Jones and Randall (1978). There is some controversy arising from a large body of data, mainly due to the fact that, depending on experimental conditions, the action of A or NA on myocardium or blood vessels may be additive or antagonistic and then eventually produce opposite haemodynamic responses. Both bradycardia or tachycardia may be observed after stress or CA infusion in elasmobranchs and teleosts with opposite effects sometimes occurring in the same species. For instance, on perfused rainbow trout heart, A exhibits a positive chronotropic effect at low temperature (6°C) and a negative chronotropic effect at high temperature (15°C) (Bennion, 1968). In dogfish perfused heart, A is positively chronotropic whereas NA is negative (Capra and Satchell, 1977).

A more consistent effect of either stress or CA on the heart is an increase of stroke volume, sometimes of tremendous proportions, which seems a more reliable mechanism for the regulation of cardiac output than the chronotropic effect in elasmobranchs (Capra and Satchell, 1977) as well as in teleosts (Stevens *et al.*, 1972; Holmgren, 1977).

Stress and CA cause adjustments of the vascular bed. Most arteries contract with CA and are responsive to α or β blockers in elasmobranchs (Nilsson *et al.*, 1975) and teleosts (Holmgren and Nilsson, 1975). Gill circulation is very responsive to CA which induce a decrease of the haemodynamic resistance and an acceleration of the perfusion rate in elasmobranchs (Davies and Rankin, 1973; Capra and Satchell, 1977) and in teleosts when at rest, only 60% of the secondary lamellae are perfused and 95% with A (Booth and Holeton, 1977). The overall result of cardiovascular adjustments following stress or CA perfusion is an increase of the aortic pressure.

At the respiratory level, acceleration of blood through the gill results in an increase of oxygen uptake by 4- to 12-fold (Jones and Randall, 1978) and of CO_2 excretion. An acceleration of ventilation has been reported in rainbow trout (Kiceniuk and Jones, 1977; see also Hughes, 1981, this volume) while in the eel, CA may elicit either acceleration or slowing of breathing seemingly according to the season (Peyraud-Waitzenegger, 1978).

(b) Osmoregulation

The osmotic repercussions of stress were long overlooked until Maetz (1974) pointed them out. They have been reviewed by Mazeaud *et al.* (1977). Most

of them can be artificially reproduced by CA injections. Data on cyclostomes and elasmobranchs are non-existent. In teleosts, there is a good
evidence that A increases the permeability of gill to water (Pic *et al.*, 1974),
which fits fairly well with the observed response to stress: in hypo-osmotic
media (fresh water), stress results in a weight gain (water imbibition) while in
hyper-osmotic media (sea water), a weight loss (water loss) occurs. A
striking illustration is provided by Farmer and Beamish (1969) in which
forced swimming of *Tilapia nilotica* resulted in an increase of plasma
osmotic pressure in seawater-adapted fish and a decrease in freshwater-
adapted fish.

In addition, CA act on ionic transfer across the gills, the net effect of stress
being an increased mineralization in sea water and demineralization in fresh
water (Pic *et al.*, 1975; Girard and Payan, 1980).

Besides these overall effects of stress or CA on the general ionic and water
balance of teleosts, other kinds of hydromineral disturbances have been
described: haemoconcentration regardless of the environmental salinity,
electrolyte shifts (see Mazeaud *et al.*, 1977), increased diuresis (Hunn, 1969;
Hickmann and Trump, 1969), some of them being possibly caused by factors
other than CA.

Another approach to the regulation of ionic balance is the relationship
between stress and gill (Na^+/K^+) ATPase. Although the effect of A on the
gill function seems mediated by cyclic AMP production (Djabali *et al.*,
1979), there is no modification of ATPase activity after transportation of
coho salmon smolts, *Oncorhynchus kisutch* (Specker and Schreck, 1980).

It may be assumed that most of the effects of stress on osmotic balance are
mediated by CA secretion which in a few minutes results in a water or in an
ionic overload, depending on whether fish are held in fresh water or sea
water, an overload from which the fish may never recover. There is some
paradox when considering CA action in this respect, because these
hormones are supposed to bring relief to the organism whereas they actually
add an osmotic disturbance to almost any kind of stress.

The light cast on the osmoregulatory disturbances induced by stress
prompted the development of a very simple way to bring relief to the fish. If
the animals are kept in an environment alleviating the osmotic burden, the
major part of the osmotic imbalance is cancelled. This practice is getting
more and more credence for freshwater and euryhaline teleosts (Miles *et al.*,
1974; Hattingh *et al.*, 1975; Kutty *et al.*, 1980). Holding chinook salmon
smolts, *Oncorhynchus tshawytscha*, in only 3‰ saline brings complete relief
from harsh handling stress which otherwise would have caused 80% fish to
die and resulted in a *Saprolegnia* bloom in the survivors (Long *et al.*, 1977;
see also Schreck, 1981, this volume). For a further discussion of the effects of
stress on osmotic and ionic regulation in teleosts the reader is referred to
Eddy (1981, this volume).

(c) Metabolic Effects

It has long been known that different kinds of stress (anoxia, struggling) induce an elevation of blood glucose in elasmobranchs (Scott, 1921), in teleosts (McCormick and MacLeod, 1925; see review in Love, 1970) and in cyclostomes (Hardisty et al., 1976). Aquaculture practices such as capture and handling almost inevitably result in hyperglycemia (Chavin and Young, 1970; Wedemeyer, 1972; Miles et al., 1974; Specker and Schreck, 1980). Most metabolic disturbances induced by stress may be reproduced by CA injection (see Fontaine, 1975). In cyclostomes, elasmobranch and teleosts, A injections consistently increase blood glucose levels. In carp 10 μg kg^{-1}, corresponding to 2×10^{-7} M instant concentration in the distribution space, produces a significant hyperglycemia and 100 μg kg^{-1} produces a maximum hyperglycemia (Mazeaud, 1964, 1969). NA appears ten times less potent than A (Mazeaud, 1965; Larsson, 1973) and is reported to cause hypoglycemia in the Holocephali (Patent, 1970).

Stress elevates blood lactic acid levels (Love, 1970; Larsson, 1973; Bilinski, 1974; Miles et al., 1974; Driedzic and Kicernuik, 1976), which may be a factor causing death in salmonids exhausted by forced swimming (Black et al., 1966), hence the existence of mechanisms preventing an excessive rise of blood lactate (Wardle, 1978).

After stress, glycogen breaks down within seconds in the muscle and within hours in the liver, and this is usually followed by a prompt recovery in the liver, although the picture may be somewhat variable (Love, 1970; Plisetskaya, 1975; Narasimhan and Sundararaj, 1971; Miles et al., 1974; Wardle, 1978). Activation of a tissue phosphorylase has been reported during forced swimming (Nakano and Tomlinson, 1967; Yamamoto, 1968) or in the presence of A (Umminger et al., 1975). The metabolic effects of stress or CA may be mediated by cyclic AMP (Nakano and Tomlinson, 1967; Yamamoto, 1968; Terrier and Perrier, 1975).

The consequences of stress or CA on lipid metabolism, especially on the plasma free fatty acid (FFA) level, are far from clear. Stress as well as A may increase or decrease the FFA, and in an extensive investigation carried out by Mazeaud (1973) in the carp, A was shown to be capable of producing either effect depending on the experiments. Research on ten species of teleosts led to similar, almost uninterpretable results. In in vitro studies, Farkas (1967) observed a poor or negative effect of A on FFA mobilization from carp adipose tissue whereas Bilinski and Lau (1969) reported an activation of lipolysis in the dark muscle of the rainbow trout. NA action on FFA is very similar to A. The recent extensive compilation of Plisetskaya (1980) does not shed too much light on this matter and the variability of CA effects on FFA mobilization in teleosts has not yet been elucidated. Besides FFA, A has been reported to induce hypercholesterolemia (Perrier et al.,

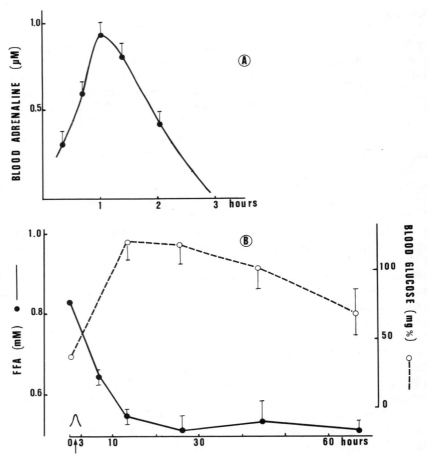

Fig. 7   Effect of a single injection of adrenaline on blood glucose and free fatty acid (FFA) in the teleost, *Cyprinus carpio*. A: Pulse of blood adrenaline after injection. B: Blood glucose and free fatty acid (FFA) levels; blood adrenaline is shown (arrowed) on the same time scale for comparison. Vertical lines indicate standard deviations (from Mazeaud *et al.*, 1977, with permission).

1972; Larsson, 1973). The major, common feature of the metabolic disturbances is their long duration (days), when compared to the short duration of stress or the rapid clearance of A from blood (minutes) as shown in Fig. 7.

(d) Colour Changes and other Secondary, Adrenergic Effects of Stress

The control of melanin aggregation of the melanophores is humoral in cyclostomes, elasmobranchs and teleosts and tyramine, dopamine, NA and

A are all very active in this respect (see Fernando and Grove, 1974). Although melanophores do receive an adrenergic innervation (Falck *et al.*, 1969), it has been observed that in carp, bleaching was strictly concomitant to the presence of A in the plasma (Mazeaud and Mazeaud, 1965). There are also indications that light emission of some bioluminescent fish is under adrenergic control (see Warner and Case, 1980). Other consequences of neuro-hormonal adrenergic responses, such as contraction of the spleen (Nilsson, 1974; Abrahamsson and Nilsson, 1975) have also been noted.

VII CONCLUSIONS

Despite some primitive characters, the adrenergic function in cyclostomes, elasmobranchs and teleosts is very responsive to stress, which results within minutes, in a massive elevation of plasma CA concentrations ($>10^{-6}$ M), seemingly compensating for a rudimentary adrenergic innervation. The fast, primary reaction to stress is followed by secondary effects of which we have attempted to identify those closely related to CA secretion. Among these secondary effects, emphasis should be put on osmoregulatory disturbances because, paradoxically, this consequence of the adrenergic response to stress seems to bring more physiological deterioration than recovery.

Besides the primary effects–secondary effects sequence, there are other remote and multicausal effects of acute or chronic stress which could tentatively be referred to as tertiary effects. Examples of these include the susceptibility to fungal infections (Mazeaud *et al.*, 1977), delayed seaward migration of smolts (Specker and Schreck, 1980), stunting and reversion of smolts (Woo *et al.*, 1978) or simply death. Resolving these effects into their various components would improve our understanding of the responses of fish to stress and help to prevent their consequences. For instance, a very common stressing factor is fright. We are not aware of many studies devoted to quantification of fright or other "psychological" influences on fish (see Schreck, 1981, this volume) whereas it would be of the utmost importance in a fish farm.

It should be borne in mind that a very common effect of stress, death, may occur several weeks after the application of stress, often without apparent warning. This raises the question of the early detection of stress in order to bring some relief to the fish if, and only if, necessary. With respect to the adrenergic function, CA may be considered as stress indicators, although in fish they are also implicated in other responses. At the present time CA determinations are difficult to perform. Moreover, the CA secretion is transient and, as shown in this review, A may have completely cleared up from the plasma before the secondary effects are apparent. Blood glucose levels are very sensitive to A or stress and as high plasma glucose levels may last for several days, they might also be witness of an earlier stress. Other stress indicators have been proposed such as the presence of haemoglobin (Smith and Ramos, 1976) and ketone bodies (Ramos and Smith, 1978) in skin mucus or the gill sialic acid content (Arillo *et al.*, 1979), but these are not strictly related to the adrenergic function.

The last question arising in this review concerns the development of practices which result in stress prevention or stress relief in fish. In order to prevent stress, training fish to improve their resistance has been attempted by several workers. Although some modifications of the muscular lactate pattern in physically conditioned rainbow trout (Hammond and Hickman, 1966) were observed, these studies have remained without practical application. Another practice is to use anaesthetization which has been shown to sometimes reduce the adrenergic response to stress. Genetic selection of low reactive strains has also been suggested (Mazeaud *et al.*, 1977). Genetic selection is a procedure which most fish culturists unknowingly practice by selecting the fast growing fish as broodstock. In order to relieve fish from deterioration following stress, our belief is that a major step has been taken with the improved knowledge of the effects of CA on fish gills. A very simple practice, manipulation of the environmental osmolarity, has been derived from complex fundamental research, resulting in excellent survival rates in heavily stressed fish.

REFERENCES

Abrahamsson, T. (1979a). Axonal transport of adrenaline, noradrenaline and phenylethanolamine-N-methyl transferase (PNMT) in sympathetic neurons of the cod *Gadus morhua*. *Acta Physiol. Scand.* **105**, 316–325.
Abrahamsson, T. (1979b). Phenylethanolamine-N-methyl transferase activity and catecholamine storage and release from chromaffin tissue of the spiny dogfish, *Squalus acanthias*. *Comp. Biochem. Physiol.* **64C**, 169–173.
Abrahamsson, T. and Nilsson, S. (1975). Effects of nerve sectioning and drugs on the catecholamine content in the spleen of the cod, *Gadus morhua*. *Comp. Biochem. Physiol.* **51C**, 231–233.
Abrahamsson, T. and Nilsson, S. (1976). Phenylethanolamine-N-methyl transferase (PNMT) activity and catecholamine content in chromaffin tissue and sympathetic neurons in the cod, *Gadus morhua*. *Acta Physiol. Scand.* **96**, 94–99.
Abrahamsson, T. and Nilsson, S. (1978). Control of catecholamine release from chromaffin tissue in a teleost fish. In *Comparative Physiology—Water Ions and Fluid Mechanics* (K. Schmidt-Nielsen, L. Bolis and S. H. P. Maddrell, eds), pp. 247–251. Cambridge: Cambridge University Press.
Abrahamsson, T., Jöhnsson, A. C. and Nilsson, S. (1979). Catecholamine synthesis in the chromaffin tissue of the African lungfish, *Protopterus aethiopicus*. *Acta Physiol. Scand.* **107**, 149–151.

Arillo, A., Margiocco, C. and Melodia, F. (1979). The gill sialic acid content as an index of environmental stress in rainbow trout, *Salmo gairdneri* R. J. *Fish Biol.* **15**, 405–410.

Augustinsson, K. B., Fänge, R., Johnels, A. and Östlund, E. (1956). Histological, physiological and biochemical studies on the heart of two cyclostomes, hagfish (*Myxine*) and lamprey (*Lampetra*). J. *Physiol., Lond.* **131**, 257.

Bilinski, E. (1974). Biochemical aspects of fish swimming. In *Biochemical and Biophysical Perspectives in Marine Biology, Vol. 1* (D. C. Malins and J. R. Sargent, eds), pp. 239–288. London and New York: Academic Press.

Bilinski, E. and Lau, Y. C. (1969). Lipolytic activity toward long-chain triglycerides in lateral line muscle of rainbow trout (*Salmo gairdneri*). J. *Fish. Res. Bd Can.* **26**, 1857–1866.

Bennion, G. R. (1968). The control of the function of the heart in teleost fish. M. S. Thesis, University of British Columbia, Vancouver, Canada.

Black, E. C., Manning, G. T. and Hayashi, K. (1966). Changes in levels of haemoglobin, oxygen, carbon dioxide, pyruvate and lactate in venous blood of rainbow trout (*Salmo gairdneri*) during and following severe muscular activity. J. *Fish. Res. Bd Can.* **23**, 738–795.

Blaschko, H. (1939). The specific action of L-dopa decarboxylase. J. *Physiol., Lond.* **96**, 50–51P.

Booth, J. and Holeton, G. F. (1977). Cf. Jones, D. R., Randall, D. J. (1978). The respiratory and circulatory systems during exercise. In *Fish Physiology, Vol. VII* (W. S. Hoar and D. J. Randall, eds), London and New York: Academic Press.

Brandenburger-Brown, E. A. and Trams, E. G. (1968). Catecholamine metabolism in elasmobranch body. *Comp. Biochem. Physiol.* **25**, 1099–1105.

Bühler, H. V., Prada, M., Haefely, W. and Picotti, G. B. (1978). Plasma adrenaline, noradrenaline and dopamine in man and different animal species. J. *Physiol., Lond.* **276**, 311–320.

Burnstock, G. (1969). Evolution of the autonomic innervation of visceral and cardiovascular systems in vertebrates. *Pharmac. Rev.* **21**, 247–324.

Busacker, G. P. and Chavin, W. (1977). Uptake, distribution and turnover of catecholamine radiolabel in the goldfish *Carassius auratus. Can. J. Zool.* **55**, 1656–1670.

Butler, P. J., Taylor, E. W., Capra, M. F. and Davison, W. (1978). The effect of hypoxia on the levels of circulating catecholamines in the dogfish *Scyliorhinus canicula. J. comp. Physiol.* **127**, 325–330.

Butler, P. J., Taylor, E. W. and Davison, W. (1979). The effect of long- term, moderate hypoxia on acid-base balance, plasma catecholamines and possible anaerobic end products in the unrestrained dogfish, *Scyliorhinus canicula. J. comp. Physiol.* **132**, 297–303.

Campbell, G. (1970). Autonomic nervous system. In *Fish Physiology, Vol. 1* (W. S. Hoar and D. J. Randall, eds), pp. 109–132. London and New York: Academic Press.

Capra, M. F. and Satchell, G. H. (1977). The differential haemodynamic responses in the elasmobranch, *Squalus acanthias*, to naturally occurring catecholamines adrenaline and noradrenaline. *Comp. Biochem. Physiol.* **58C**, 41–47.

Caravita, S. and Coscia, L. (1966). Les cellules chromaffines du coeur de lamproie (*Lampetra zanandreai*). Etude au microscope électronique avant et après traitement à la réserpine. *Archs Biol., Liège* **77**, 723–753.

Chavin, W. and Young, J. E. (1970). Factors in the determination of normal glucose levels of goldfish, *Carassius auratus. Comp. Biochem. Physiol.* **33**, 629.

Coupland, R. E. (1972). The chromaffin system. *Handb. exp. Pharmak.* **33**, 16–45.

Coupland, R. E. (1979). Catecholamines. In *Hormones and Evolution, Vol 1* (E. J. W. Barrington, ed.), pp. 309–340. London and New York: Academic Press.

Dalmaz, Y. (1972). La dopamine dans le tissu chromaffine de la roussette: analyse quantitative et rôle dans la biosynthèse de la noradrénaline. M. S. Thesis, University of Lyon, France.

Dalmaz, Y. and Peyrin, L. (1978). Occurrence of dopamine in the chromaffin tissue of a cartilaginous selachian fish, *Scyliorhinus canicula. Comp. Biochem. Physiol.* **59C**, 135–143.

Davies, D. T. and Rankin, J. C. (1973). Adrenergic receptors and vascular response to catecholamines of perfused dogfish gills. *Comp. gen. Pharmacol.* **4**, 139–148.

Djalabi, M., Compeau-Jimenez, G. and Pic, P. (1979). Temperature de l'eau de mer et AMP cyclique branchiale chez *Mugil capito*. Rôle des catécholamines endogènes. *C.r. hebd. Séanc. Acad. Sci., Paris* **289**, 861–864.

Donaldson, E. M. (1981). The pituitary–interrenal axis as an indicator of stress in fish. In *Stress and Fish* (A. D. Pickering, ed.), pp. 11–47. London and New York: Academic Press.

Driedzic, W. R. and Kiceniuk, J. W. (1976). Blood lactate levels in free-swimming rainbow trout (*Salmo gairdneri*) before and after strenuous exercise resulting in fatigue. *J. Fish. Res. Bd Can.* **33**, 173–176.

Eddy, F. B. (1981). Effects of stress on osmotic and ionic regulation in fish. In *Stress and Fish* (A. D. Pickering, ed.), pp. 77–102. London and New York: Academic Press.

Falck, B., Müntzing, J. and Rosengren, A. M., (1969). Adrenergic nerves to the dermal melanophores of the rainbow trout, *Salmo gairdneri. Z. Zellforsch. mikrosk. Anat.* **99**, 430–434.

Farkas, T. (1967). The effects of catecholamines and adrenocorticotrophic hormones on blood and adipose tissue free fatty acid levels in the fish, *Cyprinus carpio* L. *Prog. Biochem. Pharmacol.* **3**, 314–319.

Farmer, G. J. and Beamish, W. H. (1969). Oxygen consumption of *Tilapia nilotica* in relation to swimming speed and salinity. *J. Fish. Res. Bd Can.* **26**, 2807–2821.

Fernando, M. M. and Grove, D. J. (1974). Melanophore aggregation in the plaice (*Pleuronectes platessa* L.). *Comp. Biochem. Physiol.* **48A**, 711–732.

Fontaine, M., Mazeaud, M. M. and Mazeaud, F. (1963). L'adrénaline du *Salmo salar* L. à quelques étapes de son cycle vital et de ses migrations. *C.r. hebd. Séanc. Acad. Sci. Paris*, **256**, 4562–4565.

Fontaine, Y. A. (1975). Hormones in fishes. In *Biochemical and Biophysical Perspectives in Marine Biology, Vol. 2* (D. C. Malins and J. R. Sargent, eds), pp. 139–212. London and New York: Academic Press.

Fremberg, M. and Meurling, P. (1975). Catecholamine fluorescence in the pituitary of the eel, *Anguilla anguilla*, with special reference to its variation during background adaptation. *Cell Tiss. Res.* **157**, 53–72.

Gannon, B. J. (1972). Comparative and developmental studies on autonomic nerves in visceral and cardiovascular systems. Ph.D. Thesis, Univ. of Melbourne, Australia.

Gannon, B. J., Campbell, G. D. and Satchell, G. H. (1972). Monoamine storage in relation to cardiac regulation in the Port Jackson shark *Heterodontus portusjacksoni. Z. Zellforsh. mikrosk. Anat.* **131**, 437–450.

Girard, J. P. and Payan, P. (1980). Ionic exchanges through respiratory and chloride cells in fresh water and sea water adapted teleostean: adrenergic control. *Am. J. Physiol.* **238**, R260–R268.

Hammond, B. R. and Hickman, C. P. (1966). The effect of physical conditioning on the metabolism of lactate, phosphate and glucose in rainbow trout, *Salmo gairdneri*. *J. Fish. Res. Bd Can.* **23**, 65–83.

Hardisty, M. W., Zelnik, P. R. and Wright, V. C. (1976). The effects of hypoxia on blood sugar levels and on the endocrine pancreas, interrenal and chromaffin tissues of the lamprey, *Lampetra fluviatilis* (L.). *Gen. comp. Endocr.* **28**, 184–204.

Hattingh, J., Fourie, F. and Van Vuren, J. (1975). The transport of freshwater fish. *J. Fish Biol.* **7**, 447–449.

Hickman, C. P. and Trump, B. (1969). The kidney. In *Fish Physiology, Vol. 1* (W. S. Hoar and D. J. Randall, eds), pp. 91–239. London and New York: Academic Press.

Holmgren, S. (1977). Regulation of the heart of a teleost, *Gadus morhua* by autonomic nerves and circulating catecholamines. *Acta Physiol. Scand.* **99**, 62–74.

Holmgren, S. (1980). On the adrenergic control of the teleost heart. In *Animal and Environmental Fitness* (R. Gilles, ed.), pp. 165–166. Oxford: Pergamon Press.

Holmgren, S. and Nilsson, S. (1975). Effects of some adrenergic and cholinergic drugs on isolated spleen strips from the cod, *Gadus morhua*. *Eur. J. Pharmacol.* **32**, 163–169.

Holzbauer, M. and Sharman, D. F. (1972). The distribution of catecholamines in vertebrates. In *Catecholamines* (H. Blaschko and E. Muscholls, eds), pp. 110–185. Berlin: Springer.

Hughes, G. M. (1981). Effects of low oxygen and pollution on the respiratory systems of fish. In *Stress and Fish* (A. D. Pickering, ed.), pp. 121–146. London and New York: Academic Press.

Hunn, J. B. (1969). Chemical composition of rainbow trout urine following acute hypoxic stress. *Trans. Am. Fish. Soc.* **98**, 20–22.

Johnels, A. G. (1956). On the peripheral autonomic nervous system of the trunk region of *Lampetra planeri*. *Acta zool., Stockh.* **37**, 251–286.

Jones, D. R. and Randall, D. J. (1978). The respiratory and circulatory systems during exercise. In *Fish Physiology, Vol. VII* (W. S. Hoar and D. J. Randall, eds), pp. 425–501. London and New York: Academic Press.

Jonsson, A. C. and Nilsson, S. (1979). Effects of pH, temperature and Cu^{2+} on activity of dopamine-hydroxylase from the chromaffin tissue of the cod, *Gadus morhua*. *Comp. Biochem. Physiol.* **62C**, 5–8.

Kah, O., Chambolle, P. and Olivereau, M. (1978). Innervation aminergique hypothalamo-hypophysaire chez *Gambusia* sp. (Téléostéen Poecilidé) étudié par deux techniques de fluorescence. *C.r. hebd. Séanc. Acad. Sci., Paris* **286**, 705–708.

Kiceniuk, J. W. and Jones, D. R. (1977). The oxygen transport system in trout (*Salmo gairdneri*) during sustained exercise. *J. exp. Biol.* **69**, 247–260.

Kutty, M. N., Sukumaran, N. and Kasim, H. M. (1980). Influence of temperature and salinity on survival of the freshwater mullet *Rhinomugil corsula* (Hamilton). *Aquaculture* **20**, 261–274.

Laduron, P. (1972). N-methylation of dopamine to epinine in adrenal medulla: a new model for the biosynthesis of adrenaline. *Archs int. Pharmacol. Ther.* **195**, 197–200.

Larsson, A. L. (1973). Metabolic effects of epinephrine and norepinephrine in the eel, *Anguilla anguilla*. *Gen. comp. Endocr.* **20**, 155–167.

Le Bras, Y.-M. (1978). Contribution à l'étude des catécholamines circulantes et tissulaires chez quelques espèces de poissons. M.S. Thesis, University de Bretagne Occidentale, France.

Lignon, J. (1979). Responses to sympathetic drugs in the ammocoete heart: probable influence of small intensity fluorescent (SIF) cells. *J. Molec. Cell. Cardiol.* **11**, 447–465.

Long, C. W., McComas, J. R. and Monk, B. H. (1977). Use of salt (NaCl) water to reduce mortality of chinook salmon smolts, *Oncorhynchus tshawytscha*, during handling and hauling. *Mar. Fish. Rev. Paper* **1255**, 6–9.

Love, R. M. (1970). *The Chemical Biology of Fishes*. London and New York: Academic Press. 262 pp.

Maetz, J. (1974). Aspects of adaptation in hypo-osmotic and hyper-osmotic environments. In *Biochemical and Biophysical Perspectives in Marine Biology*, *Vol. 1* (D. C. Malins and J. R. Sargent, eds), pp. 1–167. London and New York: Academic Press.

Mazeaud, F. (1964). Hyperglycémie adrénalinique biphasique chez la carpe. *C.r. Séanc. Soc. Biol.* **158**, 1230–1233.

Mazeaud, F. (1965). Action de la noradrénaline sur la glycémie de la carpe. *C.r. Séanc. Soc. Biol.* **159**, 2159–2161.

Mazeaud, F. (1969). Acides gras libres plasmatiques et glycémie de la carpe (*Cyprinus carpio* L.) après asphyxie ou agitation musculaire épuisante. *C.r. Séanc. Soc. Biol.* **163**, 558–561.

Mazeaud, F. (1973). Recherches sur la régulation des acides gras libres plasmatiques et de la glycémie chez les poissons. Ph.D. Thesis, es-Sciences, Universite de Paris, France, 129pp.

Mazeaud, F. and Mazeaud, M. M. (1965). Variations de l'adrénalinemie consécutives à une surcharge d'adrénaline en fonction de la température de l'organisme. *C.r. Séanc. Soc. Biol.* **159**, 1083–1087.

Mazeaud, M. M. (1964). Influence de divers facteurs sur l'adrenalinémie et la noradrénalinémie de la carpe. *C.r. Séanc. Soc. Biol.* **158**, 2018–2021.

Mazeaud, M. M. (1969a). Adrenalinémie et noradrénalinémie chez la lamproie marine (*Petromyzon marinus* L.). *C.r. Séanc. Soc. Biol.* **163**, 349–352.

Mazeaud, M. M. (1969b). Influence du stress sur les teneurs en catecholamines du plasma et des corps axillaires chez un sélacien, *Scyliorhinus canicula* L. *C.r. Séanc. Soc. Biol.* **163**, 2262–2266.

Mazeaud, M. M. (1971). Recherches sur la biosynthèse, la sécrétion et le catabolisme de l'adrénaline et de la norardénaline chez quelques espèces de cyclostomes et de poissons. Ph.D. Thesis, ès-Sciences, Paris, France.

Mazeaud, M. M. (1972). Epinephrine biosynthesis in *Petromyzon marinus* (Cyclostoma) and *Salmo gairdneri* (Teleost). *Comp. gen. Pharmacol.* **3**, 457–468.

Mazeaud, M. M. (1974). Monoamine oxidase and catechol-O-methyl transferase in tissues of rainbow trout (*Salmo gairdneri* R., Teleost). *Comp. gen. Pharmacol.* **5**, 251–253.

Mazeaud, M. M. (1979). Catecholamine turnover rate in a salmonid the rainbow trout (*Salmo gairdneri* R.) *Ichtyophysiol. Acta* **3**, 70–82.

Mazeaud, M. M. and Mazeaud, F. (1973a). Excretion and catabolism of catecholamines in fish. Part I. Excretion rates. *Comp. gen. Pharmacol.* **4**, 183–187.

Mazeaud, M. M. and Mazeaud, F. (1973b). Excretion and catabolism of catecholamines in fish. Part II. Catabolites. *Comp. gen. Pharmacol.* **4**, 209–217.

Mazeaud, M. M., Mazeaud, F. and Donaldson, E. M. (1977). Primary and secondary effects of stress in fish: some new data with a general review. *Trans. Am. Fish. Soc.* **106**, 201–212.

McCormick, N. A. and MacLeod, J. J. R. (1925). The effect on the blood sugar of fish of various conditions including removal of the principal islets (isletectomy). *Proc. R. Soc. Lond., Ser. B*, **98**, 1–29.

Miles, H. M., Loehner, S. M., Michaud, D. T. and Salivar, S. L. (1974). Physiological responses of hatchery reared muskellunge (*Esox masquinongy*) to handling. *Trans. Am. Fish. Soc.* **103**, 336–342.

Molinoff, P. B. and Axelrod, J. (1972). Distribution and turnover of octopamine in tissues. *J. Neurochem.* **19**, 157–163.

Murray, M., Jones, H., Cserr, H. F. and Rall, D. P. (1975). The blood–brain barrier and venticular system of *Myxine glutinosa*. *Brain Res.* **99**, 17–33.

Nakano, T. and Tomlinson, N. (1967). Catecholamines and carbohydrate concentrations in rainbow trout (*Salmo gairdneri*) in relation to physical disturbances. *J. Fish. Res. Bd Can.* **24**, 1701–1715.

Narasimhan, P. V. and Sundararaj, B. I. (1971). Effects of stress on carbohydrate metabolism in the teleost, *Notopterus notopterus* (Pallas). *J. Fish Biol.* **3**, 441–451.

Nilsson, S. (1974). Autonomic innervation in teleost fish. An experimental study in the cod, *Gadus morhua*. Ph.D. Thesis, University of Göteborg, Sweden.

Nilsson, S., Holmgren, S. and Grove, D. J. (1975). Effects of drugs and nerve stimulation of the spleen and arteries of two species of dogfish, *Scyliorhinus canicula* and *Squalus acanthias*. *Acta. Physiol. Scand.* **95**, 219–230.

Nilsson, S., Abrahamsson, T. and Grove, D. J. (1976). Sympathetic nervous control of adrenaline release from the head kidney of the cod, *Gadus morhua*. *Comp. Biochem. Physiol.* **55C**, 123–127.

Oguri, M. (1960). Studies of the adrenal glands of teleosts-III. On the distribution of chromaffin cells and interrenal cells in the head kidneys of fishes. *Bull. Jap. Soc. scient. Fish.* **26**, 443–447.

Olivereau, M. (1975). Dopamine, prolactin control and osmoregulation in eels. *Gen. comp. Endocr.* **26**, 550–561.

Parent, A. (1979). Anatomical organization of monoamine- and acetyl-cholinesterase-containing neuronal systems in the vertebrate hypothalamus. In *Handbook of the Hypothalamus, Vol. 1. Anatomy of the Hypothalamus* (P. G. Morgane and J. Panksepp, eds), pp. 511–554. New York–Bâle: Marcel Dekker Inc.

Patent, G. J. (1970). Comparison of some hormonal effects on carbohydrate metabolism in an elasmobranch (*Squalus acanthias*) and a holocephalan (*Hydrolagus colliei*) *Gen. comp. Endocr.* **14**, 215–242.

Perrier, H., Perrier, C., Gudefin, Y. and Gras, J. (1972). Adrenaline-induced hypercholesterolemia in the rainbow trout (*Salmo gairdneri* R.): a separate study in male and female trout and the effect of adrenergic blocking agents. *Comp. Biochem. Physiol.* **43A**, 341–347.

Peyraud-Waitzenegger, M. (1978). Contribution à l'étude du rôle des catécholamines circulantes dans la régulation ventilatoire de deux espèces de poissons teléostéens: la carpe et l'anguille. Analyse des modifications saisonnières de réactivité. Ph.D. Thesis es-Sciences, Université de Bretagne Occidentale, France.

Peyrin, L. and Peres, G. (1970). Influence de l'hypophysectomie sur la methylation de la noradrénaline dans le tissu chromaffine de la petite roussette (*Scyliorhinus canicula* L.). *C.r. hebd. Séanc. Acad. Sci., Paris* **270**, 1002–1005.

Peyrin, L., Cier, J. F. and Peres, G. (1969). La méthylation de la noradrénaline et les interrelations cortico-médullaires chez la roussette. *Annls Endocr.* **30**, 1–38.

74 M. M. MAZEAUD AND F. MAZEAUD

Pic, P., Mayer-Gostan, N. and Maetz, J. (1974). Branchial effects of epinephrine in
the seawater-adapted mullet. I. Water permeability. Am. J. Physiol. 226, 698–
702.
Pic, P., Mayer-Gostan, N. and Maetz, J. (1975). Branchial effects of epinephrine in
the seawater-adapted mullet. II. Na⁺ and Cl⁻ extrusion. Am. J. Physiol. 228,
441–447.
Pickering, A. D. (1981). Introduction: the concept of biological stress. In Stress and
Fish (A. D. Pickering, ed.), pp. 1–9. London and New York: Academic Press.
Plisetskaya, E. M. (1975). Hormonal Regulation of Carbohydrate Metabolism in
Lower Vertebrates. Leningrad: Nauka. 215pp (in Russian).
Plisetskaya, E. M. (1980). Fatty acid levels in blood of cyclostomes and fish. Env.
Biol. Fish. 5, 273–290.
Plisetskaya, E. M. and Prozorovskaya, M. P. (1971). (in Russian) Catecholamines in
blood and heart in the lamprey (Lampetra fluviatilis) during insulin-induced
hypoglycemia. Zh. Evol. Biokhim. Fiziol. 7, 101–103.
Ramos, F. and Smith, A. C. (1978). Ketone bodies in fish skin mucus as an indicator
of starvation: a preliminary report. J. Fish Biol. 12, 105–108.
Ristori, M-Th., Rehm, J-Cl. and Laurent, P. (1979). Dosages des catécholamines
plasmatiques chez la truite au cours de l'hypoxie contrôlée. J. Physiol., Paris 75,
67A.
Rovainen, C. M. (1979). Neurobiology of lampreys. Physiol. Rev. 59, 1007–1077.
Santer, R. M. (1977). Monoaminergic nerves in the central and peripheral nervous
system of fishes. Gen. Pharmacol. 8, 157–172.
Scheline, R. P. (1962). O-methylation in fish. Nature, 195, 904–905.
Schreck, C. B. (1981). Stress and compensation in teleostean fishes: response to
social and physical factors. In Stress and Fish (A. D. Pickering, ed.), pp. 295–321.
London and New York: Academic Press.
Scott, E. L. (1921). Sugar in the blood of the dogfish and of the sand shark. Am. J.
Physiol. 55, 349–355.
Smith, A. C. and Ramos, F. (1976). Occult haemoglobin in fish skin mucus as an
indicator of early stress. J. Fish Biol. 9, 537–541.
Smith, D. G. (1978). Neuronal regulation of blood pressure in rainbow trout (Salmo
gairdneri) Can. J. Zool. 56, 1678–1683.
Specker, J. L. and Schreck, C. B. (1980). Stress responses to transportation and
fitness for marine survival in coho salmon (Oncorhynchus kisutch) smolts. Can. J.
Fish. Aquat. Sci. 37, 765–769.
Stabrovski, E. M. (1968). Adrenaline and noradrenaline in the organs of carp,
Cyprinus carpio at rest and under functional stresses (in Russian), Zh. Evol.
Biokim. Fiziol. 4, 337–341.
Stabrovski, E. M. (1969). Adrenaline and noradrenaline in the organs of
elasmobranch and teleost fishes from the Black Sea. (in Russian). Zh. Evol.
Biokim. Fiziol. 5, 38–41.
Stevens, E., Bennion, G. R., Randall, D. J. and Shelton, G. (1972). Factors affecting
arterial pressures and blood flow from the heart in intact unrestrained lingcod
Ophiodon elongatus. Comp. Biochem. Physiol. 43A, 681–695.
Terrier, M. and Perrier, H. (1975). Cyclic 3',5'-adenosine monophosphate level in
the plasma of the rainbow trout (Salmo gairdneri) following adrenaline adminis-
tration and constrained exercise. Experientia, 31, 196.
Trams, E. G. and Brandenburger-Brown, E. A. (1967). Metabolic alterations of
catecholamines and other compounds in elasmobranch tissues. Proc. Soc. Exp.
Biol. Med. 125, 253–256.

Umminger, B. L., Benziger, D. and Levy, S. (1975). *In vitro* stimulation of hepatic glycogen phosphorylase activity by epinephrine and glucagon in the killifish, *Fundulus heteroclitus. Comp. Biochem. Physiol.* **51C**, 111–115.

Ungell, A. L. and Nilsson, S. (1979). Metabolic degradation of [³H]-adrenaline in the Atlantic cod, *Gadus morhua. Comp. Biochem. Physiol.* **64C**, 137–142.

Urano, A. (1971). Monoamine oxidase in the hypothalamo-hypophysial region of the brain of the smooth dogfish, *Triakis scyllia. Endocr. Jap.* **18**, 37–46.

Von Euler, U. S. and Fänge, R. (1961). Catecholamines in nerves and organs of *Myxine glutinosa, Squalus acanthias* and *Gadus callarias. Gen. comp. Endocr.* **1**, 191–194.

Wahlqvist, I. (1980). Effects of catecholamines on isolated systemic and branchial vascular beds of the cod, *Gadus morhua. J. comp. Physiol.* **137B**, 139–144.

Wahlqvist, I. and Nilsson, S. (1980). Adrenergic control of the cardio-vascular system of the Atlantic cod, *Gadus morhua*, during "stress". *J. comp. Physiol.* **137B**, 145–150.

Wardle, C. S. (1978). Non-release of lactic acid from anaerobic swimming muscle of plaice *Pleuronectes platessa* L.: a stress reaction. *J. exp. Biol.* **77**, 141–155.

Warner, J. A. and Case, J. F. (1980). The zoogeography and dietary induction of bioluminescence in the midshipman fish, *Porichthys notatus. Biol. Bull. mar. biol. Lab., Woods Hole* **159**, 231–246.

Wedemeyer, G. A. (1972). Some physiological consequences of handling stress in juvenile coho salmon (*Oncorhynchus kisutch*) and steelhead trout (*Salmo gairdneri*). *J. Fish. Res. Bd Can.* **29**, 1780–1783.

Woo, N. Y. S., Bern, H. A. and Nishioka, R. S. (1978). Changes in body composition associated with smoltification and premature transfer to seawater in coho salmon (*Oncorhynchus kisutch*) and king salmon (*O. tschawytscha*). *J. Fish Biol.* **13**, 421–428.

Wurtman, R. J. and Axelrod, J. (1966). Control of enzymatic synthesis of adrenaline in the adrenal medulla by adrenal cortical steroids. *J. biol. Chem.* **241**, 2301–2305.

Yamamoto, M. (1968). Fish muscle glycogen phosphorylase. *Can. J. Biochem.* **46**, 423–431.

Young, J. Z. (1931). On the autonomic nervous system of the teleostean fish *Uranoscopus scaber. Q. Jl microsc. Sci.* **74**, 491–535.

Young, J. Z. (1933). The autonomic system of selachians. *Q. Jl Microsc. Sci.* **75**, 571–624.

Zambrano, D. (1975). The ultrastructure, catecholamine and prolactin contents of the rostral pars distalis of the fish *Mugil platanus* after reserpine or 6-hydroxydopamine administration. *Cell Tiss. Res.* **162**, 551–563.

4. Effects of Stress on Osmotic and Ionic Regulation in Fish

F. B. EDDY

Department of Biological Sciences, Dundee University, Scotland

Abstract. An account of the mechanism and control of osmotic and ionic regulation in fish is presented together with some current views on salt and water balance in marine, freshwater and euryhaline fish. Important topics such as branchial salt fluxes, the role of Na-K ATPases and drinking are given particular attention. An attempt is made to define those areas of osmotic and ionic regulation which are likely to be influenced by stress, the most important of which are considered to be changes in ionic content of the blood plasma and other body fluids, changes in branchial ionic fluxes, volume and composition of the urine, and drinking and salt absorption.

The effects of specific stresses are examined, and particular emphasis is placed on physiological effects of the osmotic stress of transferring fish from fresh water to sea water and the reverse. Transfer to a hypertonic medium results in large physiological changes, notably increases in blood plasma osmotic pressure and salt content together with a transitory increase in drinking. Urine volume is rapidly decreased. If the fish survives this initial "crisis" period then a slow adaptation lasting many days takes place eventually resulting in stabilized plasma ionic content, an increase in cellular ionic content, and elevated branchial salt fluxes associated with increased amounts of the branchial enzyme Na-K ATPase. The effects of certain pollutants (particularly heavy metals), anaesthetics, handling, and temperature changes on salt and water balance in fish are also considered.

I INTRODUCTION

The salt content of fish blood and body fluids corresponds to approximately one third the concentration of sea water and is regulated at a relatively constant level within a given environment. This applies not only to marine fish whose blood is considerably more dilute than the surrounding sea water but also to freshwater fish whose internal fluids are highly concentrated compared to the environment. Euryhaline fish such as the European eel, *Anguilla anguilla*, have the ability to regulate their body fluid concentration when exposed to either hypo- or hyper-osmotic waters. Each species regulates the blood and body fluid salt concentration within certain limits and departure from this range is likely to be the result of stress.

Body fluids must be regulated at all times, including the periods of sustained activity related to survival, growth and reproduction. Changes in body fluid composition may be induced by a variety of environmental factors including: changes in salinity, temperature, oxygen and carbon dioxide content of the water, and the presence of specific pollutants. Body fluid concentrations may also be altered when fish are diseased or when they are exposed to the stresses of handling, netting, capture and confinement.

The point at which the effect of such influences ceases to be normal (i.e. having a negligible effect upon ionic regulation) and becomes stressful is difficult to define but it is easy to observe the gross effects of stress. However, by the time these effects on osmotic and ionic regulation are apparent, the fish may be severely damaged.

II OSMOTIC AND IONIC REGULATION IN FISH

Before discussing the effects of stress, it is necessary to briefly review our current understanding of the mechanisms of osmotic and ionic regulation in fish and then try to determine at which point stress is likely to be important.

(a) Marine Fishes

The body fluids of marine teleost fish are approximately one-third the concentration of sea water and consequently there is a tendency for the fish to be dehydrated by osmosis. Furthermore, the inward diffusion of salts along their concentration gradients exacerbates this problem of dehydration. Salt and water movements occur mainly across the gills, the skin being relatively impermeable. It was discovered by Smith (1930) that marine fish replace osmotic water losses by drinking sea water at a rate of approximately 0.5% body wt h^{-1}. Both salts and water are absorbed by the gut and excess salts (Na^+ and Cl^-) are excreted by chloride-cells (or mitochondria-rich cells) located in the gills, as was originally suggested by Keys and Willmer (1932). The bulk of the ingested divalent ions (mainly Mg^{2+} and SO_4^{2-}) are eliminated via the rectum and the small amounts which do penetrate the gut wall are excreted via the kidney. The rate of urine production is low (about 0.05% body wt h^{-1}) and the urine is isosmotic with the body fluids. These ideas were not challenged until the use of radioactive tracers showed massive branchial Na^+ and Cl^- fluxes in seawater-adapted flounders, *Platichthys flesus*, and other marine fish (Motais, 1961). The Na^+

efflux was approximately 26 mM kg^{-1} h^{-1} or about 20% h^{-1} of the body's exchangeable Na$^+$ and was almost matched by a slightly smaller Na$^+$ influx. The difference between the two fluxes (net flux) was equivalent to the excreted salt (Table I). Similar results have now been obtained by many investigators with a variety of species but the exact nature of these branchial fluxes remains unresolved. Because the fluxes are greatly reduced when some euryhaline fish (for example flounders) are transferred to fresh water it was proposed that the greater part of the flux was exchange diffusion (Motais et al., 1966) with the remainder being an active component dependent upon the presence of external K$^+$ (Maetz, 1969b). Later work suggested that the Na$^+$ fluxes were mainly simple diffusional fluxes because the body potential of approximately 20 mV in sea water would be sufficient to prevent a net inwards diffusion of Na$^+$ whilst the potentials of about -40 mV recorded in fresh water would largely counteract a net outwards diffusion of Na$^+$ (Potts and Eddy, 1973). In other species, for example, the mullet, *Mugil capito*, (Maetz and Pic, 1975) and the lined sole, *Achirus lineatus*, (Evans and Cooper, 1976) the reduction in Na$^+$ efflux upon transfer to fresh water is thought to be an exchange diffusion or non-diffusional process largely unrelated to potential. On energetic considerations, a relatively small net flux may be optimally linked to large unidirectional ionic fluxes (Fletcher, 1980). Space does not permit further discussion of this subject and the reader is referred to reviews by Maetz and Bornancin (1975), Potts (1976), Kirschner (1979) and Evans (1980).

It is accepted that branchial salt fluxes are associated with the chloride cells. As with many other ion-secreting cells, the chloride cells contain the enzyme Na-K ATPase which is known to actively pump Na$^+$ from the cell to the extracellular space and to move K$^+$ in the opposite direction. However, the configuration of the salt pumping mechanism in chloride cells has not been satisfactorily resolved although there are a number of models which attempt to account for the known facts. For example, Silva et al. (1977) suggest that active pumping of K$^+$ into and Na$^+$ out of the chloride-cell induces a potential between the blood and sea water such that the tendency for Na$^+$ to diffuse inwards along intercellular channels, down the concentration gradient, is more or less opposed by the electrical gradient, i.e. Na$^+$ is in electrochemical balance. The ion pump also holds the inside of the cell negative so that Cl$^-$ (which enters the cell possibly linked to Na$^+$) is expelled along the electrical gradient and against the concentration gradient.

(b) Freshwater Fishes

In freshwater fishes the body fluids are much more concentrated than the surrounding medium and thus water enters osmotically and salts diffuse outwards. Excess water is removed as copious hypotonic urine (excretion

TABLE I Salt Fluxes in Various Marine and Euryhaline Fishes.

Species	Blood plasma concentration	mM litre^{-1}	Drinking	Branchial influx	Branchial efflux	Branchial net efflux	Urine
Rainbow Trout^a ($\frac{2}{3}$ sea water) 10°C	Na$^+$	139	0·95	6·67	7·62	0·95	0·05
	Cl$^-$	109	1·21	6·35	7·56	1·21	0·09
Flounder^b	Na$^+$	168	1*	22·5	26	3·5	—
Cod 12·5°C^c	Na$^+$	190	1·87	6·97	8·78	1·81	0·06
	Cl$^-$	157	2·09	3·51	5·44	1·93	0·16

Values in mM kg^{-1} hr^{-1}. ^{a} Rainbow trout (*Salmo gairdneri*), Eddy and Bath (1979a). ^{b} Flounder (*Platichthys flesus*), Maetz (1971). * Drinking rate measured on a separate group of animals. ^{c} Cod (*Gadus callarias* L.), Fletcher (1978). In each case 80–95% of the ingested salt is absorbed and rectal losses are very small.

TABLE II Salt and Water Balance in Freshwater Fish.

Species	Blood plasma concentration	mM litre^{-1}	External concentration mM litre^{-1}	Drinking	Branchial influx	Branchial efflux	Branchial net influx	Urine
Rainbow Trout^a 10°C	Na$^+$	139	0·22	0·0001	0·6909	0·6910	0	0·0057
	Cl$^-$	112	0·30	0·0001	0·2134	0·2135	0	0·0054
Goldfish^{b,c}	Na$^+$	147*	0·44	—	0·79	0·25	0·54	0·007*
	Cl$^-$	117*	0·37	—	0·48	0·35	0·13	0·005*

Values in mM kg^{-1} hr^{-1}. ^{a} *Salmo gairdneri* (Eddy and Bath, 1979a; Bath and Eddy, 1979). ^{b} Na$^+$ values, *Carassius auratus*, 16°C (Maetz, 1972). ^{c} Cl$^-$ values, 9–18°C (de Renzis, 1975). * Values from Mackay (1974), 14°C for blood ions and 10°C for urine ions. Net fluxes for goldfish are very high because they had been "salt depleted" by keeping them in deionized water for several weeks prior to flux measurements.

rate 0·15–0·42% body wt h^{-1}) whilst salt losses are replaced by active uptake mechanisms in the gills. Branchial ionic uptake increases with the external salt concentration up to about 2 mM litre^{-1} when the mechanism becomes saturated. It was suggested by Krogh (1939) that neutrality was maintained by the exchange of Na$^+$ for NH$_4^+$ and Cl$^-$ for HCO$_3^-$, a hypothesis which was subsequently confirmed by Maetz and Romeu (1964) although later it was shown that Na$^+$ could exchange for H$^+$ as well as NH$_4^+$ (Maetz, 1972). For reasons not yet understood, freshwater fish drink the medium at a rate of approximately 0·05% body wt h^{-1}. Some typical values for salt balance in freshwater fish are shown in Table II. The gills of fresh water fish contain the enzyme Na-K ATPase (Sargent and Thomson, 1974) as well as an anion stimulated enzyme Cl-K ATPase which is possibly involved in the proposed Cl/HCO$_3$ exchange (Bornancin et al., 1980).

(c) Euryhaline Fishes

Certain fish including salmon, trout, eels, flounders, mullet and many others are able, at some point in their life history, to move between fresh water and sea water. This is a very interesting phenomenon because the transition from fresh water to sea water requires a complete reversal of salt movement across the gills, from a net movement inwards in fresh water to a net movement outwards in sea water, and the mechanisms responsible for this change are far from understood. For a review of euryhalinity the reader is referred to Kirschner (1979) and Evans (1980).

III ENDOCRINOLOGY OF OSMOTIC AND IONIC REGULATION

A number of hormones have been shown to be involved in osmotic and ionic regulation but particular attention has been paid to cortisol, prolactin and the catecholamines. Stimuli which have the capacity for altering any aspect of the metabolism of these hormones must, therefore, be potentially capable of influencing osmotic and ionic regulation in fish. A detailed account of these and other hormones can be found in reviews by Bentley (1971), Johnson (1973) and Hirano and Mayer-Gostan (1978).

The secretion of cortisol influences both mineral and carbohydrate metabolism in fish and is stimulated by stresses such as handling, temperature change, exercise and spawning (see Donaldson, 1981, this volume). The involvement of cortisol in mineral balance was demonstrated by removal of the corticosteroid-producing interrenal tissues in eels, a severe procedure initially carried out by Chester-Jones et al. (1964). This was shown to result in decreased levels of circulating cortisol (Butler *et al.*, 1969). In freshwater eels, interrenalectomy leads to reduced Na^+ uptake causing a deficiency in blood plasma Na^+, which can be restored by the administration of cortisol. In seawater animals, the operation causes a reduction in the Na^+ fluxes and an elevation of blood plasma Na^+. Again cortisol administration promotes a return to normal values (Maetz, 1969a). Thus, cortisol appears to promote salt gain in freshwater fish and salt loss in seawater fish, both active processes. In eels, cortisol acts on a variety of osmoregulatory organs (gills, intestine, kidney and urinary bladder) by increasing the levels of Na-K ATPase, the net transport of Na^+ and Cl^-, and the permeability of the fish to these ions as well as to water (Hirano and Mayer-Gostan, 1978). However these effects have yet to be demonstrated in other fish species.

Prolactin (or prolactin-like substances) are important in hydromineral balance as shown by early experiments in which hypophysectomized killifish, *Fundulus heteroclitus*, survived in sea water or isotonic media but failed to survive in fresh water because of greatly increased Na^+ losses (Pickford and Phillips, 1959). Replacement therapy by means of prolactin injections reduced branchial Na^+ permeability even in seawater fish and prolonged survival in fresh water (Pickford and Phillips, 1959; Potts and Evans, 1966). Similar results have been obtained with other species including the brown trout, *Salmo trutta*, in which survival of hypophysectomizec fish in fresh water was prolonged by prolactin injections or by increasing the Ca^{2+} content of the medium to approximately 5 mM litre^{-1} (Oduleye, 1976). These physiological results are in keeping with histological studies showing that the prolactin cells in the adenohypophyseal pars distalis of the pituitary gland of yearling coho salmon, *Oncorhynchus kisutch*, are more active in freshwater fish compared to seawater fish (Nagahama *et al.*, 1977). Like cortisol, prolactin acts on a variety of osmoregulatory organs including the gills, intestine, kidney, urinary bladder and oesophagus. The primary effect of prolactin is to reduce membrane permeability to ions and water and, in some epithelia, to promote mucus secretion (Bern, 1975). Thus, cortisol and prolactin may, in certain cases, act antagonistically. For example, cortisol induces a high water permeability in the urinary bladder of *Gillichthys* sp., an effect which is inhibited by prolactin (Bern, 1975). Both prolactin and cortisol may take many hours or even days to exert their full effect and it is suggested that one function of these hormones is in cellular rearrangement of osmoregulatory epithelia (Hirano and Mayer-Gostan, 1978).

Elevation of the levels of circulating catecholamines is one of the more immediate and dramatic responses of fish to a wide variety of stresses (see Mazeaud and Mazeaud, 1981, this volume) and consequently the influence of these hormones (adrenaline in particular) on osmotic and ionic regulation in fish is of particular interest. Adrenaline injection in the seawater-adapted mullet (approximately 1 mg kg^{-1} body wt) reduces the Na$^+$ and Cl$^-$ effluxes (Pic *et al.*, 1975) and a similar effect has been observed in the isolated perfused head of seawater-adapted rainbow trout, *Salmo gairdneri*, (Girard, 1976). These results were interpreted as an adrenaline induced inhibition of the K$^+$ stimulated component of the Na$^+$ efflux. In isolated, seawater-adapted flounder gills when diffusion potentials are eliminated by both bathing and perfusing the gill with fish saline solutions the observed potential of about 10 mV is halved by the addition of 10^{-6} M adrenaline to the perfusate (Shuttleworth, 1978). This has led to the conclusion that the bioelectric ion pump, which is believed to be responsible for active transport of both Na$^+$ and Cl$^-$ (Shuttleworth *et al.*, 1974), is inhibited by adrenaline. Thus, Shuttleworth (1978) makes the important point that studies of ion fluxes may give misleading results if the fish are handled or stressed at the time of experimentation. The branchial circulation is influenced by adrenaline, which increases perfusion of the secondary lamellae. In contrast, acetylcholine decreases perfusion of the secondary lamellae but increases blood flow to the central filament sinus or "shunt pathway" (Richards and Fromm, 1969). However Booth (1979) found greater numbers of secondary lamellae perfused in the presence of adrenaline and fewer with acetylcholine, with no change in blood flow to the "shunt" pathway. In freshwater trout it has been reported that adrenaline stimulates Na$^+$ uptake (Richards and Fromm, 1970; Payan *et al.*, 1975) whilst in seawater adapted trout adrenaline appears to inhibit salt excretion although the significance of such effects remains uncertain (Girard and Payan, 1980).

Other hormones including the thyroid hormones, angiotensin and the neurohypophysial peptides vasotocin and isotocin have been implicated in osmoregulation, but their involvement in stress is little understood. A discussion of some of these hormones can be found in Bentley (1971), Babiker and Rankin (1979) and Dickhoff *et al.* (1978). The complex subject of seasonal variations in hormone levels and their metabolic effects is discussed by Hoar (1976), Matty (1978) and Simpson (1978).

IV EFFECTS OF STRESS ON OSMOTIC AND IONIC REGULATION

In fish, this subject has not been systematically studied, but many primary investigations on osmotic and ionic regulation have, to varying degrees, examined particular aspects of the effects of stress. Changes in osmoregulatory mechanisms may not occur immediately in response to a stress and could take many hours, or even days, to develop. Similarly, removal of the stress does not necessarily mean a rapid return to normality. The following account is selective in that it deals mainly with salmonids and is restricted to certain well-defined stresses.

(a) Osmotic and Ionic Stresses

These will be considered to be transfer, whether rapid or gradual, from fresh water to sea water or the reverse. Whilst there is an abundant literature concerning ionic regulation in fish adapted to sea water or dilute sea water over a period of days or weeks, the immediate physiological consequences of such transfers is a relatively neglected area. The immediate responses shown by fish upon transfer to hyperosmotic media are likely to have significant effects upon subsequent survival and adaptation (see also Wedemeyer and McLeay, 1981, this volume).

(i) *Fresh water to sea water transfer.* In rainbow trout transferred directly to sea water (32‰) one of the earliest responses is an increase in the drinking rate from about $0.5 \, \text{ml} \, \text{kg}^{-1} \, \text{h}^{-1}$ to over $25 \, \text{ml} \, \text{kg}^{-1} \, \text{h}^{-1}$ in 22‰ sea water (Bath and Eddy, 1979). A similar drinking response is seen in eels (Kirsch and Mayer-Gostan, 1973) which, as in trout, return to normal levels after a few hours in sea water. Increased drinking in the Japanese eel, *Anguilla japonica*, can be elicited by reduction in blood volume or by applying chloride solutions to the oral region (Hirano, 1974). Other changes in the rainbow trout seen during the first few hours in sea water include a dehydration of the whole body resulting in a weight loss (approximately 5% after 4 h—F. B. Eddy and J. McEwan, unpublished results) and a reduction of the blood plasma water content from 95% to 85% (Bath and Eddy, 1979). When salmon parr, *Salmo salar*, are placed in 33.9‰ sea water, the blood plasma osmotic pressure increases significantly within an hour, followed soon afterwards by death of the fish (Parry, 1960). A similar trend has been noted in salmon smolts but in this case there is a much smaller rise in osmotic pressure and a greater survival (Parry, 1960).

During their first 8 h after direct transfer from fresh water to two-thirds sea water, juvenile rainbow trout show significant increases in the Na^+ and Cl^- concentrations of the blood plasma, whole body and muscle tissues (Bath and Eddy, 1979). Chloride is the more penetrating ion, as evidenced by the Cl^- concentrations in the intracellular compartment. During this initial readjustment period an increase in the ionic effluxes has been observed both in the rainbow trout (Bath and Eddy, 1979) and in salmon smolts (Potts *et al.*, 1970). Transfer to sea water is also accompanied by a sharp decrease in both the glomerular filtration rate and urine flow. For example, Holmes (1961) reported a decrease in the urine production of rainbow trout from 3.44 ml $kg^{-1} h^{-1}$ in fresh water to 0.031 ml $kg^{-1} h^{-1}$ in sea water and decreases have also been observed in the flounder and the Japanese eel (Hickman and Trump, 1969).

Many freshwater species are intolerant of even dilute sea water. Goldfish, *Carassius auratus*, survive no more than 15‰ sea water and show increased blood plasma and exchangeable body Na^+ levels, together with higher drinking rates. Even after several days in 15‰ sea water, ionic regulation is incomplete and the Na^+ effluxes fail to match the Na^+ influxes (Lahlou *et al.*, 1969). Similarly perch, *Perca fluviatilis*, fail to survive 16‰ sea water and show signs of body dehydration together with ionic invasion (particularly Cl^-) into most tissues with the exception of the liver (Lutz, 1972).

The role of free amino acids and other non-protein nitrogenous substances in the maintenance of cellular tonicity during exposure to hyperosmotic media has been investigated in flounders (Lange and Fugelli, 1965), in *Angonus cataphractus* (Colley *et al.*, 1974) and in *Fundulus diaphanus* (Ahokas and Sorg, 1977). In all cases, tissue concentrations of these substances increased with increasing salinity, and this would appear to be an important area for future studies.

(ii) *Sea water to fresh water transfer.* Rapid transfer from sea water to fresh water has been intensely studied in a number of euryhaline fish with the main object of elucidating the physiological nature of the branchial salt fluxes. In such fish, direct entry to dilute media is accompanied by a marked reduction in both Na^+ and Cl^- effluxes. For example, in flounders the Na^+ efflux is reduced from about 25% of the total body Na^+ h^{-1} (approximately 20 mM $kg^{-1} h^{-1}$) to about 1% h^{-1} (Motais *et al.*, 1966). However, similar experiments with stenohaline marine fish such as the sea perch, *Serranus* sp., have failed to show such a reduction in ionic effluxes (Maetz, 1971). Nevertheless, the stenohaline marine fish, *Holocanthus ciliaris*, is able to survive many weeks in fresh water provided that the environmental calcium concentration is increased to the range 5–25 mM $litre^{-1}$ (Evans, 1975).

Of considerable interest is the ionic regulatory physiology of anadromous fish which feed in sea water but migrate back to fresh water to spawn. Whilst the immediate response to fresh water is unknown, migrating Atlantic salmon which have been in the river for several days show a decrease in blood plasma Na^+ (from about 211 to 181 mM $litre^{-1}$) and an increase in muscle water content together with a possible increase in the extracellular fluid salt content (Parry, 1978). Similar decreases in plasma Na^+, together with a drop in the coelomic fluid ionic concentration have been seen by Hirano *et al.* (1978) in the chum salmon, *Oncorhynchus keta*, after 7 days in fresh water.

(iii) *Adaptation to sea water.* Numerous studies have been concerned with adaptation of fish to sea water much of which is reviewed by Parry (1966), Holmes and Donaldson (1969), Conte (1969) and Hoar (1976). Survival in full strength sea water is greatly improved if fish are preadapted to dilute sea water for a few days. Successful adaptation is also dependent upon size and to some extent upon age and season of the year (Houston, 1959; Conte *et al.*, 1966). Furthermore, it is claimed that feeding the fish with a salt-loaded diet prior to transfer enhances adaptation (Zaugg and McLain, 1969; Jackson, 1977).

The main points to emerge from such studies are that adaptation to sea water is accompanied by initial disturbances to the ion regulatory system but after a few days, physiological variables stabilize, many of them at new levels. Thus, after a week or more in sea water, the drinking rate is increased compared with the fresh water value and the urine excretory rate is much reduced. Blood osmotic and ionic values are held at a constant level, generally close to the fresh water values, but the ionic content of cells may have increased. Branchial salt fluxes are elevated and this appears to be related to an increase in levels of Na-K ATPase, an enzyme found principally in the more numerous chloride cells (Giles and Vanstone, 1976; Thomson and Sargent, 1977). A reduction in the kidney tubule epithelial-cell size has been noted during sea water adaptation of eels (Olivereau and Olivereau, 1977). Many of the physiological processes involved in adaptation by rainbow trout to sea water are summarized in Fig. 1.

(b) Pollution

Much is known about the lethality of pollutants but in many cases their precise mechanisms of toxicity are unknown. Similarly the effects on osmotic and ionic regulation have received little attention. Although not dealing specifically with osmoregulation the effects of many toxic substances on fish have been reviewed by Bremner (1974), Cairns *et al.* (1975) and Alabaster and Lloyd (1980).

(i) *Inorganic pollutants.* Heavy metals are one class of pollutants which have a disruptive influence on the structural organization of the gill tissue. Because the gills are intimately associated with ionic regulation it is predictable that heavy metals will influence aspects of osmotic and ionic regulation in fish. With relatively high levels of Zn^{2+} (40 p.p.m.) rainbow trout die mainly through tissue hypoxia (Skidmore, 1970; Burton *et al.*, 1972), a major factor being disruption of the branchial respiratory epithelium (Skidmore and Tovell, 1972). Skidmore (1970) found little change in the arterial blood plasma osmotic pressure or ionic content of rainbow

OSMOTIC/IONIC BALANCE

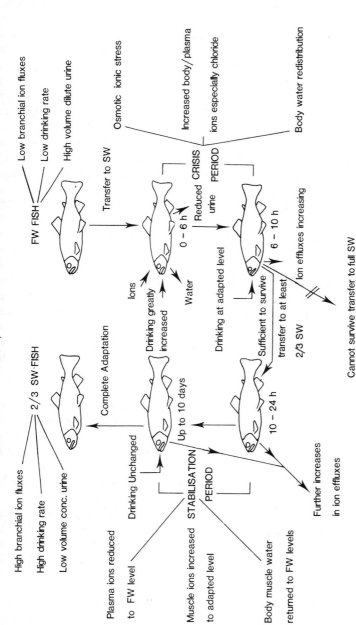

Fig. 1 Diagram outlining the main physiological events which occur when rainbow trout are transferred from fresh water to sea water. The period immediately after transfer and lasting about 8 h is characterized by major physiological changes and is referred to as the "crisis" period. This is followed by a period lasting 7–10 days when slower changes occur, resulting finally in completed adaptation, and is called the "stabilization" period (from Bath and Eddy (1979) by kind permission of *J. exp. Biol.*).

trout after Zn^{2+} treatment whereas Lewis and Lewis (1971), using rather lower Zn^{2+} concentrations over a longer period of time, found significant decreases in the plasma osmotic pressure of channel catfish, *Ictalurus punctatus*, and this was considered a major factor leading to death. They also found similar results with copper. In this connection it is interesting that in the presence of 10 μM litre^{-1} Cu^{2+} the *in vitro* activity of branchial Na-K ATPase was reduced by 43% in freshwater-adapted flounders and by 83% in seawater-adapted fish (see abstract by Stagg and Shuttleworth, 1981, this volume). An immediate, large increase in Na^+ and Cl^- effluxes, sustained ionic net loss and an eventual disruption of the gill epithelium was seen in goldfish after treatment with 2 mM litre^{-1} lanthanum (Eddy and Bath, 1979b). It was suggested that La^{3+} interferes with, and displaces Ca^{2+} from the branchial binding sites thereby increasing passive permeability to Na^+ and Cl^-, and that other polyvalent ions (for example Mn^{2+}, Cr^{2+}, Ni^{2+}) may act in a similar way.

The gill epithelium of mosquito fish, *Gambusia affinis*, is disrupted by exposure to 0·5 p.p.m. Cl_2, but recovery can be greatly improved by placing the fish in isotonic salt solutions, a treatment which presumably reduces diffusional ionic losses and the osmotic gain of water (Cohen, 1977). Zeitoun (1978) noted an increased concentration of blood plasma K^+ and Ca^{2+} but a significant decrease in Na^+ from 147 mM litre^{-1} to 125 mM litre^{-1} in rainbow trout exposed to approximately 1 mg litre^{-1} residual Cl_2. However, interpretation of these results is complicated by a massive haemoconcentration, haematocrit increasing from 41% to 53%. Recovery in Cl_2 free water was complete after 48 h.

(ii) *Accumulated excretory products.* Perhaps the two most important excretory products of teleost fish with respect to their effects on osmotic and ionic regulation are ammonia and carbon dioxide. Rainbow trout exposed to sublethal ammonia levels (up to 20 p.p.m. total NH_3.N, pH 8·1, 10°C) show an increase in urine volume from about 2 ml kg^{-1} h^{-1} to nearly 10 ml kg^{-1} h^{-1} at the highest ammonia concentrations. Similar results were noted with ammonia/phenol mixtures and with prolonged exposure to low oxygen concentrations (Lloyd and Orr, 1969; Swift and Lloyd, 1974; Lloyd and Swift, 1976). This response could result from an increase in branchial permeability or from an increase in the drinking rate. It is of interest, therefore, to note that exposure of rainbow trout to 5 mg litre^{-1} Zn^{2+} for 3 h decreased the drinking from 1·43 ml kg^{-1} h^{-1} to 0·25 ml kg^{-1} h^{-1} (S. Lovegrove, personal communication).

Hypercapnia (35 mg litre^{-1} free CO_2 for up to 24 h) causes an increase in blood plasma HCO_3^- at the expense of Cl^- in the rainbow trout (Lloyd and White, 1967) and a reduction in net Cl^- uptake and ammonia output (Lloyd and Swift, 1976). In the Arctic grayling, *Thymallus arcticus*, exposure to 1% CO_2 causes a reduction of ^{36}Cl influx but an increase in ^{22}Na influx (Cameron, 1976). For a discussion of the significance of Na^+/H^+ (NH_4^+) and Cl^-/HCO_3^- exchanges in relation to the regulation of the fish's acid base balance see Maetz (1971) and Cameron (1978). An increase in muscle K^+, Ca^{2+} and H^+ was noted in rainbow trout after prolonged exposure (many weeks) to at least 7 mmHg PCO_2 (Eddy *et al.*, 1979).

Rainbow trout returned to fresh water after a period of hypercapnia show several major physiological events during the first hour. These include a decrease in net Na^+ uptake and an increase in urine output (Lloyd and Swift, 1976) and an increase in blood pH and O_2 affinity (Eddy *et al.*, 1977). Removal of excess blood plasma HCO_3^- and its replacement by Cl^- is a much slower process taking several hours (Lloyd and White, 1967; Eddy *et al.*, 1977), presumably limited by the rate at which the branchial Cl^-/HCO_3^- exchange can operate. These experiments illustrate the point that not only is the onset and progress of stress important but also its removal may require major physiological adjustments as the animal attempts to become normal. This could be particularly important in fish exposed to periodic or intermittent stresses.

(iii) *Environmental acidification.* The progressive acidification of many poorly buffered freshwater systems has had a deleterious effect on the fish populations (Leivestad *et al.*, 1976). Acid waters, particularly those below pH 4·5 are toxic to fish (see review by Alabaster and Lloyd, 1980) and have marked effects upon the osmoregulatory processes. Thus, Packer and Dunson (1970, 1972) noted increased net Na^+ losses with a concomitant lowering of the blood plasma sodium levels of brown trout. McWilliams and Potts (1978) have shown that the gills of the brown trout are highly permeable to hydrogen ions with a significant influx of H^+ at low environmental pH. Under these conditions an inhibition of the Na^+ influx was also noted. In certain, but not all, situations this could be ameliorated by an elevation of the environmental Ca^{2+} concentration. The main reason for the increase in Na^+ efflux in acid waters appears to be related to the more positive body potential recorded in the fish (McWilliams and Potts, 1978). For a general review of the effects of acid waters on teleost fish the reader is referred to Fromm (1980).

(c) Temperature

The Arrhenius theory predicts that an increase in temperature will increase the rate of chemical or biochemical reactions. A 10°C rise in temperature will result in an approximate doubling of the rate of most biological processes ($Q_{10} = 2$), although the overall range of Q_{10} values for biological processes appears to be between 1 and 3. This relationship is of fundamental importance to poikilotherms because changes in environmental temperature will dictate corresponding changes in the metabolic rate, although in time adaptive processes may take place. General aspects of this subject are discussed by Prosser (1973). Temperature sensitivity of the biochemical reactions governing osmotic and ionic regulation has been little studied with the exception of ionic regulation in the fish intestine (Smith, 1976).

The dissociation of water into H^+ and OH^- is temperature dependant such that the pH for neutrality (when $pH = pOH$) increases with cooling. Poikilotherms such as fish do not appear to regulate body fluid pH as such but regulate the ratio $[OH^-]/[H^+]$ at approximately $30:1$ over a wide temperature range. Thus, there is an inverse relationship between blood pH and temperature, i.e. the blood is more acidic at higher temperatures (Howell *et al.*, 1970). This important relationship should not be overlooked when temperature effects on ionic regulation in fish are discussed.

(i) *Acclimation to different temperatures.* Acclimation to temperatures within the normal environmental range generally results in small changes in blood ionic content. Goldfish adapted to 5°C show a slight, but significant, reduction in blood Na^+, K^+ and Cl^- concentrations compared to those adapted to 15°C or 25°C (Prosser *et al.*, 1970). A similar pattern has been observed in carp *Cyprinus carpio* (Houston *et al.*, 1970). However, the rainbow trout does not exhibit a very marked temperature dependant variation in the ionic composition of its blood plasma (Houston *et al.*, 1968).

It has been observed that freshwater fish exposed to near freezing temperatures show a decrease in plasma electrolyte concentration although this is not necessarily accompanied by a decrease in plasma osmolarity. Umminger (1971) identified several types of compensation to extreme cold; in the brown bullhead, *Ictalurus nebulosus*, both plasma electrolytes and osmolarity are decreased without the addition of organic substances whereas carp, and to some extent killifish, keep their osmotic pressure constant despite a drop in electrolytes, presumably through addition of organic substances. Goldfish adapted to 1°C show a modest decrease in plasma osmotic pressure and Na^+, whilst Cl^- remains unchanged (Catlett and Millich, 1976).

Marine fishes, when exposed to near freezing temperatures, tend to show an increase in blood plasma osmotic pressure and electrolytes (Prosser *et al.*, 1970; Umminger, 1969a). It is not clear whether haemodilution in fresh water and haemoconcentration in sea water, induced by extreme cold is adaptive or a consequence of osmoregulatory failure. In supercooled seawater-adapted killifish the marked increases in plasma electrolytes, osmolarity and glucose are maintained indefinitely and are considered not to be indicative of osmoregulatory failure (Umminger, 1969a, b). Furthermore, certain marine fishes resist freezing by the addition of specific antifreeze substances (for example, glycoproteins or peptides) to the blood (DeVries, 1971; Dunman and DeVries, 1976).

In fresh water, higher urine flow rates were observed with increasing acclimation temperature in white suckers, *Catostomus commersonii*, (MacKay and Beatty, 1968) and rainbow trout (Lloyd and Orr, 1969) the Q_{10} values being 2·2 and 2·4 respectively. Similar coefficients were obtained for urine flow and branchial Na^+ and Cl^- net uptakes in goldfish adapted to various temperatures in the range 10°C to 30°C (MacKay, 1974).

(ii) *Sudden temperature changes.* Acute cold shock in alewives, *Alosa pseudoharengus*, from 16°C to 3°C, decreased the plasma and muscle Na^+ content in both freshwater and seawater-adapted fish. However, acute warming from 17°C to 31°C, caused an increase in Na^+ content of plasma and muscle only in seawater-adapted fish (Stanley and Colby, 1971). These authors considered that sudden exposure to cold is more harmful than sudden heating. Rainbow trout adapted to 11°C and then acutely exposed to a 10°C drop in temperature show a marked decrease in the blood plasma Na^+ and Cl^- concentrations within 6 h. This effect persists for approximately 2 days before the fish slowly regain their original plasma levels. Acute exposure to a 10°C rise in temperature results in much smaller changes (Reaves *et al.*, 1968). The rapid transfer of goldfish from 16°C to 6°C decreases their Na^+ influx ($Q_{10} = 3$) more than Na^+ efflux ($Q_{10} = 1·7$) (Maetz, 1972). This effect is reversible and the reduced efflux has been attributed to a decreased branchial Na^+ permeability. The resulting Na imbalance would result in a net loss of plasma electrolytes and is a possible explanation for the common response of a decrease in the concentration of plasma ions when freshwater fish are transferred from warm to cold water (Maetz, 1972). Results from similar rapid transfer experiments on sea perch yielded Na^+ efflux temperature coefficients in the range 1·08–2·03 (Isaia, 1972) and in the seawater-adapted eel 1·5–2·0 (Motais and Isaia, 1972). In seawater-adapted flounders, transfer between 16°C and 6°C results in reversible decreases in the efflux by a factor of 2 and in the active extrusion mechanism (Na^+/K^+ exchange) by a factor of 6 (Maetz and Evans, 1972). On the other hand, flounders rapidly transferred from 16°C to 26°C showed a 14% reduction in Na^+ efflux and elevated blood plasma Na^+ levels (201 mM litre^{-1} Na^+ compared to 167 mM litre^{-1} at 16°C). When returned to 16°C these fish continued to show low Na^+ effluxes for several days and later died suggesting irreversible damage to the salt extruding mechanism (Maetz and Evans, 1972).

Tritiated water has been used to measure diffusional water permeability in a variety of species both freshwater and marine. Temperature coefficients are generally in the range 1·5–3·0 (Evans, 1969; Isaia, 1972; Motais and Isaia, 1972). Loretz (1979) measured diffusional water permeability in goldfish adapted to 21°C then rapidly transferred to higher or lower temperatures, yielding a Q_{10} value of 2·48, except above 25°C when the value was 1·4. In contrast, diffusional water permeability measured in fish adapted to various temperatures gave Q_{10} values of 1·4 indicating that the thermal history of the fish is likely to be important in determining the properties of branchial membranes.

(d) Anaesthetics and Handling

Capture, handling and anaesthesia all have profound effects on salt and water balance in fish. This problem has long been recognized and was clearly outlined by Grafflin (1931) who found that undisturbed fish (toad fish *Opsanus tau*, sculpin *Myoxocephalus octodecimospinosus*) produced urine at a rate of approximately 4 ml kg^{-1} day^{-1} with very low Cl$^-$ concentrations. However, handled or slightly damaged fish produced urine in excess of 30 ml kg^{-1} day^{-1} with a high Cl$^-$ content. Similarly, bladder urine from freshly caught *Lophius piscatorius* was almost devoid of Cl$^-$ but later, after handling in the laboratory, the concentration of this ion increased to levels similar to those in the blood plasma (Forster and Berglund, 1953). Holliday and Blaxter (1961) concluded that damaged or descaled herrings are unlikely to survive sea water, but their chances of survival are greatly improved in 50% sea water, because of reduced osmotic stress.

Winter flounders, *Pseudopleuronectes americanus*, stressed in the laboratory by placing them upside down show a rapid increase in blood plasma osmotic pressure which tends to decrease when the fish are righted. Plasma Na$^+$ and Cl$^-$ also increase rapidly but these high values persist for many hours after stress (Fletcher, 1975). Similarly, high blood plasma ionic contents were seen in freshly captured winter flounders and in laboratory "netted" fish (Fletcher, 1975) which also showed a persistent hyperglycemia. Both rainbow trout and coho salmon subjected to handling stress show hyperglycemia and hyperchloridemia with peak values being reached after 3–4 h and returning to basal levels after 24 h. These symptoms could be reduced by placing the fish in 100 mM litre^{-1} NaCl solutions (Wedemeyer, 1972).

Many laboratory procedures, fish transport and handling require the use of anaesthetics. One of the most popular is MS222 (tricaine methane sulphonate) although a variety of others, including benzocaine (ethyl P-amino benzoate), are used (McFarland, 1960; Randall and Hoar, 1971;

Laird and Oswald, 1975; Booke *et al.*, 1978). MS222 and its derivatives are cleared from the blood of rainbow trout within 8 h and from the urine within 24 h of recovery from anaesthetization at 100 mg litre^{-1} (Hunn *et al.*, 1968), although Houston and Wards (1972) noted a more rapid clearance from the blood of the brook trout, *Salvelinus fontinalis*.

Rainbow trout anaesthetized with 100 mg litre^{-1} MS222 prior to insertion of a urinary cannula, or upon subsequent reanaesthetization, show a maximum increase in urine flow and ionic content after 2–4 h recovery. For example, after 2 h recovery the urine flow increased from 43·8 to 139 ml kg^{-1} day^{-1} and the urine Na$^+$ concentration from 4·3–8·4 mM litre^{-1}, Cl^{-1} from 5·1–6·0 mM litre^{-1} and PO$_4$ as P from 2·5 to 4·8 mM litre^{-1} (Hunn and Willford, 1970). Similar responses were seen in rainbow trout after 30 min severe hypoxia (Hunn, 1969).

Various blood parameters, including ionic content, were examined in brook trout after 15 min anaesthesia in 100 mg litre^{-1} MS222 (Houston *et al.*, 1971a). The most noticeable change was an increase in blood plasma Na$^+$ content which remained elevated for 1–2 h. Moreover, hyperglycemia together with an increase in tissue K$^+$ and a decrease in tissue Ca^{2+} content was noted for a period of several days following anaesthesia (Houston *et al.*, 1971b).

These changes in carbohydrate and blood electrolyte balance are thought to be under endocrine control and in this respect the roles of adrenaline and cortisol are particularly important (see reviews by Mazeaud and Mazeaud, 1981, and Donaldson, 1981, this volume).

A number of careful studies on the effects of anaesthetics and stress have been carried out by Soivio, using a variation of the dorsal aorta cannulation technique developed by Smith and Bell (1964). This approach allows blood parameters in fish to be monitored during the process of anaesthesia and for several days or even weeks afterwards thereby enabling resting or "unstressed" values to be obtained. Rainbow trout which were allowed 3 weeks recovery from anaesthesia (100 mg litre^{-1} unbuffered MS222) and cannulation were sampled at the beginning and end of the following 7 days, or repeatedly throughout that period. Either procedure failed to show any significant variations in blood Na$^+$, K$^+$, Ca^{2+}, lactate and glucose although repeated sampling, as might be expected, led to dilution of blood haemoglobin. Variations between restrained and freeswimming fish were negligible (Soivio and Nyholm, 1975). In a similar experiment again after 3 weeks recovery, rainbow trout were anaesthetized for 15 min to 100 mg litre^{-1} MS222 and blood samples were taken over the next 4–7 days. Blood plasma ions (Na$^+$, K$^+$, Ca^{2+}) remained more or less unchanged throughout but glucose and lactate showed modest rises during the first 12 h of recovery. If anaesthesia was preceded by stress (removal from the water for 20 sec) significant increases in the ionic content and glucose concentration of the blood were observed. A most significant finding was that MS222 seemed to act as an asphyxiant causing severely depressed blood O_2 tension and pH which returned to normal values within 20 min after recovery in fresh water (Soivio et al., 1977).

Studies of this type emphasize the importance of obtaining blood values from quiescent and unstressed fish because only then can the effects of a particular stress be assessed with certainty. In many previous studies, blood samples have been obtained by traumatic procedures such as cardiac puncture, puncture of the caudal artery or vein etc., which may involve removing the fish from water for several minutes. The data obtained can only refer to the physiology of fish under varying degrees of stress.

Effects of stress on branchial ionic fluxes have been studied on relatively few occasions. The physical disturbance of rainbow trout adapted to sea water or dilute sea water increases both the plasma Na^+ concentration as well as the Na^+ efflux and influx. Lahlou et al. (1975) have shown that under these conditions the Na^+ efflux may double to approximately $10 \, \text{mM} \, \text{kg}^{-1} \, \text{h}^{-1}$ and the Na^+ influx may increase 7-fold to $20 \, \text{mM} \, \text{kg}^{-1} \, \text{h}^{-1}$. Pic (1978) studied the potential changes and ionic effluxes in killifish immediately following anaesthesia and cannulation in ice cold water. Compared to unstressed fish, examined 18 h to 4 days later, the stressed animals in sea water showed similar Na^+ effluxes (approximately $45 \, \text{mM} \, \text{kg}^{-1} \, \text{h}^{-1}$), increased Cl^- effluxes ($48 \, \text{mM} \, \text{kg}^{-1} \, \text{h}^{-1}$ compared to $26 \, \text{mM} \, \text{kg}^{-1} \, \text{h}^{-1}$) and a potential $5 \cdot 5$ mV compared to 23 mV. Upon transfer to fresh water (achieved by replacing the medium rather than handling the fish) ionic effluxes remained elevated in stressed fish and the potential remained within a few mV of zero instead of becoming strongly negative. It was concluded that stress caused an increase in branchial Cl^- permeability. Similar results were seen in the mullet (Pic, 1978). In handled goldfish, Na^+ and Cl^- effluxes are at least five times greater than those obtained after 24 h recovery when the fish are quiescent (Eddy and Bath, 1979b).

As with blood sampling these studies illustrate the importance of obtaining physiological data from quiet unstressed fish before examining the effects of a particular procedure.

V   CONCLUDING REMARKS

Osmotic and ionic regulation in fish is a very large subject and in a short review it is impossible to outline every area where salt balance is of physiological importance and then go on to discuss effects of stress upon that particular system. Whilst several major areas have been covered, a number of subjects have been omitted, not because they are unimportant but because our knowledge of osmoregulation in these areas is small. Such topics include salt and water balance in eggs and embryos, nutritional aspects, diseased fish, and ionic regulation during swimming. Finally little is known of the cellular aspects of osmotic and ionic regulation in fish, particularly in tissues such as skin, gut and gills and this would seem to be an important area for future research.

A point often made in this review is that stress, in whatever form, has far reaching effects on osmotic and ionic regulation in fish. Thus, when experiments are designed to investigate some aspect of salt and water balance it is important to adopt procedures which minimize stress otherwise it may be impossible to differentiate the true experimental results from those attributable to stress.

REFERENCES

Ahokas, R. A. and Sorg, G. (1977). The effect of salinity and temperature on intracellular osmoregulation and muscle free amino acids in *Fundulus diaphanus*. *Comp. Biochem. Physiol.* **56A**, 101–105.

Alabaster, J. S. and Lloyd, R. (1980). *Water Quality Criteria for Freshwater Fish*. London: Butterworths. 297pp.

Babiker, M. M. and Rankin, J. C. (1979). Factors regulating the functioning of *in vitro* perfused aglomerular kidney in the angler fish *Lophius piscatorius* L. *Comp. Biochem. Physiol.* **62A**, 989–993.

Bath, R. N. and Eddy, F. B. (1979). Salt and water balance in rainbow trout (*Salmo gairdneri*) rapidly transferred from fresh water to sea water. *J. exp. Biol.* **83**, 193–202.

Bentley, P. J. (1971). *Endocrines and Osmoregulation*. New York: Springer-Verlag. 300 pp.

Bern, A. H. (1975). Prolactin and osmoregulation. *Am. Zool.* **15**, 937–948.

Booke, H. E., Hollender, B. and Lutterbie, G. (1978). Sodium bicarbonate, an inexpensive fish anaesthetic for field use. *Progve Fish Cult.* **40**, 11–13.

Booth, J. H. (1979). The effects of oxygen supply, epinephrine and acetylocholine on the distribution of blood flow in trout gills. *J. exp. Biol.* **83**, 31–39.

Bornancin, M., de Renzis, G. and Naon, R. (1980). $Cl^- - HCO_3^-$ ATPase in gills of rainbow trout: evidence for its microsomal localisation. *Am. J. Physiol.* **238**, R251–R259.

Bremner, I. (1974). Heavy metal toxicities. *Q. Rev. Biophys.* **7**, 75–124.

Burton, D. T., Jones, A. H. and Cairns, J. (1972). Acute zinc toxicity to rainbow trout (*Salmo gairdneri*): confirmation of the hypothesis that death is related to tissue hypoxia. *J. Fish. Res. Bd Can.* **29**, 1463–1466.

Butler, D. G., Clarke, W. C., Donaldson, E. M. and Langford, R. W. (1969). Surgical adrenalectomy of a teleost fish (*Anguilla rostrata* LeSueur) effect on plasma cortisol and tissue electrolyte and carbohydrate concentration. *Gen. comp. Endocr.* **12**, 503–514.

Cairns, J., Heath, A. G. and Parker, P. C. (1975). The effects of temperature upon the toxicity of chemicals to aquatic organisms. *Hydrobiologia* **47**, 135–171.

Cameron, J. N. (1976). Branchial ion uptake in arctic grayling: resting values and effects of acid base disturbance. *J. exp. Biol.* **64**, 711–725.

Cameron, J. N. (1978). Regulation of blood pH in fishes. *Respir. Physiol.* **33**, 129–144.

Catlett, R. H. and Millich, D. R. (1976). Intracellular and extracellular osmoregulation of temperature acclimated goldfish: *Carassius auratus*. *Comp. Biochem. Physiol.* **55A**, 261–269.

Chester-Jones, I., Henderson, I. W. and Mosley, W. (1964). Methods for the adrenalectomy of the European eel (*Anguilla anguilla*). *J. Endocr.* **30**, 155–156.

Cohen, G. M. (1977). Influence of cations on chlorine toxicity. *Bull. Env. Contam. Toxicol.* **18**, 131–137.

Colley, L., Fox, F. R. and Huggins, A. K. (1974). The effects of changes in external salinity on the non-protein nitrogenous constituents of parietal muscle from *Agonus cataphractus*. *Comp. Biochem. Physiol.* **48A**, 757–763.

Conte, F. P. (1969). Salt secretion. In *Fish Physiology, Vol. I* (W. S. Hoar and D. J. Randall, eds), pp. 241–292. London and New York: Academic Press.

Conte, F. P., Wagner, H. H., Fessler, J. and Grose, C. (1966). Development of osmotic and ionic regulation in juvenile coho salmon *Oncorhynchus kisutch*. *Comp. Biochem. Physiol.* **18**, 1–15.

de Renzis, G. (1975). The branchial chloride pump in the goldfish *Carassius auratus*: relationship between Cl^-/HCO_3^- and Cl^-/Cl^- exchanges and the effect of thiocyanate. *J. exp. Biol.* **63**, 587–602.

DeVries, A. L. (1971). Glycoproteins as biological antifreeze agents in Antarctic fish. *Science, N.Y.* **172**, 1152–1155.

Dickhoff, W. W., Folmar, L. C. and Gorbman, A. (1978). Changes in plasma thyroxine during smoltification of coho salmon *Oncorhynchus kisutch*. *Gen. comp. Endocr.* **36**, 229–232.

Donaldson, E. M. (1981). The pituitary–interrenal axis as an indicator of stress in fish. In *Stress and Fish* (A. D. Pickering, ed.), pp. 11–47. London and New York: Academic Press.

Dunman, J. G. and DeVries, A. L. (1976). Isolation, characterization and physical properties of protein antifreezes from winter flounder *Pseudopleuronectes americanus*. *Comp. Biochem. Physiol.* **54B**, 375–380.

Eddy, F. B. and Bath, R. N. (1979a). Ionic regulation in rainbow trout (*Salmo gairdneri*) adapted to freshwater and dilute sea water. *J. exp. Biol.* **83**, 181–192.

Eddy, F. B. and Bath, R. N. (1979b). Effects of lanthanum on sodium and chloride fluxes in the goldfish *Carassius auratus*. *J. comp. Physiol.* **129**, 145–149.

Eddy, F. B., Lomholt, J. P., Weber, R. E. and Johansen, K. (1977). Blood respiratory properties of rainbow trout (*Salmo gairdneri*) kept in water of high CO_2 tension. *J. exp. Biol.* **67**, 37–47.

Eddy, F. B., Smart, G. R. and Bath, R. N. (1979). Ionic content of muscle and urine in rainbow trout (*Salmo gairdneri* Richardson) kept in water of high CO_2 content. *J. Fish. Dis.* **2**, 105–110.

Evans, D. H. (1969). Studies on the permeability to water of selected marine freshwater and euryhaline teleosts. *J. exp. Biol.* **50**, 689–704.

Evans, D. H. (1975). Ionic exchange mechanism in fish gills. *Comp. Biochem. Physiol.* **51A**, 491–495.

Evans, D. H. (1980). Kinetics studies of ion transport by fish gill epithelium. *Am. J. Physiol.* **238**, R224–R230.

Evans, D. H. and Cooper, K. (1976). The presence of Na-Na and Na-K exchange in sodium extrusion by three species of fish. *Nature* **259**, 241–242.

Fletcher, C. R. (1978). Osmotic and ionic regulation in the cod (*Gadus callarias* L). *J. comp. Physiol.* **124**, 157–168.

Fletcher, C. R. (1980). The relationship between active transport and the exchange diffusion effect. *J. theor. Biol.* **82**, 643–661.

Fletcher, G. L. (1975). The effects of capture "stress" and storage of whole blood on red blood cells, plasma proteins, glucose and electrolytes of the winter flounder (*Pseudopleuronectes americanus*). *Can. J. Zool.* **53**, 197–206.

Forster, R. P. and Berglund, F. (1953). Total electrolyte distribution in blood and urine of the aglomerular marine teleost, *Lophius piscatorius. Anat. Rec.* **117**, 591–592.

Fromm, P. O. (1980). A review of some physiological and toxicological responses of freshwater fish to acid stress. *Envir. Biol. Fishes* **5**, 79–93.

Giles, M. A. and Vanstone, W. E. (1976). Changes in ouabain-sensitive adenosine triphosphatase activity in gills of coho salmon (*Oncorhynchus kisutch*) during parr-smolt transformation. *J. Fish. Res. Bd Can.* **33**, 54–62.

Girard, J. P. (1976). Salt excretion by the perfused head of trout adapted to sea water and its inhibition by adrenaline. *J. comp. Physiol.* **111**, 77–91.

Girard, J. P. and Payan, P. (1980). Ion exchanges through respiratory and chloride cells in freshwater and seawater adapted teleosteans. *Am. J. Physiol.* **238**, R260–R268.

Grafflin, A. L. (1931). Urine flow and diuresis in marine teleosts. *Am. J. Physiol.* **97**, 602–610.

Hickman, C. P. and Trump, B. F. (1969). The kidney. In *Fish Physiology, Vol. I* (W. S. Hoar and D. J. Randall, eds), pp. 91–239. London and New York: Academic Press.

Hirano, T. (1974). Some factors regulating water intake by the eel *Anguilla japonica. J. exp. Biol.* **61**, 737–747.

Hirano, T. and Mayer-Gostan, N. (1978). Endocrine control of osmoregulation in fish. In *Comparative Endocrinology* (P. J. Gaillard and H. H. Boer, eds), pp. 209–212. North-Holland: Elsevier.

Hirano, T., Morisawa, M. and Suzuki, K. (1978). Changes in plasma and coelomic fluid composition of the mature salmon (*Oncorhynchus keta*) during freshwater adaptation. *Comp. Biochem. Physiol.* **61A**, 5–8.

Hoar, W. S. (1976). Smolt transformation: evolution, behaviour and physiology. *J. Fish. Res. Bd Can.* **33**, 1234–1252.

Holliday, F. G. T. and Blaxter, J. H. S. (1961). The effects of salinity on herring after metamorphosis. *J. mar. biol. Ass. U.K.* **41**, 37–48.

Holmes, R. M. (1961). Kidney function in migrating salmonids. *Rep. Challenger Soc.* **3** (XIII), 23.

Holmes, W. N. and Donaldson, E. M. (1969). The body compartment and distribution of electrolytes. In *Fish Physiology, Vol. I* (W. S. Hoar and D. J. Randall, eds), pp. 1–89. London and New York: Academic Press.

Houston, A. H. (1959). Osmoregulatory adaptation of steelhead trout (*Salmo gairdneri* Richardson) to sea water. *Can. J. Zool.* **37**, 729–748.

Houston, A. H. and Wards, R. J. (1972). Blood concentrations of tricaine methanesulphonate in brook trout *Salvelinus fontinalis* during anaesthetization, branchial irrigation and recovery. *J. Fish. Res. Bd Can.* **29**, 1344–1346.

98   F. B. EDDY

Houston, A. H., Reaves, R. S., Madden, J. A. and DeWilde, M. A. (1968). Environmental temperature and the body fluid system of the fresh water teleost. I. Ionic regulation in thermally acclimated rainbow trout *Salmo gairdneri*. *Comp. Biochem. Physiol.* **25**, 563–581.

Houston, A. H., Madden, J. A. and DeWilde, M. A. (1970). Environmental temperature and the body fluid system of the fresh water teleost. IV. Water electrolyte regulation in thermally acclimated carp *Cyprinus carpio*. *Comp. Biochem. Physiol.* **34**, 805–818.

Houston, A. H., Madden, J. A., Wards, R. J. and Miles, H. M. (1971a). Some physiological effects of handling and tricaine methanesulphonate anaesthetization upon brook trout *Salvelinus fontinalis*. *J. Fish. Res. Bd Can.* **28**, 625–633.

Houston, A. H., Madden, J. A., Wards, R. J. and Miles, H. M. (1971b). Variations in blood and tissue chemistry of brook trout *Salvelinus fontinalis* subsequent to handling, anaesthesia and surgery. *J. Fish. Res. Bd Can.* **28**, 635–642.

Howell, B. J., Baumgartner, K., Bondi, K. and Rahn, H. (1970). Acid-base balance as a function of body temperature. *Am. J. Physiol.* **218**, 600–606.

Hunn, J. B. (1969). Chemical composition of rainbow trout urine following acute hypoxic stress. *Trans. Am. Fish. Soc.* **98**, 20–22.

Hunn, J. B. and Willford, W. A. (1970). The effect of anaesthetization and urinary bladder catheterization on renal function of rainbow trout. *Comp. Biochem. Physiol.* **33**, 805–812.

Hunn, J. B., Schoetlger, R. A. and Willford, W. A. (1968). Turnover and urinary excretion of free and acetylated MS222 by rainbow trout *Salmo gairdneri*. *J. Fish. Res. Bd Can.* **25**, 25–31.

Isaia, J. (1972). Comparative effects of temperature on the sodium and water permeabilities of the gills of a stenohaline freshwater fish (*Carassius auratus*) and a stenohaline marine fish (*Serranus scriba, Serranus cabrilla*). *J. exp. Biol.* **57**, 359–366.

Jackson, A. J. (1977). Reducing trout mortalities after sea water transfer. *Fish Farming Int.* **4**, 31–32.

Johnson, D. W. (1973). Endocrine control of hydromineral balance in teleosts. *Am. Zool.* **13**, 799–818.

Keys, A. B. and Willmer, E. N. (1932). "Chloride secreting cells" in the gills of fishes with special reference to the common eel. *J. Physiol., Lond.* **76**, 368–381.

Kirsch, R. and Mayer-Gostan, N. (1973). Kinetics of water and chloride exchanges during adaptation of the European eel to sea water. *J. exp. Biol.* **58**, 105–121.

Kirschner, L. B. (1979). Control mechanisms in crustaceans and fishes. In *Mechanisms of Osmoregulation in Animals* (R. Gilles, ed.), pp. 157–222. New York: John Wiley.

Krogh, A. (1939). *Osmotic regulation in aquatic animals*. Cambridge University Press. 242pp.

Lahlou, B., Henderson, I. W. and Sawyer, W. H. (1969). Sodium exchanges in goldfish (*Carassius auratus* L.) adapted to a hypertonic saline solution. *Comp. Biochem. Physiol.* **28**, 1427–1433.

Lahlou, B., Crenesee, D., Bensahla-Talet, A. and Porte-Nibelle, J. (1975). Adaptation de la truite de'elevage à l'eau de mer. *J. Physiol., Paris* **70**, 593–603.

Laird, L. M. and Oswald, R. L. (1975). A note on the use of benzocaine (Ethyl P-aminobenzoate) as a fish anaesthetic. *Fish. Mgmt.* **6**, 92–94.

Lange, R. and Fugelli, R. (1965). The osmotic adjustment in euryhaline teleosts, the flounder, eel and three-spined stickleback. *Comp. Biochem. Physiol.* **15**, 283–292.

Leivestad, M., Hendry, G., Muniz, I. P. and Snekvik, E. (1976). Effects of acid precipitation on freshwater organisms. *Res. Rep. SNSF-project, Oslo* 87-111.

Lewis, S. D. and Lewis, W. M. (1971). The effect of zinc and copper on the osmolarity of blood serum of the channel catfish *Ictalurus punctatus* Rafinesque, and golden shiner *Noternigonus crysoleucas* Mitchell. *Trans. Am. Fish. Soc.* **100**, 639–643.

Lloyd, R. and Orr, L. D. (1969). The diuretic response by rainbow trout to sublethal concentrations of ammonia. *Wat. Res.* **3**, 335–344.

Lloyd, R. and Swift, D. J. (1976). Some physiological responses by freshwater fish to low dissolved oxygen, high carbon dioxide, ammonia and phenol with particular reference to water balance. In *Effects of Pollutants on Aquatic Organisms* (A. P. M. Lockwood, ed.), pp. 47–69. Cambridge University Press.

Lloyd, R. and White, W. R. (1967). Effect of high concentrations of carbon dioxide on the ionic composition of rainbow trout blood. *Nature, Lond.* **216**, 1341–1342.

Loretz, C. A. (1979). Water exchange across fish gills: the significance of tritiated water flux measurements. *J. exp. Biol.* **79**, 147–162.

Lutz, P. (1972). Ionic and body compartment responses to increasing salinity in the perch *Perca fluviatilis*. *Comp. Biochem. Physiol.* **42A**, 711–717.

MacFarland, W. N. (1960). Use of anaesthetics for the handling and the transport of fish. *Calif. Fish Game* **46**, 407–431.

MacKay, W. C. (1974). Effect of temperature on osmotic and ionic regulation in goldfish *Carassius auratus*. *J. comp. Physiol.* **88**, 1–19.

MacKay, W. C. and Beatty, D. D. (1968). The effect of temperature on renal function in the white sucker fish *Catostomus commersonii*. *Comp. Biochem. Physiol.* **26**, 235–245.

Maetz, J. (1969a). Observations on the role of the pituitary interrenal axis in ion regulations of the eel and other teleosts. *Gen. comp. Endocr., Suppl.* **2**, 299–316.

Maetz, J. (1969b). Sea water teleosts: evidence for a sodium potassium exchange in the branchial sodium excreting pump. *Science, N.Y.* **166**, 613–615.

Maetz, J. (1971). Fish gills: mechanisms of salt transfer in fresh water and sea water. *Phil. Trans. R. Soc. Ser. B* **262**, 209–249.

Maetz, J. (1972). Branchial sodium exchange and ammonia excretion in the goldfish, *Carassius auratus*. Effects of ammonia loading and temperature changes. *J. exp. Biol.* **56**, 601–620.

Maetz, J. and Bornancin, M. (1975). Biochemical and biophysical aspects of salt excretion by chloride cells in teleosts. *Fortschr. Zool.* **23**, 322–362.

Maetz, J. and Evans, D. H. (1972). Effects of temperature on branchial sodium exchanges and extrusion mechanisms in the seawater adapted flounder *Platichthys flesus* L. *J. exp. Biol.* **56**, 565–585.

Maetz, J. and Pic, P. (1975). New evidence for a Na/K and Na/Na exchange carrier linked with the Cl^- pump in the gill of *Mugil capito* in sea water. *J. comp. Physiol.* **102**, 85–100.

Maetz, J. and Romeu, F. G. (1964). The mechanism of sodium and chloride uptake by the gills of a freshwater fish. *Carassius auratus*. II. Evidence for NH_4^+/Na^+ and HCO_3^-/Cl^- exchanges. *J. gen. Physiol.* **47**, 1209–1227.

Matty, A. J. (1978). Hormonal control. In *Rhythmic Activity in Fishes*. (J. E. Thorpe, ed.), pp. 21–31. London and New York: Academic Press.

Mazeaud, M. M. and Mazeaud, F. (1981). Adrenergic responses to stress in fish. In *Stress and Fish* (A. D. Pickering, ed.), pp. 49–75. London and New York: Academic Press.

McWilliams, P. G. and Potts, W. T. W. (1978). The effects of pH and calcium concentrations on gill potentials in the brown trout *Salmo trutta. J. comp. Physiol.* **126**, 277–286.

Motais, R. (1961). Kinetics of sodium exchange in a euryhaline teleost (*Platichthys flesus*) during successive passages from sea water, fresh water and to sea water, as a function of the period of stay in fresh water. *C.r. hebd. Séanc. Acad. Sci., Paris* **235**, 2609–2611.

Motais, R. and Isaia, J. (1972). Temperature dependence of permeability to water and to sodium of the gill epithelium of the eel *Anguilla anguilla. J. exp. Biol.* **56**, 587–600.

Motais, R., Romeu, F. G. and Maetz, J. (1966). Exchange diffusion effect and euryhalinity in teleosts. *J. gen. Physiol.* **50**, 391–422.

Nagahama, Y., Clarke, W. C. and Hoar, W. S. (1977). The influence of salinity on ultrastructure of the secretory cells of the adenohypophysis pars distalis in yearling coho salmon (*Oncorhynchus kisutch*). *Can. J. Zool.* **55**, 183–198.

Oduleye, S. O. (1976). The effects of hypophysectomy, prolactin therapy and environmental calcium on freshwater survival and salinity tolerance in the brown trout *Salmo trutta. J. Fish Biol.* **9**, 363–370.

Olivereau, M. and Olivereau, J. (1977). Effect of transfer to sea water and back to fresh water on the histological structure of the eel kidney. *J. comp. Physiol.* **115**, 223–239.

Packer, R. K. and Dunson, W. A. (1970). Effects of low environmental pH on blood pH and sodium balance in brook trout. *J. exp. Zool.* **174**, 65–72.

Packer, R. K. and Dunson, W. A. (1972). Anoxia and sodium loss associated with the death of brook trout at low pH. *Comp. Biochem. Physiol.* **41A**, 17–26.

Parry, G. (1960). The development of salinity tolerance in the salmon, *Salmo salar* L. and some related species. *J. exp. Biol.* **37**, 425–434.

Parry, G. (1966). Osmotic adaptation in fishes. *Biol. Rev.* **41**, 392–444.

Parry, G. (1978). Osmotic and ionic changes in blood and muscle of migrating salmonids. In *Readings in Ichthyology* (M. S. Love and G. M. Cailliel, eds), pp. 363–385. Santa Monica, California: Goodyear.

Payan, P., Matty, A. J. and Maetz, J. (1975). A study of the sodium pump in the perfused head preparation of the trout *Salmo gairdneri* in freshwater. *J. comp. Physiol.* **104**, 33–48.

Pic, P. (1978). A comparative study of the mechanism of Na^+ and Cl^- excretion by the gill of *Mugil capito* and *Fundulus heteroclitus*: Effects of stress. *J. comp. Physiol.* **123**, 155–162.

Pic, P., Mayer-Gostan, N. and Maetz, J. (1975). Branchial effects of epinephrine in the seawater adapted mullet II. Na^+ and Cl^- extrusion. *Am. J. Physiol.* **228**, 441–447.

Pickford, G. E. and Phillips, J. G. (1959). Prolactin a factor promoting the survival of hypophysectomised killifish in fresh water. *Science* **130**, 453.

Potts, W. T. W. (1976). Ion transport and osmoregulation in marine fish. In *Perspectives in Experimental Biology* (P. Spencer Davies, ed.), London: Pergamon.

Potts, W. T. W. and Eddy, F. B. (1973). Gill potentials and sodium fluxes in the flounder *Platichthys flesus. J. comp. Physiol.* **87**, 29–48.

Potts, W. T. W. and Evans, D. (1966). The effects of hypophysectomy and bovine prolactin on the salt fluxes in fresh water adapted *Fundulus heteroclitus. Biol. Bull. mar. biol. Lab., Woods Hole* **131**, 362–368.

Potts, W. T. W., Foster, M. A. and Stather, J. W. (1970). Salt and water balance in salmon smolts. *J. exp. Biol.* **52**, 553–564.

Prosser, C. L. (1973). *Comparative animal physiology*. 3rd edition. Philadelphia: W. B. Saunders. 457pp.

Prosser, C. L., MacKay, W. and Kato, K. (1970). Osmotic and ionic concentrations in some Alaskan fish and goldfish from different temperatures. *Physiol. Zool.* **43**, 81–89.

Randall, D. J. and Hoar, W. S. (1971). Special techniques. In *Fish Physiology, Vol. VI* (W. S. Hoar and D. J. Randall, eds), pp. 511–528. London and New York: Academic Press.

Reaves, R. S., Houston, A. H. and Madden, J. M. (1968). Environmental temperature and the body fluid system of the freshwater teleost. II. Ionic regulation in rainbow trout *Salmo gairdneri* following abrupt thermal shock. *Comp. Biochem. Physiol.* **25**, 849–860.

Richards, B. D. and Fromm, P. O. (1969). Patterns of blood flow through filaments and lamellae of isolated, perfused rainbow trout (*Salmo gairdneri*) gills. *Comp. Biochem. Physiol.* **29**, 1063–1071.

Richards, B. D. and Fromm, P. O. (1970). Sodium uptake by isolated perfused gills of rainbow trout (*Salmo gairdneri*). *Comp. Biochem. Physiol.* **33**, 303–310.

Sargent, J. R. and Thomson, A. J. (1974). The nature and properties of the inducible sodium-plus-potassium ion-dependent adenosine triphosphatase in the gills of eels (*Anguilla anguilla*) adapted to fresh water and sea water. *Biochem. J.* **144**, 69–75.

Shuttleworth, T. J. (1978). The effect of adrenaline on potentials in the isolated gills of the flounder *Platichthys flesus*. *J. comp. Physiol.* **124**, 129–136.

Shuttleworth, T. J., Potts, W. T. W. and Harris, J. N. (1974). Bioelectric potentials in the gills of the flounder *Platichthys flesus*. *J. comp. Physiol.* **94**, 321–329.

Silva, P., Solomon, R., Spokes, K. and Epstein, F. H. (1977). Ouabain inhibition of gill Na-K-ATPase: Relationship to active chloride transport. *J. exp. Zool.* **199**, 419–426.

Simpson, T. H. (1978). An interpretation of some endocrine rhythms in fish. In *Rhythmic Activity in Fishes* (J. E. Thorpe, ed.), pp. 55–69. London and New York: Academic Press.

Skidmore, J. F. (1970). Respiration and osmoregulation in rainbow trout with gills damaged by zinc sulphate. *J. exp. Biol.* **52**, 481–494.

Skidmore, J. F. and Tovell, P. W. A. (1972). Toxic effects of zinc sulphate on the gills of rainbow Trout. *Wat. Res.* **6**, 217–230.

Smith, H. W. (1930). The absorption and excretion of water and salts by marine teleosts. *Am. J. Physiol.* **93**, 480–505.

Smith, L. S. and Bell, G. R. (1964). A technique for prolonged blood sampling in free swimming salmon. *J. Fish. Res. Bd Can.* **21**, 711–717.

Smith, M. W. (1976). Temperature adaptation in fish. *Biochem. Soc. Symp.* **41**, 43–60.

Soivio, A. and Nyholm, K. (1975). A technique for repeated sampling of the blood of individual resting fish. *J. exp. Biol.* **62**, 207–217.

Soivio, A., Nyholm, K. and Huhti, M. (1977). Effects of anaesthesia with MS222 neutralised MS222 and benzocaine on the blood constituents of rainbow trout, *Salmo gairdneri*. *J. Fish Biol.* **10**, 91–101.

Stagg, R. M. and Shuttleworth, T. J. (1981). The effects of copper on osmotic and ionic regulation by the gills of the flounder, *Platichthys flesus* L. (Abstract) In *Stress and Fish* (A. D. Pickering, ed.), pp. 342–343. London and New York: Academic Press.

Stanley, J. G. and Colby, P. J. (1971). Effects of temperature on electrolyte balance and osmoregulation in the alewife (*Alosa pseudoharengus*) in fresh and sea water. *Trans. Am. Fish. Soc.* **100**, 624–638.

Swift, D. J. and Lloyd, R. (1974). Changes in urine flow rate and haematocrit value of rainbow trout (*Salmo gairdneri* Richardson) exposed to hypoxia. *J. Fish Biol.* **6**, 379–387.

Thompson, A. J. and Sargent, J. R. (1977). Changes in the levels of chloride cells and ($Na^+ + K^+$)-dependent ATPase in the gills of yellow and silver eels adapting to seawater. *J. exp. Zool.* **200**, 33–40.

Umminger, B. L. (1969a). Physiological studies on supercooled killifish (*Fundulus heteroclitus*). I. Serum inorganic constituents in relation to osmotic and ionic regulation at subzero temperatures. *J. exp. Zool.* **172**, 283–302.

Umminger, B. L. (1969b). Physiological studies on supercooled killifish (*Fundulus heteroclitus*). II. Serum organic constituents and the problem of supercooling. *J. exp. Zool.* **172**, 283–302.

Umminger, B. L. (1971). Patterns of osmoregulation in freshwater fishes at temperatures near freezing. *Physiol. Zool.* **44**, 20–27.

Wedemeyer, G. (1972). Some physiological consequences of handling stress in the juvenile coho salmon (*Oncorhynchus kisutch*) and steelhead trout (*Salmo gairdneri*). *J. Fish. Res. Bd Can.* **29**, 1780–1783.

Wedemeyer, G. A. and McLeay, D. J. (1981). Methods for determining the tolerance of fishes to environmental stressors. In *Stress and Fish* (A. D. Pickering, ed.), pp. 247–275. London and New York: Academic Press.

Zaugg, W. S. and McLain, L. R. (1969). Inorganic salt effects on growth, salt water adaptation and gill ATPase of Pacific salmon. In *Fish in Research* (O. W. Neuham and J. E. Halver, eds), pp. 293–306. London and New York: Academic Press.

Zeitoun, I. H. (1978). The recovery and haemotological rehabilitation of chlorine stressed adult rainbow trout (*Salmo gairdneri*). *Environ. Biol. Fishes* **3**, 355–359.

5. The Swelling of Erythrocytes in Relation to the Oxygen Affinity of the Blood of the Rainbow Trout, *Salmo gairdneri* Richardson

A. SOIVIO and M. NIKINMAA

Department of Zoology, University of Helsinki, SF-00100 Helsinki 10, Finland

Abstract. A series of experiments was conducted to find out if the swelling of rainbow trout erythrocytes had any influence on the oxygen binding properties of blood. The erythrocytes swelled when the fish were sampled by cardiac puncture, when the fish were subjected to hypoxia at 18°C, and when, in the course of determining the *in vivo* blood oxygen dissociation curve at 18°C, the ambient O_2 saturation decreased below 50% for the normoxic fish and below 40% for the hypoxic fish. In hypoxia at 11°C and in the determinations of the *in vivo* dissociation curves at 8°C the red blood cells did not swell appreciably.

The swelling of the erythrocytes leads to a decreased intraerythrocytic ATP concentration, which increases the oxygen affinity of the blood, as indicated by the *in vivo* oxygen dissociation curves at 18°C. The oxygen affinity increase is probably not caused by a decrease in the formation of ATP–Hb complex, as the ATP/Hb molar ratio did not change, but by an increase in the intraerythrocytic pH. In hypoxia at the low temperatures (8 and 11°C), the oxygen affinity of the blood can be increased by both these mechanisms.

I INTRODUCTION

The swelling of fish erythrocytes *in vitro* was first described by Black and Irving in 1938. They ascribed it to the increase in the blood lactic acid concentration during equilibration. Later Benditt *et al.* (1941) and Irving *et al.* (1941) suggested that an increase in the blood CO_2 tension (P_{CO_2}) during equilibration would account for the increase in cell volume. Irving *et al.* (1941) showed that when the blood of several species of trout was equilibrated with an air/carbon dioxide mixture ($P_{CO_2} = 10$ mmHg) the erythrocytes swelled, and when the carbon dioxide was removed from the equilibration gas, the cells shrank back to their original size. Also in the flounder, *Platichthys flesus* (Fugelli, 1967) and in the rainbow trout, *Salmo gairdneri* (Soivio and Nyholm, 1973) the swelling is reversible: when equilibrated under reduced oxygen tension (P_{O_2}) the erythrocytes swelled, but shrank when equilibrated with oxygen.

Holeton and Randall (1967) first showed that the erythrocytes swell also *in vivo*; the haematocrit values of rainbow trout increased with hypoxia at 15°C without a change in the red cell count. Later, Soivio *et al.* (1974b) demonstrated that the erythrocytes of asphyctic rainbow trout were swollen *in vivo*. The erythrocytes of rainbow trout and brown trout, *Salmo trutta*, also swelled when the fish were anaesthetized with MS222 or benzocaine (Soivio *et al.*, 1977; Aho, unpublished). Soivio *et al.* suggested that the reason for the swelling in this case was the low blood P_{O_2} (only 1·3 kPa); the fish were in an asphyctic state.

The situation in hypoxia seems to depend both on the depth of hypoxia and on the speed at which the water is made hypoxic. For example, it was found that rainbow trout erythrocytes swelled *in vivo* in hypoxia at 10°C when the O_2 saturation (S_{O_2}) of water was dropped from 80–90% to 25–30% within a couple of minutes (A. Soivio, K. Nyholm and K. Westman, unpublished). The erythrocytes seemed to swell most in the fish which struggled at the onset of hypoxia and least in those which stayed still. However, when the O_2 saturation of water at 11°C was decreased slowly (within 3 h) from 80 to 30%, the trout erythrocytes did not swell appreciably (Soivio *et al.*, 1980). Furthermore, Swift and Lloyd (1974) showed that no changes in the erythrocytic volume took place in hypoxia at 17°C, when the O_2 concentration of water was 4·5 mg l^{-1} ($S_{O_2} = 48\%$).

Sampling may also influence the erythrocytic volumes. Soivio *et al.* (1974a) have shown that the erythrocytes obtained by cardiac puncture from anaesthetized or stunned fish swelled when equilibrated at low oxygen tensions and shrank when equilibrated at atmospheric oxygen tension. This indicates that the erythrocytes obtained by cardiac puncture were swollen. Nikinmaa and Soivio (1979) reached the same conclusion after comparing the haematocrit value and blood oxygen capacity of unstressed fish sampled via dorsal aortic cannulae with those of stunned fish sampled by cardiac puncture. Soivio *et al.* (1977) have further shown that lifting the fish out of water for 20 s was enough to cause the swelling of erythrocytes.

On the other hand, the blood samples obtained by means of dorsal aortic cannulae from undisturbed rainbow trout do not swell when equilibrated *in vitro* with N_2, or shrink when equilibrated with air. Originally we thought that the high P_{O_2} of the sample was the reason for this situation. However, later we have found that the blood samples taken via ventral aortic cannulae, samples with low initial P_{O_2}, act in a similar way (A. Soivio, E. Railo and M. Nikinmaa, unpublished).

The swelling of the trout erythrocytes is thus associated with stress; the more disturbed the fish is the more its erythrocytes seem to swell *in vivo*. The reason for the swelling has been suggested to be any of the following factors : high P_{CO_2}, high lactate concentration, or low P_{O_2} in the blood. Although all of these are usually associated with the swelling, none of them alone can cause it. Thus, the initiation and mechanism of the swelling process are, as yet, open questions. Moreover, even though the swelling phenomenon was first observed more than 40 years ago, no physiological relevance has so far been attached to it in fish. In man, however, Bellingham *et al.* (1971) have shown that the erythrocytic swelling increases the blood oxygen affinity.

To resolve the question of the physiological relevance of the swelling of the erythrocytes in fish we have carried out several experiments which are presented here.

II MATERIALS AND METHODS

The experiments presented in this chapter were carried out at Laukaa Fish Culture Research Station in July–August 1979 and in June 1980. In all cases the fish had been acclimatized for a minimum of 2 weeks to oxygen levels of over 75% O_2 saturation at a constant temperature. The water used during the experiments was lake water supplied at a rate of 2 litres $min^{-1} kg^{-1}$ fish. The pH varied between 6·6 and 7·0, the specific conductivity at 20°C between 38 and 40 μS, and the P_{CO_2} remained below 66 Pa at all times.

The fish used were mature 3-year-old rainbow trout, *Salmo gairdneri* Richardson (weight 500–900 g) from a commercial fish farm (Savon Taimen Oy). They were cannulated either via the dorsal aorta (Soivio *et al.*, 1975) or via the bulbus arteriosus (A. Soivio, K. Nyholm and M. Nikinmaa, unpublished) and allowed to recover from the operation for a week. Forty-eight hours before the experiments, the fish were enclosed in individual restrainers (Soivio *et al.*, 1975). If the time between two successive samples was more than 48 h, the fish were allowed to swim freely in their tanks until 48 h before sampling, when they were again enclosed in the restrainers. Feeding (EWOS pelleted trout food) was in all cases stopped 48 h before sampling.

(a) Experiment 1

The influence of the sampling method of the blood oxygen binding properties was evaluated at 19°C. Blood samples (sample size 1 ml) were taken via
the ventral aortic cannula from eight fish and the blood pH, P_{O_2}, oxygen
content, haematocrit value, haemoglobin and adenosine triphosphate
(ATP) concentration, and the P_{50} values were determined (for details of the
techniques see Soivio et al., 1980).

In the determination of the P_{50} value with the mixing method, a portion of
the sample is equilibrated with nitrogen until it is fully deoxygenated and
another portion with air until it is fully oxygenated. The deoxygenated and
oxygenated blood are then mixed to give 50% oxygen saturation of the
mixture, and the P_{O_2} of the mixture is determined polarometrically. This
oxygen tension is the P_{50} value. The fish were then allowed to recover from
sampling for 24 h, after which they were lifted out of water, stunned with a
blow to the head, and a blood sample (1 ml) was taken by cardiac puncture.
The above determinations were again carried out.

(b) Experiment 2

The oxygen binding properties of hypoxic rainbow trout were evaluated at
18°C. The experimental procedure was essentially the same as in an earlier
study (Soivio et al., 1980), except that the environmental percentage O_2
saturation was slightly higher (35–40% instead of 30%). Even at this oxygen
saturation there was a high mortality amongst the fish; only three of the nine
fish which were exposed to hypoxia survived the 6-day exposure. Blood
samples were taken via cannula before the onset of hypoxia (O-sample) and
then at 1 and 6 days after the onset of hypoxic period. Samples were then
analysed for the blood pH, P_{50} value, haematocrit value, haemoglobin
concentration, ATP concentration, oxygen content and oxygen capacity as
described earlier (Soivio et al., 1980).

(c) Experiment 3

The so-called in vivo blood oxygen dissociation curves were determined at 8
and 18°C. The curves were determined for hypoxic and normoxic groups at
both temperatures. The hypoxic groups were exposed to hypoxia (25–30%
O_2 at 8°C and 35–40% O_2 at 18°C; O_2 concentration ~3·5 mg l^{-1}) for 6
days. The in vivo blood oxygen dissociation curves were determined using a
flow-through system in 50 l glass aquaria within 2 h of the end of hypoxic
period. The water in the aquarium was first aerated to 100% O_2 saturation,
the fish placed there, and thereafter the oxygen saturation was rapidly
diminished by bubbling nitrogen through the aquarium water. By this

method the oxygen saturation of the water could be decreased to less than 5% in 90 min. During this time, the water pH, P_{CO_2} or specific conductivity did not change. The oxygen saturation of water was continuously recorded and 4–7 blood samples were taken from the fish via the dorsal or the ventral cannula. The blood oxygen tension, oxygen content and oxygen capacity of these samples was determined, and the percentage blood oxygen saturation at different oxygen tensions calculated. Thus, an oxygen dissociation curve could be constructed using the fish as an "equilibration chamber". In addition to the dissociation curve, the blood pH, haematocrit value, haemoglobin concentration, lactate concentration, and ATP concentration were determined.

III   RESULTS

(a) Experiment 1

A decrease in the mean corpuscular haemoglobin concentration (MCHC) is taken as an indication of swelling of the erythrocytes. No changes in MCHC took place when the cannulated fish were sampled twice within a 24 h period at 18°C; the MCHC was $256 \cdot 0 \pm 6 \cdot 8$ ($\bar{x} \pm$ S.E.M.) in the first and $258 \cdot 5 \pm 6 \cdot 0$ g l^{-1} in the second set of samples. Against this background, the erythrocytes had swelled in the samples taken by cardiac puncture from stunned fish as compared to the samples taken via ventral aortic cannula from the same, undisturbed fish (Table I). The increase in volume, based on MCHC,

TABLE I   The Erythrocytic Adenosine Triphosphate Concentration (ATP, mM l^{-1} Erythrocytes), Adenosine Triphosphate/Haemoglobin Molar Ratio (ATP/Hb), Mean Corpuscular Haemoglobin Concentration (MCHC, g l^{-1} Erythrocytes), and P_{50} Value (P_{50}, kPa) of Rainbow Trout at 18°C.

	Ventral cannula sample	Cardiac puncture sample	Statistical significance
MCHC	$254 \cdot 3 \pm 10 \cdot 8$ (8)	$226 \cdot 1 \pm 5 \cdot 2$ (8)	*
ATP	$4 \cdot 419 \pm 0 \cdot 765$ (7)	$3 \cdot 948 \pm 0 \cdot 743$ (7)	*
ATP/Hb	$1 \cdot 29 \pm 0 \cdot 065$ (6)	$1 \cdot 34 \pm 0 \cdot 105$ (6)	NS
P_{50}	$3 \cdot 33 \pm 0 \cdot 17$ (8)	$3 \cdot 12 \pm 0 \cdot 11$ (8)	NS

Samples were taken from the same fish, first via ventral aortic cannulae and, after 24 h recovery from sampling, with cardiac puncture. Before sampling via the ventral aortic cannulae the fish were enclosed in individual restrainers for 48 h and before cardiac puncture the fish were stunned. Means ±SEM and the number of determinations are given. The groups of samples were compared with dependent t-test, asterisks indicate statistically significant differences between the groups (*$p < 0 \cdot 05$, ** $p < 0 \cdot 01$, *** $p < 0 \cdot 001$, NS = non-significant difference).

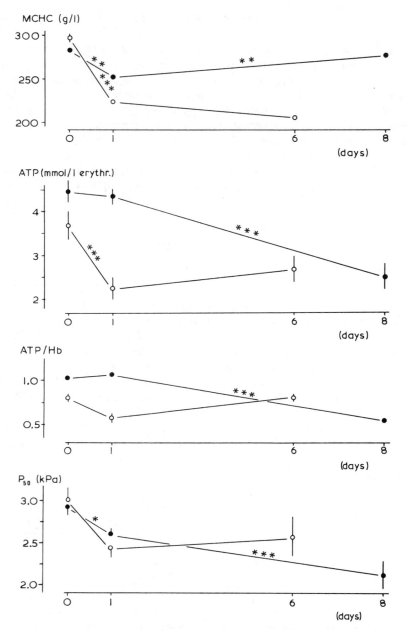

Fig. 1 The mean corpuscular haemoglobin concentration (MCHC), the erythrocytic ATP concentration, ATP/haemoglobin molar ratio and the P_{50} value for the blood of hypoxic rainbow trout at 11°C (●) (Soivio *et al.*, 1980) and 18°C (○). Bars indicate ±SEM, the asterisks indicate the statistical significance of the difference between two consecutive samples (*$p <$ 0·05, **$p < 0·01$, ***$p < 0·001$). Dependent *t*-test was used for comparisons.

is 10% ($p < 0.05$). This change in cell volume can explain the observed decrease in the erythrocytic ATP concentration, as it decreased by 10% ($p < 0.05$). That the decrease in the erythrocytic ATP concentration was due to the erythrocytic swelling was further supported by the fact that the ATP/haemoglobin molar ratio did not change as a result of the sampling method. Also the P_{50} values, as measured by the mixing method, were not significantly different, which would have been the case if the ATP/Hb ratio had changed. The mixing method cannot take into account the changes in blood O_2 affinity caused by the changes in the cell volume, because during equilibration, the erythrocyte volume changes, especially in the samples taken with cardiac puncture (Soivio et al., 1974a, b).

(b) Experiment 2

The effect of hypoxia on the erythrocyte volume at 18°C was drastic. The MCHC decreased approximately 25% within 24 h ($p < 0.001$), and this MCHC persisted throughout the 6-day experiment (Fig. 1). This led to a very significant ($p < 0.001$), 30–40% decrease in the erythrocytic ATP concentration. This ATP concentration also persisted throughout the experiment. Again it is notable that the ATP/Hb ratio, although decreasing slightly, did not change significantly in the experiment, so that most of the changes in the erythrocytic ATP can be ascribed to the swelling of the erythrocytes. A slight decrease in the P_{50} value was also observed. This hypoxic response is obviously strongly temperature dependent, because at 11°C the change in the MCHC was transient (Fig. 1). In the experiment at 11°C (Soivio et al., 1980) samples were taken at 3 h, 6 h, 1 day, 2 days, 4 days, 8 days, and 12 days from the onset of hypoxia, and the change was significant ($p < 0.01$) only after 1 day. However, the ATP/Hb ratio decreased throughout the experiment at 11°C, to about 50% of the original ratio ($p < 0.001$). This led to the increased blood oxygen affinity, as indicated by the P_{50} value ($p < 0.001$).

(c) Experiment 3

The in vivo dissociation curves for rainbow trout acclimated to hypoxia and normoxia at 8°C and 18°C are presented in Fig. 2. At 8°C, the whole dissociation curve for hypoxic fish had shifted to the left. The P_{50} value was about 1·8 kPa for the fish acclimated to hypoxia and 2·5 kPa for the fish acclimated to normoxia. The P_{90} values were 5 kPa and 15·8 kPa respectively. At 18°C, lower parts of the dissociation curves were practically identical for both groups of fish. The P_{50} value for both groups was 4·3 kPa. However, the upper end of the curve for the fish acclimated to hypoxia had

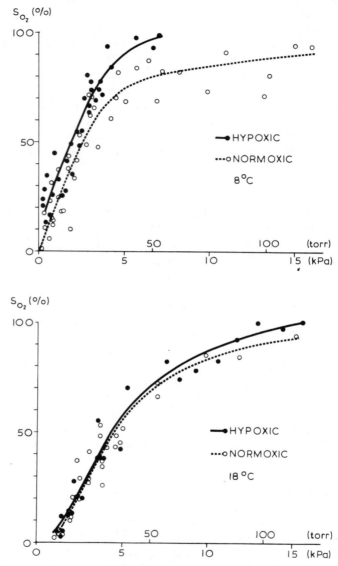

Fig. 2   The *in vivo* blood oxygen dissociation curves for normoxic and hypoxic rainbow trout at 8 and 18°C. Both curves at 18°C and the hypoxic curve at 8°C are based on data from 6 fish. The normoxic curve at 8°C is based on data from 10 fish.

shifted slightly to the left. This was shown by the P_{90} value which was 10·7 kPa for the fish acclimated to hypoxia and 12·2 kPa for the fish acclimated to normoxia. The other parameters determined for the fish in the *in vivo* blood oxygen dissociation curve experiment were chosen as to give some information concerning the reasons for the differences in these curves. In Fig. 3 the percentage change in the haematocrit value, and in Fig. 4 the percentage change in the erythrocytic ATP concentration as functions of the water O_2 saturation are given for the fish acclimated to hypoxia and normoxia at both temperatures (8°C and 18°C). In Fig. 5 the blood pH as a function of blood oxygen tension is given.

At 8°C the percentage changes in the blood haematocrit value and erythrocytic ATP concentration were practically the same, and less than 10% for both the hypoxic and normoxic groups (Figs 3 and 4). However, the erythrocytic ATP concentration of the fish acclimated to hypoxia was much lower than that of the fish acclimated to normoxia (2 mM 1^{-1} for hypoxic and 4 mM 1^{-1} for normoxic fish). The blood pH was practically the same for both groups of fish, although at very low oxygen tensions it was slightly lower (approximately 0·1 pH units) in the normoxic than in the hypoxic fish (Fig. 5).

At 18°C, on the other hand, the response of the fish acclimated to hypoxia and normoxia differed considerably. As the oxygen saturation of water was decreased, the haematocrit value increased much more for the fish acclimated to normoxia than for the fish acclimated to hypoxia (60% and 30% respectively, Fig. 3). Because no changes took place in the blood haemoglobin concentration, these changes indicate the swelling of the erythrocytes. The initial erythrocytic ATP concentration for the fish acclimated to hypoxia was 3·5 mM 1^{-1} and for the fish acclimated to normoxia 5·0 mM 1^{-1}. However, when the water oxygen saturation was decreased, the red cell ATP concentration of the fish acclimated to hypoxia first increased by about 30%, and started to decrease when the oxygen saturation of water decreased below 40% (Fig. 4). By comparison, the erythrocytic ATP concentration of the fish acclimated to normoxia had already started to decrease when the oxygen saturation of water decreased below 50%. The changes in the blood pH and lactate concentration were similar in both groups at every water oxygen saturation level.

IV DISCUSSION

In this study, the MCHC has been used as an indicator of the erythrocytic swelling. The changes in cell volume have been confirmed *in vitro* with a Coulter Counter ZBI cell size analyzer (Nikinmaa and Soivio, 1980).

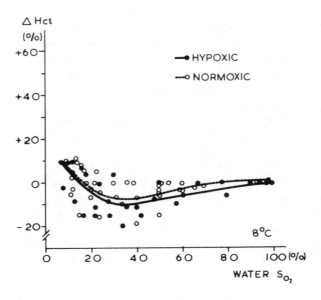

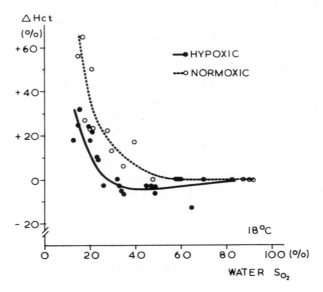

Fig. 3 The percentage change in the blood haematocrit as a function of the O_2 saturation of the water in the *in vivo* blood oxygen dissociation curve experiment at 8 and 18°C. The change is calculated by comparing the haematocrit values at the other water O_2 saturations to those at 100% O_2.

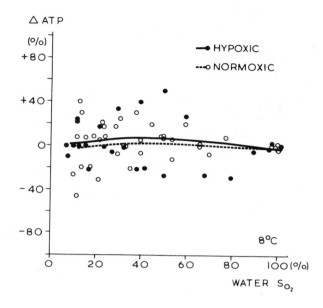

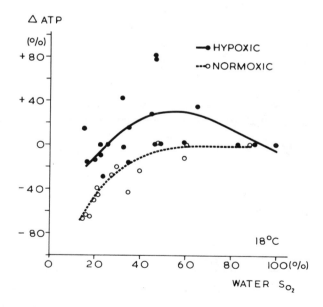

Fig. 4 The percentage change in the erythrocytic ATP concentration (mM l^{-1} erythrocytes) as a function of the oxygen saturation of water in the *in vivo* blood oxygen dissociation curve experiment at 8 and 18°C. The percentage change is calculated as in Fig. 3.

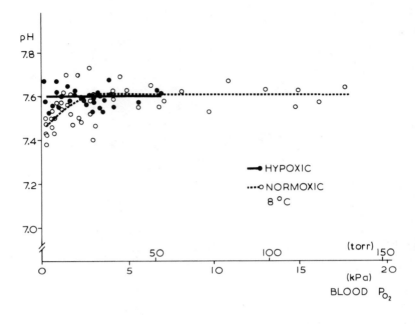

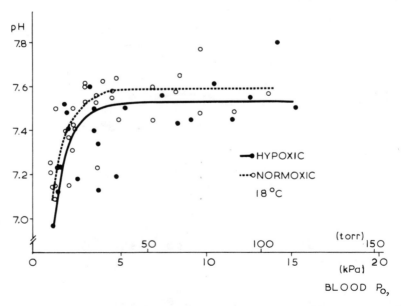

Fig. 5 The blood pH as a function of the blood oxygen tension in the *in vivo* blood oxygen dissociation curve experiment at 8 and 18°C.

Because the MCHC is the ratio of blood haemoglobin concentration to the haematocrit, it is not dependent on the blood volume or on the number of red cells per unit volume. Only if new red cells, with a different haemoglobin content from the existing red cells, were liberated to the circulation, would the cell volume deductions based on the MCHC be faulty. Although such cells probably appear during anaemia induced by bleeding (Lane, 1979; McLeod et al., 1978), they only appear in the circulation 3–4 days after bleeding and are not released during hypoxia (McLeod et al., 1978).

It is thus highly unlikely that appreciable numbers of new red cells would have been formed during the course of the experiments presented in this paper. Furthermore, the hypoxia-induced changes in the weight of the spleen, probably the most likely site for the liberation of erythrocytes (see McLeod et al., 1978), represent only 2% increase in the blood volume (A. Soivio, M. Nikinmaa and S. Egginton, unpublished). Even if the red cells liberated from the spleen were totally devoid of haemoglobin, their effect on the MCHC would be only 6–8%, a change far smaller than the change actually observed. So, even if new red cells appear, their appearance cannot invalidate the deductions about the cellular swelling.

The changes in the mean corpuscular haemoglobin content due to the different sampling methods agree well with previous studies (Soivio et al., 1974a, b). This indicates that the erythrocytes obtained by cardiac puncture from stunned fish had swelled by about 10%. In addition, the MCHC values of the 6-day hypoxia at 18°C agree well with the findings of Holeton and Randall (1967) indicating a marked swelling of the erythrocytes during severe hypoxia. In hypoxic exposure at 11°C the swelling of the erythrocytes was transient (Soivio et al., 1980).

Swift and Lloyd (1974) reported that the erythrocytes did not swell during hypoxia at 12–13°C and 17–18°C. The situation at 12–13°C closely resembles the findings of Soivio et al. (1980) at 11°C, in which the oxygen capacity increased with practically no change in the MCHC. On the other hand the O_2 concentration at 17–18°C in Swift and Lloyd's investigation was $4\cdot5$ mg l^{-1}, and on the basis of Fig. 3, a swelling of the erythrocytes would not be expected at this concentration.

The swelling of the erythrocytes caused a significant decrease in the erythrocytic ATP concentration in the present experiments. ATP affects the blood oxygen affinity by two mechanisms: by a specific binding with haemoglobin and by influencing the intraerythrocytic pH via an influence on the Donnan distribution of hydrogen ions across the red cell membrane (Wood and Johansen, 1973). Because the swelling of the erythrocytes decreases the ATP concentration without a change in the ATP/Hb ratio, it would not be expected to have much of an influence on the specific binding of ATP to haemoglobin. However, the decrease in the ATP concentration as such would still influence the Donnan distribution of hydrogen ions and, by increasing the intraerythrocytic pH, increase the oxygen affinity of blood. M. Nikinmaa and A. Soivio (unpublished) have, indeed, shown that the increase in the intraerythrocytic pH in hypoxia at 18°C occurs simultaneously with the swelling of the erythrocytes. In addition, swelling of the erythrocytes can increase the blood oxygen affinity by diluting the haemoglobin inside the cells. Lykkeboe and Weber (1978) have shown that decreasing the concentration of haemoglobin solution increases its oxygen affinity even if the nucleotide triphosphate (NTP)/Hb ratio is kept constant.

The effect of the erythrocytic swelling on the *in vivo* blood oxygen affinity is clearly demonstrated by the *in vivo* oxygen dissociation curves and simultaneous measurements of the haematocrit values, ATP concentrations and plasma pH values at 18°C. At the upper end of the curve (Fig. 2), the normoxic curve lies somewhat to the right from the hypoxic one, most probably due to the initial differences in the erythrocytic ATP levels. However, the initial shrinking of the erythrocytes of the hypoxia acclimated fish and the swelling of the erythrocytes of the normoxia acclimated fish abolishes this difference in the erythrocytic ATP concentrations, when the water oxygen saturation goes down to 40%. Below 40% water O_2 saturation the erythrocytes of both fish groups swell so that the erythrocytic ATP concentration stays similar in both groups. This is seen in the lower parts of the *in vivo* blood oxygen dissociation curves, which are essentially the same for both groups of fish.

It is quite obvious that the *in vivo* dissociation curves presented here are not comparable to those obtained with the *in vitro* technique (e.g. Nikinmaa and Soivio, 1979), because neither the pH nor the P_{CO_2} of the blood stay constant in the fish as the environmental oxygen saturation is decreased. The P_{50} value read from the *in vivo* curve is slightly higher 4·2 kPa (32 mmHg) than the P_{50} value 3·6 kPa (27 mmHg) at 18°C obtained with mixing method, and corrected to the *in vivo* pH value of blood (Nikinmaa *et al.*, 1980). The *in vivo* dissociation curve shows how the oxygen binding properties of blood of individual fish acclimated to certain environmental conditions respond to sudden changes in the water oxygen saturation.

The changes in pH probably affect the shape of the *in vivo* dissociation curves, thereby making them different from those obtained with *in vitro* equilibration at 18°C. However, the curves for normoxia- and hypoxia-acclimated fish can be compared with each other as the pH changes *in vivo* were similar for both groups. At 8°C, on the other hand, the *in vivo* P_{50} value of normoxia-acclimated fish, 2·5 kPa (19 mmHg), is the same as the *in vitro* P_{50} value calculated from the data of Nikinmaa *et al.* (1980). This similarity is clearly due to the fact that at 8°C practically no changes took place in either the blood pH or the red cell volume during the determination of the *in vivo* dissociation curve.

The strong shift to the left of the *in vivo* dissociation curve of hypoxia-acclimated fish at 8°C cannot be based on the swelling of the erythrocytes, as both fish groups had similar haematocrit values throughout the experiment. The main reason for the increased oxygen affinity in this case must be the low initial ATP concentration of the erythrocytes. This low ATP concentration was also seen as a low ATP/Hb molar ratio, and probably reflects a decrease in oxidative phosphorylation due to hypoxia (Greaney and Powers, 1978). The decrease in ATP/Hb ratio during acclimation to hypoxia has been described in several studies; with the eel, *Anguilla anguilla* (Weber *et al.*, 1976), with the carp, *Cyprinus carpio* (Weber and Lykkeboe, 1978), and also with rainbow trout (this study, calculations based on the data from Soivio *et al.*, 1980). In the study of Soivio *et al.* (1980) the water temperature was 11°C, and at that temperature it seems that the changes in the oxygen affinity are based totally on the decrease in the ATP/Hb ratio (i.e. the absolute amount of ATP) and not at all on the changes in the red cell volume.

It seems that the ATP concentration inside the erythrocytes can be decreased by two mechanisms, both of these leading to an increased blood oxygen affinity. As a result of hypoxia, oxidative phosphorylation decreases thus leading to a decrease in the erythrocytic ATP concentration and the ATP/Hb molar ratio. This mechanism therefore affects the blood oxygen affinity in two ways, by decreasing the formation of ATP–Hb complexes, and by increasing the intracellular pH to achieve a new Donnan equilibrium (Wood and Johansen, 1973). In this case a steady-state level in ATP concentration is only reached after several days of hypoxia (Soivio *et al.*, 1980), so this response is of particular importance in long-term stresses. As shown by the experiments at 8°C and 11°C this seems to be the only response at work during hypoxia at lower temperatures.

At high temperatures, on the other hand, swelling of the erythrocytes may also decrease the erythrocytic ATP concentration. This change, however, does not influence the ATP–Hb complex formation, as the ATP/Hb molar ratio does not change, but it may influence the blood oxygen affinity by increasing the intraerythrocytic pH. This response takes place immediately at the onset of stress, thus being of importance in acute, hypoxic stresses.

ACKNOWLEDGEMENTS

This study was partly supported by a grant from the Alfred Kordelin foundation.

REFERENCES

Bellingham, A. J., Detter, J. C. and Lenfant, C. (1971). Regulatory mechanisms of haemoglobin oxygen affinity in acidosis and alkalosis. *J. clin. Invest.* **50**, 700–706.

Benditt, E., Morrison, P. and Irving, L. (1941). The blood of the Atlantic salmon during migration. *Biol. Bull. mar. biol. Lab.*, *Woods Hole* **80**, 429–440.

Black, E. G. and Irving, L. (1938). The effect of hemolysis upon the affinity of fish blood for oxygen. *J. cell. comp. Physiol.* **12**, 255–262.

Ferguson, J. K. W. and Black, E. G. (1941). The transport of CO_2 in the blood of certain freshwater fishes. *Biol. Bull. mar. biol. Lab.*, *Woods Hole* **80**, 139–152.

Fugelli, K. (1967). Regulation of cell volume in flounder (*Pleuronectes flesus*) erythrocytes accompanying a decrease in plasma osmolarity. *Comp. Biochem. Physiol.* **22**, 253–260.

Greaney, G. S. and Powers, D. A. (1978). Allosteric modifiers of fish hemoglobins: *in vitro* and *in vivo* studies of the effect of ambient oxygen and pH on erythrocyte ATP concentrations. *J. exp. Zool.* **203**, 339–350.

Holeton, G. F. and Randall, D. J. (1967). The effect of hypoxia upon the partial pressure of gases in the blood and water afferent and efferent to the gills of rainbow trout. *J. exp. Biol.* **46**, 317–327.

Irving, L., Black, E. G. and Safford, V. (1941). The influence of temperature upon the combination of oxygen with the blood of trout. *Biol. Bull. mar. biol. Lab.*, *Woods Hole* **80**, 1–17.

Lane, H. C. (1979). Some haematological responses of normal and splenectomized rainbow trout *Salmo gairdneri* to a 12% blood loss. *J. Fish Biol.* **14**, 159–164.

Lykkeboe, G. and Weber, R. E. (1978). Changes in the respiratory properties of the blood in the carp, *Cyprinus carpio*, induced by diurnal variation in ambient oxygen tension. *J. comp. Physiol.* **128**, 117–125.

McLeod, T. F., Sigel, M. M. and Yunis, A. A. (1978). Regulation of erythropoiesis in the Florida gar, *Lepisosteus platyrhincus*. *Comp. Biochem. Physiol.* **60A**, 145–150.

Nikinmaa, M. and Soivio, A. (1979). Oxygen dissociation curves and oxygen capacities of blood of a freshwater fish, *Salmo gairdneri*. *Annls Zool. fenn.* **16**, 217–221.

Nikinmaa, M. and Soivio, A. (1980). The volumes of rainbow trout (*Salmo gairdneri*) erythrocytes incubated with air and with nitrogen. *5th Symposium on the Physiology of Aquatic Animals, University of Turku, Abstracts. Reports Dept. Biol., University of Turku* No. 1 1980.

Nikinmaa, M., Tuurala, H. and Soivio, A. (1980). Thermoacclimatory changes in blood oxygen binding properties and gill secondary lamellar structure of *Salmo gairdneri*. *J. comp. Physiol.* **140**, 255–260.

Soivio, A. and Nyholm, K. (1973). Notes on haematocrit determinations on rainbow trout, *Salmo gairdneri*. *Aquaculture* **2**, 31–35.

Soivio, A., Westman, K. and Nyholm, K. (1974a). Changes in the haematocrit values in blood samples treated with and without oxygen: a comparative study with four salmonid species. *J. Fish Biol.* **6**, 763–769.

Soivio, A., Westman, K. and Nyholm, K. (1974b). The influence of changes in oxygen tension on the haematocrit value of blood samples from asphyctic rainbow trout. *Aquaculture* **3**, 395–401.

Soivio, A., Nyholm, K. and Westman, K. (1975). A technique for repeated sampling of the blood in individual resting fish. *J. exp. Biol.* **62**, 207–217.

Soivio, A., Nyholm, K. and Huhti, M. (1977). Effects of anaesthesia with MS222, neutralized MS222 and benzocaine on the blood constituents of rainbow trout, *Salmo gairdneri. J. Fish Biol.* **10**, 91–101.

Soivio, A., Nikinmaa, M. and Westman, K. (1980). The blood oxygen binding properties of hypoxic *Salmo gairdneri. J. comp. Physiol.* **136**, 83–87.

Swift, D. J. and Lloyd, R. (1974). Changes in urine flow rate and haematocrit value of rainbow trout (*Salmo gairdneri* Richardson) exposed to hypoxia. *J. Fish Biol.* **6**, 379–387.

Weber, R. E. and Lykkeboe, G. (1978). Respiratory adaptations in carp blood. Influences of hypoxia, red cell organic phosphates, divalent cations and CO_2 on hemoglobin-oxygen affinity. *J. comp. Physiol.* **128**, 127–137.

Weber, R. E., Lykkeboe, G. and Johansen, K. (1976). Physiological properties of eel haemoglobin: hypoxic acclimation, phosphate effects and multiplicity. *J. exp. Biol.* **64**, 75–88.

Wood, S. C. and Johansen, K. (1973). Organic phosphate metabolism in nucleated red cells: influence of hypoxia on eel Hb O_2 affinity. *Neth. J. Sea Res.* **7**, 328–338.

6. Effects of Low Oxygen and Pollution on the Respiratory Systems of Fish

G. M. HUGHES

Research Unit for Comparative Animal Respiration, University of Bristol, Bristol, England

Abstract. The respiration of fish involves the transfer of oxygen from a medium in which it is contained at a relatively low concentration via the blood and thence to the sites of oxidative metabolism in the cells. The main stages in this transfer are points at which interference may occur with consequent lack of oxygen. Consideration of such stages provides one way in which different types of hypoxia can be classified. Most commonly, environmental hypoxia is used by experimental biologists because it provides a good method of assessing the performance of control mechanisms regulating gaseous exchange. In addition to the degree of hypoxia, the time course of its development and its duration are known to influence the responses observed. Some of these effects may influence not only those parts concerned with oxygen transport but may also influence other features of the internal medium of the fish. These in their turn are also affected by the nature of the water in which the fish lives. The use of some recent techniques which enable such studies to be made are discussed together with the extent to which the action of pollutants can be interpreted against this background of fish respiratory physiology. In view of the many mechanisms that operate under conditions of lowered environmental oxygen, individual variations need to be taken into account.

I THE RESPIRATORY CHAIN

At a symposium concerned with homeostasis, the concept of a respiratory chain in fish was proposed (Hughes, 1964) in order to emphasize the different components of the path along which oxygen molecules pass from the environment to the mitochondrial sites, where they are utilized. At all stages in this chain there are resistances to gas transfer and the driving force is a difference in oxygen tension (P_{O_2}) across them. Correspondingly, there are changes in tension of carbon dioxide (P_{CO_2}) from the cellular level to its release at the gas exchange surfaces. Emphasis was laid upon the possibility that adaptation could occur at any of the many different parts of the respiratory chain, and that the time course of such adaptive changes could vary from immediate responses to long-term, genetic changes (Hughes, 1964). During the past 15 years many more of these adaptations have been investigated in a variety of fish species and have amply illustrated this general concept.

Correspondingly, there are possibilities of interference with the supply of oxygen to the mitochondria at all stages of the respiratory chain (Hughes, 1973). Under normal conditions, environmental oxygen tensions are about 150 mmHg and the greatest drop in tension (about 50 mmHg) is found at the water/blood barrier in the gills of fish (Fig. 1). This barrier constitutes the

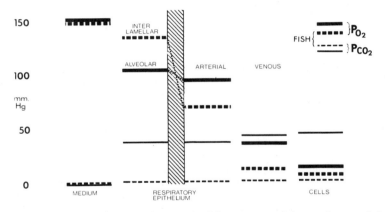

Fig. 1 Diagram to show the P_{O_2} and P_{CO_2} in different parts of the respiratory chain of a teleost fish (broken lines) and a mammal (full lines). Gradients in P_{O_2} between the respiratory medium and mitochondria are present in both types, but in fishes there is a marked drop at the water/blood barrier whereas in mammals the P_{O_2} difference between alveolar gas and pulmonary blood is very slight. P_{CO_2}s are higher in mammals; in aquatic organisms they rarely exceed 5 mmHg. Mammalian regulatory mechanisms control the alveolar P_{CO_2} at about 40 mmHg.

greatest resistance to oxygen transfer and contrasts very strongly with the situation in the mammalian lung where the difference between the alveolar oxygen tension and that in the blood of the pulmonary vein is extremely small (Fig. 1). Because it constitutes a major resistance to gas transfer, the gill is, therefore, a part of the system where interference can have a very marked effect. Hypoxia at the cellular level can develop following interference at any point along the chain as, for example, during anaemia produced as a result of bleeding or by the action of certain chemicals which might block the oxygen-carrying properties of haemoglobin. Figure 1 also shows the extremely low levels of carbon dioxide in fish which rarely exceed 5 mmHg. This, of course, is because of the high solubility of CO_2 in water and consequently a much lower tension than that obtained when the same quantity of oxygen is dissolved in an equal volume of water.

These differences in physical properties of the respiratory gases result in different problems faced by animals using water or air as respiratory media. Nevertheless, the respiratory chain concept emphasizes the continuity between the environment and the organism and the basic similarities between all respiratory systems. A reduction in the supply of oxygen, however produced, in the external or internal environment has as its end result a reduction in oxygen pressure within the cells. Such reductions in oxygen levels produce a constraint on the system which, because of built in equilibria, becomes modified to restore equilibrium at a new level. A notable part of the mechanisms involved in such compensatory responses involves nervous pathways in which receptors are present both on the external gill surface of the fish and internally within the tissues. Of particular importance is the direct action of the blood on receptive elements in the central nervous system. Unfortunately, information about the precise nature and location of such receptors is incomplete (Hughes and Ballintijn, 1968; Eclancher, 1972; Randall and Jones, 1973; Bamford, 1974; Daxboeck and Holeton, 1978; Smith and Jones, 1978). There is little doubt, however, that the efferent responses from the central nervous system are largely mediated by nervous pathways. Such responses include changes in the frequency and depth of the ventilatory movements and similar changes of the cardiac pump. Co-ordination between the activities of these two pumps is also regulated during the response to hypoxia (Hughes, 1973). The net result of these responses is to increase the supply of oxygen at the tissue level. Most commonly, experiments are carried out in which variations are made in the environmental oxygen levels and this is probably the situation which leads to tissue hypoxia in the natural environment.

Before discussing the nature and adaptive significance of some of these responses it is of interest to consider whether or not some of this type of response should be referred to as "stress". A number of authors, including myself, have referred to these conditions of environmental hypoxia as producing "respiratory stress"; "CO_2 stress" etc. In the sense that many of the responses which are observed are mediated through mainly neural pathways, this use of the term is perhaps inappropriate as it is commonly used to indicate conditions under which blood levels of corticosteroids or catecholamines are increased in the blood (Mazeaud et al., 1977). This is not to say that such changes in blood concentrations do not occur for it is certainly known that environmental hypoxia may be followed by an increased concentration of catecholamines which produce important adaptive effects including enhanced blood flow to the gill secondary lamellae which increases their effectiveness in oxygen uptake. The levels of hypoxia which lead to such increases in catecholamines are within the normal range of activity of the fish and in this sense cannot be considered stressful (for further discussion of the concept of stress see Pickering, 1981, this volume).

In the rest of this article I therefore propose not to use the term stress unless it represents some extreme hypoxic condition of the fish and/or persists for very lengthy periods. Even when environmental hypoxia is continued for prolonged periods, however, the adaptive changes within the respiratory chain usually compensate and lead to the restoration of new equilibria (see also Soivio and Nikinmaa, 1981, this volume).

II CRITICAL LEVELS FOR RESPONSES ALONG THE RESPIRATORY CHAIN

Many experiments have been carried out with different fish species in which oxygen consumption has been measured as the oxygen tension in the environment is reduced. In general, these responses have been classified into two types the first of these being the so-called independent types of respiration in which the oxygen consumption ($\dot{V}_{O_2}$) remains constant in spite of a fall in the oxygen tension of the water (Pw_{O_2}). In other species of fish the oxygen uptake falls gradually as Pw_{O_2} decreases; such species are said to show dependent respiration. The so-called critical oxygen tension (T_c) is the P_{O_2} at which respiration changes from being independent to being dependent. These two types were originally recognized with respect to the "active" metabolism; the corresponding transition for the "standard" metabolism being named the "incipient lethal level". As most measurements that have been made are best described as "routine" the terms dependent and independent and T_c have been extended to these relationships. In fact, very few directly determined relationships for "standard" $\dot{V}_{O_2}$ are available, most having been obtained by extrapolation of the active metabolic relationships to zero activity (e.g. Fry and Hart, 1948; Beamish, 1964; Webb, 1971). T_c varies according to temperature and other environmental conditions and is by no means constant for a given species (Fry and Hart, 1948; Beamish, 1964; Spitzer et al., 1969). Although the T_c concept seems clear cut, in practice it is often more difficult to show such a marked transition. For example, plots shown in Fig. 3 are typical for three species of American fishes and represent mean values plotted from computerized data (Marvin and Heath, 1968). An illustration of the practical

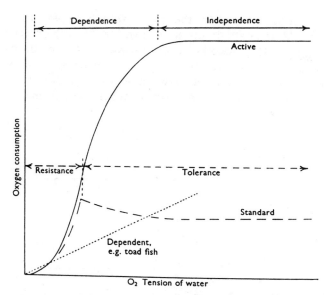

Fig. 2 Generalized diagram showing relationships between oxygen consumption of a fish and water P_{O_2}. Although the zones of "dependence" and "independence" were originally defined with respect to the active metabolic rate and "resistance" and "tolerance" to the equivalent regions of the standard oxygen uptake curve, nowadays the terms dependent and independent respiration are quite often applied to standard $\dot{V}_{O_2}$ (from Hughes, 1964, with permission).

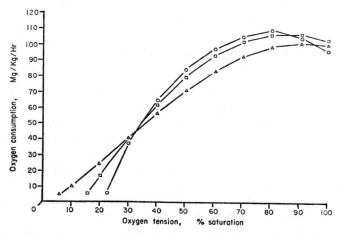

Fig. 3 Oxygen consumption of three species of freshwater fish subjected to gradual hypoxia, catfish ($\triangle - \triangle$), rainbow trout ($\bigcirc - \bigcirc$) and bluegill ($\square - \square$). Polynomial lines were fitted to grouped data by computer (from Marvin and Heath, 1968, with permission).

difficulties is shown in Fig. 4 for the carp, *Cyprinus carpio*, at two different temperatures. All the data points are shown for seven specimens of fish at 20°C and seven at 10°C together with possible lines to be drawn through these points assuming a sharp transition at a particular P_{O_2}. (Many publications in the literature do not show the actual data points and give the impression of a very clearcut relationship.) When measurements are made

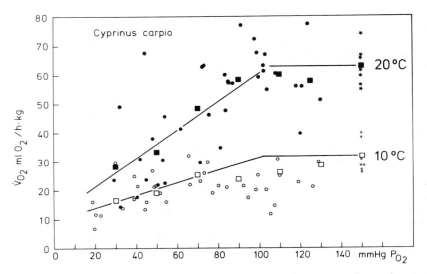

Fig. 4 *Cyprinus carpio*. Relationship between environmental oxygen tension and oxygen uptake for 7 fish at each temperature (10° and 20°C). Lines drawn on the basis of mean values from 7 fish at 150 mmHg for the horizontal portions and slope of line in hypoxic zone is drawn as regression line for values between 29 and 90 mmHg. Squares show mean values for each class of 20 mmHg (from Hughes *et al.*, 1981a, with permission).

with fish at "rest" in respirometers with a small water flow, the overall figures obtained are "routine" consisting of high values when the fish may be more active and low figures when it is truly at rest. By selecting only the latter values, lines can be drawn which represent a good approximation to "standard". The accuracy of such procedures depends a great deal on the time constant of the flow-through respirometer in use. If the respirometer is large, allowing the fish greater freedom of movement, the time constant is also large and effectively dampens out fluctuations in the P_{O_2} of the outlet water, and consequently of the $\dot{V}_{O_2}$ measurements.

Another recent example is given in Fig. 5a in which a line is drawn through mean values obtained from many specimens of yellowtail, *Seriola quinqueradiata*, over particular ranges of oxygen content. As in a number of

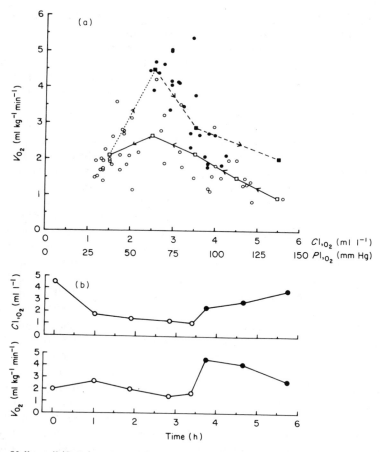

Fig. 5 Yellowtail (*Seriola quinqueradiata*) (a) Oxygen uptake of fish which were confined in a closed circuit circulation which produced a lowering in the environmental P_{O_2}. Open circles are during hypoxia and closed circles during recovery. Line is drawn through mean values obtained for each 1 ml l^{-1} O_2 content of the water. (b) Time course of oxygen uptake during hypoxia and recovery of a single specimen to show the marked increase of oxygen uptake during the recovery phase (from Hughes *et al.*, 1981b, with permission).

studies, these data suggest an increase in oxygen uptake shortly before a marked decline as the environmental oxygen tension is reduced. Similar data have been obtained for the carp (Beamish, 1964) and for the rainbow trout, *Salmo gairdneri*, by a number of authors (Marvin and Heath, 1968; Hughes and Saunders, 1970). It has commonly been supposed that this increased oxygen uptake is due to the extra work of breathing following the hyperventilatory response. Recent estimates (Hughes, 1973; Jones and

Schwarzfeld, 1974) suggest that 10% of the standard metabolism is required for the ventilatory movements under these conditions.

In addition to the many studies of T_c other critical levels have been investigated which include the "critical value for normal life" (T_L, Table I). Such a concept is important in fish culture and indicates the minimum oxygen level which does not interfere with normal growth or reproduction of a particular population. Determination of such values involves long term investigations with many ponds in which it is difficult to maintain constant levels of oxygen tension for prolonged periods (see also Smart, 1981, this volume). Many fish culturists have wished to obtain estimates of this value using short term experiments. One possible physiological correlate for both T_L and T_c is the oxygen dissociation curve of the blood. Fish blood has a high affinity and remains fully saturated until quite low oxygen tensions. It is possible that the point at which there is a sudden fall in saturation with lowering oxygen tension might provide the basis for restrictions on the oxygen consumption of the whole fish. In general, however, the values obtained from such curves are significantly lower than those for T_c and T_L. A closer approximation to the latter values is obtained by inspecting the relationship between the P_{O_2} of the dorsal aorta blood. Itazawa (1974) showed a close similarity between such values and those reported for the T_L by fish culturists for eel, *Anguilla japonica*, carp and rainbow trout.

When $\dot{V}_{O_2}$ of a fish is determined following its recovery from hypoxia, some species show a marked increase which is usually taken to indicate the paying-off of an oxygen debt (Fig. 5b). Trout, *Salmo clarki*, bluegill, *Lepomis macrochirus*, and dragonet, *Callionymus lyra*, also show the paying-off of an O_2 debt following hypoxia (Heath and Pritchard, 1965; Hughes and Umezawa, 1968). Other species (e.g. goldfish, *Carassius auratus*, and catfish, *Ictalurus nebulosus*), do not show such responses even though there is evidence that they obtain additional energy from anerobic pathways during hypoxia (Beamish, 1964; Kutty, 1968; Marvin and Burton, 1973). One way in which this has been investigated is by determining the concentration of lactate in the muscles of fish which have been subjected to different levels of hypoxia. An early investigation of this type indicated that the lactate levels in both red and white muscles of crucian carp, *Carassius carassius*, rose sharply below 33 mmHg (Johnston, 1975). It is thus possible to think in terms of a critical level at which these anaerobic mechanisms become operative. In crucian carp such sources of energy become available at oxygen tensions below those at which the oxygen consumption is significantly reduced from normoxic levels. Similar findings with other species of fish that have been investigated recently (Burton and Heath, 1980) suggest that this situation might be considered more typical than that found in rainbow trout where the critical level for anaerobiosis appears to be

TABLE I Oxygen Tensions at which Marked Transitions Occur in some Respiratory Measurements of Fish.

Fish species	"Critical" tension (mmHg)	Physiological measurement	Temp °C	Reference
Rainbow trout (Salmo gairdneri)	90	$\dot{V}_{O_2}$ Routine	12	Marvin and Heath (1968)
	75	Ventil. freq. falls	12	
	112	Bradycardia	12	
	80–100	Bradycardia	8·5–15	Randall and Smith (1967)
	100	P_aO_2 (O_2 tension of dorsal aorta blood)	2–9	Itazawa (1971)
	80–90	Critical value normal life (T_L)	11	Sawato et al. (1969)
	80	$\dot{V}_{O_2}$ Routine	15	Kutty (1968)
	75	R. Q. Rises	15	
	75–85	Anaerobic threshold (muscle lactate)	15	Burton and Heath (1980)
	54	$\dot{V}_{O_2}$ Resting	11	Nakanishi and Itazawa (1974)
	59	Bradycardia	11	
	20·8	$\dot{V}_{O_2}$ Standard	10	Ott et al. (1980)
	22·0	$\dot{V}_{O_2}$ Standard	15	
	27·4	$\dot{V}_{O_2}$ Standard	20	
Brook trout (Salvelinus fontinalis)	80	$\dot{V}_{O_2}$ Standard	10	Beamish (1964)
	75–85	$\dot{V}_{O_2}$ Standard	15	
Carp (Cyprinus carpio)	55	$\dot{V}_{O_2}$ Routine	10	Hughes et al. (1981)
	83	$\dot{V}_{O_2}$ Routine	20	
	20·2	$\dot{V}_{O_2}$ Standard	10	Ott et al. (1980)
	20·7	$\dot{V}_{O_2}$ Standard	15	
	20·2	$\dot{V}_{O_2}$ Standard	25	
	60	$\dot{V}_{O_2}$ Standard	20	Beamish (1964)
	50	$\dot{V}_{O_2}$ Standard	10	
	20–50	$\dot{V}_{O_2}$ Routine		Itazawa and Takeda (1979)
	30	C_aO_2 (no CO_2)	24·5	Takeda and Itazawa (1979)
	70	P_aO_2 (O_2 content of dorsal aorta blood		Itazawa and Takeda (1979)
	40	Haematocrit		Itazawa and Takeda (1979)
	55	Ventil. freq. rises	24–26	
	20	Ventil. str. vol		
	31	Ventil. freq. falls	12	Nakanishi and Itazawa (1974)
	34	Heart rate falls	12	
	39	$\dot{V}_{O_2}$ Routine	12	
	73–76	"Normal life" (T_L)	20–30	Chiba (1965)
	78	P_aO_2	13–23	Itazawa (1959)

TABLE I   (*continued*)

Fish species	"Critical" tension (mmHg)	Physiological measurement	Temp °C	Reference
Crucian carp (*Carassius carassius*)	15	Muscle (White) lactate	15	Johnston (1975)
	38	Red muscle succinate	15	
Goldfish (*Carassius auratus*)	34	$\dot{V}_{O_2}$ Active	20	Fry and Hart (1948)
	40	$\dot{V}_{O_2}$ Active	35	
	18	$\dot{V}_{O_2}$ Standard (calc)	20	
	25	$\dot{V}_{O_2}$ Standard (calc)	35	
	75	$\dot{V}_{O_2}$ Routine	20	Kutty (1968)
	65–75	R. Q. rises	20	
	10%	$\dot{V}_{O_2}$ Routine	20	
	30	$\dot{V}_{O_2}$ Standard	10	Beamish (1964)
	65	$\dot{V}_{O_2}$ Standard	20	
Bluegill (*Lepomis macrochirus*)	60–70	$\dot{V}_{O_2}$ Routine	13	Spitzer *et al.* (1969)
	90–100	$\dot{V}_{O_2}$ Routine	25	
	19–40	Anaerobic metabol. muscle lactate	20	Burton and Heath (1980)
	115	Heart Rate	25	Marvin and Heath (1968)
	120	$\dot{V}_{O_2}$ Routine	25	
	60	Ventil. freq.	25	
Brown bullhead (*Ictalurus nebulosus*)	9	Muscle lactate	20	Burton and Heath (1980)
	37	Muscle lactate	5	
	115	Ventil. freq.		Marvin and Heath (1968)
Largemouth bass (*Micropterus salmonoides*)	8·2 mg l^{-1}	Growth	26	Stewart *et al.* (1967)
	40	$\dot{V}_{O_2}$ Routine	20	Cech *et al.* (1979)
	40–50	$\dot{V}_{O_2}$ Routine	25	
	50–60	$\dot{V}_{O_2}$ Routine	30	
	50	$P_a O_2$ pH (HLa?)	30	
	5	P_{50} (Tension at which blood is 50% saturated with oxygen)	20	

very close to T_c. This latter situation would appear to be ideal from the fishes point of view as it would help to maintain an adequate supply of energy at a lower level of environmental oxygen. In addition to the lactate/pyruvate mechanism it is known that other anaerobic pathways exist among fishes subjected to hypoxia (e.g. Hughes and Johnston, 1978; Hochachka, 1980).

In addition to the critical oxygen levels discussed above, there are also levels at which other marked changes occur, e.g. the initiation of bradycardia

(Table I). Although not investigated so far, there are presumably particular degrees of hypoxia at which increases in circulatory catecholamines will be initiated. Changes of this latter type, and possibly for corticosteroids, would clearly be of particular interest in the present context as they might be taken to indicate those degrees of hypoxia to which the term "stress" might be applied most appropriately.

III EFFECTS OF HYPOXIA ON ACID-BASE BALANCE

The production of lactate and other organic acids circulating in the blood must inevitably lead to some adjustment in the acid/base equilibrium of a normoxic fish. The investigation of such adjustments has been greatly facilitated by recent developments in techniques for sampling the blood and making suitable measurements on it. Figure 6 is an X-ray photograph of a carp with its dorsal aorta cannulated using the method of Soivio *et al.* (1975) which has greatly improved the condition of cannulated fish used in extended experiments during which blood samples are taken. The relatively narrow cannula inserted into the dorsal aorta interferes minimally with the blood circulation (see also Soivio and Nikinmaa, 1981, this volume). When such a carp is subjected to hypoxia, changes in arterial pH are observed which are often correlated with increasing concentrations of blood lactate. In quite a number of experimental animals, however, the pH does not fall as much as might be expected from the increases in lactate. Evidently some adjustment is taking place to maintain the normal pH levels, and in a number of fish the pH actually rises. Such increases in pH are probably related to the marked hyperventilation (Fig. 7). In carp the ventilation changes from an intermittent to a more regular rhythm of higher frequency, but there is also a marked increase in ventilatory amplitude as shown by pressure records from the buccal cavity (Fig. 7). In fact the most relevant parameter is that of ventilation volume which in this case was estimated from the relationship

$$\text{Ventilation volume } \dot{V}_G = \dot{V}_{O_2}/(P_{insp} - P_{exp})\alpha_w O_2$$

where $\dot{V}_{O_2}$ = oxygen consumption unit time^{-1}; $P_{insp} - P_{exp}$ is the difference in oxygen tension between the water in the buccal and opercular cavities; $\alpha_w O_2$ is the absorption coefficient for O_2 in the water at the appropriate temperature and salinity.

In many studies not specifically concerned with respiration, changes in ventilatory frequency are monitored, but it is less common for the amplitude to be observed and very rare for the ventilation volume to be determined. Observations of frequency alone can be misleading as for example in the yellowtail, which may show a very marked increase in ventilation volume

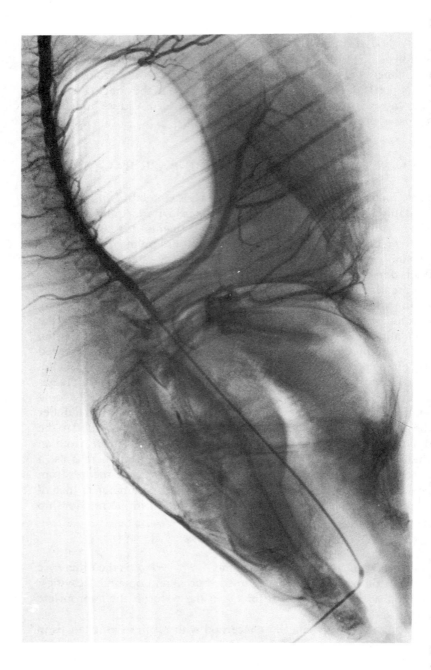

Fig. 6 X-ray photograph of a specimen of *Cyprinus carpio* with a cannula inserted into the dorsal aorta. This cannula is exteriorized through a wider polyethylene tube which has been inserted into the roof of the mouth. The cannula is kept in position by a "bubble" formed at the junction where the cannula makes an almost right-angled bend along the roof of the mouth before entering the dorsal aorta. Notice how much narrower the cannula is than the dorsal aorta (Hughes *et al.*, 1981, with permission).

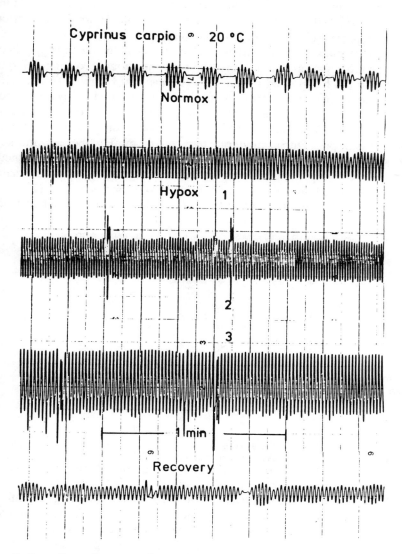

Fig. 7 Recordings of pressure changes in the buccal cavity of a carp during an hypoxia experiment (50 mmHg). The initial intermittent rhythm is replaced by a regular waveform of much greater amplitude. During recovery not only is there a reduction in the amplitude and frequency, but the rhythm begins to be intermittent (from Hughes *et al.*, 1981, with permission).

although frequency of the opercular movements remains almost constant (Hughes *et al.*, 1981). In the dragonet frequency falls although ventilation volume increases (Hughes and Umezawa, 1968).

In some recent studies of acid/base changes occurring during hypoxia of trout, the introduction of a new method for continuous recording of blood oxygen and pH has proved invaluable (Thomas and Hughes, 1981). With this technique an extracorporeal circulation is established following cannulation of the subclavian artery and subclavian vein. Such a circulation only includes about 4% of the total blood volume and reduces the necessity to take blood samples. During moderate hypoxia (60 mmHg) there is a marked hyperventilation associated with the washing-out of CO_2 and a consequent increase in blood pH. Compensation for this respiratory alkalosis occurs during the next 24 h as the blood pH returns to normoxic values (7·9) but with a corresponding decrease in bicarbonate levels (Fig. 8). When trout

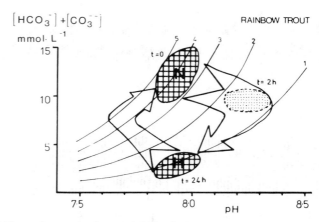

Fig. 8   Acid/base changes in the arterial blood of a rainbow trout subjected to moderate hypoxia followed by recovery. Approximate times during the main phases of the changes in acid/base balance are indicated (from Thomas and Hughes, 1981, with permission).

were subjected to a deeper and more rapid hypoxia (30 mmHg) the initial changes were similar to those described above (Fig. 9), but about 15 minutes after the initiation of hypoxia there was a sudden decrease in blood pH to values of less than 7·0. During the next 10 minutes the pH value rose once again, but during these relatively rapid changes in pH the blood P_{CO_2} continued to fall continuously. The compensatory responses during deep hypoxia once more established normal pH values.

The experimental observations with the extracorporeal circulation during deep hypoxia are of general interest to all of us who are more accustomed to monitoring changes in blood values by occasional sampling methods. Thus, a

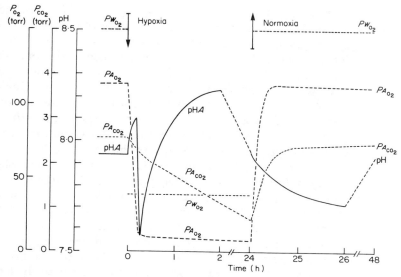

Fig. 9 Time course of changes in pH and P_{O_2} of arterial blood recorded as it passes through an extra-corporeal circulation in a trout subjected to severe hypoxia (30 mmHg) (from Thomas and Hughes, 1981, with permission).

blood sample taken in this type of experiment after 15 min will give a very much lower value than one taken 5 or 25 min after the onset of hypoxia. The ability to make such extracorporeal circulations is clearly restricted and, even when possible, only certain blood parameters can be determined continuously. Perhaps future developments will enable such techniques to provide more comprehensive information about the time course of changes in blood characteristics following specific environmental modifications.

IV SOME EFFECTS OF HEAVY METAL POLLUTION ON RESPIRATORY MECHANISMS OF RAINBOW TROUT

As discussed earlier, respiratory physiologists envisage the possibility of interference with gas exchange by reference to the respiratory chain. Pollutants can influence such mechanisms at all parts of the chain. Particular emphasis has often been laid on the effect of dissolved pollutants on the gills which may not only restrict gas transfer, but their irritant effect can also interfere with ventilation. For example, "coughs" are a regular feature of the ventilatory rhythm of many fish and in polluted water their frequency tends to increase. This is especially true for suspended solid pollutants

(Hughes, 1975). Such pollutants can also precipitate upon the gill surfaces (Herbert *et al.*, 1961) and interfere with the diffusion of oxygen into the blood. More detailed investigation of the effects of some heavy metal pollutants on the secondary lamellae themselves has been carried out using morphometric methods which make it possible to quantify such influences (Hughes and Perry, 1976). The results of the pilot study of this type (Hughes *et al.*, 1979) have shown the way in which, following exposure to some pollutants, there is a reduction in the morphological basis for the diffusing capacity—a physiological term indicating the quantity of oxygen transferred for an oxygen tension gradient of 1 mmHg. As shown in Fig. 1, the P_{O_2} difference across the water/blood barrier is very marked in fishes. Morphometrically, diffusing capacity is directly proportional to surface area and inversely proportional to the mean diffusion distance between the water and the blood (Hughes, 1972). Diffusing capacity of the gills is reduced following the action of pollutants such as zinc and nickel, and consequently there is a fall in the oxygen supply to the tissues which become hypoxic and mechanisms are initiated which include responses similar to those following reductions in environmental oxygen. In early studies, relatively large concentrations of zinc were employed (Skidmore, 1970) but more recently, effects of sublethal concentrations have been investigated (Hughes and

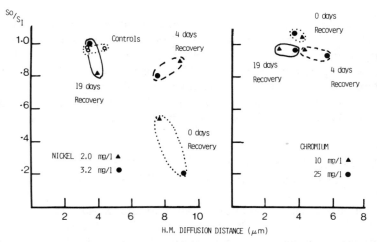

Fig. 10   Plots of harmonic diffusion distance across the water/blood barrier to the nearest red blood cell in rainbow trout following treatment with nickel and chromium. Vertical axis is an index of surface area (S_O/S_I, the ratio of the outer surface of the gill secondary lamella and the internal surface as defined by the basement membrane). Both nickel treatments lead to an increase in diffusion distance and a decrease in area which return to control values after 19 days of recovery. Relatively little change occurs in these parameters following chromium treatment (from Hughes, 1980b, with permission).

Adeney, 1977). A morphometric study using nickel, chromium, and cadmium indicated that there were clear effects of low doses of nickel, but for chromium, changes in barrier thickness and area were less well defined (Fig. 10). Following return of the fish to clean waters, diffusing capacity rose to normal (Hughes *et al.*, 1979). Because of the natural variations in gill structure it is necessary to carry out such studies on larger numbers of individuals if the effects of these sublethal concentrations are to be detected.

Interference with gas transfer will reduce oxygen levels within the blood circulating to the brain where responses are initiated by the diffusely located respiratory centre (Hughes and Shelton, 1962; Ballintijn and Bamford, 1975). Co-ordinated cardiovascular responses can also result from such changes and, in addition to these nervous pathways, there will also be effects upon the hormonal system as it is known that some pollutants produce increases in circulating catecholamine levels. Some of the latter effects may be directly related to the pollution but others will be secondary effects due to the resulting hypoxia. It has now become recognized that recording of physiological parameters is one way of assaying pollutant levels both in the laboratory and in natural environments. Using closed circuit circulation, previous studies in this laboratory have shown effects of zinc on the ventilation frequency, heart rate and coughing of fish (Skidmore, 1970; Hughes and Adeney, 1977). Recent studies, using concentrations below 15 p.p.m. added zinc (=p.p.m.a. Zn), have extended this work. The particular circulation used was necessitated by local conditions of water supply. Known amounts of zinc were added and the concentration monitored during the period of exposure of fish which had been previously acclimated to the experimental system. It was found that the concentration of zinc declined exponentially, the precise form depending upon the particular concentration. Under such conditions it was found that the LC50 was about 13·75 p.p.m.a. Zn. Fish were exposed for a total period of 48 h to concentrations of 12·5, 10 and 5·0 p.p.m.a. Zn and many controls with no added zinc were also carried out. The buccal pressure waveform gave information regarding ventilatory frequency and amplitude, and ECG wires enabled the recording of heart rate. Many variations were found between individuals in the response to the sudden addition of zinc to the water circulation. The effects could be divided into short term responses of 1–2 h and longer term responses of 24–48 h (Hughes, 1981). A summary of the latter is given in Table II where it can be seen that as the Zn concentration is reduced there is a gradual reduction in the occurrence of responses of the ventilatory system. As found for higher concentrations, there is usually an increase in both the frequency and amplitude of the buccal pressure waveform. In these particular experiments, over a 48 h period it was found that heart rate was an

TABLE II   Rainbow Trout. The Effect of Four Concentrations of Zinc on Ventilatory Frequency, Ventilatory Amplitude and Cardiac Frequency.

Zn p.p.m.a.	12.5			10			5			0		
Type of response	↑	↓	→	↑	↓	→	↑	↓	→	↑	↓	→
Ventilatory frequency	8	0	1	6	3	1	4	2	4	3	2	5
Ventilatory amplitude	6	0	3	5	4	1	4	1	5	4	2	4
Cardiac frequency	3	2	2	2	2	4	4	1	2	2	3	3
Number of fish	9			10			10			10		

Values summarize the effects recorded in experiments with 10 fish in each group (9 in 12·5 p.p.m.a). Key: ↑ increase over 48 h treatment; ↓ decrease over 48 h treatment; → no consistent change during 48 h.

unreliable indicator of pollution because the changes in average frequency did not appear to be correlated with the concentration of Zn.

In view of the conditions under which zinc was administered in these experiments, these data are not strictly comparable with most studies of this kind, but perhaps have some analogy with situations which might occur when there is a sudden and brief release of a large concentration of effluent into a river. A fish some distance downstream would experience a rapid increase in zinc followed by a decay in concentration which may be exponential as found in the present experimental circulation. Certainly, under these conditions it can be affirmed that even where concentrations are below the 48 hour LC50 there can be significant effects upon ventilation, and consequently gas exchange, by the fish.

Another approach has been to test the effect of zinc upon responses of trout to environmental hypoxia. It seems possible that although some pollutants might not have a very significant effect upon the respiratory and cardiovascular systems at rest, nevertheless they might influence the abilities of the fish to respond to environmental changes and reduce their chances of survival. The experimental procedure was to subject the fish to a quite marked hypoxia (50 mmHg) for 50 min and the same treatment 48 h later. One group of fish was kept in the same water circulation throughout the whole experimental period whereas the other was treated for 24 h with 12·5 p.p.m.a. Zn prior to the second hypoxia. It was thus possible to test whether any changes in the responses occurred as a result of maintaining the fish under constant conditions and if so whether similar changes occurred when fish were treated with sublethal concentrations of Zn between the two hypoxias.

Results showed a great similarity in all the responses to hypoxia—namely an increased ventilatory frequency and amplitude, usually a reduction in

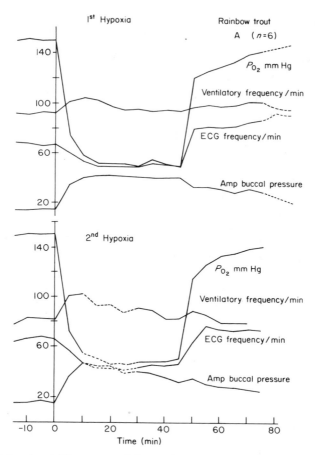

Fig. 11 Rainbow trout. Time course of changes in ventilatory frequency and amplitude and heart frequency during hypoxia. Between the first and second hypoxia these fish were treated with 12·5 p.p.m.a. zinc for 24 h. Mean values are plotted.

cardiac frequency followed by tachycardia when the fish returned to normoxic conditions (Fig. 11). These changes are shown in Fig. 12 where values are plotted relative to the normoxic values immediately prior to the commencement of hypoxia. From the mean values shown it would appear that there are some differences between the responses to the first and second hypoxia and perhaps these are different in the two groups of fish. For example, the amplitude of the buccal pressure waveform shows a very marked increase during hypoxia, but this effect is not so great in the second hypoxia with the control group. On the other hand, the second group of trout showed a similar increase in amplitude during the first hypoxia but this was

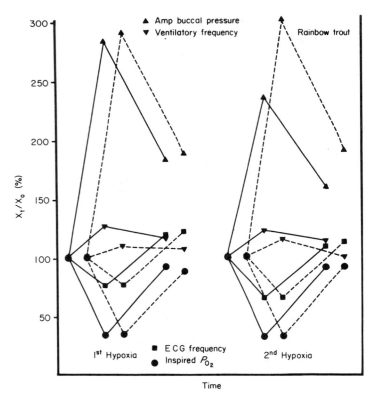

Fig. 12 Summary of double hypoxia experiments showing the effects of zinc treatment on ventilatory frequency and amplitude, and heart frequency for two groups of fish. Full lines show control fish, broken lines are for fish treated for 24 h in 12·5 p.p.m.a. Zn between two equivalent hypoxias. Values before the commencement of each hypoxia are taken as 100%. The other two points plotted in each case are those which occur 15 min after the commencement of hypoxia and 15 min following the restoration of normoxic water to the circulation. All points are mean values.

increased still further during the second hypoxia. Correspondingly, the increase in ventilatory frequency is reduced in the second hypoxia of normal fish whereas after zinc there is an increase in the increment of frequency during hypoxia. Thus, both frequency and amplitude show greater increases during hypoxia following zinc treatment. Changes in cardiac frequency of the two groups were extremely similar. In both cases the bradycardia of hypoxia was increased during the second hypoxia.

When the responses of individual fish were observed it was found that these mean values did not tell the whole story, but that in all cases there was a difference between the response to first and second hypoxic treatments and that these were more amplified following the zinc treatment. Whether such changes would become clear following detailed statistical analysis remains doubtful. It may be concluded that perhaps in this test we were operating at the limit of the possible value of this type of approach. Presumably if a higher Zn concentration had been used or treatment was more prolonged, or perhaps a deeper and/or longer hypoxia been given then limitations in the ability of the zinc-treated fish to respond might have become more clear cut. The evidence, in so far as it goes, supports the view that sublethal concentrations of zinc do have some effect upon the ability of fish to respond to a change in environmental oxygen and under certain conditions this might lead to a reduction in survival. Clearly, further work is needed in this important area of research.

V CONCLUSIONS

It is clear that fish show many adaptive responses to lowering of oxygen in the inspired water. Most of these responses concern the ventilatory system and are reflex in nature, initiated by exteroceptors probably on the surfaces of the gills or associated regions such as the pseudobranch. There is also evidence that there may be interoceptors which respond to changes in blood oxygen levels after it has left the gills and circulates to the brain (Hughes and Ballintijn, 1968). Ventilatory responses mainly serve to increase the total amount of oxygen brought into contact with the gas exchange surfaces. Correspondingly on the blood side of the exchanger there are cardiovascular changes which improve the effectiveness of oxygen uptake by the blood. Many of these changes are responses to stimulation of sense organs and are effected via reflex pathways from the CNS (Hughes and Shelton, 1962; Smith and Jones, 1978). These responses mainly alter the cardiac output and its distribution not only to the tissues but perhaps more importantly to the gills themselves in a way that again improves the effectiveness of oxygen uptake. It is also known that catecholamines can affect both the branchial and systemic circulation (see Mazeaud and Mazeaud, 1981, this volume). Changes in their concentration in the blood have been observed especially under conditions of deep and prolonged hypoxia. Some of the experiments in which such effects have been demonstrated, however, are complicated because the fish were brought out of water and in addition to the reduction in available oxygen there are other factors which can be more effective in initiating chemical changes within the blood stream.

These responses of the ventilatory and cardiac pumps to hypoxia result in an increased energy demand by both pumps which consume significant proportions of the standard oxygen uptake of a fish (Hughes and Saunders, 1970; Jones and Schwazfeld, 1974). As the available oxygen becomes reduced this may result in an increased oxygen uptake, but eventually the point is reached where the aerobic mechanisms are insufficient to satisfy these requirements and either the oxygen consumption must fall, with consequent reductions in activity, or there must be an increase in other mechanisms which enable the continuation of an adequate supply of energy. It would appear that the presence of anaerobic pathways within fish and their importance varies according to the species, presumably in relation to their particular life habits (Hughes and Johnston, 1978; Hochachka, 1980). But there is no doubt that such mechanisms play an important part in responses to hypoxia just as they have been known to be important during exercise of fish. The precise level of hypoxia at which these become initiated again varies according to the species. There seem to be very few studies of the nervous and hormonal mechanisms which may be involved in these responses. During deeper and more prolonged hypoxia it seems probable that other mechanisms such as compensatory responses regulating acid/base balance of the blood become important and these are more likely to require the involvement of hormonal systems which have often been discussed as the basis for the so-called "stress" reactions of fish.

Figure 13 represents, diagrammatically, some of the possible routes for these different responses to lowered oxygen. Much of the work carried out by fish respiratory physiologists has concentrated upon mechanisms which

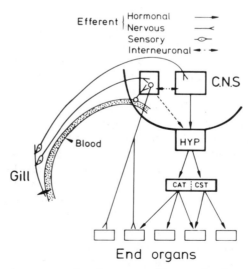

Fig. 13 Diagrammatic representation of nervous and hormonal pathways involved in responses of the fish respiratory mechanisms. The extent of the involvement of the neuro-hormonal systems which liberate catecholamines (CAT) and corticosteroids (CST) into the blood requires more detailed investigation.

are probably most directly concerned with the nervous system both on the sensory and efferent side whereas indicated above and in the diagram, some of the effector systems can be influenced not only by nervous pathways but also by circulating catecholamines (Peyraud-Waitzenegger, 1979) and probably circulating corticosteroids. In addition, it is probable that some effector systems only respond to one or both of the two latter hormones. Thus, it would seem that the term "stress" is best applied to those parts of the system which involve the catecholamines and corticosteroids. If this sort of definition is adopted, then respiratory physiologists should not use the term stress for those parts of the system where there is little evidence for the involvement of such substances. The most important result of such a view must be, however, to emphasize the need for both types of worker not to forget either the nervous or the neuro-endocrine functions. For example, in a previous review (Hughes, 1964) little mention was made of the neuro-endocrine control mechanisms. Correspondingly, in their helpful review of stress responses of fish Mazeaud et al. (1977) pay little attention to the purely neural mechanisms. As depicted in Fig. 13, it is clear that both types of mechanisms are important parts of the total response mechanisms of fish which enable them to survive under adverse conditions. All these mechanisms are important, therefore, in maintaining this particular feature of the homeostasis of the fish which enable it to survive in a remarkable range of environments in spite of the very severe limitations imposed upon its respiration.

REFERENCES

Ballintijn, C. M. and Bamford, O. S. (1975). Proprioceptive motor control in fish respiration. J. exp. Biol. 62, 99–114.

Bamford, O. S. (1974). Respiratory neurones in rainbow trout (Salmo gairdneri). Comp. Biochem. Physiol. 48A, 77–83.

Beamish, F. W. H. (1964). Respiration of fishes with special emphasis on standard oxygen consumption. III. Influence of oxygen. Can. J. Zool. 42, 355–366.

Burton, D. T. and Heath, A. G. (1980). Ambient oxygen tension (P_{O_2}) and transition to anaerobic metabolism in three species of freshwater fish. Can. J. Fish. Aquat. Sci. 37, 1216–1224.

Cech Jr. J. J., Campagna, C. G. and Mitchell, S. J. (1979). Respiratory responses of largemouth bass (Micropterus salmoides) to environmental changes in temperature and dissolved oxygen. Trans. Am. Fish. Soc. 108, 166–171.

Chiba, K. (1965). A study of the influence of oxygen concentration on the growth of juvenile common carp. [J. e]. Bull. Freshwat. Fish. Res. Lab., Tokyo 15, 35–47.

Daxboeck, C. and Holeton, G. F. (1978). Oxygen receptors in the rainbow trout, Salmo gairdneri. Can. J. Zool. 56, 1254–1259.

Eclancher, B. (1972). Action des changements de P_{O_2} de l'eau sur la ventilation de la truite et de la tanche. J. Physiol., Paris 65, 397A.

Fry, F. E. J. and Hart, J. S. (1948). The relationship of temperature to oxygen consumption in the goldfish. *Biol. Bull. mar. biol. Lab.*, *Woods Hole* **94**, 66–77.

Heath, A. G. and Pritchard, A. W. (1965). Effects of severe hypoxia on carbohydrate energy stores and metabolism in two species of freshwater fish. *Physiol. Zool.* **38**, 325–334.

Herbert, D. W. M., Alabaster, J. S., Dart, M. C. and Lloyd, R. (1961). The effect of china-clay wastes on trout streams. *Int. J. Air Wat. Pollut.* **5**, 56–74.

Hochachka, P. W. (1980). *Living Without Oxygen*. Cambridge, Mass.: Harvard University Press. 181pp.

Hughes, G. M. (1964). Fish respiratory homeostasis. *Symp. Soc. exp. Biol.* **18**, 81–107.

Hughes, G. M. (1972). Morphometrics of fish gills. *Respir. Physiol.* **14**, 1–25.

Hughes, G. M. (1973). Respiratory responses to hypoxia in fish. *Am. Zool.* **13**, 475–489.

Hughes, G. M. (1975). Coughing in the rainbow trout (*Salmo gairdneri*) and the influence of pollutants. *Revue suisse Zool.* **82**, 47–64.

Hughes, G. M. (1980a). Functional morphology of fish gills. In *Epithelial Transport in the Lower Vertebrates* (B. Lahlou, ed.), pp. 15–36. Cambridge: Cambrilge University Press.

Hughes, G. M. (1980b). Morphometry of fish gas exchange organs in relation to their respiratory function. In *Environmental Physiology of Fishes* (M. A. Ali, ed.), pp. 33–56. New York and London: Plenum Press.

Hughes, G. M. (1981). Some effects on the respiration of rainbow trout subjected to Zn for periods of 24–48 hours. (In preparation).

Hughes, G. M. and Adeney, R. J. (1977). The effects of zinc on the cardiac and ventilatory rhythms of rainbow trout (*Salmo gairdneri*, Richardson) and their responses to environmental hypoxia. *Wat. Res.* **11**, 1069–1077.

Hughes, G. M. and Ballintijn, C. M. (1968). Electromyography of the respiratory muscles and gill water flow in the dragonet. *J. exp. Biol.* **49**, 583–602.

Hughes, G. M. and Johnston, I. A. (1978). Some responses of the electric ray (*Torpedo marmorata*) to low ambient oxygen tensions. *J. exp. Biol.* **73**, 107–117.

Hughes, G. M. and Perry, S. F. (1976). Morphometric study of trout gills: a light-microscope method suitable for the evaluation of pollutant action. *J. exp. Biol.* **64**, 447–460.

Hughes, G. M. and Saunders, R. L. (1970). Response of the respiratory pumps to hypoxia in rainbow trout *Salmo gairdneri*. *J. exp. Biol.* **53**, 529–545.

Hughes, G. M. and Shelton, C. (1962). Respiratory mechanisms and their nervous control in fish. In *Advances in Comparative Physiology and Biochemistry*, 1 (O. Lowenstein, ed.), pp. 275–364. London and New York: Academic Press.

Hughes, G. M. and Umezawa, S. I. (1968). On respiration in the dragonet (*Callionymus lyra* L.). *J. exp. Biol.* **49**, 565–582.

Hughes, G. M., Perry, S. F. and Brown, V. M. (1979). A morphometric study of effects of nickel, chromium and cadmium on the secondary lamellae of rainbow trout gills. *Wat. Res.* **13**, 665–679.

Hughes, G. M., Albers, C., Muster, D. and Götz, K. (1981a). Respiration of carp (*C. carpio*) at 10° and 20°C and the effects of hypoxia. (in preparation).

Hughes, G. M., Yamamoto, Y., Itazawa, Y. and Kobayashi, S. (1981b). Respiratory responses to confinement in a marine carangid fish. (in preparation).

Itazawa, Y. (1959). Gas content of the blood in response to that of medium water in fish—II: comparison of the responses in several species. *Bull. Jap. Soc. scient. Fish.* **25**, 301–306.

Itazawa, Y. (1971). An estimation of the minimum level of dissolved oxygen in water required for normal life of fish. *Bull. Jap. Soc. scient. Fish.* **37**, 273–276.

Itazawa, Y. and Takeda, T. (1979). An estimation of the minimum level of dissolved oxygen in water required for normal life of fish—II: an experiment with carp under carbon dioxide accumulation. *Bull. Jap. Soc. scient. Fish.* **45**(3), 323–327.

Johnston, I. A. (1975). Anaerobic metabolism in the carp (*Carassius carassius* L.) *Comp. Biochem. Physiol.* **51B**, 235–241.

Jones, D. R. and Schwazfeld, T. (1974). The oxygen cost to the metabolism and efficiency of breathing in trout (*Salmo gairdneri*). *Resp. Physiol.* **21**, 241–254.

Kutty, M. N. (1968). Respiratory quotients in goldfish and rainbow trout. *J. Fish. Res. Bd Can.* **25**, 1689–1728

Marvin, D. E. Jr. and Burton, D. T. (1973). Cardiac and respiratory responses of rainbow trout, bluegills and brown bullhead catfish during rapid hypoxia and recovery under normoxic conditions. *Comp. Biochem. Physiol.* **46A**, 755–765.

Marvin, D. E. and Heath, A. C. (1968). Cardiac and respiratory responses to gradual hypoxia in three ecologically distinct species of fresh-water fish. *Comp. Biochem. Physiol.* **27**, 349–355.

Mazeaud, M. M. and Mazeaud, F. (1981). Adrenergic responses to stress in fish. In *Stress and Fish* (A. D. Pickering, ed.), pp. 49–75. London and New York: Academic Press.

Mazeaud, M. M., Mazeaud, F. and Donaldson, E. M. (1977). Primary and secondary effects of stress in fish: some new data with a general review. *Trans. Am. Fish. Soc.* **106**, 201–212.

Nakanishi, T. and Itazawa, Y. (1974). Effects of hypoxia on the breathing rate, heart rate and rate of oxygen consumption in fishes. *Rpt. Fish. Res. Lab. Kyushu Univ.* **2**, 41–52.

Ott, M. E., Heisler, N. and Ultsch, G. R. (1980). A re-evaluation of the relationship between temperature and the critical oxygen tension in freshwater fishes. *Comp. Biochem. Physiol.* **67A**, 337–340.

Peyraud-Waitzenegger, M. (1979). Simultaneous modifications of ventilation and arterial P_{O_2} by catecholamines in the eel, *Anguilla anguilla* L.: Participation of α and β effects. *J. comp. Physiol.* **129**, 343–354.

Pickering, A. D. (1981). Introduction: the concept of biological stress. In *Stress and Fish* (A. D. Pickering, ed.), pp. 1–9. London and New York: Academic Press.

Randall, D. J. and Jones, D. R. (1973). The effect of deafferentiation of the pseudobranch on the respiratory response in hypoxia of the trout (*Salmo gairdneri*). *Respir. Physiol.* **17**, 291–301.

Randall, D. J. and Smith, J. C. (1967). The regulation of cardiac activity in fish in a hypoxic environment. *Physiol. Zool.* **40**, 104–113.

Sawato, M., Nomura, M., Abe, K., Motonishi, A. and Matsushima, S. (1969). Annual Meeting of Jap. Soc. Sci. Fish. Tokyo.

Skidmore, J. F. (1970). Respiration and osmoregulation in rainbow trout with gills damaged by zinc sulphate. *J. exp. Biol.* **52**, 484–494.

Smart, G. R. (1981). Aspects of water quality producing stress in intensive fish culture. In *Stress and Fish* (A. D. Pickering, ed.), pp. 277-293 London and New York: Academic Press.

Smith, F. M. and Jones, D. R. (1978). Localization of receptors causing hypoxic bradycardia in trout (*Salmo gairdneri*). *Can. J. Zool.* **56**, 1260–1265.

Soivio, A. and Nikinmaa, M. (1981). The swelling of erythrocytes in relation to the oxygen affinity of rainbow trout blood. In *Stress and Fish* (A. D. Pickering, ed.), pp. 103–119. London and New York: Academic Press.

146 G. M. HUGHES

Soivio, A., Nyholm, K. and Westman, K. (1975). A technique for repeated sampling of the blood of individual resting fish. *J. exp. Biol.* **62**, 207–217.

Spitzer, K. W., Marvin, D. E. and Heath, A. C. (1969). The effect of temperature on the respiratory and cardiac response of the bluegill sunfish to hypoxia. *Comp. Biochem. Physiol.* **30**, 83–90.

Stewart, N. E., Shumway, D. L. and Doudoroff, P. (1967). Influence of oxygen concentration on the growth of juvenile largemouth bass. *J. Fish. Res. Bd Can.* **24**, 475–494.

Takeda, T. and Itazawa, Y. (1979). An estimation of the minimum level of dissolved oxygen in water required for normal life of fish—III: an experiment with carp avoiding carbon dioxide accumulation. *Bull. Jap. Soc. scient. Fish.* **45**(3), 329–333.

Thomas, S. and Hughes, G. M. (1981). A study of the effects of hypoxia on rainbow trout using an extracorporeal blood circulation. *Respir. Physiol.* (in press).

Webb, P. W. (1971). The swimming energetics of trout. II. Oxygen consumption and swimming efficiency. *J. exp. Biol.* **55**, 521–540.

7. Stress and the Modulation of Defence Mechanisms in Fish

A. E. ELLIS

DAFS Marine Laboratory, Aberdeen, Scotland

Abstract. It has long been recognized that stress and resistance to disease are related, but the mechanisms of this relationship are extremely complex and little understood. Stress causes many changes in the physiological systems of the body including the defence systems which are comprised of such responses as tissue repair, phagocytosis, inflammation and the multitude of specific and non-specific responses mediated by the lymphoid system. The complex interactions of factors modulating the defence mechanisms are only beginning to be understood and as yet there is little relevant information in this field concerning fish. This review attempts to bring together data concerning modulating influences on the defence systems which are relevant to stress.

Stress modulates many of the defence mechanisms, suppressing some and exaggerating others. This may be advantageous or injurious to the animal concerned depending upon the complex interactions between the stress factors and the animal's physiological state which will eventually determine how well the animal will adapt to the situation.

Topics discussed include the effects of the endocrine system on phagocytic cells, both direct and indirect through lymphokines, acute phase proteins and other endogenous mediators. The effects of stress and hormones on lymphocyte function are discussed with reference to cell traffic, proliferative responses of lymphocytes (mitogen stimulation and mixed lymphocyte reactions) and the ontogenetic development of lymphocyte function. Immuno-suppressive factors reviewed include stress "pheromones", factors released by parasites, macrophage products, α-2 macroglobulin, temperature effects, endogenous seasonal rhythms, nature of antigenic exposure in induction of immunological tolerance and antibiotics.

I INTRODUCTION

In 1936 Selye published the morphological indices of stress in mammals which became the basis of the General Adaptation Syndrome. These morphological criteria of stress were: enlarged adrenals, atrophy of lymphoid tissues and ulcers in the gastro-intestinal tract. It is now well established that the hypothalamus–hypophysis–adrenocortical axis plays a central role in homeostasis and, as Selye recognized, in the regulation of disease phenomena. However, the mechanism of the effect of stress on disease is still very little understood. Selye (1973) suggested that derangements in the secretion of hormones can lead to "diseases of adaptation". These are not due directly to the effects of pathogens themselves but rather to faulty adaptive responses to the stress of pathogenic challenges or to other factors. The main purpose of the defence mechanisms is to localize irritants and present a hostile barrier to destroy them. Sometimes disease is caused by the defence mechanisms themselves and their suppression can be advantageous if the foreign agent is itself innocuous (e.g. allergic responses). Defence systems are under regulatory mechanisms which include hormonal controls (e.g. corticoids) and if these are modified during stress, there may be resultant derangements of the defence mechanisms and the appearance of disease.

The primary effects of stress occur in the endocrine system which, in turn, mediates the secondary effects characterized by metabolic changes in other organ systems as the animal attempts to maintain homeostasis. One of the major adaptation responses to aggressors is the immune system. In its widest sense this refers to a variety of tissue reactions ranging from repair of damaged tissue to phagocytosis, inflammation and the multitude of specific and non-specific responses mediated by the lymphoid system. It is the mechanism of controlling the defence systems and the effects of stress upon them that is still only partially understood. However, it is now recognized that stress can cause a derangement of the defence systems with a consequent suppression or exaggeration of responses which may disturb the balance of other physiological systems and ultimately result in disease.

In mammals, the effects of stress upon the defence mechanisms are not fully understood and there is even less known in fish. This review, therefore, will of necessity draw heavily upon data obtained from work with mammals, but there is much to suggest that the mechanisms in mammals and fish are very similar. Nevertheless, there are also some notable differences between mammals and fish, perhaps the principal one being the effect of environmental temperature on immune responsiveness. Because of the lack of knowledge concerning the detailed effects of stress on the immune response, a broad based approach to physiologically mediated suppression of the defence system will be taken. This will include factors which may not be directly stress mediated but which may have interrelated underlying mechanisms. As the primary effects of stress are seen in the endocrine system, the effects of hormones on defence mechanisms will be discussed first, followed by a discussion of the effects of other factors which may be regarded as endogenous or exogenous stresses although their underlying mechanisms of action are not fully understood.

II HORMONAL MODULATION OF DEFENCE MECHANISMS

Data from mammalian studies indicate that during ontogeny and in the adult stage, the neuro-endocrine system and the immune system are inter-dependent, each influencing and conditioning the other. Pierpaoli and Besedovsky (1975) suggested that the thymus plays an essential endocrine function in early ontogeny and is required for the final functional organization of the hypothalamus. Data also suggest that the interaction between antigen and the lymphoid system triggers, via the release of substances such as lymphokines and prostaglandins, certain rapid changes in the hormonal status which in turn cause a hormone-dependent alteration of the initially antigen-stimulated cells.

(a) Macrophages and Phagocytosis

The reticulo-endothelial system is an important defence system both directly, by its phagocytic capacity to destroy pathogenic material, and indirectly, by its helper role in antibody production by B lymphocytes. A variety of hormones in mammals have been shown to affect the rate of clearance of foreign particles such as carbon, chromium phosphate, foreign erythrocytes or trypan blue. Most have an enhancing effect although the effects of corticosteroids are complex and both enhancement and suppression of phagocytic rates have been reported with low doses of these hormones (Table I).

Macrophages and monocytes have specific receptor sites for cortisol, corticosterone and progesterone (Werb et al., 1978). Glucocorticoids administered in vivo cause a monocytopenia and reduction in the numbers of monocytes accumulating in inflammatory sites (Leibovich and Ross, 1975). In in vitro studies using physiological concentrations of glucocorticoids, there is suppression of differentiation and growth of monocytic and granulopoietic colonies from bone marrow precursors (Werb, 1978). The metabolic and secretory activity of mature macrophages (e.g. secretion of elastase, collagenase, non-specific neutral proteases, endogenous pyrogens and prostaglandins) is also suppressed (Werb, 1978). This suppression may be mediated directly via the corticosteroid receptors on the macrophages or indirectly, by other cells such as lymphocytes and hepatocytes (which release factors which in turn may influence the macrophages) or via the enhanced

TABLE I   The Effects of Several Hormones on the Phagocytic Rate of
Macrophages (adapted from White and Goldstein, 1972).

Hormone	Direction of effect	Reference
Somatotropin	None	
Thyroxine and triiodothyronine	Increase	
Corticosteroids	Increase (small doses)	
	Decrease (large doses)	
	Suppressed activation	Dimitriu (1976)
	(small doses)	Werb (1978)
Oestrogens	Increase	
Progesterone	None	
Androgens	None	
Thymus	None	

production of certain factors by the macrophages themselves (e.g. α-2 macroglobulin) which suppress the secretion of other macrophage products.

Direct effects of corticoids on macrophages include the stabilization of lysosomes which may prevent the lysosomal exocytosis employed in certain cytotoxic properties of macrophages (Hibbs, 1974). Glucocorticoids are also known to block the effect on macrophages of certain lymphokines such as macrophage arming factor (MAF). The release of MAF by antigen-stimulated T lymphocytes is unaffected by corticoids but its uptake by macrophages and their subsequent increased cytotoxic activity is inhibited *in vitro* by physiological concentrations of these hormones (Dimitriu, 1976). The production of another lymphokine, migration inhibition factor (MIF), is not suppressed by corticosteroids but it has been claimed that these hormones suppress the ability of macrophages to respond to it (Balow and Rosenthal, 1973).

The indirect effects of corticoids lead to very complex regulatory mechanisms which are only just beginning to be understood. For example, glucocorticoids are known to decrease the secretion of endogenous mediators by neutrophils and macrophages. These mediators, such as endogenous pyrogens, are potent elicitors of acute phase protein (e.g. α-2 macroglobulin) production by the liver (for further discussion of acute phase proteins (APR) the reader is referred to Fletcher, 1981, this volume). However, glucocorticoids do not cause suppression of APR production. On the contrary, Gordon and Limaos (1979) have shown an increased production of APR to endotoxin (which causes macrophages to release endogenous pyrogen) after administration of cortisol.

Macrophages themselves also secrete α-2 macroglobulin which may affect the secretion of proteases by macrophages. Glucocorticoids increase the secretion of α-2 macroglobulin by macrophages (James, 1980), but decrease their secretion of prostaglandins (Werb, 1978). Both of these factors have suppressive and enhancing effects on the immune system and so the regulation of the relative secretion rates of these and other substances by hormones and their effects on the endocrine system may provide complex regulatory mechanisms which modulate both the immune and hormonal status of an animal (see Pierpaoli and Maestroni, 1978, for elaboration of these possible mechanisms). Progesterone antagonizes the suppressive effects of glucocorticoids on protease secretion by macrophages (Werb, 1978) and it is possible that progesterone may modulate the suppressive activity of glucocorticoids on macrophages *in vivo*.

(b) The Lymphoid System

Much work has been done on the immuno-suppressive effects of hormones, particularly the corticosteroids, but most of this work has been based on investigations leading to an understanding of their pharmacological immuno-suppressive effects rather than their physiological effects in relation to stress. I do not intend to discuss the pharmacological data in this review but it is frequently difficult to discern which category results fall into and it should be borne in mind that not all the immuno-suppressive effects attributed to certain hormones *in vitro* may operate *in vivo* during physiological stress.

The effects of hormones on the numbers of lymphocytes present in lymphoid tissues are summarized in Table II.

TABLE II A Summary of the Effects of Hormones on the Numbers of Lymphocytes Present in Lymphoid Tissues.

Hormone	No. of lymphocytes in lymphoid tissues	Reference
Somatotropin	Increase	Sorkin (1969)
Thyrotropin, thyroxine, triiodothyronine	Increase (in hyperthyroidism)	Sorkin (1969)
Corticotropin, cortisol, corticosterone	Decrease	Dougherty (1952) Pearson *et al.* (1978)
Oestrogens	Increase	Dougherty (1952)
Androgens	Decrease	Dougherty (1952)
Thymosin	Increase	Goldstein and White (1971) Pierpaoli and Besedovsky (1975)

Earlier literature stressed the lymphocytotoxic properties of ACTH and corticosteroids (e.g. Dougherty, 1952) but these observations were probably due to the high pharmacological doses of these hormones administered in experiments. This review will attempt to concentrate on the effects of physiological doses of these hormones which may throw light on to the events occurring in the immune systems during stress.

(i) *Blood leucocyte numbers.* Stress has been shown in mammals and fishes to result in lymphocytopenia, monocytopenia and neutrophilia (Pearson *et al.*, 1978; Weinreb, 1958; McLeay, 1975; Ball and Hawkins, 1976; Johansson-Sjöbeck *et al.*, 1978). Lymphocytes in all vertebrates circulate around the body from blood to lymph, returning to the blood again via the peripheral lymphoid organs. In teleosts, lymphocytes pass from the blood and take up residence for a period of time in the lymphoid tissues of the kidney and spleen (Ellis and de Sousa, 1974). In mammals, the lymphocytopenia has recently been shown to result from a sequestration of circulating T lympho-cytes mainly into the bone marrow and less so into the lymph nodes (Pearson *et al.*, 1978). Administration of corticosteroids in physiological amounts caused a lymphocytopenia in 4–6 h with a return to normal levels in 24 h. The mechanism for the sequestration into the bone marrow is not known but changes in the surface characteristics of lymphocytes or the vascular endo-thelium have been suggested.

The lymphocytopenic effects of corticosteroids may have bearings on defence mechanisms as there will be a reduced access for lymphocytes to inflammatory sites where immunological reactions normally occur. Certainly the lymphopenia due to corticosteroid administration *in vivo* results in decreased responsiveness of lymphocytes remaining in the circu-lation as measured by *in vitro* assays such as antigen and mitogen responses, natural cytotoxicity, mixed lymphocyte responses (MLR) and immuno-globulin (Ig) synthesis (Pearson *et al.*, 1978). The explanation for this is probably the sequestration of reactive lymphocytes into the bone marrow although physiological concentrations of corticosteroids are known to suppress lymphocyte function *in vitro* (Smith *et al.*, 1977).

The literature on the effects of stress and the pituitary–interrenal axis on circulating leucocytes in fish needs careful scrutiny. Firstly, the effects on total leucocyte numbers are not always so useful. Stress results in a lympho-cytopenia and neutrophilia but these events may not be synchronous, so that data based on total leucocyte numbers do not necessarily reflect what is happening to the lymphocyte population. Secondly, the effects of stress and corticosteroid administration vary depending upon the physiological status of the fish. For example, Slicher (1961) found that in the killifish, *Fundulus heteroclitus*, cortisol caused either lymphocytopenia or lymphocytosis depending upon the state of maturity and the sex. In the same species, Pickford *et al.* (1971) also found a differential response to cortisol. A leucocytosis occurred in sexually mature and hypophysectomized fish, whereas a leucopenia arose in sexually regressed, intact fish.

The mechanisms of lymphopenia, neutrophilia and leucopenic–leucocytosis oscillations resulting from stress in fish have been investigated by several workers. Weinreb (1958) suggested the lymphopenia resulted from release of corticosteroids from the interrenal and the neutrophilia was under pituitary ACTH control but not the interrenal. Pickford *et al.* (1971) studied the effects of cold shock stress and the pituitary–interrenal axis on modulation of circulating leucocyte numbers but no attempt was made to differentiate the leucocytes. They described a complex oscillation of leucocyte numbers in the killifish resulting from cold-shock stress. A leucopenia occurred within 3 min followed by a leucocytosis at 15 min, leucopenia at 30–60 min, leucocytosis at 2 h and then a gradual return to normal. Hypophysectomy abolished the second leucocytosis phase but had no effect on the earlier phases. However, injection of the catecholamine, epinephrine, completely simulated the cold shock sequence. The authors postulated that catecholamines may control the leucopenic phases and cortisol the leucocytosis phases. Indeed, the concentration of plasma epinephrine does increase rapidly after stress in fish along with cortisol levels (Mazeaud *et al.*, 1977; Mazeaud and Mazeaud, 1981, this volume).

Ball and Hawkins (1976) described a fall in the blood leucocyte concentration in *Poecilia latipinna* after hypophysectomy and a return to normal levels by the administration of ACTH or cortisol at doses which restored plasma cortisol to normal resting levels. Other pituitary hormones (e.g. growth hormone (GH) and prolactin) although capable of restoring plasma cortisol to normal levels, had no effect on the circulating leucocytes. By comparison, TSH completely restored leucocyte numbers but only partially restored cortisol levels. Thyroxine was able to partially restore leucocyte numbers. This suggests the GH and prolactin antagonize the normalizing influence of cortisol (see van Dijk and Jacobse-Geels, 1979), whereas TSH and thyroxine may act directly on leucocyte circulation.

McLeay (1975) has presented evidence which suggests that in the coho salmon, *Oncorhynchus kisutch*, raised cortisol levels resulting from stress or seasonal factors can cause lymphopenia. In fish exposed to high temperatures and crowding stress he observed a lymphopenic response. Exposure to a pulp-mill effluent had similar results. He also reported seasonal variations in pituitary–interrenal activity and circulating lymphocyte numbers. From histiometric data it was concluded that the pituitary–interrenal axis was inactive during spring and summer in fingerling coho, but active during winter for all fish and in spring for smolting fish. The numbers of small lymphocytes in the blood were negatively correlated with histiometric indices of pituitary–interrenal activity whilst numbers of neutrophils and thrombocytes were not correlated. He concluded that with a decrease in environmental temperature there was an increased activity of the pituitary–interrenal axis which resulted in a decrease in the numbers of circulating small lymphocytes.

(ii) *Proliferative responses of lymphocytes.* It was generally accepted that lymphocytes were insensitive to corticosteroids until they are stimulated by specific antigen or mitogens. This induced an early glucocorticoid-sensitive phase before resistance again supervened at the time of full morphological blast transformation and mitosis (Baxter and Harris, 1975). However, Smith *et al.* (1977) showed that lymphocytes, regardless of their state of activation, are sensitive to metabolic inhibition by physiological levels of glucocorticoids and that blast transformation is associated with a striking increase in the number of corticosteroid receptor sites per cell which may make them even more sensitive to regulation by these hormones.

(iii) *Ontogenetic development of lymphocyte function.* Van Dijk and Jacobse-Geels (1979) recently demonstrated that the presence of the adrenal gland was necessary for proper development of cell-mediated immunity in mammals. The blocking of secretion by the adrenal gland in mice by administration of aminoglutethimide phosphate (AGP) results in thymic hyperplasia, lymph node hypoplasia, leucocytosis and potentiation of the delayed hypersensitivity (DH) reaction. Within 2 weeks of withdrawal of AGP treatment, normality returned. However, when young mice under 4 weeks of age were similarly treated with AGP there was a similar reaction, but on withdrawal of AGP there was a persistently diminished DH response. These authors suggested there was an early requirement of the adrenal gland for proper functional development of the lymphoid system as this did not occur with AGP treatment of older animals. In fish, there is virtually no information available on the role of the interrenal in ontogenetic development of lymphocyte function although cortisol phosphate failed to affect the development of the lymphoid organs of the rainbow trout, *Salmo gairdneri*, when applied at doses of 1 mg l^{-1} to the tank water during the first months of histogenesis (see abstract by Manning *et al.*, 1981, this volume).

(iv) *Modulation of the immune response.* In mammals, immunosuppressive properties of short-term and long-term exposures to various stresses have been established. For example, Monjan and Collector (1977) subjected mice to noise stress, killed groups of individuals at sequential periods after onset of stress and assayed the spleen, bone marrow and thymus cells for mitogen responsiveness. They also studied *in vitro* cytotoxicity responses where mice were injected with P815 tumour cells 9 days before killing. The results indicate (Fig. 1) that for both mitogen and cytotoxicity responses, short-term exposure to the stress one week prior to immunization with tumour cells or *in vitro* mitogen exposure clearly depressed the responsiveness of the lymphocytes. However, enhanced responses occurred with longer exposure to the sound stress. Such enhancement of immune responsiveness during adaptation to stress has not been widely recognized and its

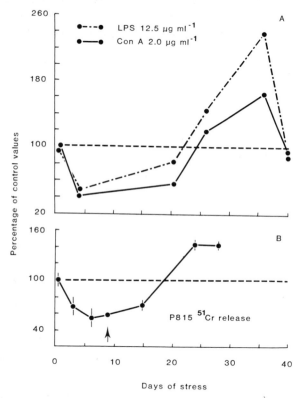

Fig. 1 Stress-induced modulation of immune function in mice. (A) *In vitro* response of splenic lymphocytes to mitogens LPS or Con A following stimulation (*in vivo*) of mice with sound stress for 1 h per day for up to 39 days. (B) Ability of immune lymphocytes to kill target cells *in vitro* following stimulation (*in vivo*) of mice with sound stress for 3 h per day for up to 28 days. Arrow indicates that mice were immunized with P815 cells 9 days before they were killed. Some animals had their daily sound stress periods initiated prior to immunization (represented by points to the right of the arrow) while others had their stress sessions started after immunization represented by points to the left of the arrow. Reproduced with the kind permission of Dr A. A. Monjan. Copyright 1977 by the American Association for the Advancement of Science (Monjan and Collector, 1977).

mechanism is not understood. Plasma cortisol assays (Fig. 2) showed elevated levels during the stage of depressed immune responsiveness. During
the whole stress period, a decrease in the numbers of splenic leucocytes was
noted so the suppression could not simply be explained by changes in
lymphocyte traffic. These data support the view that immune suppression is
mediated by corticosteroid release, but what is the mechanism of immune
enhancement? Possibly, stress operates on the immune system via the
pituitary in a complex manner. Gisler *et al.* (1971) were able to depress the
antibody response in mice to sheep erythrocytes by injections of adrenocorticotropic hormone (ACTH). With time, the responsiveness recovered but
only if the animals had intact pituitaries. Hypophysectomized mice would

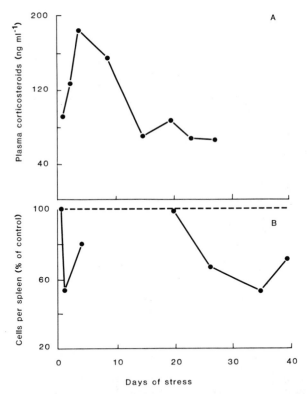

Fig. 2 Humoral and splenic changes induced by long-term exposure to sound stress. (A)
Plasma corticosteroid levels of mice subjected to sound stress for 3 h per day for up to 28 days.
(B) Viable nucleated splenocytes recovered per spleen from mice subjected to sound stress for
1 h per day for up to 39 days. Reproduced and modified with the kind permission of Dr A. A.
Monjan. Copyright 1977 by the American Association for the Advancement of Science
(Monjan and Collector, 1977).

not regain normal immune responsiveness unless the administration of ACTH was preceded by administration of somatotropic, or growth, hormone (GH).

When mice are injected with sheep erythrocytes there is a sudden increase in prostaglandins in the spleen. This response appears to be dependent upon the presence of T lymphocytes. Within 2 h of antigen injection there is a rise in the LH, FSH and corticosterone concentration of plasma (Pierpaoli and Maestroni, 1978), but no change in GH or prolactin. Pierpaoli and Maestroni (1978) have investigated the significance of these transient increases in hormone levels on the immune response by administering certain drugs which are known to block pituitary function. Administration of such drugs just prior to antigen injection in mice, rats and monkeys abrogated the subsequent release of LH and completely suppressed antibody production to the antigen. This suppression was found to be antigenically specific and persistent. The degree of suppression was drug-dose dependent and complete only when the drugs were given just before or at the same time as antigen. When administered after antigen injection, the drugs only diminished but did not completely block the antibody response. Cell mediated immunity, as measured by allograft rejection, could only be partially blocked by administration of the drugs. Suppression of the immune response could be alleviated if a mixture of LH, FSH and ACTH were also injected at the same time or just before the antigen/drug inoculum. A significant alleviation of the suppression was achieved only when the three hormones were given together.

In concluding this section on hormonal suppression of the immune response it must be said that stress causes a variety of changes in the hormonal status of an animal and these changes may result in modulation of the immune response in a variety of ways. The immune system itself, on interaction with antigen, causes changes in the hormonal balance which in turn affects the further progress of the immune response. Clearly, environmental factors interact with the physiological status of an animal in a complex manner which is still little understood. I will now turn to a discussion of immuno-suppressive factors which may operate through stress-induced hormonal changes.

III IMMUNOSUPPRESSIVE FACTORS

(a) Biological Interaction

There are many reports of diseases in fish which have been associated with stress (see review by Wedemeyer, 1970) but there are few studies of the effects of stress on the defence mechanisms in fish. Most fish which live in groups organize themselves into dominance hierarchies. Barrow (1955) found that amongst carp, *Cyprinus carpio*, held at 20°C only the dominant members produced antibodies to experimental infection. with trypanosomes. In a recent paper, Scott and Currie (1980) claimed from histiometric data that the subordinate individuals in a hierarchy of *Xiphophorus helleri* had more active interrenal tissue. Thus, raised levels of corticosteroids in subordinate individuals may result in stress-induced suppression of immunity.

Stress pheromones have been implicated in mediating immune suppression in fish. Pfuderer *et al.* (1974) found a substance which could be extracted from the flesh and the water in which carp were kept under crowded conditions and which caused depression of heart and growth rates of uncrowded carp. Perlmutter *et al.* (1973) discovered a similar "crowding pheromone" in the blue gourami, *Trichogaster trichopterus*. In this species, a reduction in the immune responsiveness of the fish to IPN virus was found in fish held under crowded conditions. The immune suppression was removed if the water in which the fish were kept was extracted with methyl-chloroform.

(b) Macrophage activity

The effects of hormones on macrophages and monocytes, and the ways in which these cells may be altered resulting in suppression of certain defence mechanisms, has already been discussed. In this section, some of the effects the macrophages themselves exert over other cell populations involved in defence mechanisms will be described (for more complete review see Allison, 1979). There are as yet no data from studies on fish in this important area of immunology.

Mammalian macrophages can be activated to produce a variety of factors, many of which have not yet been biochemically characterized, which exert enhancing and suppressive effects on the immune response. Macrophages are activated by numerous different stimuli (e.g. endotoxin, bacterial, fungal and yeast cell walls; polyanions; *Corynebacterium parvum*) most of which are thought to act via the complement system with the generation of C3b, a potent macrophage activator. Many infections are associated with immuno-suppressive effects which may result from macrophage products. For example, mouse lactate dehydrogenase virus infection results in a severe depletion of cortical thymocytes and lymphocytes in thymus-dependent areas in lymph nodes and spleen. The mouse LDH virus grows selectively in the macrophages and destruction of T lymphocytes occurs even in adrenalectomized animals. Thus, the lymphocyte depletion is not due to corticosteroid release. It has been suggested that the infected macrophages release cytotoxic factors for T lymphocytes or lymphoblasts. Amongst the products released from activated macrophages and which are considered to have suppressive effects on lymphocyte function are thymidine, prostaglandins, arginase, interferon, complement cleavage products and α-2 macroglobulin (see Allison, 1979).

(c) Parasites

Parasites employ a variety of means to protect themselves against destruction by the host defence mechanisms. For example, trypanosomes may exhibit antigenic variation whereas helminths, such as *Schistosoma*, employ other techniques including masking themselves with host-derived antigens. In addition to these mechanisms of immune avoidance, protozoan and helminth parasites are known to suppress the host's immune response.

Camus *et al.* (1979) have shown that during *Schistosoma mansoni* infection of rat and mouse, the splenic lymphocytes show an increased mitogen proliferation response during the first two weeks of infection but during the third and fourth week, lymphocyte responses are suppressed, returning to normal by week 7. Two mechanisms working concurrently have been suggested. When lymphocytes from infected rats are cultured with normal syngeneic lymphocytes, the mitogen responses of the latter are suppressed, suggesting the presence of suppressor cells in the infected animals. However, the parasite was also found to produce, both *in vitro* and *in vivo*, a small molecular weight, dialysable factor (suppressor cell factor is non-dialysable) which suppressed rat, mouse and human lymphocyte proliferation regardless of whether the latter was elicited specifically by *S. mansoni* antigen or non-specifically by mitogens (PHA, Con A, or LPS) or allogeneic cells in mixed lymphocyte reactions.

The biological significance of these substances has not yet been assessed and to date there are no data on their production by fish parasites but they may be of extreme importance in the still unknown mechanisms of biological balance in host-parasite relationships.

(d) α-2 Macroglobulins

Alpha-2 macroglobulin is, in many mammals, an acute phase protein and its corticosteroid related synthesis has already been referred to. It is thought to be produced by the liver in response to endogenous mediators of inflammation released from neutrophils and macrophages but macrophages themselves also synthesize it (Hibbs, 1974). This protein (or group of proteins) has a plethora of homeostatic effects, which are principally anti-protease in nature but it has also been implicated as a suppressive factor of many inflammatory and immunological responses (see review by James, 1980).

An α-globulin with many similar properties to mammalian α-2 macro-globulin is present in high concentrations in normal salmonid sera and has been shown to have anti-proteolytic and *Aeromonas salmonicida* exotoxin neutralizing properties (Munro *et al.*, 1979). Very little is known of these α-globulins in fish but their importance is likely to be wide ranging.

(e) Temperature

This subject has been extensively investigated and reviewed by Avtalion *et al.* (1976, 1980) but has become a controversial field of research in recent times (see Rijkers *et al.*, 1980a).

Humoral and cell-mediated immune responses in poikilothermic verte-brates are well known to be temperature dependent. The optimum temperature for development of immunity in fish is related to the natural environmental temperatures experienced by the species. Certain workers have reported diminished levels and rate of production of antibodies in fish at low temperatures (Paterson and Fryer, 1974), and others have reported a complete absence of antibody production (Avtalion, 1969; Fryer *et al.*, 1976).

Present data suggest that the first phase of the immune response involving antigen processing and recognition is temperature-independent (Cone and Marchalonis, 1972). The first temperature-sensitive phase is thought to be the subsequent interaction between T and B-like cells (Avtalion *et al.*, 1976). The mechanism has been suggested to involve a block in "T-helper" cell activity (Cuchens and Clem, 1977) or an increase in "T-suppressor" activity at low temperatures (Avtalion *et al.*, 1980). The subsequent multi-plication and differentiation of activated B-like cells into plasma cells is thought to be independent of temperature (Avtalion *et al.*, 1976) with a final temperature-sensitive phase involving synthesis and release of antibodies by plasma cells (Azzolina, 1978).

Avtalion's group have reported that carp were incapable of antibody production in a primary response to bovine serum albumin (BSA) when held below 15°C. However, normal secondary responses could be elicited, after primary stimulation at high temperature, even when the fish were held at 12°C. They demonstrated that the temperature-dependent phase of the primary response was during antibody induction in the first few days after immunization. Thereafter, antibody production was normal with increasing titres developing at low temperatures. In a series of elegant experiments, Avtalion's groups have obtained data which are consistent with an interpretation based on the existence of helper and suppressor cells in the carp and the induction of helper-cell function being suppressed at low temperatures.

Other workers have not been able to confirm the "all or none" effect of temperature on antibody production. Rijkers *et al.* (1980a), using a plaque forming cell (PFC) assay for antibody production to sheep erythrocytes in the carp, have reported a humoral response obtained at temperatures between 8–28°C. They found a delay in the PFC response at lower temperatures but the magnitude of the primary response was unaffected by temperature. However, the secondary response, characterized by an earlier appearance of PFC and higher peak numbers, was absent at temperatures below 18°C.

A further difference in temperature effects on antibody production was reported by Azzolina (1978). Goldfish, *Carassius auratus*, were acclimated to 4°C and 22°C, and the splenic antibody forming cell (AFC) response and humoral antibody response to polymerized flagellin (POL) were assayed. The AFC response in the two groups of fish was identical but whilst the time course of humoral antibody production was similar, the peak titre was lower for the low temperature acclimated group. This was interpreted as reflecting a lower anabolic activity at low temperature and a more efficient retention of immune capacity in fish to bacterial antigens.

The nature of the antigen may well be important in studies concerning the effect of temperature on the antibody response in fish. In mammals, POL is a T-independent antigen and according to Avtalion's interpretation, POL unlike BSA (a T-dependent antigen in higher vertebrates), may not require participation of a "T-helper" function. However, sheep erythrocytes, used by Rijkers *et al.* (1980a), are also T-dependent antigens in mammals and their finding of a normal, though delayed, humoral response in the carp to this antigen is not entirely consistent with Avtalion's results, although the lack of a secondary response at temperatures below 18°C also suggests the absence of development of a memory function at low temperatures. It is possible that the antigenic properties of BSA, for unknown reasons, tends to stimulate suppressor-cell function more effectively than helper-cell function in carp held at low temperatures. Species differences may also be important since Avtalion also demonstrated that soluble BSA is tolerogenic in carp but not in *Tilapia* (Avtalion *et al.*, 1980).

It is worth recalling McLeay's observations (1975) that at low temperatures there is an increased output of corticosteroids in salmonids so there may be a corticosteroid mediated inhibition of lymphocyte function in fish held at low temperatures rather than, or as well as, a direct temperature-dependent effect on lymphocyte/plasma cell metabolism. This has not been tested.

One other important feature of the temperature/immune response relationship is worth noting. Work on salmonids has shown a quantitative temperature dependency of antibody production. Fryer *et al.* (1976) immunized coho salmon with *Aeromonas salmonicida* cells in complete Freund's adjuvant at a variety of different temperatures ranging from 4–18°C. There was a stepwise reduction in peak titre and delayed onset of antibody production with lower temperature regimes and virtually no humoral response in the fish held at 4°C. However, oral vaccination of coho salmon with formalin-killed *Vibrio anguillarum* cells was found to be effective at all temperatures from 4–18°C as measured by resistance to natural exposure of the fish in an infected water body. (However, low temperature vaccinated fish had to be acclimated to ambient temperature, 12°C, for one week prior to exposure.) No serum agglutinin antibodies were found in any group of fish and the mechanism of this immunity is not understood but may result from factors discussed in the section on the nature of the antigenic exposure.

(f) Seasonal Rhythms

Some workers have reported that many poikilotherms have a poorer immune response during the winter periods (as compared with summer) even though temperature was held constant. Ambrosius (1976) studied the seasonal influence on antibody production in the tortoise, *Testudo hermanni*. Animals were kept at 25°C all the year round. When immunized in spring, there was a rapid increase in antibody levels with a latent period of about 10 days. However, animals immunized in October, showed a latent period of antibody production of over 60 days, although subsequent kinetics of antibody production were similar to the spring-immunized animals. The antigens used were serum proteins. However, if they were administered in complete Freund's adjuvant, no seasonal variation in antibody response was observed.

Seasonal variation of immune responsiveness and organization of the lymphoid tissues have been reported in other reptiles by Hussein *et al.* (1978) and Badir (1980). Recently, Yamaguchi *et al.* (1980) have reported seasonal suppression of antibody formation in rainbow trout even when the temperature was held constant at 18°C. Fish were selected for uniformity of age, sex and dosage of antigen. When fish were immunized with *Aeromonas salmonicida* or sheep erythrocytes prior to spring, antibody levels were much higher than in fish immunized prior to winter. The kinetics of antibody production were also seasonally dependent. Furthermore, there were seasonal differences in the heat stability of antibodies, their electrophoretic mobility and sedimentation coefficients (winter-immunized fish had serum antibodies in the 7S fraction as well as 19S fraction whereas spring-immunized fish only had antibodies in the 19S fraction). These workers suggested that antibody production in fish was controlled by unknown, internal mechanisms related to seasonal rhythms.

(g) Immunological Tolerance and the Nature of Antigenic Exposure

The mechanism of signal discrimination whereby the nature of exposure to antigen results in a different form of immune response is not fully understood. Antigenic exposure may induce or suppress an immune response thereby resulting in memory or tolerance, or it may stimulate a humoral or cell-mediated response to differing degrees or induce a localized rather than a systemic response which, in higher vertebrates, involves the production of different classes of immunoglobulins.

In vitro exposure of the neonatal mammal to antigen may induce immunological unresponsiveness. In the adult mammal, injection of large doses of antigen tends to induce tolerance following the production of small amounts of antibody. Conversely, a so-called low zone tolerance is known for certain serum protein antigens and flagellin after very small doses of these antigens are injected. Theories concerning the mechanism of tolerance-induction centre on clonal deletion but the details are not fully understood (Mitchinson, 1972). Evidence is becoming available to suggest that antigen exposure in early larval life in fish may induce tolerance. Teleost fish may not become immunologically competent until some weeks after hatching. In *Salmo salar*, lymphocyte surface immunoglobulin (sIg$^+$) markers and mixed lymphocyte responsiveness do not appear until the onset of feeding and development of the spleen (Ellis, 1977). Van Loon et al. (1980), in studies on the carp, also found that while lymphocytes were present 4 days after fertilization, the first sIg$^+$ lymphocytes were not seen until day 14, coinciding with differentiation of the spleen. Injection of 4-week-old carp with sheep erythrocytes did not result in a PFC response and only a negligible response was elicited after a second injection 3 months later. This suggests tolerance-induction due to exposure to antigen in early life.

Tolerance-induction using a combination of dosage, temperature, physicochemical nature and route of injection of antigen, has also been reported in carp. Avtalion et al. (1980) found that BSA in complete Freund's adjuvant (CFA) was immunogenic while soluble BSA was not, unless the carp had first been primed with BSA in CFA or with acetylated BSA in CFA which itself is not immunogenic. Furthermore, a primary injection with soluble BSA given intra-cardially, but not intra-peritoneally, induced specific tolerance to BSA injected later in CFA. Tolerance-induction was found not only to be route dependent but also dose and temperature dependent. Low and high doses of BSA injected intra-cardially induced tolerance when fish were kept at 25°C. However, when fish were injected with soluble BSA at 12°C only the high doses (>10 mg) induced tolerance to a challenge with BSA in CFA given at 25°C. These findings were not confirmed in *Tilapia* by the same authors. This species was capable of responding to soluble BSA at all doses, routes and temperatures without the induction of tolerance.

Other workers have not found tolerance-induction in fish related to dosage or route effects. However, slight differences in the antibody response have been reported according to antigen dosage, route of administration and timing of booster injections (Fletcher and White, 1973; Croy and Amend, 1977; O'Neill, 1979; Jayaraman *et al.*, 1979; Rijkers *et al.*, 1980a).

(h) Antibiotics

The effect of antibiotic treatment on the immune response in mammals is controversial and contradictory with reports of enhancement and suppression (see Rijkers *et al.*, 1980b). Antibiotics and antimetabolites have been shown to delay allograft rejection in fish (Levy, 1963; Cooper, 1976) and in a recent study by Rijkers *et al.*, (1980b) oxytetracycline, although having growth promoting properties was also found to have immuno-suppressive effects in the carp. Oral administration of therapeutic doses resulted in normal allograft responses but depressed humoral responses. Injection of the antibiotic depressed both cell-mediated and humoral responses, some fish having completely suppressed antibody production. Treated fish had increased numbers of granulocytes in the spleen and the authors speculated that whilst specific defence mechanisms may be blocked by antibiotic treatment there may be an increase in the activity of the phagocytic system.

IV   CONCLUDING REMARKS

An attempt has been made to review the effects on defence mechanisms which are, or are likely to be, associated with the stress response in vertebrates. It is generally thought that stress results in a suppression of the defence mechanisms, but this is only partly true. Stress modulates the defence system as it does other physiological systems and while certain aspects of defence may be suppressed by stress, others are enhanced. Also, it must be remembered, the systems are dynamic. The degree of stress and the animals ability to adapt to it, is important in determining the direction of the effect on a particular aspect of the defence system and this direction will fluctuate during the course of the adaptation period. For example, Monjan and Collector (1977) showed not only a phase when the immune response was suppressed in mice subjected to a continuous noise stress but also a phase of enhanced immune responsiveness.

The physiological significance of the mechanisms operating to modulate the defence mechanisms in vertebrates is little understood even at an experimental level, let alone that operating during the stress response. There are many areas of research in which mammalian data are available but nothing is known for fish; conversely, there is much known about the modulating effects of temperature on defence mechanisms in fish, a phenomenon of little importance in mammals. Therefore, much of the data reviewed comes from mammalian work and while details may prove to be different in fish, the basic principles are likely to be similar.

The stress–stress response concept is an important area of biology (one might say one of the most important) but is comprised of extremely complex interactions between the animal's physiological systems and the environment. Horridge (1977) wrote "Reductionism is description not explanation". In order to understand and explain the mechanisms and physiological significance of the stress–stress response phenomenon, biologists need to adopt a multidisciplinary synthetic approach rather than the reductionist one which has proved so successful for understanding mechanistic aspects of biology but is inadequate for explaining the significance of physiological events in functional terms, which is surely, the crux of biology.

REFERENCES

Allison, A. C. (1979). Macrophages and their products in immunoregulation (as effector cells and as targets for adjuvants). In *The Pharmacology of Immunoregulation* (G. H. Werner and F. Floc'h, eds), pp. 181–186. London and New York: Academic Press.

Ambrosius, H. (1976). Immunoglobulins and antibody production in reptiles. In *Comparative Immunology* (J. J. Marchalonis, ed.), pp. 298–334. Oxford: Blackwell Scientific Publications.

Avtalion, R. R. (1969). Temperature effect on antibody production and immunological memory in carp (*Cyprinus carpio*) immunised against bovine serum albumin (BSA). *Immunology* **17**, 927–931.

Avtalion, R. R., Weiss, E. and Moalem, T. (1976). Regulatory effects of temperature upon immunity in ectothermic vertebrates. In *Comparative Immunology* (J. J. Marchalonis, ed.) pp. 227–238. Oxford: Blackwell Scientific Publications.

Avtalion, R. R., Wishkovsky, A. and Katz, D. (1980). Regulatory effect of temperature on specific suppression and enhancement of the humoral response in fish. In *Immunological Memory* (M. J. Manning, ed.). Amsterdam, North-Holland: Elsevier. (In press).

Azzolina, L. S. (1978). Antigen recognition and immune response in goldfish *Carassius auratus* at different temperatures. *Dev. comp. Immunol.* **2**, 77–86.

166   A. E. ELLIS

Badir, N. (1980). Effect of seasonal changes on humoral immune responses of the lizard, *Chalcides ocellatus*. In *Aspects of Developmental and Comparative Immunology*, Vol. 1 (J. B. Solomon, ed.), pp. 515–516. Oxford: Pergamon Press. (In press).

Ball, J. N. and Hawkins, E. F. (1976). Adrenocortical (Interrenal) responses to hypophysectomy and adenohypophysial hormones in the teleost *Poecilia latipinna*. *Gen. comp. Endocr.* **28**, 59–70.

Balow, J. E. and Rosenthal, A. S. (1973). Glucocorticoid suppression of macrophage migration inhibitory factor. *J. exp. Med.* **137**, 1031–1041.

Barrow, J. H. (1955). Social behaviour in fresh-water fish and its effect on resistance to trypanosomes. *Proc. Nat. Acad. Sci. U.S.A.* **41**, 676–679.

Baxter, J. D. and Harris, A. W. (1975). Mechanism of glucocorticoid action: general features, with reference to steroid mediated immunosuppression. *Transplantation Proc.* **7**, 55–65.

Camus, D., Dessaint, J. P., Fischer, E. and Capron, A. (1979). Immunomodulating substances from parasites. Their role in the regulation of the immune response. In *The Pharmacology of Immunoregulation* (G. H. Werner and F. Floc'h, eds), pp. 253–265. London and New York: Academic Press.

Cone, R. E. and Marchalonis, J. J. (1972). Cellular and humoral aspects of the influence of environmental temperature on the immune response of poikilothermic vertebrates. *J. Immunol.* **108**, 952–957.

Cooper, E. L. (1976). *Comparative Immunology*. Englewood Cliffs, U.S.A.: Prentice-Hall Inc. 338pp.

Croy, T. R. and Amend, D. F. (1977). Immunization of sockeye salmon (*Oncorhynchus nerka*) against vibriosis using the hyperosmotic infiltration technique. *Aquaculture* **12**, 317–325.

Cuchens, M. and Clem, L. W. (1977). Phylogeny of lymphocyte heterogeneity. II. Differential effects of temperature on fish T-like and B-like cells. *Cell. Immunol.* **34**, 219–230.

Dimitriu, A. (1976). Suppression of macrophage arming by corticosteroids. *Cell. Immunol.* **21**, 79–87.

Dougherty, T. F. (1952). The effect of hormones on lymphatic tissue. *Physiol. Rev.* **32**, 379–402.

Ellis, A. E. (1977). Ontogeny of the immune response in *Salmo salar*. In *Developmental Immunology* (J. B. Solomon and J. D. Horton, eds), pp. 225–231. Amsterdam, North-Holland: Elsevier.

Ellis, A. E. and de Sousa, M. A. B. (1974). Phylogeny of the lymphoid system. I. A study of the fate of circulating lymphocytes in the plaice. *Eur. J. Immunol.* **4**, 338–343.

Fletcher, T. C. (1981). Non-antibody molecules and the defence mechanisms of fish. In *Stress and Fish* (A. D. Pickering, ed.), pp. 171–184. London and New York: Academic Press.

Fletcher, T. C. and White, A. (1973). Antibody production in the plaice after oral and parenteral immunisation with *Vibrio anguillarum* antigens. *Aquaculture* **1**, 417–428.

Fryer, J. L., Pitcher, K. S., Sanders, J. E., Rohovec, J. S., Zinn, J. L., Groberg, W. J. and McCoy, R. H. (1976). Temperature, infectious diseases and the immune response in salmonid fish. *US Department of Commerce. National Technical Information Service, PB-253 191.*

Gisler, R. E., Bussard, A. E., Mazie, J. C. and Hess, R. (1971). Hormonal regulation of the immune response. 1. Induction of an immune response *in vitro* with lymphoid cells from mice exposed to acute systemic stress. *Cell. Immunol.* **2**, 634–645.

Goldstein, A. L. and White, A. (1971). Role of thymosin and other thymic factors in the development, maturation and functions of lymphoid tissue. In *Current Topics in Experimental Endocrinology, Vol. 1* (V. H. T. James and L. Martini, eds), pp. 122–149. London and New York: Academic Press.

Gordon, A. H. and Limaos, E. A. (1979). Effects of bacterial endotoxin and corticosteroids on plasma concentrations of $\alpha2$ macroglobulin, haptoglobin and fibrinogen in rats. *Br. J. exp. Path.* **60**, 434–440.

Hibbs, J. B. (1974). Heterocytolysis by macrophages activated by bacillus Calmette-Guérin: lysosome exocytosis into tumor cells. *Science, N.Y.* **184**, 468–471.

Horridge, G. A. (1977). Mechanistic teleology and explanation in neuroethology. *Bioscience* **27**, 725–732.

Hussein, M. F., Badir, N., El Ridi, R. and Akef, M. (1978). Effect of seasonal variation on lymphoid tissues of the lizards, *Mabuya quinquetaenatia* Licht and *Uromastyx aegyptia* Forsk. *Dev. comp. Immunol.* **2**, 469–478.

James, K. (1980). Alpha 2 macroglobulin and its possible importance in immune systems. In *Trends in Biochemical Sciences* (J. Tooze, ed.), pp. 43–47. Netherlands: Elsevier.

Jayaraman, S., Mohan, M. and Muthukkaruppan, V. R. (1979). Relationship between migration inhibition and plaque-forming cell responses to sheep erythrocytes in the teleost, *Tilapia mossambica. Dev. comp. Immunol.* **3**, 67–75.

Johansson-Sjöbeck, M.-L., Göran, D., Larsson, A., Lewander, K. and Lidman, U. (1978). Haematological effects of cortisol in the European eel, *Anguilla anguilla* L. *Comp. Biochem. Physiol.* **60A**, 165–168.

Leibovich, S. J. and Ross, R. (1975). The role of the macrophage in wound repair. A study with hydrocortisone and antimacrophage serum. *Am. J. Pathol.* **78**, 71–100.

Levy, L. (1963). Effect of drugs on goldfish scale homograft survival. *Proc. Soc. exp. Biol. Med.* **114**, 47–50.

Manning, M. J., Ruglys, M., Grace, M. F. and Botham, J. W. (1981). Ontogenetic development of the immune system in fish. (Abstract). In *Stress and Fish* (A. D. Pickering, ed.), pp. 327–328. London and New York: Academic Press.

Mazeaud, M. M. and Mazeaud, F. (1981). Adrenergic responses to stress in fish. In *Stress and Fish* (A. D. Pickering, ed.), pp. 49–75. London and New York: Academic Press.

Mazeaud, M. M., Mazeaud, F. and Donaldson, E. M. (1977). Primary and secondary effects of stress in fish: Some new data with a general review. *Trans. Am. Fish. Soc.* **100**, 624–638.

McLeay, D. J. (1975). Variations in the pituitary–interrenal axis and the abundance of circulating blood-cell types in juvenile coho salmon, *Oncorhynchus kisutch*, during stream residence. *Can. J. Zool.* **53**, 1882–1891.

Mitchison, N. A. (1972). Dose, frequency and route of administration of antigen. In *Immunogenicity* (F. Borek, ed.), pp. 87–111. Amsterdam: North-Holland Publishing Co.

Monjan, A. A. and Collector, M. I. (1977). Stress-induced modulation of the immune response. *Science* **196**, 307–308.

Munro, A. L. S., Hastings, T. S., Ellis, A. E. and Liversidge, J. (1981). Studies on an ichthyotoxic material produced extracellularly by the furunculosis bacterium *Aeromonas salmonicida*. In *Fish Diseases* (W. Ahne, ed.), pp. 98–106. Heidelberg: Springer-Verlag.

O'Neill, J. G. (1979). The immune response of the brown trout, *Salmo trutta* L., to MS2 bacteriophage: immunogen concentration and adjuvants. *J. Fish Biol.* **15**, 237–248.

Paterson, W. D. and Fryer, J. L. (1974). Effect of temperature and antigen dose on the antibody response of juvenile coho salmon (*Oncorhynchus kisutch*) to *Aeromonas salmonicida* endotoxin. *J. Fish. Res. Bd Can.* **31**, 1743–1749.

Pearson, C. M., Clements, P. J. and Yu, D. T. Y. (1978). The effects of corticosteroids on lymphocyte functions. *Eur. J. Rheumatol. Inflammation* **1**, 216–225.

Perlmutter, A., Sarot, D. A., Uy, M., Fillozola, R. J. and Seeley, R. J. (1973). The effect of crowding on the immune response of the blue gourami (*Trichogaster trichopterus*) to infectious pancreatic necrosis (IPN) virus. *Life Sci.* **13**, 363–375.

Pfuderer, P., Williams, P. and Francis, A. A. (1974). Partial purification of the crowding factor from *Carassius auratus* and *Cyprinus carpio*. *J. exp. Zool.* **187**, 375–382.

Pierpaoli, W. and Besedovsky, H. O. (1975). Role of the thymus in programming of neuroendocrine functions. *Clin. exp. Immunol.* **20**, 323–338.

Pierpaoli, W. and Maestroni, G. J. M. (1978). Pharmacological control of the immune response. II. Blockade of antibody production by a combination of drugs acting on neuroendocrine functions. Its prevention by gonadotropins and corticotrophin. *Immunology* **34**, 419–430.

Pickford, G. E., Srivastava, A. K., Slicher, A. and Pang, P. K. T. (1971). The stress response in the abundance of circulating leucocytes in the killifish *Fundulus heteroclitus*. *J. exp. Zool.* **177**, 89–118.

Rijkers, G. T., Frederik-Wolters, E. M. H. and van Muiswinkel, W. B. (1980a). The immune system of cyprinid fish. Kinetics and temperature dependence of antibody-producing cells in carp (*Cyprinus carpio*). *Immunology* **41**, 91–97.

Rijkers, G. T., Teunissen, A. G., van Oosterom, R. and van Muiswinkel, W. B. (1980b). The immune system of cyprinid fish. The immunosuppressive effect of the antibiotic oxytetracycline in carp (*Cyprinus carpio*). *Aquaculture* **19**, 177–190.

Scott, D. B. C. and Currie, C. E. (1980). Social hierarchy in relation to adrenocortical activity in *Xiphophorus helleri* Heckel. *J. Fish Biol.* **16**, 265–277.

Selye, H. (1936). A syndrome produced by diverse nocuous agents. *Nature, Lond.* **138**, 32.

Selye, H. (1973). The evolution of the stress concept. *Am. Scient.* **61**, 692–699.

Slicher, A. M. (1961). Endocrinological and hematological studies in *Fundulus heteroclitus* (Linn.). *Bull. Bingham oceanogr. Coll.* **17**, 1–55.

Smith, K. A., Crabtree, G. R., Kennedy, S. J. and Munck, A. U. (1977). Glucocorticoid receptors and glucocorticoid sensitivity of mitogen stimulated and unstimulated human lymphocytes. *Nature, Lond.* **267**, 523–525.

Sorkin, E. (Ed.). (1969). *The Immune Response and its Suppression*. New York: Karger.

van Dijk, H. and Jacobse-Geels, H. E. L. (1979). The involvement of corticosterone in the ontogeny of the cellular immune apparatus of the mouse. In *The Pharmacology of Immunoregulation* (G. H. Werner and F. Floc'h, eds), pp. 57–61. London and New York: Academic Press.

van Loon, J. J. A., van Oosterom, R. and van Muiswinkel, W. B. (1980). Development of the immune system in carp. In *Aspects of Developmental and Comparative Immunology, Vol. I* (J. B. Solomon, ed.), pp. 469–470. Oxford: Pergamon Press.

Wedemeyer, G. (1970). The role of stress in the disease resistance of fishes. In *A Symposium on Diseases of Fishes and Shellfishes* (S. F. Snieszko, ed.), pp. 30–35. Washington, D.C.: American Fisheries Society.

Weinreb, E. L. (1958). Studies on the histology and histopathology of the rainbow trout, *Salmo gairdneri*. I. Haematology: under normal and experimental conditions of inflammation. *Zoologica, N.Y.* **43**, 145–154.

Werb, Z. (1978). Biochemical actions of glucocorticoids on macrophages in culture. *J. exp. Med.* **147**, 1695–1712.

Werb, Z., Foley, R. and Munck, A. (1978). Interaction of glucocorticoids with macrophages. *J. exp. Med.* **147**, 1684–1694.

White, A. and Goldstein, A. L. (1972). Hormonal regulation of host immunity. In *Immunogenicity* (F. Borek, ed.), pp. 334–364. *Frontiers of Biology, Vol. 25*. Amsterdam: North-Holland Publishing Co.

Yamaguchi, N., Teshima, C., Kurashige, S., Saito, T. and Mitsuhashi, S. (1980). Seasonal modulation of antibody formation in fish (*Salmo gairdneri*) against heterologous erythrocytes and bacterial antigen. In *Aspects of Developmental and Comparative Immunology, Vol. 1* (J. B. Solomon, ed.), pp. 483–485. Oxford: Pergamon Press.

8. Non-antibody Molecules and the Defence Mechanisms of Fish

T. C. FLETCHER

N.E.R.C. Institute of Marine Biochemistry, Aberdeen, Scotland

Abstract. The effects of environmental stressors on various aspects of fish metabolism are considered. Attention is given to the skin and mucus production and to non-antibody humoral factors. The latter are illustrated by reference to our work on acute phase proteins, especially C-reactive protein, and the influence of inflammatory stimuli and exogenous cortisol. There is a speculative discussion on the role of fever in fish.

I INTRODUCTION

"Whenever a large number of facts accumulates concerning any branch of knowledge, the human mind feels the need for some unifying concept with which to correlate them. Such integration is not only artistically satisfying, by bringing harmony into what appeared to be discord; it is also practically useful. It helps one to see a large field from a single point of view. When surveyed from a great elevation, some details in the landscape become hazy, or even invisible; yet it is only from there that we can see the field as a whole, in order to ascertain where more detailed exploration of the ground would be most helpful for its further development." (Selye, 1976).

Esch *et al.* (1975) defined stress as "the *effect* of any force which tends to extend any homeostatic or stabilizing process beyond its normal limit, at any level of biological organization". By this definition, stress is thus the product of the causal force or stressor. Regardless of the type of stressor, Selye (1950) recognized a general pattern of response in the effort to maintain stability: the general adaptation syndrome (GAS). The three stages of the GAS pass from the alarm reaction, through the stage of resistance and finally to exhaustion. These reactions, mediated by the hypothalamus–pituitary–adrenocorticoid axis, ultimately result in stimulation of the adrenal cortex and a rise in serum corticosteroids. There are situations however, where environmental stressors extend the homeostatic limits but do not cause the GAS. Esch *et al*. (1975) quote the example of the change in immunological responsiveness with temperature. Accepting that the GAS might not be generated in all stressful conditions, then a simplified definition would be that stressors are factors causing exaggerated responses and these responses constitute stress (for further discussion of the concept of stress see Pickering, 1981, this volume).

Aspects of stress in fish have been reviewed by Love (1970); Wedemeyer *et al*. (1976); Mazeaud *et al*. (1977), and at the ecosystem level by Esch and Hazen (1978), and gain increasing significance with the growth in aquaculture. Intensive culture methods readily show the effects of environmental stressors on the health of fish. If an animal cannot adapt, the stress will be lethal but even if less severe, it will still predispose to disease if pathogens are present (Bullock and Snieszko, 1969). Observations on the effects of changing environmental conditions on some of the non-specific defence mechanisms of fish (Fletcher, 1978; Ingram, 1980) will be discussed in this chapter.

II SKIN AND MUCUS

The skin, gills and to a lesser extent the alimentary tract, usually provide the first contact with any environmental stressor and hence their response to perturbation will often determine whether the stress remains localized. The basic adaptive response of all vertebrates to tissue injury is inflammation: local injury leading to the local accumulation of fluid and blood cells. A detailed description of the inflammatory response in rainbow trout, *Salmo gairdneri*, was given by Finn and Nielson (1971). Our studies have been confined to an acute or immediate response in the skin of flatfish, which is initiated by the introduction of specific parasite extracts (Fletcher and Baldo, 1974). The principal characteristic of the response however, is that it is non-specific and can be elicited by any injurious agent. In mammals, the ability to respond to the local stressor is impaired when the whole body is under stress, so that there is a balanced relationship between the local response and the GAS (discussed by Selye, 1976), central to which are the anti-inflammatory glucocorticoids. These have many effects on stages of the inflammatory process, but in general have greater effects on leucocyte traffic than on function and on cellular rather than humoral processes (Parrillo and Fauci, 1979). The pro-inflammatory corticoids must also be involved in mammals, but because of the uncertainty still surrounding their distribution in fish, comparable studies have not been reported.

The erythematous skin reaction we described in the plaice, *Pleuronectes platessa*, (Fletcher and Baldo, 1974) results from the release of pharmacological mediators. The only active material, so far identified from *in vitro* studies, is prostaglandin E_2 (PGE_2) (Anderson *et al.*, 1979). The plaice skin is extremely sensitive to PGE_2, since 1 $\mu g\ ml^{-1}$ gives an erythematous response comparable to 10 $\mu g\ ml^{-1}$ PGE_1; 100 $\mu g\ ml^{-1}$ compound 48/80; 1 $mg\ ml^{-1}$ bradykinin and 10 $mg\ ml^{-1}$ histamine or 5-hydroxytryptamine (A. A. Anderson and T. C. Fletcher, unpublished). Although the prostaglandin synthetase inhibitor, indomethacin, completely inhibits the *in vitro* release of PG from plaice skin, the *in vivo* response is only completely and consistently inhibited by disodium cromoglycate (Baldo and Fletcher, 1975) and it was concluded that PG was not the only mediator involved. Carnuccio *et al.* (1980) reported that cortisol (10 $\mu g\ ml^{-1}$) inhibited PG generation in rat leucocytes by the induction of a factor, probably protein or polypeptide in nature, which inhibits phospholipase A_2. Cortisol (1 $mg\ ml^{-1}$) did not however inhibit the *in vitro* release of PGE_2 from plaice skin, or the *in vivo* reaction when given once intravenously (10 $mg\ kg^{-1}$ fish) or intraperitoneally (5 $mg\ kg^{-1}$ fish) on 5 consecutive days before challenge. Similarly, chronic dosing with corticosterone did not inhibit the *in vivo* response (A. A. Anderson and T. C. Fletcher, unpublished). If the action of glucocorticoids is primarily on the traffic of cells, then it is perhaps not unexpected that cortisol has no effect on the immediate release of mediators from cells already present at the site of insult and effects would only be manifest in delayed responses dependent on leucocytic infiltration (for further details of the effects of corticosteroids on fish leucocytes see Ellis, 1981, this volume). Weinreb (1959) observed that cortisone delayed the cellular inflammatory response in rainbow trout. In tagging experiments, Morgan and Roberts (1976) reported that Atlantic salmon parr, *Salmo salar*, stressed by severe exercise at a high temperature developed extensive necrotic lesions at the site of tag insertion, but the effect of stressors on the inflammatory sequence has still to be detailed. Catecholamines can influence the release of pharmacological mediators in mammals (Piper, 1974) but at present we have no evidence for this in the acute cutaneous responses of the plaice, since intravenous adrenaline (10 $mg\ kg^{-1}$ fish) prior to challenge did not affect the erythema.

Epidermal ulceration is a characteristic of many fish diseases but the involvement of pharmacological mediators has not been established. Ulceration at sites of erythema in the plaice has not been observed during 6 weeks following injection of mediators. Atlantic salmon and rainbow trout exposed to the stressors of UV-A light and dietary photosensitizing compounds, present a dermatopathology with a marked resemblance to the lesions of Ulcerative Dermal Necrosis (Bullock and Roberts, 1979; see also abstract by Bullock, 1981, this volume). A dermal inflammatory response is only developed when the basement membrane is ruptured and vascular elements involved. The susceptibility of the skin to damage is however influenced by the physical properties imposed by the thickness of the epidermis and its mucous secretions, which in turn are under hormonal influence. There is a marked increase in epidermal thickness in salmonids during sexual maturation: greater thickness occurring in the male. Hay et al. (1976) examined androgen metabolism in the skin of the rainbow trout since it had been observed that 17α-methyltestosterone or 11-oxotestosterone induced skin thickening in immature or gonadectomized adult salmonids. Pickering (1977) observed changes in epidermal thickness of hatchery-reared brown trout, Salmo trutta, while during the spawning season the males had significantly fewer epidermal mucous cells than the females. In salmonids, saprolegniaceous fungal infection is often associated with sexual maturity (Neish, 1977), and data from Richards and Pickering (1978) indicate a greater incidence of infection in sexually mature ripe males than females, prior to spawning. Neish (1977) discussed the positive correlation between the incidence of saprolegniasis and the increased plasma corticosteroid levels observed during the normal maturation of the sockeye salmon and concluded this to be a stress related disease. However, more recent evidence from Pickering and Christie (1981), working with hatchery-reared brown trout, indicates that fungal infection in this species causes an elevation of plasma cortisol levels rather than the reverse (i.e. elevated cortisol levels predispose the fish to fungal infection).

Stressors which affect mucus production will interfere with its protective role (Fletcher, 1978). The stress of pH extremes (reviewed by Fromm, 1980), caused hypertrophy of mucous cells and stimulated mucus production in Salvelinus fontinalis (Daye and Garside, 1976). The effects of handling stress on the skin of the char, Salvelinus alpinus, revealed no significant change in size of mucous cells or in epidermal thickness, although a single handling increased the concentration of superficial goblet cells, with a doubling in numbers after one week. Repeated handling did not however maintain the elevated concentration (Pickering and Macey, 1977). Studies where "stress hormones", such as cortisol, have been used, have related to their osmoregulatory effects. In the euryhaline cottid, Leptocottus armatus, the goblet cells of the gill epithelium, but not the skin, are reduced in number by hypophysectomy but may be maintained by ovine prolactin (Marshall, 1979). Treatment of 5% SW-adapted Leptocottus with cortisol, decreased the number of goblet cells on the efferent face of the gill, mimicking the effects of SW acclimation, but had no effect on the skin (Marshall, 1979). The fish had received 10 μg cortisol g^{-1} fish in ten daily injections. A similar dose of adrenaline given to the mud-eel, Macrognathus aculeatum, resulted in both an increase in size and number of mucous cells in the gills within 2 h of injection (Ojha and Munshi, 1974).

The mucus can act as a carrier for alarm pheromones although substances in the urine from stressed fish might also be involved (Todd *et al.*, 1967). There is also some evidence from *Tilapia mossambica*, that stocking density can be controlled by a substance originating in the mucus and causing the release of pharmacological mediators in other individuals (Henderson-Arzapalo *et al.*, 1980). The explosive discharge of mucus from the epidermis of plaice subjected to enforced activity was shown by Murray and Fletcher (1976). The violence of the reactions perhaps depends on the degree of alarm evoked, because Pickering and Macey (1977) found no evidence for mucus discharge in the handled char. The release of haemoglobin into the cutaneous mucus of teleosts has been observed within 2–4 min of stressing and Smith and Ramos (1976) have suggested the presence of haemoglobin as a rapid test for assessing stress.

The type of glycoprotein, whether acid or neutral, produced in the goblet cells of the skin and gills of a freshwater (rainbow trout), estuarine (flounder, *Platichthys flesus*) and marine (plaice) species, was established (Fletcher *et al.*, 1976) as a basis for studying the effects of environmental stressors. Amongst these were sublethal concentrations (2 p.p.m.) of Cd^{2+}, to which plaice were exposed for 28 days. We observed no change in the sulphated glycoproteins of the skin mucous cells but the proportion of acid glyco-proteins in the gill filaments increased from 48 to 88%; the increase being in neuraminidase resistant sialomucins (R. Jones, T. C. Fletcher and L. Reid, unpublished). A similar histochemical shift to the production of acid glyco-proteins has been reported in the goblet cells of rat respiratory epithelia exposed to tobacco smoke (Jones *et al.*, 1973). The biochemical mechanism has not been elucidated but it is possible that this shift may represent some common response to an adverse environment: hormone levels perhaps affecting the synthesis of a particular class of glycoprotein. There is also the possibility that changes in glycoprotein type might influence the viscosity. Measurement of the viscosity of plaice sulphated cutaneous mucus at a shear rate of 1350 s^{-1} was 0·029 poise and was less viscous than a sialylated mucus (Lopez-Vidriero *et al.*, 1980).

III BLOOD

The final manifestation of the sequence of responses initiated by a stressor can appear to be far removed from an elevation in the level of a circulating hormone. However, it is by measurement of the latter, usually of cortisol in fish, that particular conditions can be recognized as stressors (e.g. Barton *et al.*, 1980). Monitoring other blood components can also provide information on the state of the fish. Woodward *et al.* (1979) observed accelerated fibrinolysis in fingerling coho salmon subjected to decompression stress and suggested that the rate of lysis might give some indication of the severity of stressors affecting the haemostatic system. Cairns and Christian (1978) found that plasma levels of lactic dehydrogenase (LDH) and creatine phosphokinase in rainbow trout were significant indicators of the stress due to repeated blood sampling. The same two enzymes increased when rainbow trout were infected with *Aeromonas* (Racicot *et al.*, 1975) and we have also found them elevated in turpentine-injected plaice (T. C. Fletcher and A. White, unpublished). These enzymes are a measure of stressor-induced tissue damage rather than the direct effects of hormones. The elevation of glucose however, is one of the general responses to stressors (Selye, 1950) and this was demonstrated in newly-captured plaice (Wardle, 1972) while Harbell *et al.* (1979) also found increased glucose, together with LDH, in coho salmon infected with *Vibrio anguillarum* (for a summary of stressor-induced changes in fish blood the reader is referred to Wedemeyer and McLeay, 1981, this volume).

In mammals, inflammation usually leads to an increase in serum copper, together with the copper-binding protein ceruloplasmin (Beisel, 1976). The latter, is one of a group of plasma proteins whose production is accelerated by most forms of tissue injury, infection or inflammation and are known as acute phase reactants (Gordon, 1976). A protein analogous to ceruloplasmin has been described in plaice serum and is elevated by 40% after exposure of the fish to 2 p.p.m. Cd^{2+} for 7 days (Syed *et al.*, 1979). An anti-inflammatory role has been described for ceruloplasmin in Sprague–Dawley rats (Denko, 1979) and its stressor-induced synthesis is perhaps an example of the resistance stage of the GAS. Similarly the metallothionein protein induced in the liver of plaice by Cd^{2+} (Overnell and Coombs, 1979) appears to protect against heavy metals. Stress can thus be a protective mechanism because glucocorticoids, through their ability to regulate protein synthesis, affect the biosynthesis of metallothionein (Etzel *et al.*, 1979) which can also regulate plasma zinc concentration.

Acute phase reactants have not been extensively studied in fish, although proteins resembling the classical reactant, C-reactive protein (CRP), have been identified in many teleosts (Baldo and Fletcher, 1973) and further characterized in *Cyclopterus lumpus* (White *et al.*, 1978) and the plaice (Pepys *et al.*, 1978). Many of the acute phase proteins are produced in the liver, although this has not yet been confirmed for fish. However, the mechanism connecting inflammation with synthesis of acute phase proteins is not completely explained although leucocytic endogenous mediators and hormones are involved (discussed by Gordon and Limaos, 1979). Since cortisol is known to be released as a result of injury and is found in the plaice (Wingfield and Grimm, 1977), we examined the effect of exogenous cortisol on the levels of CRP in serum from plaice subjected to inflammatory stimuli. At 24 h after injection, and taking the starting value as 100%, *E. coli* endotoxin (40 μg 100 g^{-1} fish, intraperitoneally) caused an elevation of CRP to 109% whilst turpentine (0·5 ml, subcutaneously) caused a decrease to 82% and saline controls to 93% (White *et al.*, 1981). Turpentine is a potent inflammatory agent in fish (Weinreb, 1959) and in mammals induces CRP (Kushner and Feldmann, 1978). The endotoxin elevation was significant when compared with the controls ($p < 0.01$, no. of fish = 15). Cortisol alone (2 mg 100 g^{-1} fish, intraperitoneally) also caused an elevation to 106% and when given with endotoxin appeared to be additive (116%). It had no effect on the response to turpentine however, which still declined to 86%. No simple explanation can be given for these results. Turpentine appeared to be a more severe stressor as judged by elevated blood glucose at 24 h, whereas endotoxin caused a slight decrease in glucose identical with the controls. Endotoxin from *E. coli* has been reported to cause a marked cortisol production in rainbow trout when given as 2·5 mg 100 g^{-1} fish, an amount far in excess of the levels in our experiment (Wedemeyer, 1969). Useful information would be obtained if endogenous cortisol could be eliminated. It would seem that inflammation *per se* does not cause an increase in CRP in the plaice, which is dependent on the type of inflammatory agent used. Although we do not know the function of CRP in fish, its evolutionary persistence would argue for its possible importance. In nature the fish is likely to encounter bacterial endotoxins and if these induce an elevation of plasma cortisol which enhances the production of CRP we are again encountering a beneficial effect of stress. We have only explored the influences governing CRP production but a whole battery of piscine homologues of other acute phase proteins, such as anti-proteases, complement components and fibrinogen, await comparable investigations.

IV FEVER

The relationship between environmental temperature and fish diseases has been discussed by Roberts (1975) whilst more theoretical aspects of temperature-stressors are considered by Künnemann and Precht (1979) and Elliott (1981, this volume). Each species has an optimum range, outside which it cannot survive. Short term temperature stressors can, however, induce changes originating from the GAS. Goldfish, *Carassius auratus*, acclimated to 22°–24°C and exposed to 2°C for 4 min, exhibit a decrease of 24% in the number of circulating lymphocytes, within 1 h of the cold shock, while neutrophils increase by 78% (Bennett and Neville, 1975). Changes in leucocyte numbers will in turn influence mechanisms such as phagocytosis.

Another, but rather different phenomenon related to temperature, is behavioural fever in fish (Covert and Reynolds, 1977). This is manifested as an increase in preferred temperature following injection of bacteria or other pyrogenic substances. Bacterial endotoxin has been found to cause fever in goldfish, the fish selecting a temperature 5·9°C above baseline (Reynolds *et al.*, 1978). Since the second stage of the GAS is one of adaptation, it would seem that behavioural thermoregulation might be a stress response to infection. It may have survival value, since goldfish injected with *Aeromonas hydrophila* show 84% survival if allowed to maintain a febrile temperature of 30·5°C compared with 64% survival at their baseline, afebrile temperature of 28°C (Covert and Reynolds, 1977). The absolute temperature does not seem to be as important as elevation above the temperature normal for the species. We have not had the opportunity of observing febrile reactions in our endotoxin-injected plaice. The stress of toxic substances, including organochlorines, organophosphates and heavy metals has been reported to affect the preferred temperature of juvenile *Salmo salar* (Peterson, 1976). There were indications that substances increasing the preferred temperature were more toxic at low temperatures and *vice versa*.

Amongst the multiplicity of reactions of mammals to endotoxin (Bradley, 1979) is a marked elevation of body temperature. Fever can also be caused in man by etiocholanolone, a naturally occurring steroid metabolite, arising from androgens but with no known hormonal activity. Correlated with the amount of fever it induces, is an increase in CRP (McAdam *et al.*, 1978). In plaice however, etiocholanolone causes a slight decrease in CRP levels, comparable with the controls and distinct from the elevation in CRP caused by endotoxin over the same period (White *et al.*, 1981). Diverse pyrogens share a final common pathway (in mammals), whereby many phagocytic leucocytes produce and release a small molecular weight protein, known as leucocytic or endogenous pyrogen (EP). It is this substance which is thought to trigger the biochemical reactions in the hypothalamic thermoregulatory centre, resulting in the elevation of the temperature set point. It is not known whether the activators of fever induce the production of an EP-like protein in the fish, although clearly some mediator must be responsible. The drug, acetaminophen, an anti-pyretic drug for mammals also results in attenuation of fever in the sunfish, *Lepomis macrochirus* (Reynolds, 1977).

A leucocytic endogenous mediator (LEM) obtained from rabbit peritoneal granulocytes, caused elevation in plasma levels of CRP and body temperature and a decrease in plasma zinc and iron, when injected into rabbits (Merriman *et al.*, 1975). Evidence is presented by Kampschmidt *et al.* (1978) that EP and LEM are similar and may in fact be identical. The decrease in iron (discussed by Kluger, 1979) could reduce the growth of pathogenic organisms and have protective value. It has been reported that the inhibitory effect of lumpsucker serum on fungal growth, is reversed by the addition of iron (Fletcher and Popat, 1979).

It appears that regardless of the type of pathogen, a group of reactions, seemingly of a defensive nature, can be initiated from the activation of a class of compounds described from their origin as leucocytic endogenous mediator(s). It has not been established whether "stress hormones" are involved in the formation and/or release of LEM, but adrenal glucocorticoids are necessary for the synthesis of some acute phase proteins in conjunction with LEM (Thompson et al., 1976). One might speculate that the responses induced by LEM are an extension of the second stage of the GAS, forming a subsidiary, general resistance syndrome.

V CONCLUDING REMARKS

Since by my definition, any factor that causes an exaggerated response in an organism might be considered a stressor, I have had a vast amount of literature from which to draw. I have however selected what might, at least in the case of acute phase proteins and fever, be elements not usually considered in relation to stress in fish. These reflect my own interests and my efforts to arrange the facts relating to defence mechanisms in fish into some unified concept. I acknowledge my debt to my collaborators, especially Ann White and Brian Baldo, who have contributed many of the facts. Although I may not yet be able to view them from sufficient distance to see a coherent pattern, the facts remain, and later workers will perhaps arrange them in a more harmonious whole.

REFERENCES

Anderson, A. A., Fletcher, T. C. and Smith, G. M. (1979). The release of prostaglandin E$_2$ from the skin of the plaice, *Pleuronectes platessa* L. *Br. J. Pharmac.* **66**, 547–552.
Baldo, B. A. and Fletcher, T. C. (1973). C-reactive protein-like precipitins in plaice. *Nature, Lond.* **246**, 145–146.
Baldo, B. A. and Fletcher, T. C. (1975). Phylogenetic aspects of hypersensitivity: immediate hypersensitivity reactions in flatfish. In *Immunologic Phylogeny* (W. H. Hildemann and A. A. Benedict, eds), pp. 365–372. London and New York: Plenum Press.
Barton, B. A., Peter, R. E. and Paulencu, C. R. (1980). Plasma cortisol levels of fingerling rainbow trout (*Salmo gairdneri*) at rest, and subject to handling, confinement, transport and stocking. *Can. J. Fish. Aquat. Sci.* **37**, 805–811.

Beisel, W. R. (1976). Trace elements in infectious processes. *Med. Clins N. Am.* **60**, 831–849.

Bennett, M. F. and Neville, C. G. (1975). Effects of cold shock on the distribution of leucocyte in goldfish, *Carassius auratus. J. comp. Physiol.* **98**, 213–216.

Bradley, S. G. (1979). Cellular and molecular mechanisms of action of bacterial endotoxins. *A. Rev. Microbiol.* **33**, 67–94.

Bullock, A. M. (1981). The effect of ultraviolet radiation on teleost epidermis (Abstract). In *Stress and Fish* (A. D. Pickering, ed.), pp. 345–346. London and New York: Academic Press.

Bullock, A. M. and Roberts, R. J. (1979). Induction of UDN-like lesions in salmonid fish by exposure to ultraviolet light in the presence of phototoxic agents. *J. Fish Dis.* **2**, 439–441.

Bullock, G. L. and Snieszko, S. F. (1969). Bacteria in blood and kidney of apparently healthy hatchery trout. *Trans. Am. Fish. Soc.* **98**, 268–271.

Cairns, M. A. and Christian, A. R. (1978). Effects of hemorrhagic stress on several blood parameters in adult rainbow trout (*Salmo gairdneri*). *Trans. Am. Fish. Soc.* **107**, 334–340.

Carnuccio, R., Di Rosa, M. and Persico, P. (1980). Hydrocortisone-induced inhibitor of prostaglandin biosynthesis in rat leucocytes. *Br. J. Pharmac.* **68**, 14–16.

Covert, J. B. and Reynolds, W. W. (1977). Survival value of fever in fish. *Nature, Lond.* **267**, 43–45.

Daye, P. G. and Garside, E. T. (1976). Histopathologic changes in surficial tissues of brook trout, *Salvelinus fontinalis* (Mitchill), exposed to acute and chronic levels of pH. *Can. J. Zool.* **54**, 2140–2155.

Denko, C. W. (1979). Protective role of ceruloplasmin in inflammation. *Agents and Actions*, **9**, 333–336.

Elliott, J. M. (1981). Some aspects of thermal stress on freshwater teleosts. In *Stress and Fish* (A. D. Pickering, ed.), pp. 209–245. London and New York: Academic Press.

Ellis, A. E. (1981). Stress and the modulation of defence mechanisms in fish. In *Stress and Fish* (A. D. Pickering, ed.), pp. 147–169. London and New York: Academic Press.

Esch, G. W. and Hazen, T. C. (1978). Thermal ecology and stress: a case history for red-sore disease in largemouth bass. In *Energy and Environmental Stress in Aquatic Systems* (J. H. Thorp and J. W. Gibbons, eds), pp. 331–363. Technical Information Center, U.S. Department of Energy. CONF-771114.

Esch, G. W., Gibbons, J. W. and Bourque, J. E. (1975). An analysis of the relationship between stress and parasitism. *Am. Midl. Nat.* **93**, 339–353.

Etzel, K. R., Shapiro, S. G. and Cousins, R. J. (1979). Regulation of liver metallothionein and plasma zinc by the glucocorticoid dexamethasone. *Biochem. biophys. Res. Commun.* **89**, 1120–1126.

Finn, J. P. and Nielson, N. O. (1971). The inflammatory response of rainbow trout. *J. Fish Biol.* **3**, 463–478.

Fletcher, H. J. and Popat, Y. H. (1979). Inhibition of germination of *Trichophyton mentagrophytes* by sera. *Trans. Br. mycol. Soc.* **72**, 154–155.

Fletcher, T. C. (1978). Defence mechanisms in fish. In *Biochemical and Biophysical Perspectives in Marine Biology* (D. C. Malins and J. R. Sargent, eds), Vol. 4, pp. 189–222. London and New York: Academic Press.

Fletcher, T. C. and Baldo, B. A. (1974). Immediate hypersensitivity responses in flatfish. *Science, N.Y.* **185**, 360–361.

Fletcher, T. C., Jones, R. and Reid, L. (1976). Identification of glycoproteins in goblet cells of epidermis and gill of plaice (*Pleuronectes platessa* L.); flounder (*Platichthys flesus* (L.)) and rainbow trout (*Salmo gairdneri* Richardson). *Histochem. J.* **8**, 597–608.

Fromm, P. O. (1980). A review of some physiological and toxicological responses of freshwater fish to acid stress. *Environ. Biol. Fish.* **5**, 79–93.

Gordon, A. H. (1976). The acute phase plasma proteins. In *Plasma Protein Turnover* (R. Bianchi, G. Mariani and A. S. McFarlane, eds), pp. 381–394. London: Macmillan Press Ltd.

Gordon, A. H. and Limaos, E. A. (1979). Effects of bacterial endotoxin and corticosteroids on plasma concentrations of α_2 macroglobulin, haptoglobin and fibrinogen in rats. *Br. J. exp. Path.* **60**, 434–440.

Harbell, S. C., Hodgins, H. O. and Schiewe, M. H. (1979). Studies on the pathogenesis of vibriosis in coho salmon *Oncorhynchus kisutch* (Walbaum). *J. Fish Dis.* **2**, 391–404.

Hay, J. B., Hodgins, M. B. and Roberts, R. J. (1976). Androgen metabolism in skin and skeletal muscle of the rainbow trout (*Salmo gairdneri*) and in accessory sexual organs of the spur dog-fish (*Squalus acanthias*). *Gen. comp. Endocr.* **29**, 402–413.

Henderson-Arzapalo, A., Stickney, R. R. and Lewis, D. H. (1980). Immune hypersensitivity in intensively cultured *Tilapia* species. *Trans. Am. Fish. Soc.* **109**, 244–247.

Ingram, G. A. (1980). Substances involved in the natural resistance of fish to infection—a review. *J. Fish Biol.* **16**, 23–60.

Jones, R., Bolduc, P. and Reid, L. (1973). Goblet cell glycoprotein and tracheal gland hypertrophy in rat airways: the effect of tobacco smoke with or without the anti-inflammatory agent phenylmethyloxadiazole. *Br. J. exp. Path.* **54**, 229–239.

Kampschmidt, R. F., Pulliam, L. A. and Merriman, C. R. (1978). Further similarities of endogenous pyrogen and leukocytic endogenous mediator. *Am. J. Physiol.* **235**, C118–C121.

Kluger, M. J. (1979). *Fever: its biology, evolution and function.* 195 pp. Princeton, N.J.: Princeton University Press.

Künnemann, H. and Precht, H. (1979). The influence of environmental temperature and salinity on animals, I and II. *Zool. Anz.* **202**, 145–162.

Kuschner, I. and Feldmann, G. (1978). Control of the acute phase response. *J. exp. Med.* **148**, 466–477.

Lopez-Vidriero, M. T., Jones, R., Reid, L. and Fletcher, T. C. (1980). Analysis of skin mucus of plaice *Pleuronectes platessa* L. *J. comp. Path.* **90**, 415–420.

Love, R. M. (1970). *The Chemical Biology of Fishes.* 547 pp. London and New York: Academic Press.

Marshall, W. S. (1979). Effects of salinity acclimation, prolactin, growth hormone, and cortisol on the mucous cells of *Leptocottus armatus* (Teleostei; Cottidae). *Gen. comp. Endocr.* **37**, 358–368.

Mazeaud, M. M., Mazeaud, F. and Donaldson, E. M. (1977). Primary and secondary effects of stress in fish: some new data with a general review, *Trans. Am. Fish. Soc.* **106**, 201–212.

McAdam, K. P. W. J., Elin, R. J., Sipe, J. D. and Wolff, S. M. (1978). Changes in human serum amyloid A and C-reactive protein after etiocholanolone-induced inflammation. *J. clin. Invest.* **61**, 390–394.

182   T. C. FLETCHER

Merriman, C. R., Pulliam, L. A. and Kampschmidt, R. F. (1975). Effect of leukocytic endogenous mediator on C-reactive protein in rabbits. *Proc. Soc. exp. Biol. Med.* **149**, 782–784.

Morgan, R. I. G. and Roberts, R. J. (1976). The histopathology of salmon tagging IV. The effect of severe exercise on the induced tagging lesion in salmon parr at two temperatures. *J. Fish Biol.* **8**, 289–292.

Murray, C. K. and Fletcher, T. C. (1976). The immunohistochemical localization of lysozyme in the plaice (*Pleuronectes platessa* L.) tissues. *J. Fish Biol.* **9**, 329–334.

Neish, G. A. (1977). Observations on saprolegniasis of adult sockeye salmon, *Oncorhynchus nerka* (Walbaum). *J. Fish Biol.* **10**, 513–522.

Ojha, J. and Munshi, J. S. D. (1974). Histochemical and histophysiological observations on the specialised branchial glands of a fresh water mud-eel *Macrognathus aculeatum* (BLOCH) (Mastacembelidae, Pisces). *Mikroskopie*, **30**, 1–16.

Overnell, J. and Coombs, T. L. (1979). Purification and properties of plaice metallothionein, a cadmium-binding protein from the liver of the plaice (*Pleuronectes platessa*). *Biochem. J.* **183**, 277–283.

Parrillo, J. E. and Fauci, A. S. (1979). Mechanisms of glucocorticoid action on immune processes. *A. Rev. Pharmac. Toxic.* **19**, 179–201.

Pepys, M. B., Dash, A. C., Fletcher, T. C., Richardson, N., Munn, E. A. and Feinstein, A. (1978). Analogues in other mammals and in fish of human plasma proteins, C-reactive protein and amyloid P component *Nature, Lond.* **273**, 168–170.

Peterson, R. H. (1976). Temperature selection of juvenile Atlantic salmon (*Salmo salar*) as influenced by various toxic substances. *J. Fish. Res. Bd Can.* **33**, 1722–1730.

Pickering, A. D. (1977). Seasonal changes in the epidermis of the brown trout *Salmo trutta* (L.). *J. Fish Biol.* **10**, 561–566.

Pickering, A. D. (1981). Introduction. In *Stress and Fish* (A. D. Pickering, ed.), pp. 1–9. London and New York: Academic Press.

Pickering, A. D. and Christie, P. (1981). Changes in the concentrations of plasma cortisol and thyroxine during sexual maturation of the hatchery-reared brown trout, *Salmo trutta* L. *Gen. comp. Endocr.* **44** (in press).

Pickering, A. D. and Macey, D. J. (1977). Structure, histochemistry and the effect of handling on the mucous cells of the epidermis of the char *Salvelinus alpinus* (L.). *J. Fish Biol.* **10**, 505–512.

Piper, P. J. (1974). Mediators of anaphylactic hypersensitivity. In *Progress in Immunology II* (L. Brent and J. Holborow, eds), Vol. 4, pp. 51–59. Amsterdam: North-Holland Publ. Co.

Racicot, J. G., Gaudet, M. and Leray, C. (1975). Blood and liver enzymes in rainbow trout (*Salmo gairdneri* Rich.) with emphasis on their diagnostic use: study of CCl$_4$ toxicity and a case of *Aeromonas* infection. *J. Fish Biol.* **7**, 825–835.

Reynolds, W. W. (1977). Fever and antipyresis in the blue gill sunfish, *Lepomis macrochirus*. *Comp. Biochem. Physiol.* **57C**, 165–167.

Reynolds, W. W., Covert, J. B. and Casterlin, M. E. (1978). Febrile responses of goldfish *Carassius auratus* (L.) to *Aeromonas hydrophila* and to *Escherichia coli* endotoxin. *J. Fish Dis.* **1**, 271–273.

Richards, R. H. and Pickering, A. D. (1978). Frequency and distribution patterns of *Saprolegnia* infection in wild and hatchery-reared brown trout *Salmo trutta* L. and char *Salvelinus alpinus* (L.) *J. Fish Dis.* **1**, 69–82.

Roberts, R. J. (1975). The effects of temperature on diseases and their histopathological manifestations in fish. In *The Pathology of Fishes* (W. E. Ribelin and G. Migaki, eds), pp. 477–496. Madison, Wisconsin: The University of Wisconsin Press.

Selye, H. (1950). Stress and the general adaptation syndrome. *Br. med. J.* **1**, 1383–1392.

Selye, H. (1976). *The Stress of Life.* 515pp. New York: McGraw–Hill Book Co.

Smith, A. C. and Ramos, F. (1976). Occult haemogloblin in fish skin mucus as an indicator of early stress. *J. Fish Biol.* **9**, 537–541.

Syed, A., Coombs, T. L. and Keir, H. M. (1979). Effects of cadmium on copper-dependent enzymes in the plaice, *Pleuronectes platessa. Biochem. Soc. Trans.* **7**, 711–713.

Thompson, W. L., Abeles, F. B., Beall, F. A., Dinterman, R. E. and Wannemacher, R. W. (1976). Influence of the adrenal glucocorticoids on the stimulation of synthesis of hepatic ribonucleic acid and plasma acute-phase globulins by leucocytic endogenous mediator. *Biochem. J.* **156**, 25–32.

Todd, J. H., Atema, J. and Bardach, J. E. (1967). Chemical communication in social behaviour of a fish, the yellow bullhead (*Ictalurus natalis*). *Science, N.Y.* **158**, 672–673.

Wardle, C. S. (1972). The changes in blood glucose in *Pleuronectes platessa* following capture from the wild: a stress reaction: *J. mar. biol. Ass. U.K.* **52**, 635–651.

Wedemeyer, G. A. (1969). Pituitary activation by bacterial endotoxins in the rainbow trout (*Salmo gairdneri*). *J. Bact.* **100**, 542–543.

Wedemeyer, G. A. and McLeay, D. J. (1981). Methods for determining the tolerance of fishes to environmental stressors. In *Stress and Fish* (A. D. Pickering, ed.), pp. 247–275. London and New York: Academic Press.

Wedemeyer, G. A., Meyer, F. P. and Smith, L. (1976). *Environmental Stress and Fish Diseases.* 192pp. Neptune, N.J.: T.F.H. Publ. Inc.

Weinreb, E. L. (1959). Studies on the histology and histopathology of the rainbow trout, *Salmo gairdneri irideus*. II. Effects of induced inflammation and cortisone treatment on the digestive organs. *Zoologica, N.Y.* **44**, 45–52.

White, A., Fletcher, T. C., Towler, C. M. and Baldo, B. A. (1978). Isolation of a C-reactive protein-like precipitin from the eggs of the lumpsucker (*Cyclopterus lumpus* L.). *Comp. Biochem. Physiol.* **61C**, 331–336.

White, A., Fletcher, T. C., Pepys, M. B. and Baldo, B. A. (1981). The effect of inflammatory agents on C-reactive protein and serum amyloid P-component levels in plaice (*Pleuronectes platessa* L.) serum. *Comp. Biochem. Physiol.* (in press).

Wingfield, J. C. and Grimm, A. S. (1977). Seasonal changes in plasma cortisol, testosterone and oestradiol-17β in the plaice, *Pleuronectes platessa* L. *Gen. comp. Endocr.* **31**, 1–11.

Woodward, J. J., Casillas, E., Smith, L. S. and D'Aoust, B. G. (1979). Rapid decompression stress accelerates fibrinolysis in fingerling salmon. *J. Fish. Res. Bd Can.* **36**, 592–594.

9. Stress, Environment and Reproduction in Teleost Fish

R. BILLARD, C. BRY and C. GILLET

Laboratoire de Physiologie des Poissons, I.N.R.A., 78350 Jouy-en-Josas, France

---

Abstract. The effects of acute or chronic stress on reproduction and hormone levels are well documented in higher vertebrates. On the contrary, little information is available on fish. It is known that some aspects of fish reproduction are changed by various modifications to the environment and that some of these changes may occur under conditions of stress. Reproduction can be stimulated or inhibited by environmental factors such as temperature, photoperiod, food availability and water quality, by overcrowding and social interaction and by other stresses such as handling, captivity and confinement. Under these conditions, several steps of the reproductive cycle can be blocked: gametogenesis (initiation, completion, quantity of eggs [fecundity] and quality of gametes); oocyte maturation and ovulation; spermiation; spawning behaviour.

There are only a few data in fish showing interactions between gonadotrope and corticotrope systems and the effect of environmental factors on the endocrinology of reproduction.

I INTRODUCTION

The fish's environment is a complex system with varying water quality (physical and chemical composition), current velocity, abundance and type of aquatic vegetation, light intensity and periodicity, temperature, food availability and social interaction. In the case of cultivated or managed species, man's influence is of major importance when fish are extensively or intensively reared in captivity for breeding, stocking or human consumption. Under these conditions the fish are submitted to confinement, handling, grading and drug treatment. Man may also have an indirect effect on fish *via* changes made in the natural environment and through pollution. Most of the environmental factors fluctuate throughout the year in both temperate and tropical zones, and fish are adapted in various ways to these changes. Some fish are even adapted for survival in an apparently hostile environment, tolerating sub-zero temperatures and high pressure in the ocean as well as dry conditions. Fish respond to these environmental changes in many ways by modifying their hormone or neuro-hormone secretion, metabolism and behaviour (for a review see Chavin, 1973).

A stress response may be defined as the series of rather non-specific reactions of an organism to any of the exacting demands made on it (for further discussion of this concept see Pickering, 1981, this volume). This phenomenon involves both physiological and behavioural reactions which may help the fish adapt to a new situation. A stress maintained over a long period may exceed the adjustment capabilities of the animal, severely disturbing growth and reproduction. Neuro-endocrine activation, among other reactions, has been shown to occur under adverse conditions in various fish species, leading to the secretion of corticosteroids and catecholamines (see Mazeaud *et al.*, 1977; Strange *et al.*, 1977). The interrenal gland however may also be activated in natural, non-stressful situations, especially in the female fish at ovulation and spawning time. Thus, the same endocrine system (pituitary–interrenal axis) may be activated by factors inhibiting reproduction and by others triggering final maturation. Moreover, the nature of the response to external elements depends upon internal factors and endogenous rhythms, and also varies according to the species and between individuals of the same species. For example, Mitton and Koehn (1976) noted individual differences in the response of *Fundulus heteroclitus* to temperature. Similarly, Sawara and Egami (1977) demonstrated differences in the gonadal response of *Oryzias latipes* collected from different localities to photoperiod changes and Weibe (1968) showed that the environmental factors which stimulate gametogenesis in *Cymatogaster aggregata* are not the same for males and females. The response of fish to changes in the environment also varies with respect to the degree of domestication of the species.

The present paper deals with the effects of environmental factors, including situations which can be considered stressful, on the reproductive function in teleost fish.

II FACTORS INTERFERING WITH REPRODUCTION

(a) Temperature, Thermoperiod and Photoperiod

Temperature level and changes in temperature and photoperiod during the year are the main physical environmental factors in the control of fish reproduction in the temperate zones. The importance of these factors varies with the species and the stage of the reproductive cycle.

The water temperature directly affects fish physiology, mode of reproduction, growth rate and population dynamics and structure. Hokanson (1977) classified temperate zone fish as stenotherms, mesotherms and eurytherms, according to their thermal requirements (Table I—for a further discussion of temperature relationships in fish the reader is referred to Elliott, 1981, this volume). An optimal temperature level is necessary for reproduction. In cyprinids, gametogenesis is sensitive to both low and high temperatures (Gillet et al., 1977a, b); low temperatures are required to initiate gametogenesis (Ahsan, 1966; de Vlaming, 1974; Gillet et al., 1977a, b), whilst high temperatures stimulate gonadotropin (maturational hormone) secretion and temporarily inhibit gametogenesis (Gillet et al., 1977b; Gillet and Billard, 1977; Gillet et al., 1978). Warm-water fish such as the guppy, Poecilia reticulata, show optimal spermatogenesis at 25°C (Billard, 1968), coinciding with the thermal preference (Billard, 1968; Johansen and Cross, 1980). In rainbow trout, Salmo gairdneri, gameto- genesis occurs at either 8 or 18°C (Billard and Breton, 1977), but the fish do not ovulate and the early stages of embryonic development are perturbed at 18°C (K. Goriczko, personal communication; Kazakov, 1971). Salmonid gamete physiology is also affected by temperature; the fertilization rate decreases slightly when artificial insemination is carried out near 0°C (Billard, 1980).

During the year, the temperature varies simultaneously with the photo- period, and the effects of these two variables can only be distinguished by experimentation. The extensive data in the literature on this subject have been thoroughly reviewed by de Vlaming (1974), Htun-Han (1977) and Peter and Crim (1979). A typical example of a strong photoperiodic influence on reproduction is that of salmonid gametogenesis (sper- matogenesis and vitellogenesis) which occurs normally under decreasing photoperiod but which can be advanced if the decreasing photoperiod is artificially advanced (Breton and Billard, 1977) or if the annual photoperiod is contracted into a 6-month period (Whitehead et al., 1978). However, other external or internal factors must also be involved because there are several indications that gametogenesis occurs normally when trout are kept under constant light or constant dark from hatching (Pyle, 1969; Bieniarz, 1973). The photoperiodic effect is more subtle in other teleost fish; the increasing daylength in late winter facilitates gonad growth in goldfish, Carassius auratus (Gillet et al., 1978), and tench, Tinca tinca (Quillier, 1981), and induces nycthemeral fluctuations in plasma gonadotropin (Hontela and Peter, 1978; Gillet et al., 1980). A slight photoperiodic effect is evident in Couesius plumbeus when kept at low temperatures (Ahsan,

TABLE I Classification of some Temperate Climate Freshwater Fish According to Water Temperature Requirements: Effects of Temperature and Photoperiod on Gametogenesis and Spawning.

Classification	Ultimate upper incipient lethal temperature	Physiological optimum	Gametogenesis			Spawning		Examples
			Season	Temp.	Photop.	Season	Temp.	
Temperate stenotherm	<26°C	<20°C	Summer	<20°C	↗	Autumn to spring	5–15°C	Salmonids
Temperate mesotherm	28–34°C	20–28°C	Summer to winter	<12°C	↘	Spring	2–23°C	Percids Pike
Temperate eurytherm	>34°C	>28°C	Summer and spring	>10–12°C	↖	Spring and summer	>15–18°C	Cyprinids

1966). Long days are necessary for gonad growth in the stickleback, *Gasterosteus aculeatus*, (Baggerman, 1969) whose photostimulatory sensitivity shows a daily rhythm with an optimum 14 to 16 h after the onset of the light period (Baggerman, 1972).

In conclusion, changes in temperature and light are the obvious cues for temperate zone fish. Circannual changes in photoperiod act mainly on long-term processes like gametogenesis, while temperature fluctuation influences the short-term processes such as spermiation, oocyte maturation, ovulation and oviposition. Light and temperature may interact in goldfish where ovulation is synchronized with circadian changes in light (Stacey *et al.*, 1979a, b).

(b) Water Quality

The physico-chemical properties of the water, represented by such factors as current velocity, dissolved oxygen content, pH and salinity are prime factors in the survival of aquatic animals and may be critical for reproduction. For example, the water current velocity has been shown to influence the spawning activities of *Tilapia nilotica* (Maruyama and Nagashima, 1978).

(i) *Acidic waters.* The effect of acidic water on fish physiology is now well documented (see review by Fromm, 1980). Low pH decreases fecundity and egg fertility in fathead minnows, *Pimphales promelas* (Mount, 1973), flagfish, *Jordanella floridae* (Ruby *et al.*, 1977; Craig and Baski, 1977) and brook trout, *Salvelinus fontinalis* (Menendez, 1976). The final part of the reproductive cycle is also disturbed. For example, Beamish (1976) noted that female fish did not release their ova in acidic waters and low pH is reported to adversely affect successful fertilization (Billard, 1980), embryogenesis (Daye and Garside, 1980) and hatching (Johansson *et al.*, 1973; Mount, 1973; Peterson *et al.*, 1980). In acid water, *Catostomus commersoni* shows a reduced feeding response and weight loss which may interfere with reproduction (Beamish, 1972).

(ii) *Dissolved oxygen content.* Little information is available concerning the direct effect of reduced water oxygen levels on reproduction. A low level of dissolved oxygen depresses the growth of the gonad in goldfish (Gillet *et al.*, 1981) and an oxygen concentration of less than 1 mg l^{-1} prevents spawning in the fathead minnow (Brungs, 1971). Similarly, $2\text{--}4 \text{ mg l}^{-1}$ dissolved oxygen prevents spawning in the black crappie, *Pomoxis nigromaculatus* (Siefert and Herman, 1977; Carlson and Herman, 1978).

(iii) *Salinity.* In some euryhaline species, several stages of the reproductive process are inhibited in fresh water. For instance in Israel, *Mugil cephalus* kept in fresh water do not reproduce; ovarian development is inhibited when the females are kept in freshwater ponds and ovulation is inhibited in Lake Kinneret (Abraham and Blanc, 1966; Blanc and Abraham, 1968; Eckstein, 1975). However, Stequert (1972) stated that *Mugil labrosus* spawns normally in fresh water in the Arcachon Basin in France although he also indicated that confinement of female sea bass, *Dicentrarchus labrax*, in fresh water inhibits oocyte maturation and ovulation. Nevertheless, it seems that complete spermatogenesis and spermiation may occur in male sea bass in salinities as low as 1–2‰ (Roblin, 1980).

(iv) *Pollution*. The effects of numerous pollutants are detrimental to gametogenesis and reproduction. Global studies show that fish fecundity is reduced in a polluted environment (Zalewski, 1979). Sometimes, the depressed reproduction observed in polluted water cannot be related to any particular factor, which suggests a possible synergism of the various sources of pollution (Dean and Bailey, 1979).

Pollutants such as selenium (Cumbie and Van Horn, 1979), copper (Benoit, 1975), mercury (Kihlstrom et al., 1971), waste-oil (Hedtke and Puglisi, 1980) and the pesticides PCB (Nebeker et al., 1974; Bengtsson, 1980), parathion (Billard and de Kinkelin, 1970) and DDT (Macek, 1968a; Saxena and Garg, 1978) may alter or inhibit various steps in fish reproduction. In addition, pesticides accumulated in the ovaries can be harmful during embryogenesis and reduce hatching and fry survival (Burdick et al., 1964, 1972). Brook trout fed a sublethal concentration of DDT are more sensitive to stress, and the mortality of DDT-exposed fish is caused by interactions with various factors, including the physiological state associated with spawning (Macek, 1968b).

(c) Food Availability

Availability of food is also an important factor affecting reproduction. A lack of food usually leads to decreased fecundity in the plaice, *Pleuronectes platessa* (Bagenal, 1966), salmonids (Scott, 1962; Bagenal, 1969), the roach, *Rutilus rutilus* (Kuznetzov and Khalitov, 1978) and in the guppy (Dahlgren, 1979). Starved females tend to produce fewer eggs but the egg size remains the same. However, the decreased egg diameter in severely starved brown trout, *Salmo trutta* L., fed dry pellets at a rate of 0·4% body wt day^{-1} is accompanied by a reduction of absolute fecundity but an increased relative fecundity (Fig. 1). The problem of food availability, linked to the size of the territory, may be different for males and females (Ebersole, 1980). A decrease in fecundity was also attributed to a copepod infestation in rainbow trout (Gall et al., 1972).

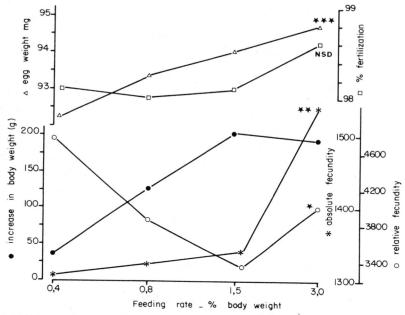

Fig. 1   Effect of feeding rate on absolute (total number of eggs stripped per female) and relative (number of eggs kg^{-1} body wt) fecundity, egg weight and egg fertility of the brown trout. Body weight increase corresponds to the feeding period from March to September (Billard and de Fremont, 1980. Comparison by analysis of variance: one star $p < 0.05$, two stars $p < 0.01$, three stars $p < 0.001$.

(d) Social Environment

Social pressure caused by overcrowding may interfere with fecundity and the final step of reproduction independently of food availability. In poecilids, the follicles show atresia and vitellogenesis is inhibited by high population densities (Ball, 1960) and a decreased fecundity has been reported in pike which is possibly related to high population density (Kipling and Frost, 1969). Social pressure may be direct (aggression) or indirect (pheromonal mediation). There is increasing evidence of pheromonal intervention in fish. Inhibiting or crowding factors reduce fecundity in guppies (Rose, 1959) and inhibit spawning in goldfish (Swingle, 1953; Greene, 1964; Whiteside and Richan, 1969), the zebrafish *Brachydanio rerio* (Yu and Perlmutter, 1970) and largemouth bass, *Micropterus salmoides* (Chew, 1972). These crowding factors (sometimes metabolites) reduce growth and cardiac activity, induce embryonic mortality and shorten the life-span. Pfuderer *et al.* (1974) attempted to extract the crowding factors;

some biological activity was found in the pthalate esters associated with neutral lipids. It appears then that overcrowding affects reproduction *via* food availability, visual interactions and also pheromone release. Overcrowding may be deterimental to spawning activities, especially if there are too many females for the number of spawning sites. In some species, adult males fight vigorously if stocked too densely.

Pheromones are also positively involved in reproductive migrations (review by Solomon, 1977; Saglio, 1979a) and spawning. Sex pheromones are implicated in the attraction between males and females during spawning in salmonids (Newcombe and Hartman, 1973, Emanuel and Dodson, 1979) and in other species (for review see Saglio, 1979b). In the female zebrafish, *Brachydanio rerio*, a pheromone released by the male stimulates ovulation and counteracts the repressive effect of the metabolites produced by the fish (Chen and Martinich, 1975). In the same species, a sex pheromone attracting conspecifics repels a closely related species, *B. albolineatus* (Bloom and Perlmutter, 1978).

(e) Stress Associated with Fish Cultivation

Man is a generator of numerous stresses especially when fish are bred in captivity. The fish are often confined and are captured by net, electricity or even poison! They undergo transport, transfer, handling and drug treatment and are subjected to changes in water quality and flow rate. This may result in physical injury and various endocrine and metabolic responses.

We have little detailed information on the effect of such procedures on reproduction in fish. According to a study by Vincent (1960), domesticated brook trout, hatchery-bred for 90 years, were less sensitive, in terms of mortality, to the concentration of accumulated water metabolites and to high temperature but had less stamina than wild trout. Domestication resulted in better growth in hatchery conditions but higher mortality in small streams. Therefore, experimental results depend on the history of the fish population studied.

Some effects of handling on reproduction have been reported and most are deleterious. A typical example was given by de Montalambert *et al.* (1978) who showed inhibition of the ovarian response to exogenous gonadotropin and follicular atresia after handling and captivity in pike, *Esox lucius* (Fig. 2). Horseman *et al.* (1976) and Meier and Horseman (1977) observed that various species of vertebrates, when handled daily at the same time of day, showed marked changes in gonad weight. In *Tilapia aurea*, noise or mechanical stimulation, when given 16 h after lights-on, induced a *rise* in testis weight. The case of *Mugil cephalus* (Abraham and Blanc, 1966) is interesting: oogenesis does not occur in freshwater ponds probably due to

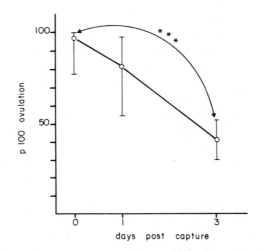

Fig. 2   Effect of time between capture (day 0) and hypophysation with a salmon pituitary extract on ovulation rate in female pike. After capture the fish were transported for 6 h, then kept in captivity until ovulation (vertical bars show confidence limits at the 95% level of probability). Number of fish: 8 (day 0), 7 (day 1), 8 (day 3). *** $p < 0.001$. (From de Montalembert *et al.*, 1978).

confinement but it is completed in lakes; if fish are kept in fresh water, they do not ovulate. Oogenesis and ovulation occur in sea water, except when fish are kept in ponds, again underlining the deleterious effect of confinement. Scott (1979) mentioned that the transfer of female minnows, *Phoxinus phoxinus*, from the natural environment to an aquarium tank resulted in massive atresia of vitellogenic oocytes within a few days. A decrease of ova fertilizability has been reported after ovulated females (Marriott, 1973) or embryos (Godfrey, 1957; Marriott, 1973) were given an electric shock. However, fecundity was not modified after immature rainbow trout were exposed to a direct pulsating current (Maxfield *et al.*, 1971).

(f) Synergism and Interaction between Factors

Some of the factors mentioned above were tested independently. Recent studies have tried to show the interaction of several factors affecting fish in the wild and influencing reproduction. An example of such an interaction was reported by Scott (1979) who repeated Bullough's experiments (1939, 1942) in the minnow showing that final vitellogenesis could be stimulated by increasing the photoperiod in late spring. Scott (1979) observed that the GSI increased under a rising photoperiod only when the rearing temperature was high. The GSI rose to 10% and 10% of the oocytes were yolk-laden; these values are higher in nature (12–14% and 20%, respectively). A similar elevation was obtained after a sudden increase in daylength from 8 to 15 h within one week in February–March. Ecological observation showed that when the temperature is less than 8°C in nature, the minnow stays in relative darkness under stones during the daytime. Above that temperature, it swims in open water and is, consequently, exposed to a relatively long photoperiod. In nature, therefore, temperature-sensitive behavioural changes may lead to a sudden exposure to the photoperiod thereby generating the maximum vitellogenic yield; this could not be obtained in a conventional laboratory experiment because the environmental changes imposed are not based on the ecology of fish in nature. Other examples showing the interactive effects of environmental factors have been reported by Stacey *et al.* (1979b), experimenting on ovulation and oviposition in goldfish. It was first observed that a warm shock induced ovulation which was synchronized with the photoperiod. Females kept under a regime of 16 h light : 8 h dark ovulated in the latter half of the dark phase, regardless of the time of day at which they were warmed to 20°C (Stacey *et al.*, 1979a). It was then shown that ovulation was influenced by both water temperature and vegetation (Table II). The additive effect of two stimuli, one visual and the other chemical, has been demonstrated in the angelfish, *Pterophyllum scalare* (Chien, 1973).

TABLE II   The Influence of some Environmental Conditions on Ovulation of the Goldfish kept under a Photoperiod of 12 h Light : 12 h Dark. The Initial Temperature for all Groups was 12°C (from Stacey *et al.*, 1979a).

Group	Temperature °C	Flowing water	Standing water	Aquatic vegetation	Male courtship	No. of females Total	No. of females Ovulated
1	12	−	+	+	+	9	0
2	22	−	+	+	+	10	10
3	21	+	−	+	+	7	7
4	21	+	−	−	−	10	3
5	21	+	−	+	−	9	9
6	21	+	−	−	+	8	1

III   MECHANISMS OF ACTION

We have shown that various environmental factors influence reproduction in fish, some of which are stimulatory and others, especially those due to man, are inhibitory. Whether these effects are mediated *via* the General

Adaptation Syndrome (Selye, 1946) is still open to debate. In fish as in other vertebrates, a drastic environmental change or aggression is followed by an elevation of the levels of plasma corticosteroids and catecholamines, a primary stress response. These hormones also appear to be normal components of the natural reproductive endocrine pattern in fish, so that hormonal fluctuations due to aggression may interfere with reproduction. More generally, responses to environmental changes involve the whole endocrine system which has been considered as a chemical link between the organism and its environment (Hoar, 1965).

It is now known that handling, loading, transport, confinement and temperature change result in an elevation of circulating corticosteroids in various salmonids (Strange et al., 1977; Strange and Schreck, 1978; Barton et al., 1980; Specker and Schreck, 1980) and in goldfish (Spieler, 1974; Fryer, 1975). Similarly, cortisol increases were observed after fish were exposed to copper, but not after they were exposed to cadmium (Schreck and Lorz, 1978) or chromium (Hill and Fromm, 1968). Social aggression between eels, Anguilla anguilla, under conditions of captivity and confinement also results in a rise of cortisol in the subordinate fish (Peters et al., 1980). For a full review of the role of the pituitary–interrenal axis in the stress responses of fish, the reader is referred to Donaldson (1981, this volume). Changes in catecholamines are not so well documented, but available information has been reviewed by Mazeaud et al. (1977) and Mazeaud and Mazeaud (1981, this volume).

Other hormones are involved in the response after handling or physical injury. For instance, in goldfish a short-term prolactin decrease was seen 9 to 17 min after capture (Spieler and Meier, 1976). Furthermore, Brown et al. (1978) demonstrated that physical injury such as removal of blood or saline injection causes a temporary elevation of plasma thyroxine (T4) in rainbow trout. Several hormones (corticosteroids or cortisol, prolactin, thyroid hormone) have been shown to have diel and annual rhythms in fish (for review see Spieler, 1979). This is interesting because the temporal hormonal synergism probably helps the fish to seasonally integrate into the changing environment.

The action of seasonal environmental factors on reproduction is mediated through specific endocrine changes, and the endocrine mechanisms controlling reproduction are roughly similar in fish and higher vertebrates. Gonadotropin-releasing hormone (Gn-RH) stimulates the secretion of gonadotropic hormone (GTH). GTH stimulates spermatogenesis and oogenesis and induces the gonads to produce sex steroids which, in turn, exert a negative feedback on the hypothalamo–pituitary axis.

Corticosteroids, often identified in plasma or ovaries, appear as normal components of the reproductive endocrine pattern. In adult fish, many authors have shown seasonal variations in blood corticosteroid levels in several species. The metabolic clearance rate, volume of distribution and calculated rate of cortisol and cortisone secretion have been studied. In several salmonid species, corticosteroids rise during sexual maturation (sometimes associated with spawning migration) (Schmidt and Idler, 1962; Donaldson and Fagerlund, 1968, 1970; Fagerlund and Donaldson, 1970) and a hyperplasia of the interrenal gland coincides with ovarian development (Robertson and Wexler, 1960). Fuller *et al.* (1976) also observed high levels of cortisol in mature, female *Coregonus lavaretus* caught on the spawning grounds, but not in those outside the spawning grounds. Similarly, Pickering and Christie (1981) demonstrated a rise in the plasma cortisol levels of the mature, female brown trout at a time coincident with the onset of ovulation in the population. By comparison, no such elevation was found in immature fish kept under identical conditions. In goldfish, Peter *et al.* (1978) identified plasma cortisol and showed that maturing females (in full vitellogenesis) had a higher level with wider fluctuations than fully mature females (at the end of vitellogenesis). However, Cook *et al.* (1980) discovered a sharp peak of cortisol just before the ovulatory GTH surge. Ovulation was induced experimentally in ayu, *Plecoglossus altivelis*, after the injection of very high doses of cortisol (Hirose and Ishida, 1974). Similarly, the injection of 11-deoxycortisol to female guppies induced parturition (Kujala, 1978). The possibility that ovarian corticosteroid peaks might affect ovulation in teleosts has been discussed by Colombo *et al.* (1973).

Sundararaj and Goswami (1977) suggested that 11-deoxycortisol might be one of the steroids mediating GTH action on oocyte maturation and ovulation in the Indian catfish, *Heteropneustes fossilis*. Jalabert (1976) demonstrated that corticosteroids potentiate GTH action on oocyte maturation (Fig. 3) and hypothesized that some fish, cyprinids for example, show an elevation of plasma corticosteroids associated with the true ovulatory surge (see also Breton *et al.*, 1972; Stacey *et al.*, 1979b). This rise may be indirectly responsible for ovulation by lowering the oocyte sensitivity threshold to GTH or by displacing the plasma equilibrium between protein-bound and free 17α-hydroxy-20β-dihydroprogesterone.

Other mediators such as catecholamines, which are involved in the primary stress response, also seem to play a natural role in the process of ovulation; Jalabert (1976) noted that epinephrine induces ovulation of matured oocytes *in vitro*.

There are a few data showing that adverse environmental conditions or aggression may interfere with reproduction via a decrease of plasma GTH. For instance, Gillet *et al.* (1980) observed a decline in both plasma and pituitary GTH in goldfish kept under conditions of starvation (Fig. 4). However, starvation probably inhibited all synthesis of gonadotropic

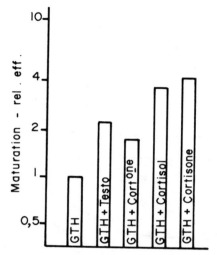

Fig. 3   Corticosteroid amplification of gonadotropin effect on *in vitro* oocyte maturation of rainbow trout follicles (redrawn from Jalabert, 1975).

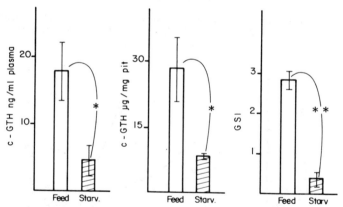

Fig. 4.   Effect of starvation on plasma and pituitary gonadotropin (c-GTH) and gonadosomatic index (GSI) in male goldfish kept for 3 months under 16 h light : 8 h dark photoperiod at 30°C. Blood was sampled at 8 a.m. at the onset of the light period. Vertical bars indicate ±SEM, number of fish are 6 (feed) and 5 (starv.) (from Gillet *et al.*, 1981). $*p < 0.05$, $**p < 0.01$.

hormone, due to a lack of adequate material, rather than inhibited the secretion of the hormone. Similarly, a decrease of plasma GTH and GSI was observed in male goldfish kept at 30°C under hypoxic conditions (1·5 and 3 mg l^{-1} O_2 (Fig. 5)). During a study involving catheterization of the dorsal aorta in rainbow trout (Bry and Zohar, 1980; Zohar, 1980), one fish failed to

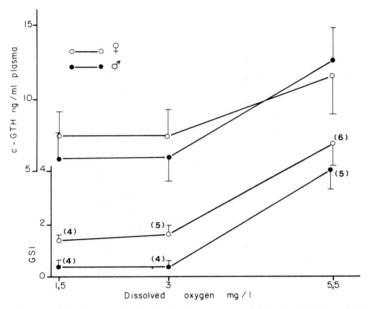

Fig. 5 Influence of dissolved oxygen in the rearing water on GSI and c-GTH in goldfish after 3 months of rearing. Vertical lines indicate ±SEM, the number of fish are shown in brackets (from Gillet *et al.*, 1981).

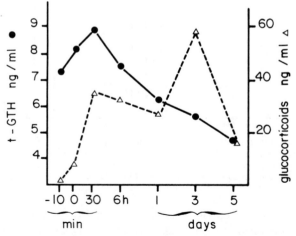

Fig. 6 Changes in glucocorticoids and gonadotropin (t-GTH) in a catheterized rainbow trout for 5 days after cannulation of the dorsal aorta. Time 0 indicates the end of surgery (cannula implantation). The example given is a female ill-adjusting to catheterization and not resuming feeding after the operation (from Bry and Zohar, 1980; Zohar, 1980).

acclimate to the experimental conditions and did not resume feeding. It is interesting that this severely stressed fish (as evidenced by a prolonged elevation of plasma glucocorticoids) also showed a marked decline in plasma gonadotropin after the operation (Fig. 6). On the other hand, when rainbow trout were netted and left struggling out of the water for 3 min, no significant change in plasma gonadotropin was observed after 10 min, 30 min or 24 h (Fig. 7; C. Bry unpublished data).

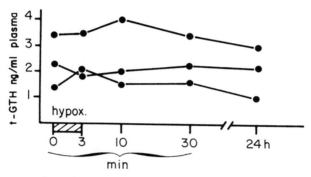

Fig. 7   Plasma gonadotropin (t-GTH) profiles in three catheterized and unanaesthetized rainbow trout after they had struggled for 3 min out of water (hypoxia).

The effects of deleterious changes in the environment on the other main area of reproductive endocrinology, that of oestrogen and androgen metabolism by the gonads, has received very little attention. Androgen metabolism is reported to be modified in brook trout exposed to sublethal levels of cadmium (Sangalang and Freeman, 1974; see also the abstract by Freeman et al., 1981, this volume) but the whole relationship between environmental stress and sex steroid metabolism is a field in which much more research is needed.

IV   CONCLUSIONS

The various steps of reproduction depend largely on environmental changes and involve many factors (Fig. 8). Circannual changes influence long-term processes such as gametogenesis. On the contrary, short-term phenomena such as ovulation may be more dependant upon sudden changes in the environment (fluctuation of temperature, rain, salinity, water quality). Fish species which release small eggs with a short incubation period normally ovulate in the spring after these sudden variations, which coincide with the climatic changes initiating or increasing food production in the water. These

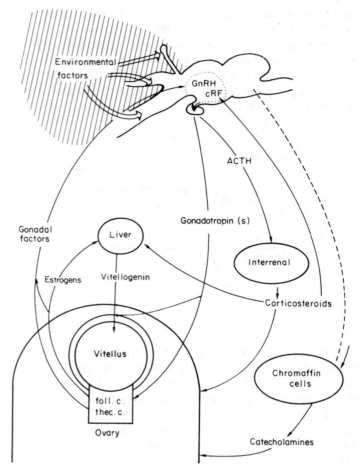

Fig. 8. Some endocrine interrelations between reproduction, corticosteroids and catecholamines in the female teleost fish.

environmental cues are responsible for egg-laying and synchronize hatching
with food availability.

Some of these modifications may cause an increase in circulating cortisol
levels. The hypothesis that environmental stress may incite the final step of
gametogenesis, i.e. oocyte maturation and ovulation, has been put forward
by Jalabert (1976). The situation in males may be different; spermiation
usually starts earlier than ovulation and no GTH surge occurs when
spermiation is initiated. On the other hand, Mazeaud *et al.* (1977) observed
sex-dependent differences in plasma corticosteroids in salmonids; female

corticosteroid levels were higher than male levels; when the fish were left struggling, these levels rose markedly in males but not in females which already had high levels.

The stressful environment created by man when handling and breeding fish in captivity in overcrowded ponds seems to be overcome by domestication. After several generations, it is possible that some cultivated fish species become adapted (by selection) to their new environment. This should be emphasized now when man is trying to rear wild species intensively. Research is needed to minimize the consequences of stressful conditions on survival, growth and reproduction and to define optimal rearing conditions. Furthermore, the rearing conditions must be adapted to the various physiological rhythms of the fish (see Spieler, 1977).

Environmental factors may stimulate or inhibit reproduction in fish and a given factor may be either inhibitory or stimulatory, depending on the time of the year or day or the stage of sexual development. The where, when and why of these phenomena need further study.

ACKNOWLEDGEMENTS

Thanks are due to Ms Alice Daifuku for editing the manuscript in English.

REFERENCES

Abraham, M. and Blanc, N. (1966). Oogenesis in five species of grey mullets (Teleostei, Mugilidae) from natural and landlocked habitats. *Israel J. Zool.* **15**, 155–172.

Ahsan, S. N. (1966). Effects of temperature and light on the cyclical change in the spermatogenetic activity of the lake chub *Couesius plumbeus* (Agassiz). *Can. J. Zool.* **44**, 161–171.

Bagenal, T. B. (1966). The ecological and geographical aspects of the fecundity of the plaice. *J. mar. biol. Ass. U.K.* **46**, 161–186.

Bagenal, T. B. (1969). The relationship between food supply and fecundity in brown trout *Salmo trutta* L. *J. Fish Biol.* **1**, 167–182.

Baggerman, B. (1969). Influence of photoperiod and temperature on the timing of breeding season in the stickleback, *Gasterosteus aculeatus*. *Gen. comp. Endocr.* **13**, 491.

Baggerman, B. (1972). Photoperiodic responses in the stickleback and their control by a daily rhythm of photosensitivity. *Gen. comp. Endocr. Suppl.* **3**, 466–476.

Ball, J. N. (1960). Reproduction in female bony fish. *Symp. zool. Soc., Lond.* **1**, 105–135.

Barton, B. A., Peter, R. E. and Paulencu, C. R. (1980). Plasma cortisol levels of fingerling rainbow trout (*Salmo gairdneri*) at rest, and subjected to handling, confinement, transport, and stocking. *Can. J. Fish. Aquat. Sci.* **37**, 805–811.

Beamish, R. J. (1972). Lethal pH for the white sucker *Catostomus commersoni* (Lacépède). *Trans. Am. Fish. Soc.* **2**, 355–358.

Beamish, R. J. (1976). Acidification of lakes in Canada by acid precipitation and resulting effects on fishes. *Wat. Air Soil Pollut.* **6**, 501–514.

Bengtsson, B. E. (1980). Long-term effects of PCB (clophen A 50) on growth, reproduction and swimming performance in the minnow, *Phoxinus phoxinus. Wat. Res.* **14**, 681–687.

Benoit, D. A. (1975). Chronic effects of copper on survival, growth, and reproduction of the bluegill (*Lepomis macrochirus*). *Trans. Am. Fish. Soc.* **104**, 353–358.

Bieniarz, K. (1973). Effect of light and darkness on incubation of eggs, length, weight and sexual maturity of sea trout (*Salmo trutta* L.) brown trout (*Salmo trutta fario* L.) and rainbow trout (*Salmo irideus* Gibbons). *Aquaculture* **2**, 299–315.

Billard, R. (1968). Influence de la température sur la durée et l'efficacité de la spermatogénèse du guppy *Poecilia reticulata. C.r. hebd. Séanc. Acad. Sci., Paris* **266**, 2287–2290.

Billard, R. (1980). Reproduction and artificial insemination in teleost fish. *9th Int. Congr. anim. Reprod., Madrid* Vol. II, 327–337.

Billard, R. and Breton, B. (1977). Sensibilité à la température des différentes étapes de la reproduction chez la truite arc-en-ciel. *Cah. Lab. Montereau* **5**, 5–24.

Billard, R. and de Kinkelin, P. (1970). Stérilisation des testicules de guppies par des doses non léthales de parathion. *Annls Hydrobiol.* **1**, 91–99.

Billard, R. and de Fremont, M. (1980). Taux d'alimentation pendant le gametogenese et performance de reproduction chez la truite fario. *Bull. Franc. Pisc.* **279**, 49–56.

Blanc, N. and Abraham, M. (1968). Evaluation du pouvoir gonadotrope dans l'hypophyse de *Cyprinus carpio* et *Mugil cephalus. C.r. hebd. Séanc. Acad. Sci., Paris* **267**, 958–961.

Bloom, H. D. and Perlmutter, A. (1978). Possible pheromone mediated reproductive isolation in two species of cyprinid fishes of the genus *Brachydanio. J. Fish Biol.* **13**, 47–50.

Breton, B. and Billard, R. (1977). Effects of photoperiod and temperature on plasma gonadotropin and spermatogenesis in the rainbow trout *Salmo gairdneri* Richardson. *Annls Biol. anim. Biochim. Biophys.* **17**, 331–340.

Breton, B., Billard, R., Jalabert, B. and Kann, G. (1972). Dosage radioimmunologique des gonadotropines plasmatiques chez *Carassius auratus* au cours du nycthémère et pendant l'ovulation. *Gen. comp. Endocr.* **18**, 463–468.

Brown, S., Fedoruk, K. and Eales, J. G. (1978). Physical injury due to injection or blood removal causes transitory elevations of plasma thyroxine in rainbow trout, *Salmo gairdneri. Can. J. Zool.* **56**, 1998–2003.

Brungs, W. A. (1971). Chronic effects of low dissolved oxygen concentrations on the fathead minnow (*Pimephales promelas*). *J. Fish. Res. Bd Can.* **20**, 1119–1123.

Bry, C. and Zohar, Y. (1980). Dorsal aorta catheterization in rainbow trout (*Salmo gairdneri*): glucocorticoid levels, hematological data and resumption of feeding during five days after surgery. *Reprod. Nutr. Develop.* **20**, 1825–1834.

Bullough, W. S. (1939). A study of the reproduction cycle of the minnow in relation to the environment. *Proc. zool. Soc., Lond.* **109A**, 79–102.

Bullough, W. S. (1942). Gametogenesis and some endocrine factors affecting it in the adult minnow (*Phoxinus laevis* L.). *J. Endocr.* **3**, 211–219.

Burdick, G. E., Harris, E. J., Dean, H. J., Walker, T. M., Skea, J. and Colby, D. (1964). The accumulation of DDT in lake trout and the effect on reproduction. *Trans. Am. Fish. Soc.* **93**, 127–136.

Burdick, G. E., Dean, H. J., Harris, E. J., Skea, J., Karcher, R. and Frisa, C. (1972). Effect of rate and duration of feeding DDT on the reproduction of salmonid fishes reared and held under controlled conditions. *N.Y. Fish Game J.* **19**, 99–115.

Carlson, A. R. and Herman, L. J. (1978). Effect of long-term reduction and diel fluctuation in dissolved oxygen on spawning of black crappie, *Pomoxis nigroma-culatus. Trans. Am. Fish. Soc.* **107**, 742–746.

Chavin, W. (1973). *Responses of Fish to Environmental Changes.* Springfield, Illinois: C. Thomas.

Chen, L. C. and Martinich, R. L. (1975). Pheromonal stimulation and metabolite inhibition of ovulation in the zebrafish, *Brachydanio rerio. Fishery Bull. Fish Wildl. Serv. U.S.* **73**, 889–894.

Chew, R. L. (1972). The failure of largemouth bass, *Micropterus salmoides floridanus* (Le Sueur), to spawn in eutrophic, over-crowded environments. *Proc. a. Conf. South. Ass. Game Fish Commn.* **26**, 1–28.

Chien, A. K. (1973). Reproductive behaviour of the angelfish *Pterophyllum scalare* (Pisces: Cichilidae) II. Influence of male stimuli upon the spawning rate of females. *Anim. Behav.* **21**, 457–463.

Colombo, L., Bern, H. A., Pieprzyk, J. and Johnson, D. W. (1973). Biosynthesis of 11-deoxycorticosteroids by teleost ovaries and discussion of their possible role in oocyte maturation and ovulation. *Gen. comp. Endocr.* **21**, 168–178.

Cook, A. F., Peter, R. E. and Stacey, N. E. (1980). Periovulatory changes in serum cortisol levels in the goldfish, *Carassius auratus. Gen. comp. Endocr.* **40**, 507–510.

Craig, G. R. and Baksi, W. F. (1977). The effects of depressed pH on flagfish reproduction, growth and survival. *Wat. Res.* **11**, 621–626.

Cumbie, P. M. and Van Horn, S. L. (1979). Selenium accumulation associated with fish mortality and reproductive failure. *Proc. a. Conf. S. East. Assoc. Fish Wildl. Agencies* **32**, 612–624.

Dahlgren, B. T. (1979). The effects of population density on fecundity and fertility in the guppy, *Poecilia reticulata* (Peters). *J. Fish Biol.* **15**, 71–91.

Daye, P. G. and Garside, E. T. (1980). Structural alterations in embryos and alevins of the Atlantic salmon, *Salmo salar* L., induced by continuous or short-term exposure to acidic levels of pH. *Can. J. Zool.* **58**, 27–43.

Dean, J. and Bailey, H. (1979). Reproductive repression of largemouth bass in a heated reservoir. *Proc. a. Conf. S. East. Assoc. Fish Wildl. Agencies* **31**, 463–470.

de Vlaming, V. L. (1974). Environmental and endocrine control of teleost reproduction. In *Control of Sex in Fishes* (C. B. Schreck, ed.), Blacksburg, Virginia: Virginia Polytechnic and State University.

Donaldson, E. M. (1981). The pituitary–interrenal axis as an indicator of stress in fish. In *Stress and Fish* (A. D. Pickering, ed.), pp. 11–47. London and New York: Academic Press.

Donaldson, E. M. and Fagerlund, U. H. M. (1968). Changes in the cortisol dynamics of sockeye salmon (*Oncorhynchus nerka*) resulting from sexual maturation. *Gen. comp. Endocr.* **11**, 552–561.

Donaldson, E. M. and Fagerlund, U. H. M. (1970). Effect of sexual maturation and gonadectomy at sexual maturity on cortisol secretion rate in sockeye salmon (*Oncorhynchus nerka*). *J. Fish. Res. Bd Can.* **27**, 2287–2296.

Ebersole, J. P. (1980). Food density and territory size: an alternative model and a test on the reef fish *Eupomacentrus leucostictus. Am. Nat.* **115**, 492–508.

Eckstein, B. (1975). Possible reasons for the infertility of grey mullets confined to fresh water. *Aquaculture* **5**, 9–17.

Elliott, J. M. (1981). Some aspects of thermal stress on freshwater teleosts. In *Stress and Fish* (A. D. Pickering, ed.), pp. 209–245. London and New York: Academic Press.

Emanuel, M. E. and Dodson, J. J. (1979). Modification of the rheotropic behavior of male rainbow trout (*Salmo gairdneri*) by ovarian fluid. *J. Fish. Res. Bd Can.* **36**, 63–68.

Fagerlund, U. H. M. and Donaldson, E. M. (1970). Dynamics of cortisone secretion in sockeye salmon (*Oncorhynchus nerka*) during sexual maturation and after gonadectomy. *J. Fish. Res. Bd Can.* **27**, 2323–2331.

Freeman, H. C., Sangalang, G. B. and Uthe, J. F. (1981). The effects of pollutants on steroid hormone metabolism in fish. (Abstract). In *Stress and Fish* (A. D. Pickering, ed.), pp. 332–333. London and New York: Academic Press.

Fromm, P. O. (1980). A review of some physiological and toxicological responses of freshwater fish to acid stress. *Env. Biol. Fish* **5**, 79–93.

Fryer, J. N. (1975). Stress and adrenocorticosteroid dynamics in the goldfish, *Carassius auratus*. *Can. J. Zool.* **53**, 1012–1020.

Fuller, J. D., Scott, D. B. C. and Fraser, R. (1976). The reproductive cycle of *Coregonus lavaretus* (L.) in Loch Lomond, Scotland, in relation to seasonal changes in plasma cortisol concentration. *J. Fish Biol.* **9**, 105–117.

Gall, G. A. E., McClendon, E. L. and Schafer, W. E. (1972). Evidence on the influence of the copepod (*Salmincola californiensis*) on the reproductive performance of a domesticated strain of rainbow trout (*Salmo gairdneri*). *Trans. Am. Fish. Soc.* **2**, 345–346.

Gillet, C. and Billard, R. (1977). Stimulation of gonadotopin secretion in goldfish by elevation of rearing temperature. *Annls Biol. anim. Biochem. Biophys.* **17**, 673–678.

Gillet, C., Billard, R. and Breton, B. (1977a). Influence de la température sur la reproduction du poisson rouge (*Carassius auratus* L.). *Cah. Lab. Montereau* **5**, 25–42.

Gillet, C., Billard, R. and Breton, B. (1977b). Effets de la température sur le taux de gonadotropine plasmatique et la spermatogénèse du poisson rouge *Carassius auratus*. *Can. J. Zool.* **55**, 242–245.

Gillet, C., Breton, B. and Billard, R. (1978). Seasonal effects of exposure to temperature and photoperiod regimes on gonad growth and plasma gonadotropin in goldfish (*Carassius auratus*). *Annls Biol. anim. Biochim. Biophys.* **18**, 1045–1049.

Gillet, C., Billard, R. and Breton, B. (1981). La reproduction du poisson rouge *Carassius auratus* élevé à 30°C. Effet de la photopériode, de l'alimentation et de l'oxygénation. *Cah. Lab. Montereau* **11**, 49–56.

Godfrey, H. (1957). Mortalities among developing trout and salmon ova following shock by direct current electrical fishing gear. *J. Fish. Res. Bd Can.* **14**, 153–164.

Greene, N. (1964). A reproduction control factor in fishes. Ph.D. Thesis, Auburn University, Auburn, Alabama, U.S.A.

Hedtke, S. F. and Puglisi, F. A. (1980). Effects of waste oil on the survival and reproduction of the American flagfish, *Jordanella floridae*. *Can. J. Fish. Aquat. Sci.* **37**, 757–764.

Hill, C. W. and Fromm, P. O. (1968). Response of the interrenal gland of rainbow trout (*Salmo gairdneri*) to stress. *Gen. comp. Endocr.* **11**, 69–77.

Hirose, K. and Ishida, R. (1974). Effects of cortisol and human chorionic gonadotrophin (HCG) on ovulation in ayu *Plecoglossus altivelis* (Temminck and Schlegel) with special reference to water and ion balance. *J. Fish Biol.* **6**, 557–564.

Hoar, W. S. (1965). The endocrine system as a chemical link between the organism and its environment. *Trans. R. Soc. Can.* **3**, 175–200.

Hokanson, K. E. F. (1977). Temperature requirements of some percids and adaptations to the seasonal temperature cycle. *J. Fish. Res. Bd Can.* **10**, 1524–1550.

Hontela, A. and Peter, R. E. (1978). Daily cycles in serum gonadotropin levels in the goldfish: effects of photoperiod, temperature and sexual condition. *Can. J. Zool.* **56**, 2430–2442.

Horseman, N. D., Meier, H. and Culley, D. D. (1976). Daily variations in the effects of disturbance on growth, fattening and metamorphosis in the bullfrog (*Rana catesbeiana*) tadpole. *J. exp. Zool.* **198**, 353–358.

Htun-Han, M. (1977). The effects of photoperiod on reproduction in fishes: an annotated bibliography. *Library Inf. Leaflet, MAFF, Lowestoft*, **6**, 30pp.

Jalabert, B. (1975). Modulation par différents stéroides non maturants de l'efficacité de la 17-hydroxy-20-dihydroprogesterone ou d'un extrait gonadotrope sur la maturation intrafolliculaire *in vitro* des ovocytes de la truite arc-en-ciel *Salmo gairdneri*. *C.r. hebd. Séanc. Acad. Sci., Paris (Ser. D.)* **281**, 811–814.

Jalabert, B. (1976). *In vitro* oocyte maturation and ovulation in rainbow trout (*Salmo gairdneri*), northern pike (*Esox lucius*), and goldfish (*Carassius auratus*). *J. Fish. Res. Bd Can.* **33**, 974–988.

Johansen, P. H. and Cross, J. A. (1980). Effects of sexual maturation and sex steroid hormone treatment on the temperature preference of the guppy, *Poecilia reticulata* (Peters). *Can. J. Zool.* **58**, 586–588.

Johansson, N., Kihlstrom, J. E. and Wahlber, G. (1973). Low pH values shown to affect developing fish eggs *Brachydanio rerio* (Ham-Buch). *Ambio* **2**, 1–2.

Kazakov, R. V. (1971). Effect of alternative temperature while incubating eggs of the Atlantic salmon upon survival and growth rates of embryos and larvae (Russian-English summary). *Isv. GOS. Nauk Ichyol. Oser* **75**, 56–66.

Kihlstrom, J. E., Landery, C. and Hulth, L. (1971). Number of eggs and young produced by zebrafishes (*Brachydanio rerio*, Ham-Buch) spawning in water containing small amounts of phenylmercuric acetate. *Env. Res.* **4**, 355–359.

Kipling, C. and Frost, W. E. (1969). Variations in the fecundity of pike *Esox lucius* L. in Windermere. *J. Fish Biol.* **1**, 221–237.

Kujala, G. A. (1978). Corticosteroid and neurohypophyseal hormone control of parturition in the guppy, *Poecilia reticulata*. *Gen. comp. Endocr.* **36**, 286–296.

Kuznetsov, V. A. and Khalitov, N. Kh. (1978). Alterations in the fecundity and egg quality of the roach, *Rutilus rutilus*, in connection with different feeding conditions. *J. Ichthyol.* **18**, 63–70.

Macek, K. J. (1968a) Reproduction in brook trout (*Salvelinus fontinalis*) fed sublethal concentrations of DDT. *J. Fish. Res. Bd Can.* **25**, 1787–1796.

Macek, K. J. (1968b). Growth and resistance to stress in brook trout fed sublethal levels of DDT. *J. Fish. Res. Bd Can.* **25**, 2443–2451.

Marriott, R. A. (1973). Effects of electric shocking on fertility of mature pink salmon. *Progve Fish Cult.* **35**, 191–194.

Maruyama, T. and Nagashima, K. (1978). Effect of water current on growth and spawning activity of *Tilapia nilotica*. *Bull. Freshwat. Fish Res. Lab., Tokyo* **28**, 201–210.

Maxfield, G. H., Lander, R. H. and Liscom, K. L. (1971). Survival, growth, and fecundity of hatchery-reared rainbow trout after exposure to pulsating direct current. *Trans. Am. Fish. Soc.* **3**, 546–552.

Mazeaud, M. M. and Mazeaud, F. (1981). Adrenergic responses to stress in fish. In *Stress and Fish* (A. D. Pickering, ed.), pp. 49–75. London and New York: Academic Press.

Mazeaud, M. M., Mazeaud, F. and Donaldson, E. M. (1977). Primary and secondary effects of stress in fish: some new data with a general review. *Trans. Am. Fish. Soc.* **106**, 201–212.

Meier, A. H. and Horseman, N. D. (1977). Stimulation and depression of growth, fat storage, and gonad weight by daily stimulus in the teleost fish, *Tilapia aurea*. *Proc. a. World maricult. Soc.* **8**, 135–143.

Menendez, R. (1976). Chronic effects of reduced pH on brook trout (*Salvelinus fontinalis*). *J. Fish. Res. Bd Can.* **33**, 118–123.

Mitton, J. B. and Koehn, R. K. (1976). Morphological adaptation to thermal stress in a marine fish, *Fundulus heteroclitus*. *Biol. Bull. mar. biol. Lab., Woods Hole* **151**, 548–559.

de Montalembert, G., Bry, C. and Billard, R. (1978). Control of reproduction in northern pike. *Spec. Publs Am. Fish. Soc.* **11**, 217–225.

Mount, D. I. (1973). Chronic effect of low pH on fathead minnow survival, growth and reproduction. *Wat. Res.* **7**, 987–993.

Nebeker, A. V., Puglisi, F. A. and Defoe, D. L. (1974). Effect of polychlorinated biphenyl compounds on survival and reproduction of the fathead minnow and flagfish. *Trans. Am. Fish. Soc.* **103**, 562–568.

Newcombe, C. and Hartman, G. (1973). Some chemical signals in the spawning behaviour of rainbow trout (*Salmo gairdneri*). *J. Fish. Res. Bd Can.* **30**, 995–997.

Peter, R. E. and Crim, L. W. (1979). Reproductive endocrinology of fishes: Gonadal cycles and gonadotropin in teleosts. *A. Rev. Physiol.* **41**, 323–335.

Peter, R. E., Hontela, A., Cook, A. F. and Paulencu, C. R. (1978). Daily cycles in serum cortisol levels in the goldfish: effects of photoperiod, temperature, and sexual condition. *Can. J. Zool.* **56**, 2443–2448.

Peters, G., Delventhal, H. and Klinger, H. (1980). Physiological and morphological effects of social stress in the eel (*Anguilla anguilla* L.) *Arch. FischWiss.* **30**, 157–180.

Peterson, R. H., Daye, P. G. and Metcalfe, J. L. (1980). Inhibition of Atlantic salmon (*Salmo salar*) hatching at low pH. *Can. J. Fish. Aquat. Sci.* **37**, 770–774.

Pfuderer, P., Williams, P. and Francis, A. A. (1974). Partial purification of the crowding factor from *Carassius auratus* and *Cyprinus carpio*. *J. exp. Zool.* **187**, 375–382.

Pickering, A. D. (1981). Introduction. In *Stress and Fish* (A. D. Pickering, ed.), pp. 1–9. London and New York: Academic Press.

Pickering, A. D. and Christie, P. (1981). Changes in the concentrations of plasma cortisol and thyroxine during sexual maturation of the hatchery-reared brown trout, *Salmo trutta* L. *Gen. comp. Endocr.* **44**, (in press).

Pyle, E. A. (1969). The effect of constant light and darkness on the growth and sexual maturity of brook trout. *Fish. Res. Bull., NY* **31**, 13–19.

Quillier, R. (1981). Influence de photoperiodes constantes sur l'activité testiculaire de la tanche (*Tinca tinca* L.). *Bull. Franc. Pisc.* (in press).

Robertson, O. H. and Wexler, B. C. (1960). Histological changes in the organs and tissues of migrating and spawning Pacific salmon (Genus *Oncorhynchus*). *Endocrinology* **66**, 222–238.

Roblin, C. (1980). Etude comparée de la biologie du dévelopement (gonadogénèse, croissance, nutrition) du loup (*Dicentrarchus labrax*) en milieu naturel et en élevage contrôlé. *Acad. de Montpellier Thèse 3ème cycle, Univ. Sci. Techn. Languedoc.*

Rose, S. M. (1959). Population control in guppies. *Am. Midl. Nat.* **62**, 474–481.

Ruby, S. M., Aczel, J. and Craig, G. R. (1977). The effects of depressed pH on oogenesis in flagfish *Jordanella floridae. Wat. Res.* **11**, 757–762.

Saglio, P. (1979a). Communication chimique et migration reproductrice chez les salmonidés. *Bull. Franc. Pisc.* **275**, 72–82.

Saglio, P. (1969b). Interactions sociales chez les poissons: les pheromones. *Bull. Franc. Pisc.* **273**, 173–184.

Sangalang, G. B. and Freeman, H. C. (1974). Effects of sublethal cadmium on maturation and testosterone and 11-ketotestosterone production *in vivo* in brook trout. *Biol. Reprod.* **11**, 429–435.

Sawara, Y. and Egami, N. (1977). Note on the differences in the response of the gonad to the photoperiod among population of *Oryzias latipes* collected in different localities. *Annotnes zool. jap.* **50**, 147–150.

Saxena, P. K. and Garg, M. (1978). Effect of insecticidal pollution on ovarian recrudescence in the fresh water teleost *Channa punctatus. Ind. J. exp. Biol.* **16**, 689–691.

Schmidt, P. J. and Idler, D. R. (1962). Steroid hormones in the plasma of salmon at various states of maturation. *Gen. comp. Endocr.* **2**, 204–214.

Schreck, C. B. and Lorz, H. W. (1978). Stress response of coho salmon (*Oncorhynchus kisutch*) elicited by cadmium and copper and potential use of cortisol as an indicator of stress. *J. Fish. Res. Bd Can.* **35**, 1124–1129.

Scott, D. B. C. (1979). Environmental timing and the control of reproduction in teleost fish. *Symp. Zool. Soc., Lond.* **44**, 105–132.

Scott, D. P. (1962). Effect of food quantity on fecundity of rainbow trout, *Salmo gairdneri. J. Fish. Res. Bd Can.* **19**, 715–730.

Selye, H. (1946). The general adaptation syndrome and the diseases of adaptation. *J. clin. Endocr.* **6**, 117–230.

Siefert, R. E. and Herman, L. J. (1977). Spawning success of the black crappie *Pomoxis nigromaculatus* at dissolved oxygen concentrations. *Trans. Am. Fish. Soc.* **106**, 376–378.

Solomon, D. J. (1977). A review of chemical communication in freshwater fish. *J. Fish Biol.* **11**, 369–376.

Specker, J. L. and Schreck, C. B. (1980). Stress responses to transportation and fitness for marine survival in coho salmon (*Oncorhynchus kisutch*) smolts. *Can. J. Fish. Aquat. Sci.* **37**, 765–769.

Spieler, R. E. (1974). Short-term serum cortisol concentrations in goldfish (*Carassius auratus*) subjected to serial sampling and restraint. *J. Fish. Res. Bd Can.* **31**, 1240–1242.

Spieler, R. E. (1977). Diel and seasonal changes in response to stimuli: a plague and a promise for mariculture. *Proc. a. World Maricult. Soc.* **8**, 865–874.

Spieler, R. E. (1979). Diel rhythms of circulating prolactin, cortisol, thyroxine, and triiodothyronine levels in fishes: a review. *Rev. Can. Biol.* **38**, 301–315.

Spieler, R. E. and Meier, H. (1976). Short-term serum prolactin concentrations in goldfish (*Carassius auratus*) subjected to serial sampling and restraint. *J. Fish. Res. Bd. Can.* **33**, 183–186.

Stacey, N. E., Cook, A. F. and Peter, R. E. (1979a). Spontaneous and gonadotropin induced ovulation in the goldfish, *Carassius auratus* L. effects of external factors. *J. Fish Biol.* **15**, 349–361.

Stacey, N. E., Cook, A. F. and Peter, R. E. (1979b). Ovulatory surge of gonadotropin in the goldfish, *Carassius auratus. Gen. comp. Endocr.* **37**, 246–249.

Stequert, B. (1972). Contribution a l'étude de la biologie du bar (*Dicentrarchus labrax* L.) des réservoirs à poissons de la région d'Arcachon. *Thèse 3ème cycle, Univ. Bordeaux.*

Strange, R. J. and Schreck, C. B. (1978). Anaesthetic and handling stress on survival and cortisol concentration in yearling chinook salmon (*Oncorhynchus tshawytscha*). *J. Fish. Res. Bd Can.* **35**, 345–349.

Strange, R. J., Schreck, C. B. and Golden, J. T. (1977). Corticoid stress responses to handling and temperature in salmonids. *Trans. Am. Fish. Soc.* **106**, 213–218.

Sundararaj, B. I. and Goswami, S. V. (1977). Hormonal regulation of *in vivo* and *in vitro* ovocyte maturation in the catfish, *Heteropneustes fossilis* (Bloch). *Gen. comp. Endocr.* **32**, 17–28.

Swingle, H. S. (1953). A repressive factor controlling reproduction in fishes. *Proc. Pacif. Sci. Congr.* **38**, 865–871.

Vincent, R. E. (1960). Some influences of domestication upon three stocks of brook trout (*Salvelinus fontinalis* Mitchill). *Trans. Am. Fish. Soc.* **89**, 35–52.

Whitehead, C., Bromage, N. R., Forster, J. R. M. and Matty, A. J. (1978). The effects of alterations in photoperiod on ovarian development and spawning time in the rainbow trout (*Salmo gairdneri*). *Annls Biol. anim. Biochim. Biophys.* **18**, 1035–1043.

Whiteside, B. G. and Richan, F. J. (1969). Repressive factors controlling reproduction in goldfish. *Progve Fish Cult.* **31**, 165.

Wiebe, J. P. (1968). The reproductive cycle of the viviparous seaperch, *Cymatogaster aggregatas* Gibbons. *Can. J. Zool.* **40**, 1221–1234.

Yu, M. L. and Perlmutter, A. (1970). Growth inhibiting factors in the zebrafish (*Brachydanio rerio*) and the blue gourami (*Trichogaster trichopterus*). *Growth* **34**, 153–175.

Zalewski, M. (1979). The effect of pollution on the fecundity of roach *Rutilus rutilus* L. from river of barbel region. *3rd Europ. Ichthyol. Cong. Warszawa. 18–25 Sept. 1979.*

Zohar, Y. (1980). Dorsal aorta catheterization in rainbow trout (*Salmo gairdneri*): Its validity in the study of blood gonadotropin patterns. *Reprod. Nutr. Develop.* **20**, 1811–1823.

10. Some Aspects of Thermal Stress on Freshwater Teleosts

J. M. ELLIOTT

Freshwater Biological Association, Far Sawrey, Nr. Ambleside, Cumbria, England

Abstract. Thermal stress is defined as any temperature change that produces a significant disturbance in the normal functions of a freshwater teleost and thus decreases the probability of survival. As stress responses at the population and community level are very complex and poorly understood, thermal stress is considered only at the level of the individual fish and emphasis is placed on ecological, rather than physiological, effects.

The thermal limits, optimum temperature range and preferred temperatures of freshwater teleosts are reviewed, and information on 27 European species is summarized. The concepts of tolerance and resistance to thermal stress are discussed and illustrated by original work on brown trout, *Salmo trutta*. Some comparisons are made between fish species with examples of cold-water stenotherms, mesotherms, and warm-water eurytherms. The temperature limits for spawning and egg development are shown to be much narrower than the normal thermal limits for older fish. Some factors that may affect thermal tolerance are briefly discussed.

The subtle effects of thermal stress within the normal tolerance range are discussed and illustrated by work on brown trout. Within the lethal limits, temperature can act as a loading stress by affecting functions such as growth and metabolism, especially when food intake is reduced. Temperature can also act as an inhibiting stress by affecting functions such as feeding and spawning.

Changes in body temperature and thermoregulation are briefly discussed. As well as combating thermal stress by tolerance, resistance and metabolic adjustments, fish may be able to change their body temperature by physiological regulation in a few species and by behavioural regulation in many species. The latter response is one of the chief factors responsible for fish movements.

I INTRODUCTION

There is little uniformity in the use of the term "thermal stress" (see also Pickering, 1981, this volume). In the present contribution, thermal stress will be used to refer to any temperature change that produces a significant disturbance in the normal functions of a freshwater teleost and thus decreases the probability of survival. This definition is similar to that proposed by Brett (1958) and assumes that the response is a stochastic variable that can be measured quantitatively. It also assumes that thermal stress is harmful. Although this is a reasonable assumption for the individual fish it is not always true for the population or community. For example, increased mortality in a crowded population may be beneficial to the fish population as a whole if space and/or food resources are limited. An extreme example is the death of the entire population through the severe stress of a thermal discharge, but even this may be beneficial to other members of the community.

It has been traditionally assumed in ecology that increasing complexity or diversity in a community produces increasing stability (e.g. Elton, 1958), but a more recent proposition is that complexity begets instability not stability, and that ecological communities persist despite, not because of, their complexity (e.g. May, 1973, 1976; Pimm and Lawton, 1980). It is, therefore, not surprising that stress responses at the population and community level are very complex and that little is known about the response of a freshwater ecosystem (for general reviews of stress and ecosystems see Odum, 1967, 1974; Slobodkin and Sanders, 1969; Gibbons, 1976; Lugo, 1978; Leffler, 1978). Therefore the present paper considers thermal stress only at the level of the individual fish.

The responses of a fish to stress can be broadly classed as either primary or secondary. Primary responses include neuro-endocrine and endocrine reactions which are reviewed in detail elsewhere in this volume (see contributions by Donaldson, 1981; Mazeaud and Mazeaud, 1981). Examples of primary responses to thermal stress include work on juvenile coho salmon, *Oncorhynchus kisutch* (Wedemeyer, 1973), goldfish, *Carassius auratus* (Fryer, 1975), juvenile sockeye salmon, *Oncorhynchus nerka* (Mazeaud *et al.*, 1977), and juvenile cutthroat trout, *Salmo clarki* (Strange *et al.*, 1977). As the fish were subjected to rapid increases of 10–15°C in these experiments, it is not surprising that the primary responses were so large. Such temperature increases rarely occur naturally in fresh water, and it would be of more ecological value to know the primary responses to smaller temperature changes at different acclimation temperatures and the level of temperature change at which there is no significant primary response.

There are numerous secondary responses to thermal stress and these include disturbances in osmotic and ionic regulation, metabolic processes, growth, reproduction and behaviour. The ultimate response is death. Metabolic and osmoregulatory disturbances during stress are effected by neuro-humoral changes (see reviews by Love, 1970; Maetz, 1974; Fontaine,

1975; Mazeaud *et al.*, 1977; Eddy, 1981, this volume; Mazeaud and Mazeaud, 1981, this volume). The marked effects of thermal stress on the cardiovascular and respiratory system of freshwater fish have been described in detail by several workers (e.g. Hughes, 1964; Hughes and Shelton, 1962; Hughes and Roberts, 1970; Shelton, 1970; Heath and Hughes, 1973; Randall and Cameron, 1973; Burton, 1979), and the large amount of information on the relationship between temperature and metabolic rates of whole fish or their organs and tissues is summarized in several reviews (e.g. Brett, 1956, 1970; Fry, 1957, 1967, 1971; Fry and Hochachka, 1970; Hochachka and Somero, 1971). There is therefore an enormous literature on the physiological responses of freshwater fish to thermal stress, and there is a similar amount of information on thermal discharges and their effects on fish (see recent reviews by Esch and McFarlane, 1976, Coutant and Talmage, 1975, 1976, 1977; Talmage and Coutant, 1978, 1979; Alabaster and Lloyd, 1980).

The present paper cannot deal with all these effects and emphasizes those aspects of thermal stress that directly affect the ecology of freshwater teleosts. These are: thermal limits and the optimum temperature range, thermal tolerance and resistance, subtle effects of thermal stress within the normal tolerance range, body temperature changes and thermoregulation. Extensive use has been made of the excellent work of F. E. J. Fry and J. R. Brett. Although their approach to the problem has usually been through the laboratory experiment, they have always asked questions that are relevant to the ecology of the fish. Their influence on my own thinking is therefore considerable and evident in this contribution.

II THERMAL LIMITS, OPTIMUM TEMPERATURE RANGE AND PREFERRED TEMPERATURES

Fish are obligate poikilotherms (ectotherms) some of which can perceive temperature changes of less than 0·5°C (Murray, 1971). Their gills are an effective heat exchanger, but most heat transfer is by conduction directly through the body wall and heat transfer at the gills accounts for only 10–30% of the total heat exchange between the fish and the surrounding water (Stevens and Sutterlin, 1976; Beitinger *et al.*, 1977; Erskine and Spotila, 1977; Kubb *et al.*, 1980). Although there is some thermoregulation by local conservation of muscular heat in at least two groups, the tunas and the lamnid sharks (Fry and Hochachka, 1970; Stevens and Neill, 1978), most fish lack a mechanism to maintain an independent body temperature and are therefore essentially thermal conformers. When the water temperature changes, the rate of thermal equilibration is usually rapid. The thermoregulatory mechanism in the central nervous system is similar to that of other vertebrates but the interrelationship between thermal acclimation and the thermoregulatory centres is somewhat ambiguous (see review by Crawshaw, 1977).

Although fish occur in habitats with temperatures from $-2\cdot5$°C to 44°C, no species can survive over this entire range and each species has a characteristic range with upper and lower lethal limits. At one extreme are the polar species that live under ice and in ice tunnels, and have a narrow thermal range with limits of $-2\cdot5$°C and 6°C (Sholander *et al.*, 1957; Somero and de Vries, 1967; Crawshaw and Hammel, 1971). The North American desert pupfish (*Cyprinodon* spp.) are at the other extreme and are the most eurythermal of fish with limits of about 2°C and 44°C (Lowe and Heath, 1969; Brown and Feldmuth, 1971; Otto and Gerking, 1973). Although different species may live within different thermal ranges, their metabolic rates may be similar. For example, the respiration rates of tissues from polar species (*Trematomus* spp.) are as high at 0–5°C as the rates of comparable tissues from goldfish at 20–25°C (Somero and de Vries, 1967). Freshwater teleosts in temperate regions usually live within the range 0–30°C. Minimum temperatures may reach 0°C in upland streams in winter, and maximum values may exceed 30°C in shallow ponds in summer or in waters that receive a thermal discharge. Brown trout, *Salmo trutta*, and carp, *Cyprinus carpio*, are good examples of temperate stenotherms and eurytherms respectively, and the marked contrast in their thermal requirements is illustrated in Fig. 1. Thermal stress, or even death, in each species occurs at temperatures that are optimal for feeding in the other species, but both species have a relatively narrow range for egg development.

Information on the thermal limits of common European species that also occur in Britain is summarized in Tables I and III. These tabulated values are my own interpretation of the data, and the number of references is a rough index of the amount of information on each species. Although the methods and objectives of studies on the same species often vary considerably, there is usually a remarkable similarity in the estimates of thermal limits. Other useful compilations have been made by Coutant (1977) who summarizes information on the "preferred" temperatures and upper and lower "avoidance" temperatures for 110 species from North America, and Alabaster and Lloyd (1980) who list the upper lethal and "disturbing" temperatures for 23 species, using data chiefly from Eastern Europe.

The "optimum temperature range" in Table I is the range over which feeding occurs and there are no external signs of abnormal behaviour, i.e. thermal stress is not obvious. This range is similar to the "normal physiological range" of some workers and is usually slightly wider than the range for growth and maturation. The optimum temperature range usually meets

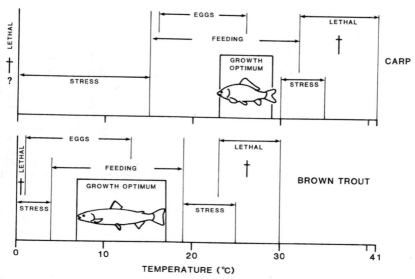

Fig. 1   Comparison of the thermal requirements of carp, *Cyprinus carpio*, and brown trout, *Salmo trutta*.

or overlaps the upper and lower critical temperature ranges (defined in Section III(a)) in Table I, but this does not occur for a few species because of a lack of reliable information.

Many workers have also used the concept of a "selected" or "preferred" temperature (see review of Richards *et al.*, 1977). The preferred temperature is often defined as the temperature at which fish are most frequently found when they are allowed to move freely in a temperature gradient. Usually the value is the modal, median or mean selected temperature and the fish generally occur over a temperature range rather than at one specific temperature. This preferred range is usually similar to, or lies within, the optimum temperature range. A second definition of preferred temperature is the value at which acclimation and preference temperatures are equal. The two definitions have led to different experimental designs. Methods for determining the final preferendum include temperature-gradient tanks, electronic shuttleboxes, body-core-temperature telemetry and calorimetry (McCauley, 1977).

As there are two definitions, several methods and additional variability due to differences in acclimation temperature, age, size and physiological conditions of the fish, it is not surprising that estimates of a single preferred temperature often vary considerably for the same species. For example, values in different studies ranged from about 21°C to 29°C for carp (Fry and Hochachka, 1970) and from 11·6°C to 19°C for rainbow trout (Spigarelli

TABLE I Summary of Optimum Temperature Range, Upper and Lower Critical Ranges for Different Freshwater Species (All Values to Nearest °C).

Species	Common name	Optimum range (°C)	Lower critical range (°C)	Upper critical range (°C)	No.	Reference
Coregonus lavaretus	whitefish	8–15		20–25	2	Hellawell (1969, 1971)
Thymallus thymallus	grayling	4–18		18–24	2+	Jones (1959), Bishai (1960),
Salmo salar	Atlantic salmon	6–20		20–34	6+	Spaas (1960), Garside (1973)
Salmo trutta	brown trout	4–19	0–4	19–30	8+	Spaas (1960), Frost and Brown (1967), Elliott (Tables II, IV)
Salmo gairdneri	rainbow trout	10–22	0–9	19–30	10+	Bidgood and Berst (1969), McCauley and Huggins (1976), Kaya (1978)
Salvelinus alpinus	charr	5–16	c.0	c.22–27	0+	McCauley (1958), Swift (1964), Johnson (1980)
Salvelinus fontinalis	American brook trout (speckled trout)	8–20	0–7	20–29	14+	Fry *et al.* (1946), McCormick *et al.* (1972), Hokanson *et al.* (1973)

Esox lucius	pike		9–25	30–34	5
Cyprinus carpio	carp	.0–15	15–32	30–41	7 + Aston and Brown (1978)
Carassius carassius	crucian carp		c.27	35–38	2
Carassius auratus	goldfish	0–17	16–30	27–42	6 + Fry *et al.* (1942)
Gobio gobio	gudgeon			27–37	3
Tinca tinca	tench		20–26	26–39	3 + Weatherley (1959)
Abramis brama	bream		8–28	28–36	3
Alburnus alburnus	bleak		?–20	20–38	2
Phoxinus phoxinus	minnow	c.0	13–25	23–31	1 + Frost (1943), Barrington and Matty (1954), Fortune (1955)
Scardinius erythrophthalmus	rudd		14–28	29–38	3
Rutilus rutilus	roach	0–12	8–25	25–38	2
Leuciscus cephalus	chub		8–25	27–39	1
Anguilla anguilla	eel	0–8	8–29	30–39	3 + Aston and Brown (1978), Sadler (1979)
Gasterosteus aculeatus	3-spine stickleback		4–20	22–37	0 + Baggerman (1957), de Sylva (1969), Jordan and Garside (1972), Wootton (1976)
Perca fluviatilis	perch		8–27	23–36	3 + Hokanson (1977)
Stizostedion lucioperca	zander		12–30	32–37	3 + Hokanson (1977)
Cottus gobio	bullhead		c.10–15		0 + Mann (1971)
Ctenopharyngodon idella	grass carp	0–2	20–30	34–39	1 + Stott (1977), Timmermans (1978)

The number of references is given for each species, and references are given if they are not in Reichenbach-Klinke (1976), Coutant (1977) or Alabaster and Lloyd (1980).

and Thommes, 1979). Therefore the concept of a single preferred temperature is difficult to apply to most species, and the preferred temperature
range, which is usually similar to the optimum temperature range, is
probably a more realistic concept in studies on thermal stress. The role of
temperature preference in relation to thermoregulation is discussed in the
second part of Section V.

III TOLERANCE AND RESISTANCE TO THERMAL STRESS

(a) Upper and Lower Critical Ranges

The "critical temperature ranges" in Table I are the ranges over which a
significant disturbance in the normal behaviour of a fish may occur, i.e. there
may be obvious signs of thermal stress. As most work on thermal stress has
been to predict the effects of thermal discharges on fish, information on the
upper critical range is more numerous than on the lower critical range. The
lowest value in the upper critical range is close to the "avoidance", "rest-
lessness" or "disturbing" temperature of other workers (see references in
Coutant, 1977; Alabaster and Lloyd, 1980), whilst the highest value is the
maximum temperature ("critical thermal maximum" of some workers) at
which fish can survive for brief periods.

As temperature increases within the upper critical range, the stress
response of the fish can be divided into three progressive phases. The first
external indications of abnormal behaviour are a reluctance to feed, sudden
bursts of activity with frequent collisions with the side of a tank in the
laboratory, rolling and pitching, defaecation and rapid ventilatory movements. In the second phase, the fish becomes quiescent with short bursts of
weak swimming, often floats on its side or back, may rapidly change colour
and increases its ventilatory movements. Movements are restricted in the
third phase to the opercula, pectoral fins and eyes, and cease with the death
of the fish. I have observed all three phases in brown trout and have found
that when fish are transferred to cooler well-oxygenated water, they usually
recover from the first and second phases, but never from phase three.
Cocking (1959) has made similar observations on roach, *Rutilus rutilus*,
subjected to thermal stress.

The occurrence of thermal stress in the critical ranges is affected by several
variables, the most important being the period of exposure to the critical
temperature and the acclimation temperature, i.e. the temperature at which
the fish are kept prior to the change in temperature. The different experimental methods of investigating the upper limits of thermal tolerance can be
divided into two broad categories. In the first group are the methods used to

determine the "critical thermal maximum" by raising the temperature from ambient acclimation level at a constant rate so that there is no significant time lag between the water temperature and the internal temperature of the fish. The critical thermal maximum is usually defined as the temperature at which the fish loses its ability to escape from lethal conditions, and is quickly followed by the lethal maximum when temperature continues to rise. In the second group of methods, the fish are kept at an acclimation temperature and then abruptly transferred to a higher constant temperature. This method is frequently used to determine the "incipient lethal temperature" which is the temperature beyond which the fish cannot live for an indefinite period. Some workers also determine the temperatures at which the fish can live for shorter periods of time, often 100 and 1000 min. Both groups of methods have their supporters and critics (see Fry, 1947, 1967, 1971; Hutchison, 1976; Becker and Genoway, 1979). Acclimation temperature is a common variable to both groups, but the important effects of the exposure period to the critical temperature are not included in the first group whilst the effects of rate of change in temperature are not included in the second group. In general, methods in the second group provide more information on the overall thermal tolerance and resistance of a fish, but have the added disadvantage that the final stress response may be due not only to thermal stress but also to handling stress when the fish are transferred from the acclimation temperature to the new temperature.

The complexity of thermal stress within the critical ranges can be illustrated by original work on brown trout. These experiments were performed to provide background data for a detailed study on feeding, growth and energetics (Elliott, 1972, 1975a, b, c, d, 1976a, b, c). The trout were in three distinct size groups with mean lengths (to nearest cm) and live weights (range to nearest g) of 10 cm and 10–12 g, 15 cm and 37–40 g, 25 cm and 175–185 g. The experimental tanks are described in detail by Swift (1961). Each tank contained about 100 litres of water that was stirred and aerated by compressed air (oxygen concentration >85% saturation) and maintained within ±0·1–0·2°C of a constant temperature. The tanks were covered with transparent polyethylene so that there was natural illumination with a light intensity at the water surface of c. 100 lux during the day.

Trout of similar size were acclimated to the same constant temperature (either 5, 10, 15, 20 or 22°C) for two weeks with one fish in each tank. Water temperature was then raised at a rate of about 1°C h^{-1} so that the final mean temperature in each tank was either 18, 20, 22, 24, 26 or 28°C. For acclimation temperatures of 20 and 22°C, there was an additional final temperature of 30°C but no final temperatures of 18–20°C and 18–22°C respectively. The rate of temperature increase was chosen because it is similar to mean rates of change in upland trout streams in summer, but rates as high as $2 \cdot 2–2 \cdot 5°C\,h^{-1}$ occasionally occur (Macan, 1958; Crisp and Le Cren, 1970; J. M. Elliott, unpublished). Two fish were kept at the acclimation temperature throughout the experiment and served as controls. Freshly killed *Gammarus pulex* were fed to the fish at satiation levels which had been determined from other experiments (Elliott, 1975a). Therefore the trout were not subjected to the additional stresses of handling and food deprivation. These stresses are ignored in most studies of thermal stress but are clearly important. When trout were handled during early experiments on feeding and growth, they refused to feed for periods between 1–6 days after handling, even when the fish were simply transferred between tanks with the same water temperature.

The survival and feeding rate (see Elliott, 1975b for experimental details) of the trout were recorded every 10 min for the first 100 min, every 100 min for the period 100–1000 min, and every 1000 min for the period 1000–10 080 min (= 7 days). These observations were used to record the highest temperature for normal feeding and survival over 10 min, 100 min, 1000 min and 7 days. The normal rate of feeding was determined in a separate series of experiments (Elliott, 1975b), and there was usually no problem in detecting a marked decrease in this rate because feeding became spasmodic or ceased. The experiment was repeated five times with different fish to give five estimates for each size group of fish at each acclimation temperature. As there were no significant differences ($p > 0 \cdot 05$) between the values for the three size groups at the same acclimation temperature, the samples were combined to give 15 values which were used to calculate arithmetic means and standard errors (Table II).

Several fish that survived for 7 days were kept at the same temperature for up to a month and it was therefore assumed that values for 7 days survival are the "incipient lethal levels", i.e. the temperatures that define a "tolerance zone" within which the fish can live for a considerable time (all definitions follow the terminology of Fry, 1947, 1971). The upper, incipient lethal temperature increased linearly with increasing acclimation temperature until the latter was just above 15°C. Above this level, there was no increase with increasing acclimation temperature and an ultimate upper incipient lethal temperature of $24 \cdot 7 \pm 0 \cdot 25°C$ was reached (Table II). Values for survival at 10 min, 100 min and 1000 min followed a similar pattern at slightly higher temperatures and were within the "zone of thermal resistance" outside the tolerance zone and between the incipient lethal temperature and ultimate lethal temperature. The latter temperature was estimated by the temperature for survival over 10 min. There was an exponential relationship between the "resistance time" (or "effective time" of some workers) to death and the lethal temperature (Fig. 2). Trout acclimated at 15, 20 or 22°C were able to survive at temperatures close to

TABLE II *Salmo trutta*: Highest and Lowest Temperatures (°C) for Survival over 10 min, 100 min, 1000 min and 7 days or Longer, and for Normal Feeding; all Values are Arithmetic Means ±SE ($n = 15$).

	Acclimation temperature				
	5°C	10°C	15°C	20°C	22°C
Highest temp. for:					
Survival over 10 min	25·6±0·21	27·3±0·25	—	29·9±0·13	29·7±0·18
100 min	24·3±0·18	25·9±0·31	27·7±0·18	27·9±0·13	27·7±0·18
1000 min	22·7±0·37	24·4±0·21	25·6±0·35	26·5±0·31	26·7±0·25
7 days +	21·5±0·36	22·9±0·38	24·4±0·45	24·7±0·25	24·7±0·25
Normal feeding	18·7±0·25	19·5±0·41	19·1±0·27	None	None
A and D, survival 100 min	23·9 (6°C)	—	27·4	28·2	—
1000 min	23·2 (6°C)	—	26·0	26·4	—
B, survival 1000 min	24·3 (6°C)	—	25·9	26·7	—
7 days	22	23	—	23	—
F and B, survival 7 days	22·5	24·2	24·5	24·8	25·3 (23°C)
Lowest temp. for:					
Survival over 100 min	0	0	0	0	0
1000 min	0	0	0	0	0·3±0·18
7 days +	0	0	0	0·7±0·25	1·3±0·25
Normal feeding	0·4±0·21	2·9±0·27	3·6±0·29	4·3±0·18	None

Values of other workers are included for comparison: A and D = Alabaster and Downing (1966), B = Bishai (1960), F and B = Frost and Brown (1967) who reproduced data from the Ph.D. thesis of E. S. Gibson (1951, University of Toronto).

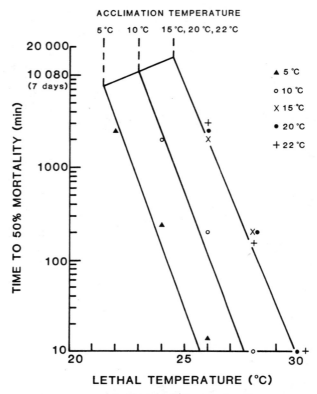

Fig. 2   Relationship between the time (min) for 50% mortality of brown trout, *Salmo trutta*,
and the lethal temperature (°C) at different acclimation temperatures.

28°C for 100 min and 30°C for 10 min. Therefore, trout can survive for short
periods at temperatures that would be eventually lethal. This resistance to
the lethal effects of thermal stress enables the fish to survive in waters where
daily maximum values exceed the incipient lethal temperature.

The highest temperatures for survival were very similar to those obtained
in three other studies on brown trout (cf. values in Table II), in spite of the
different experimental methods and fish sizes. Methods and sizes are not
given for the data quoted by Frost and Brown (1967), but in both the other
studies the fish were transferred abruptly from the acclimation temperature
to the higher temperature, and the trout were newly-hatched alevins (Bishai,
1960) and either 7·4 cm or 10·1 cm long (Alabaster and Downing, 1966).
These comparisons show that sudden or slower ($1°C\,h^{-1}$) changes in
temperature, some handling and size differences within the length range *c.*

2–25 cm had no obvious effects on the temperatures for survival over different periods.

The trout did not feed at acclimation temperatures of 20°C and 22°C, and the normal rate of feeding decreased markedly at temperatures above c. 19°C in the other experiments (Table II). As a marked decrease or a cessation of feeding will obviously have an important effect on the growth and ultimately the survival of the fish, it must be considered a stress response within the tolerance zone. Therefore, thermal stress can occur at temperatures that are below the incipient lethal level.

Detailed information on the lower critical range is scarce, but there are several records of "cold shock" during sudden decreases in temperature (see references in Brett, 1956; Ash et al., 1974; Block, 1974). As the freezing point of the body fluids of freshwater fish is close to $-0.5°C$, there is little danger of death through freezing. In lakes that freeze to the bottom, some species such as the Arctic black fish, Dallia pectoralis, and the crucian carp, Carassius carassius, avoid freezing by burrowing into the warmer mud at the bottom (de Vries, 1971). Thermal stress within the lower critical range usually produces a cessation of feeding and sudden bursts of activity followed by a state of coma in which there is failure of the respiratory centre and the ion-osmoregulatory mechanism (see references in Fry, 1971; see also Eddy, 1981, this volume). It is often difficult to determine when death occurs in comatose fish and death in the following experiments was assessed by the ability of the trout to recover when transferred to warmer water. It is worth noting that the gradual cooling of fish to less than 4°C (depending on the species and its thermal history) is one of the oldest methods of anaesthetizing fish (Randall and Hoar, 1971).

The experimental procedure used to determine lower temperature limits for brown trout was very similar to that used to determine upper limits. The same acclimation temperatures were used but the water temperature was then lowered at about $1°C\,h^{-1}$ to final mean temperatures of 0, 2, 4, 6°C (not 6°C for acclimation temperature of 5°C). This rate was close to the maximum rate of decrease in upland trout streams (Crisp and Le Cren, 1970; J. M. Elliott, unpublished). It was difficult to control the temperature at 2°C or less and iced water had to be added to maintain a temperature near 0°C. Records were made of the lowest temperatures for normal feeding and survival over 100 min, 1000 min and 7 days. Once again, there were no significant differences ($p > 0.05$) between the values for the three size groups of fish at each acclimation temperature and therefore the data were combined for the final estimates of means and standard errors.

Most fish survived for at least 7 days at temperatures close to 0°C, but some fish died at 0°C after acclimation at 20°C and 22°C, and the lowest temperatures for survival were therefore just above 0°C (Table II). The ultimate lower incipient lethal temperature could not be determined because it was obviously below the freezing point of freshwater. The lowest temperature at which normal feeding occurred increased with increasing acclimation temperature. Trout did not feed at acclimation temperatures of 20°C and 22°C, but those at 20°C started to feed at 4°C and 6°C. To check if trout could survive sudden decreases in temperature, fish kept at about 10°C in the laboratory were transferred abruptly in winter to outdoor tanks containing water to which snow was frequently added. The trout survived for 7 days, but refused to feed, at temperatures in the range 0·5–2°C, and were then returned to the laboratory where they soon returned to their normal feeding behaviour.

(b) Tolerance of Different Freshwater Species

The results presented in the last section were used to construct a thermal tolerance diagram for brown trout (Fig. 3). Thermal stress is lethal outside the tolerance zone enclosed by the incipient lethal level and death is a function of the exposure time to the thermal stress. The incipient lethal level

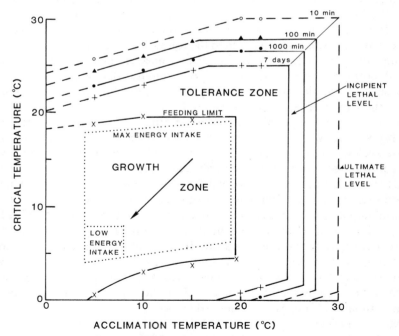

Fig. 3   Thermal tolerance diagram for brown trout, *Salmo trutta*, showing the tolerance zone, feeding zone and growth zone which decreases with decreasing energy intake.

is therefore the boundary between tolerance and resistance. Within the tolerance zone, temperature acts as a "loading" and "inhibiting" stress by limiting functions such as feeding, spawning, growth and metabolism (see Section IV).

Thermal tolerance diagrams provide a useful method for comparisons between species, but the detailed information required to construct such a diagram is lacking for most species. Notable exceptions (based on the work of Fry et al., 1942, 1946; Cocking, 1959) are compared in Fig. 4. The

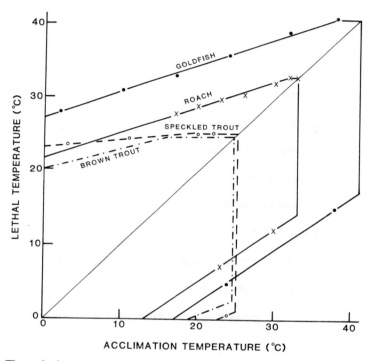

Fig. 4   Thermal tolerance diagrams for four species: brown trout, speckled trout or American brook trout (Fry et al., 1946), roach (Cocking, 1959), and goldfish (Fry et al., 1942).

thermal tolerance of brown trout and American brook trout, *Salvelinus fontinalis*, is very similar and both species are typically cold-water steno-therms. Roach have a much higher tolerance and the extremely high tolerance of goldfish shows why they can survive in habitats varying from a small lake to a jam-jar or polyethylene bag full of water! A 1°C increase in the upper incipient lethal temperature below the ultimate lethal level requires an increase in acclimation temperature of about 7°C for American brook trout, about 5°C for brown trout and about 3°C for roach and goldfish. The area of the tolerance zone is a useful index of thermal tolerance and is usually expressed as °C squared. The value of $583°C^2$ for brown trout is slightly lower than that of $625°C^2$ for American brook trout, but much lower than $770°C^2$ and $1220°C^2$ for roach and goldfish respectively. Brett (1956) gives values for 23 species from North America, and these decrease from goldfish to five *Oncorhynchus* spp. with extremely low values between 450 and $529°C^2$. There is a lack of detailed information on the temperature tolerance of most species in Table I, but a simple comparison between families (Fig. 5) shows the marked contrast between the cold-water stenotherms (Coregonidae, Thymallidae, Salmonidae), mesotherms (Esocidae, most Cyprinidae, Gasterosteidae, Percidae, Anguillidae), and the warm-water eurytherms (Cyprinidae: carp, goldfish, grass-carp).

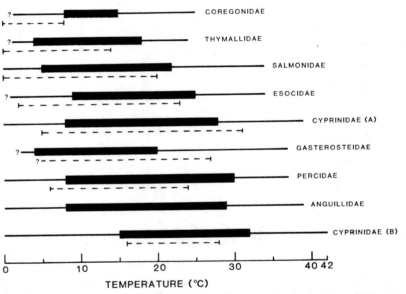

Fig. 5   Thermal tolerance of different families, using data for different species in Tables I and III: single line indicates upper and lower critical limits, solid bar indicates the optimum range, and broken line indicates the limits for development of the eggs (carp, goldfish and grass-carp constitute Cyprinidae B, all others in Cyprinidae A).

There is usually an inverse relationship between tolerance and resistance to thermal stress. Cold-water stenotherms have fairly low tolerance but high resistance (e.g. brown trout in Figs. 2, 3), whilst warm-water eurytherms usually have high tolerance but low resistance, i.e. the resistance time to temperatures outside the tolerance zone is very short (e.g. goldfish).

(c) Temperature Limits for Spawning and Egg Development

Information on the temperature range for spawning and the limits for egg development is summarized in Table III, and the tolerance ranges for the eggs of different families are compared in Fig. 5. It is obvious that the critical limits for successful spawning and egg development are narrower than those for older fish (see also Fig. 1). An extreme example is the desert pupfish with critical thermal limits of 2–44°C but a reproductive tolerance range of only 24–30°C (Shrode and Gerking, 1977; Gerking et al., 1979). Therefore, for most species, the eggs are more stenothermal than the juvenile or older fish and are the most vulnerable stage in the life cycle to the effects of thermal stress. These effects will influence not only the survival of the individual fish but also the ultimate survival of the population.

(d) Other Factors that may Affect Thermal Tolerance

Most workers agree that acclimation temperature and the period of exposure to temperatures outside the tolerance zone are the two most important factors that affect thermal tolerance and ultimately the lethal temperature for fish. There is less agreement over other factors, some of which are now considered. A full review is impossible because of lack of space and therefore only a selection of relevant examples can be given.

It is generally agreed that the egg is the critical stage for thermal stress (see previous section) but there is less agreement over a relationship between thermal tolerance and the age or size of the fish. Lack of any influence of size has been reported in the majority of studies, especially on upper temperature tolerance (see references in Brett, 1970). Smaller juvenile Pacific salmon (Oncorhynchus spp.) were more susceptible than larger juvenile fish to extremes of low temperature but not to high temperature (Brett, 1952). It has already been shown that values for brown trout in the size range c. 2–25 cm were not significantly different, but Spaas (1960) did find that as age and size increased, there was a corresponding increase in the upper lethal temperatures for brown trout and salmon, Salmo salar, with respective values close to 25°C and 28°C for alevins, 26°C and 29°C for yearlings and 29°C and 30°C for parr. These differences may be partially due to differences in experimental technique.

There may be seasonal variations in thermal tolerance and these variations are often related to changing photoperiod. Fish maintained on a long-day photoperiod may be more resistant to higher temperatures than those on a short-day photoperiod, e.g. goldfish (Hoar, 1956, 1965), carp (Roberts, 1961). Increased heat resistance under a long photoperiod and increased cold resistance under a short photoperiod may be of adaptive

TABLE III Summary of Usual Temperatures and Months for Spawning and Lethal Temperatures for Eggs of each Species (all Values to Nearest °C).

Species	Spawning range (°C)	months	Lethal for eggs Lower (°C)	Upper (°C)	No.	References
Coregonus lavaretus	0–4	October–January	c. 0	>8	3+	Bagenal (1970)
Thymallus thymallus	6–10	March–May	c. 0	>14	4+	Kokurewicz et al. (1980)
Salmo salar	0–8	October–January	c. 0	>16	3+	Peterson et al. (1977)
Salmo trutta	1–10	September–January	c. 0	>13	4	
Salmo gairdneri	4–19	October–March (May)	c. 0	>20	4+	Kwain (1975), Kaya (1977)
Salvelinus alpinus	3–15	September–April	c. 0	>8	0+	Frost (1965), Swift (1965a)
Salvelinus fontinalis	2–16	October–March	c. 0	>12	1+	Embody (1934), Needham (1961), Webster (1962), Hokanson et al. (1973)
Esox lucius	4–17	February–May	<2	>23	12+	Swift (1965b), Lillelund (1966)
Cyprinus carpio	12–30	May–July	<16	>26	6+	Sigler (1958), Swee and McCrimmon (1966)
Carassius carassius	16–18+	May–June			2	
Carassius auratus	17–24	May–July		>28	2+	Yamazaki (1965)

Species					
Barbus barbus	14–20	May–July	<14?	>20	3 + Hancock (1975)
Gobio gobio	c.12	May–June			1
Tinca tinca	18–27	May–July	<14	>31	6
Abramis brama	8–24	May–July	<8	>28	11
Alburnus alburnus	14–28	April–June	<14	>31	4
Phoxinus phoxinus	c.17–20	April–August			0+ Papadopol and Weinberger (1975)
Scardinius erythrophthalmus	14–28	April–June	<14	>31	7
Rutilus rutilus	5–22	April–June	<5	>27	14
Leuciscus cephalus	c.18	April–June		>30	1
Leuciscus leuciscus	5–10+	March–May	<16		3 + Kennedy (1969)
Gasterosteus aculeatus	12–18	April–June		>27	0+ Craig–Bennett (1931), Baggerman (1957), de Sylva (1969)
Perca fluviatilis	5–19	February–August	<6	>16	9 + Swift (1965b), Guma'a (1978), Hokanson (1977)
Stizostedion lucioperca	4–26	February–July	<9	>24	9 + Hokanson (1977)
Cottus gobio	7–14	February–June			0+ Fox (1978)
Ctenopharyngodon idella	c.20–30	May?–July	<20	>28	0+ Stott (1977), Timmermans (1978)

The number of references is given for each species, and references are given if they are not in Reichenbach-Klinke (1976) or Alabaster and Lloyd (1980).

value in temperate and polar regions (Hoar and Robinson, 1959; Tyler, 1966), but there are no really detailed studies on the seasonal effect or the extent to which changes in photoperiod can modify the lethal temperature. A clear demonstration of endocrine involvement is that the pituitary must be intact for a goldfish to acclimate to a higher temperature (Johansen, 1967). There may be also diel changes in thermal tolerance, similar to those shown by reptiles and amphibians (Hutchison, 1976), but there is no comparable evidence for fish, except that they may show diel changes in the "preferred" temperature (see Section V).

Thermal tolerance may be affected by diet and nutritional status, and varies in relation to levels of fats, cholesterol and phospholipids in the diet of goldfish (Hoar and Dorchester, 1949; Hoar and Cottle, 1952; Irvine et al., 1958). There is considerable evidence that thermal tolerance to high temperature is related to the reduction of free, body water (Fry, 1958). A high fat content and a low water content is usually indicative of fish in good condition. The "condition" of a fish (ratio of body mass to length^3) will therefore affect its thermal tolerance because fish in poor condition exchange heat more rapidly than those in good condition (Kubb et al., 1980).

Although two different rates of change in temperature (abrupt transfer and a slow change of $1°C\,h^{-1}$) had no obvious effects on the thermal tolerance of brown trout (cf. values in Table II), an increase from $1°C\,h^{-1}$ to $60°C\,h^{-1}$ increased the upper lethal temperature by about 4°C for juvenile coho salmon and young pumpkinseed fish, Lepomis gibbosus (Becker and Genoway, 1979), and an increase of $6°C\,h^{-1}$ to $60°C\,h^{-1}$ elevated the critical thermal maximum of bluegill, Lepomis macrochirus, by about 3°C (Cox, 1974). Most workers use constant acclimation temperatures in experimental studies, but there is some evidence that thermal tolerance and resistance increase if slightly fluctuating acclimation temperatures are used or there is a brief exposure to sublethal high temperatures (see references in Heath, 1963; Hutchison, 1976).

There may be geographical or genetic differences in thermal tolerance between populations of the same species, i.e. there may be physiological races (see references in Hart, 1952; McCauley, 1958). An example of the perils of assuming genetic differences is a study of a geothermal river where both brown and rainbow trout were apparently unaffected by daily maximum values of 28·8°C in summer (Kaya, 1977). The trout were therefore found at temperatures which are normally regarded as lethal (Table II), and it would have been easy to conclude that these populations were genetically different from other populations. However, it was later shown experimentally that the rainbow trout had not developed a greater resistance to high temperatures when they were compared with trout from two hatcheries (Kaya, 1978). Some of the apparent geographical variation in the thermal tolerance of the same or closely related species, may be due to differences in experimental technique and acclimation temperatures (Brett, 1956). There may be also different interpretations of the same data. For example, Hall *et al.* (1978) concluded that the preference temperatures of three populations of white perch, *Morone americana*, were significantly different and thus provided an example of geographical variation in temperature response, but Mathur and Silver (1980) later showed that these apparent differences were not significant when the correct number of degrees of freedom was used in the analysis.

IV THERMAL STRESS WITHIN THE TOLERANCE ZONE

To obtain a complete picture of the possible effects of thermal stress, it is important to know how temperature affects the various functions of a fish. The most complete information is for sockeye salmon and Brett (1971) has collated information on 25 responses to temperature. A similar summary is now possible for 19 responses of brown trout (Nos 1–19 in Table IV). Tolerance and preference (Nos 1, 2, 3) were discussed in Sections II and III, but it is worth noting that the upper lethal temperature is the only response with an increase to an upper plateau. If the rather short response of lower lethal temperature is excluded, there are four responses with a continuous increase to a maximum, namely rate of gastric evacuation (No. 7), energy losses of fish deprived of food (No. 15), standard metabolic rate (No. 9) and maintenance energy intake (No. 13). The two latter aspects also determine the lower limits of the "scope for activity" and "scope for growth" respectively (Fig. 6c, d).

All the remaining responses show an increase with increasing temperature to maximum values at optimum temperatures, and then a decrease as temperature continues to increase. Feeding rate (No. 6) has the widest optimum range of 7–19°C, whilst both appetite, as measured by voluntary food intake, and satiation time (Nos 4, 5) have narrower ranges of 13–18°C (Figs 6a, b). The active metabolic rate, maximum energy intake and scopes for activity and growth (Nos 10, 11, 12, 16) all have maximum values at about 18°C (Figs 6c, d), but there is a lower optimum of about 15°C for the optimum energy intake (No. 14), i.e. the value that produces the greatest growth for the least energy intake at each temperature. Although the scope for growth is greatest at *c.* 18°C, the energy losses in the faeces and excretory products increase markedly with temperature and therefore the energy available for growth is greatest in the narrow range 13–14°C. This is the optimum temperature for growth of all sizes and ages of trout on maximum rations (No. 17), but the growth rates at all temperatures decrease with

TABLE IV Responses of Brown Trout to Temperature Increases (Information is from Table II for Aspects 1 and 2, from Coutant (1977), Reynolds and Casterlin (1979) for Aspect 3, and from Elliott (1972, 1975a, b, c, d, 1976a, b, c, 1979) for Other Aspects).

Function	No.	Fig.	Aspect	(a) Continuous increase to maximum (range in °C)	(b) Increase to optimum, then decrease (optimum in °C)	(c) Increase to upper plateau (Plateau range in °C)
Tolerance	1	3	Upper lethal temp.			25–30
	2	3	Lower lethal temp.	0–c.2		
Preference	3	—	Selected temp.			
Appetite + feeding	4	6a	Voluntary food intake		10–14	
	5	6b	Satiation time		13–18	
	6	—	Feeding rate		13–18	
Digestion	7	—	Gastric evacuation rate	4–19	7–19	?
Metabolism + growth	8	—	% energy intake		14→4	
Metabolism	9	6c	Standard metabolic rate	4–20	c. 18	
	10	6c	Active metabolic rate		c. 18	
	11	6c	Scope for activity		c. 18	
Energetics + growth	12	6d	Maximum energy intake	4–20		
	13	6d	Maintenance energy intake		c. 15	
	14	6d	Optimum energy intake			
	15	—	Energy losses (starvation)	4–20		
	16	6d	Scope for growth		c. 18	?
	17	6e	Growth rate (max. rations)		13–14	
	18	6e	Growth rate (reduced rations)		14→4	
	19	6f	Gross efficiency (all rations)		8–11	

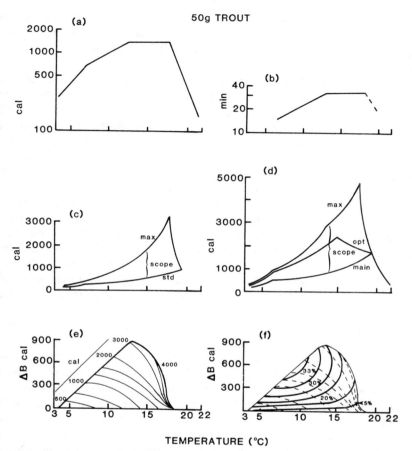

Fig. 6 Examples of some of the responses of brown trout (live weight 50 g) to temperature: (a) appetite (energy intake per meal); (b) satiation time (min); (c) daily energy requirements for standard (std) and active (max) metabolic rates with scope for activity; (d) maintenance (main), optimum (opt) and maximum (max) energy intake with scope for growth; (e) energy available for growth (ΔB) for different levels of energy intake (C cal day^{-1}); (f) gross efficiency isopleths (%).

increasing size and age (Elliott, 1979). When the energy intake (ration level) is reduced progressively, there is a corresponding reduction in the optimum temperature for the maximum growth rate (No. 18) and for the proportion of the energy intake available for growth and metabolism (No. 8). There is also a reduction in the upper temperature at which growth occurs, e.g. range for growth in 50 g trout is about 4–19°C on maximum rations but only about 4–8°C at a ration of 500 cal day^{-1} (Fig. 6e). The lowest optimum temperature range is for gross efficiency (energy for growth as a percentage of energy

232   J. M. ELLIOTT

intake) at all ration levels (No. 19). For 50 g trout, gross efficiency exceeded 33% in the range 8–11°C and then decreased with both increasing and decreasing values for temperature, energy intake and energy available for growth (Fig. 6f).

Although this brief summary of temperature effects on brown trout is no substitute for the detailed descriptions in the original publications, it does show that the form of the response to temperature and the optimum temperatures are not always the same for different functions, and that the optimum temperature for the response may change if there is a change in another factor such as energy intake. Some of these responses can be used to illustrate the subtle effects of stress within the tolerance zone, but some further concepts of stress must first be defined.

Fry (1947, 1971) classified environmental effects into five groups of factors: lethal, controlling, limiting, masking and directive. This approach was followed by Brett (1958) who divided stresses on fish into four categories: lethal (self-explanatory), limiting (restriction in the supply of essential metabolites or interference with the chain of energy release), inhibiting (reduction in the ability of the fish to carry out its normal functions, and hence a reduction in its probability of survival), and loading (an undue burden on the fish with a rapid or steady release of energy). Limiting, inhibiting and loading stresses may also be lethal when they continue over a long period.

The effects of temperature as a lethal stress outside the tolerance zone have been discussed in detail in Section III. An example of temperature as an inhibiting stress is cessation of feeding and this has also been discussed in Section III. Temperature limits for feeding at the normal rate were used to construct a feeding zone within the tolerance zone (Fig. 3). The range between the feeding limit and the incipient lethal level is the "zone of resistance to starvation", using a concept similar to that for the zone of thermal resistance, and the resistance time to death within this starvation zone is also a function of temperature (see No. 15 in Table IV), and the size and body composition of the fish (Elliott, 1975d, 1976a, b). Another example of temperature as an inhibiting stress is the limited range for spawning (Table III). Outside this range, temperature may be acting as an inhibiting stress by affecting the normal endocrine balance necessary for spawning (Brett, 1958).

The best example of temperature as a loading stress is the limit for growth and activity. In brown trout on maximum rations, growth occurs between 4°C and 19°C, and the lack of energy for growth outside this range is due to a combination of reduced energy intake, high energy losses in waste products, high metabolic demands above 19°C and perhaps the inhibition of metabolism below 4°C. These limits were used to construct a growth zone within the feeding zone (Fig. 3). Thermal stress can continue even within this growth zone when there are also limiting stresses, e.g. reductions in oxygen concentration, enzyme substrates, nutrients and essential ions (see review of Fry, 1971). It has already been shown that when the food supply is reduced, both the optimum temperature and temperature range for growth are reduced (Fig. 6e). These changes are due to the combined effects of two stresses: the limiting stress of reduced energy intake and the loading stress of temperature. As the energy intake is reduced, there is a marked decrease in the upper limits of the growth zone (Fig. 3).

These examples have shown that thermal stress is not only lethal outside the tolerance zone, but can also act subtly within the tolerance zone as an inhibiting stress, a loading stress, or a loading stress in conjunction with other limiting stresses. All these effects are within the definition of thermal stress in the introduction and show that thermal stress can affect most functions of a fish.

V BODY TEMPERATURE AND THERMOREGULATION

Body temperature is usually less than 0·6°C above water temperature but the excess body temperature usually increases slightly as a function of fish size and weight (Stevens and Fry, 1970, 1974; Spigarelli et al., 1974). For example, body temperatures of brown trout were measured with a thermistor (precision at least 0·05°C, see Mortimer and Moore, 1970) inserted 1–2 cm inside the anal aperture. The measurements were made within 30 s of the removal of the fish from the water. Mean values (±SE) for samples of 10 trout kept at 15°C or 6°C were 15·07±0·02°C and 6·07±0·02°C for trout with a mean length of 10 cm (live weight 10–12 g), 15·12±0·02°C and 6·13±0·02°C for 15 cm trout (37–40 g), 15·28±0·03°C and 6·25±0·03°C for 25 cm trout (175–185 g). Other workers have measured body temperatures by implanting thermistors or using miniature transmitters that are small enough to be swallowed (see review by McCauley, 1977).

Rates of thermal equilibration in body temperature following a change in water temperature are affected by many factors, including rates of gill ventilation and blood flow, circulatory anatomy, water movement and the shape, size and activity of the fish (see references in Crawshaw, 1977; Kubb et al., 1980). Between 70 and 90% of the heat transfer occurs through the body wall, rather than the gills, and body diameter, insulation thickness and tissue thermal conductivity are the chief factors affecting heat transfer. It is therefore not surprising that rates of heat exchange are generally related to body size and weight.

These changes are illustrated by original data for brown trout in three size groups with mean lengths of 10 cm, 15 cm, 25 cm (see above for weight ranges). Ten fish in each size group were transferred abruptly from 15°C to 6°C or the reverse, and one fish was then removed every minute after the transfer so that ten measurements of anal temperature were made with a thermistor. The temperature difference (ΔT °C) between body temperature and water temperature decreased exponentially with time for both cooling (15 to 6°C) and warming (6 to 15°C), but the exponential rate was not the same for the two processes nor for the different size groups (Fig. 7a, b). The exponential relationship follows Newton's law of cooling and has been used by other workers (e.g. Stevens and Fry, 1970, 1974).

As the mean temperatures of the trout in each size group were already known for water temperatures of 15°C and 6°C (see above), exponential rates of change in body temperature were estimated for each fish (R °C per min per ΔT °C, where $R = (\log_e \Delta T_t - \log_e \Delta T_0)/t$ and ΔT_0 and ΔT_t were the temperature differences at the beginning and end of a period of t min). When the values of R for the three size groups and a small number of trout of intermediate weights were plotted against the live weight (Wg) of the fish (Fig. 7c), the relationship between the two variables followed a power law with a negative exponent ($R = aW^{-b}$ where a and b are constants). The rate of cooling was clearly lower than the rate of warming for trout of similar weight, and both rates decreased as the weight of the trout increased (for cooling: $a = 1.862$, $b \pm 95\% CL = 0.390 \pm 0.033$, $r^2 = 0.95$, $n = 32$; for warming: $a = 2.290$, $b \pm 95\% CL = 0.375 \pm 0.025$, $r^2 = 0.97$, $n = 30$). These relationships can be used to estimate the time taken to reach thermal equilibrium for trout of different weights exposed to different changes in temperature. Sudden changes in water temperature rarely exceed 2°C but may be as high as 5–7°C when a thermal discharge enters a river, or as high as 10°C when a fish crosses the thermocline in a stratified lake. If trout are exposed to these changes within the extremes of 2°C to 10°C, the time taken to attain thermal equilibrium is only 3–6 min for 10 g trout, but about 7–15 min for 100 g trout, and about 23–35 min for cooling and 18–27 min for warming in 1000 g trout. Other workers have also found that the internal temperature of smaller fish (<100 g) changes rapidly, usually in less than 10 min, to the ambient temperature whereas larger fish may require over an hour (Spigarelli et al., 1974; Kubb et al., 1980). Several studies have also shown that rates of heat exchange are usually higher for warming than for cooling, at least in larger fish (McCauley and Huggins, 1976; Reynolds, 1977; Beitinger et al., 1977). Some physiological changes may be responsible for this difference, e.g. circulatory rates may decrease with cooling and thereby reduce the rate of heat exchange across the gills.

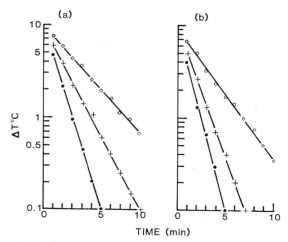

Fig. 7a, b Relationship between the temperature difference ($\Delta T°C$ = difference between body and water temperatures) and time (min) for brown trout subjected to (a) cooling (15 to 6°C) and (b) warming (6 to 15°C); mean lengths of trout were 10 cm (●), 15 cm (+) and 25 cm (○).

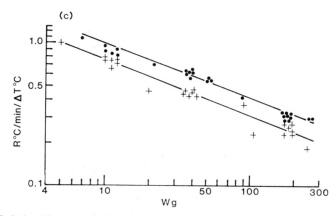

Fig. 7c Relationship between the exponential rate of change in body temperature ($R°C$ per min per $\Delta T°C$) and the live weight of brown trout (Wg) subjected to warming (●) and cooling (+).

Rates of change in body temperature are important because they determine the time lag in thermal equilibration. This time lag increases as fish weight increases and therefore the short-term fluctuations in the body temperature of larger fish are less than temperature fluctuations in the surrounding water. For example, gut temperatures of 200 g rainbow trout remained within $16 \pm 0.5°C$ whilst water temperatures varied continuously within about $13.5–18.5°C$ (McCauley and Huggins, 1976). Thus, the body temperatures of larger fish are independent of small and rapid fluctuations in water temperature. Freshwater teleosts do not show any physiological thermoregulation by local conservation of muscular heat as seen in tunas and lamnid sharks (Fry and Hochachka, 1970; Stevens and Neill, 1978), but there may be a limited control of heat exchange by a restriction of blood circulation through the gills (Fry and Hochachka, 1970).

The only other mechanism available to a freshwater fish is behavioural thermoregulation. Fish can detect temperature changes of less than $0.5°C$ (Murray, 1971) and are able to select a particular temperature or range of temperatures. The concept of "selected" or "preferred" temperatures has already been discussed in Section II. A spectacular demonstration of temperature preference is the work of Rozin and Mayer (1961) who trained goldfish to press a lever and cause a fall in water temperature when it was too warm. Thus, the goldfish maintained their environmental temperature at about 34°C and their precision was similar to that achieved by a rat in a similar experiment. Thermoregulatory behaviour has not been adequately studied in many species and is not well understood (see reviews of Fry and Hochachka, 1970; Richards et al., 1977). It is remarkable that several species show diel rhythms of preferred temperature, e.g. goldfish (Reynolds, 1977; Reynolds et al., 1978), brown trout (Reynolds and Casterlin, 1979), but other species do not, e.g. striped bass, *Morone saxatilis* (Coutant and Carroll, 1980). These rhythms may be related to varying temperature optima for different physiological functions (see Section IV). The diel migration of sockeye salmon smolts into deep, cold water may be due to a lower ration level and hence a lower optimum temperature for growth (Brett, 1971). Brown trout of 50 g live weight will not grow on a daily energy intake of about 1000 cal at $14.5°C$, but growth will be about 350 cal day^{-1} for the same energy intake at 8°C (Fig. 6e). Therefore trout may also move into colder water, especially in lakes, when the food supply is reduced (Elliott, 1979). Both these examples show that thermoregulatory behaviour is one of the chief factors responsible for fish movements, but a discussion of fish movements in relation to temperature is beyond the scope of this contribution.

VI GENERAL CONCLUSIONS

This account has shown that a fish is subjected to a hierarchy of thermal stresses, ranging from lethal effects outside the tolerance zone to inhibiting and loading effects within the tolerance zone. The fish can counteract these effects by resistance, acclimation with metabolic adjustment, and thermo-regulation chiefly by behaviour. There is clearly a need for more complete studies on the effects of temperature on various functions connected with feeding, metabolism and growth. It is also important to know more about the thermal requirements of different species in the field and the critical limits for all forms of thermal stress. Although they have not been discussed in the present contribution, fish movements and the synergistic effects of temperature in conjunction with other stresses are clearly important aspects of thermal stress. Effects at the population and community levels are probably the least understood aspects of thermal stress and are probably the most important in relation to the impact of man's activities on the freshwater ecosystem.

REFERENCES

Alabaster, J. S. and Downing, A. L. (1966). A field and laboratory investigation on the effect of heated effluents on fish. *Fishery Invest., Lond.* Ser. I, **6**, 1–42.
Alabaster, J. S. and Lloyd, R. (1980). *Water Quality Criteria for Freshwater Fish.* London: Butterworths. pp. 297.
Ash, G. R., Chymko, N. R. and Gallup, D. N. (1974). Fish kill due to "cold shock" in Lake Wabamum, Alberta. *J. Fish. Res. Bd Can.* **31**, 1822–1824.
Aston, R. J. and Brown, D. J. A. (1978). Fish farming in heated effluents. In *Proc. Conference on fish farming and wastes* (C. M. R. Pastakia, ed.), pp. 39–62. London: Institute of Fisheries Management.
Bagenal, T. B. (1970). Notes on the biology of the schelly *Coregonus lavaretus* (L.) in Haweswater and Ullswater. *J. Fish Biol.* **2**, 137–154.
Baggerman, B. (1957). An experimental study of the timing of breeding and migration in the three-spined stickleback, (*Gasterosteus aculeatus* L.) *Archs Néerl. Zool.* **7**, 105–318.
Barrington, E. J. W. and Matty, A. J. (1954). Seasonal variation in the thyroid gland of the minnow, *Phoxinus phoxinus* L., with some observations on the effect of temperature. *Proc. zool. Soc. Lond.* **124**, 89–95.
Becker, C. D. and Genoway, R. G. (1979). Evaluation of the critical thermal maximum for determining thermal tolerance of freshwater fish. *Environ. Biol. Fishes*, **4**, 245–256.
Beitinger, T. L., Thommes, M. M. and Spigarelli, S. A. (1977). Relative roles of conduction and convection in the body temperature change of gizzard shad, *Dorosoma cepidianum. Comp. Biochem. Physiol.* **57A**, 275–279.
Bidgood, B. F. and Berst, A. H. (1969). Lethal temperatures for Great Lakes rainbow trout. *J. Fish. Res. Bd Can.* **26**, 456–459.
Bishai, H. M. (1960). Upper lethal temperatures for larval Salmonids. *J. Cons. int. Explor. Mer.* **25**, 129–133.
Block, R. M. (1974). Effects of acute cold shock on the channel catfish. In *Thermal Ecology* (J. W. Gibbons and R. R. Sharitz, eds), pp. 109–118. NTIS Conference Report CONF-730505.

Brett, J. R. (1952). Temperature tolerance in young Pacific salmon, genus *Oncorhynchus*. *J. Fish. Res. Bd Can.* **9**, 265–323.

Brett, J. R. (1956). Some principles in the thermal requirements of fishes. *Q. Rev. Biol.* **31**, 75–87.

Brett, J. R. (1958). Implications and assessments of environmental stress. In *Investigations of Fish-power Problems* (P. A. Larkin, ed.), pp. 69–83. H. R. MacMillan Lectures in Fisheries, University of British Columbia.

Brett, J. R. (1970). Environmental factors, Part 1, Temperature. In *Marine Ecology*, *Vol. 1* (O. Kinne, ed.), pp. 513–560. London: Wiley.

Brett, J. R. (1971). Energetic responses of salmon to temperature. A study of some thermal relations in the physiology and freshwater ecology of sockeye salmon (*Oncorhynchus nerka*). *Am. Zool.* **11**, 99–113.

Brown, J. H. and Feldmuth, C. R. (1971). Evolution in constant and fluctuating environments: thermal tolerances of desert pupfish (*Cyprinodon*). *Evolution* **25**, 390–398.

Burton, D. T. (1979). Ventilation frequency compensation responses of three eurythermal estuarine fish exposed to moderate temperature increases. *J. Fish Biol.* **15**, 589–601.

Cocking, A. W. (1959). The effect of high temperatures on roach, (*Rutilus rutilus*). II. The effects of temperature increasing at a known constant rate. *J. exp. Biol.* **36**, 217–226.

Coutant, C. C. (1977). Compilation of temperature preference data. *J. Fish. Res. Bd Can.* **34**, 739–745.

Coutant, C. C. and Carroll, D. S. (1980). Temperatures occupied by ten ultrasonic-tagged striped bass in freshwater lakes. *Trans. Am. Fish. Soc.* **109**, 195–202.

Coutant, C. C. and Talmage, S. S. (1975). Thermal effects. *J. Wat. Pollut. Control Fed.* **47**, 1656–1711.

Coutant, C. C. and Talmage, S. S. (1976). Thermal effects. *J. Wat. Pollut. Control. Fed.* **48**, 1486–1544.

Coutant, C. C. and Talmage, S. S. (1977). Thermal effects. *J. Wat. Pollut. Control. Fed.* **49**, 1369–1425.

Cox, D. K. (1974). Effects of three heating rates on the critical thermal maximum of bluegill. In *Thermal Ecology*, *Vol. 1* (J. W. Gibbons and R. R. Sharitz, eds), pp. 158–163. CONF-730505, Nat. Tech. Inf. Serv., Springfield, Va.

Craig-Bennett, A. (1931). The reproductive cycle of the three-spined stickleback, *Gasterosteus aculeatus* (L.). *Phil. Trans. R. Soc. Lond. B.* **219**, 197–279.

Crawshaw, L. I. (1977). Physiological and behavioral reactions of fishes to temperature change. *J. Fish. Res. Bd Can.* **34**, 730–734.

Crawshaw, L. I. and Hammel, H. T. (1971). Behavioral thermoregulation in two species of antarctic fish. *Life Sci.* **10**, 1009–1020.

Crisp, D. T. and Le Cren, E. D. (1970). The temperature of three different small streams in northwest England. *Hydrobiologia* **35**, 305–323.

de Sylva, D. P. (1969). Theoretical considerations on the effects of heated effluents on marine fishes. In *Biological Aspects of Thermal Pollution* (P. A. Krenkel and F. L. Parker, eds), pp. 229–293. Nashville: Vanderbilt University Press.

de Vries, A. L. (1971). Freezing resistance in fishes. In *Fish Physiology*, *Vol. VI* (W. S. Hoar and D. J. Randall, eds), pp. 157–190. London and New York: Academic Press.

Donaldson, E. M. (1981). The pituitary-interrenal axis as an indicator of stress in fish. In *Stress and Fish* (A. D. Pickering, ed.), pp. 11–47. London and New York: Academic Press.

Eddy, F. B. (1981). Effects of stress on osmotic and ionic regulation in fish. In *Stress and Fish* (A. D. Pickering, ed.), pp. 77–102. London and New York: Academic Press.

Elton, C. S. (1958). *The ecology of invasions by animals and plants.* London: Methuen. 181 pp.

Elliott, J. M. (1972). Rates of gastric evacuation in brown trout, *Salmo trutta* L. *Freshwat. Biol.* **2**, 1–18.

Elliott, J. M. (1975a). Weight of food and time required to satiate brown trout, *Salmo trutta* L. *Freshwat. Biol.* **5**, 51–64.

Elliott, J. M. (1975b). Number of meals in a day, maximum weight of food consumed in a day and maximum rate of feeding for brown trout, *Salmo trutta* L. *Freshwat. Biol.* **5**, 287–303.

Elliott, J. M. (1975c). The growth rate of brown trout (*Salmo trutta* L.) fed on maximum rations. *J. Anim. Ecol.* **44**, 805–821.

Elliott, J. M. (1975d). The growth rate of brown trout (*Salmo trutta* L.) fed on reduced rations. *J. Anim. Ecol.* **44**, 823–842.

Elliott, J. M. (1976a). Body composition of brown trout (*Salmo trutta* L.) in relation to temperature and ration size. *J. Anim. Ecol.* **45**, 273–289.

Elliott, J. M. (1976b). Energy losses in the waste products of brown trout (*Salmo trutta* L.). *J. Anim. Ecol.* **45**, 561–580.

Elliott, J. M. (1976c). The energetics of feeding, metabolism and growth of brown trout (*Salmo trutta* L.) in relation to body weight, water temperature and ration size. *J. Anim. Ecol.* **45**, 923–948.

Elliott, J. M. (1979). Energetics of freshwater teleosts. *Symp. zool. Soc., Lond.* **44**, 29–61.

Embody, G. C. (1934). Relation of temperature to the incubation periods of eggs of four species of trout. *Trans. Am. Fish. Soc.* **64**, 281–292.

Erskine, D. J. and Spotila, J. R. (1977). Heat-energy-budget analysis and heat transfer in the largemouth blackbass (*Micropterus salmoides*). *Physiol. Zool.* **50**, 157–169.

Esch, G. W. and McFarlane, R. W. (Eds) (1976). *Thermal Ecology, Vol. II.* ERDA Symp. Ser. CONF-750425. Natl. Inf. Serv., Springfield, Va.

Fontaine, Y. A. (1975). Hormones in fishes. In *Biochemical and Biophysical Perspectives in Marine Biology, Vol. 2* (D. C. Malins and J. R. Sargent, eds), pp. 139–212. London and New York: Academic Press.

Fortune, P. Y. (1955). Comparative studies of the thyroid function in the teleosts of tropical and temperate habitats. *J. exp. Biol.* **32**, 504–513.

Fox, P. J. (1978). Preliminary observations on different reproduction strategies in the bullhead (*Cottus gobio* L.) in northern and southern England. *J. Fish Biol.* **12**, 5–11.

Frost, W. E. (1943). The natural history of the minnow, *Phoxinus phoxinus. J. Anim. Ecol.* **12**, 139–162.

Frost, W. E. (1965). Breeding habits of Windermere charr, *Salvelinus willughbii* (Gunther), and their bearing on speciation of these fish. *Proc. R. Soc. Lond. B*, **163**, 232–284.

Frost, W. E. and Brown, M. E. (1967). *The Trout.* London: Collins. 286 pp.

Fry, F. E. J. (1947). Effects of the environment on animal activity. Univ. Toronto Stud. Biol. Ser. 55, Publs. Ont. Fish. Res. Lab. **68**, 5–62.

Fry, F. E. J. (1957). The aquatic respiration of fish. In *The Physiology of Fishes, Vol. I* (M. E. Brown, ed.), pp. 1–63. London and New York: Academic Press.

Fry, F. E. J. (1958). Laboratory and aquarium research. II. The experimental study of behaviour in fish. *Proc. Indo–Pacif. Fish. Coun.* 37–42.

Fry, F. E. J. (1967). Responses of vertebrate poikilotherms to temperature. In *Thermobiology* (A. H. Rose, ed.), pp. 375–409. London and New York: Academic Press.

Fry, F. E. J. (1971). The effect of environmental factors on the physiology of fish. In *Fish Physiology, Vol. VI* (W. S. Hoar and D. J. Randall, eds), pp. 1–98. London and New York: Academic Press.

Fry, F. E. J. and Hochachka, P. W. (1970). Fish. In *Comparative Physiology of Thermoregulation, Vol. 1. Invertebrates and Non-mammalian Vertebrates* (G. Causey Whitton, ed.), pp. 79–134. London and New York: Academic Press.

Fry, F. E. J., Brett, J. R. and Clawson, G. H. (1942). Lethal limits of temperature for young goldfish. *Rev. Can. Biol.* **1**, 50–56.

Fry, F. E. J., Hart, J. S. and Walker, K. F. (1946). Lethal temperature relations for a sample of young speckled trout, *Salvelinus fontinalis*. *Univ. Toronto Stud. Biol. Ser.* 54, *Publs. Ont. Fish. Res. Lab.* **66**, 9–35.

Fryer, J. N. (1975). Stress and adrenocorticosteroid dynamics in the goldfish, *Carassius auratus*. *Can. J. Zool.* **53**, 1012–1020.

Garside, E. T. (1973). Ultimate upper lethal temperature of Atlantic salmon *Salmo salar* L. *Can. J. Zool.* **51**, 898–900.

Gerking, S. D., Lee, R. and Shrode, J. B. (1979). Effects of generation long temperature acclimation on reproductive performance of the desert pupfish *Cyprinodon n. nevadensis*. *Physiol. Zool.* **52**, 113–121.

Gibbons, J. W. (1976). Thermal alteration and the enhancement of species populations. In *Thermal ecology, Vol. II*, ERDA Symposium Series, 1975. (G. W. Esch and R. M. McFarlane, eds), pp. 27–31. CONF-750425, NTIS.

Guma'a, S. A. (1978). The effects of temperature on the development and mortality of eggs of perch, *Perca fluviatilis*. *Freshwat. Biol.* **8**, 221–227.

Hall, L. W. Jr, Hocutt, C. H. and Stauffer, J. R. Jr (1978). Implication of geographic location on temperature preference of white perch, *Morone americana*. *J. Fish. Res. Bd Can.* **35**, 1464–1468.

Hancock, R. S. (1975). The spawning behaviour of barbel, *Barbus barbus*. *Proc. 7th Br. coarse Fish Conf.* 54–58.

Hart, J. S. (1952). Geographic variations of some physiological and morphological characters in certain freshwater fish. *Univ. Toronto Biol. Ser.* 60, *Publs Ont. Fish. Res. Lab.* **72**, 1–79.

Heath, A. G. and Hughes, G. M. (1973). Cardiovascular and respiratory changes during heat stress in rainbow trout (*Salmo gairdneri*). *J. exp. Biol.* **59**, 323–338.

Heath, W. G. (1963). Thermoperiodism in sea-run cutthroat trout (*Salmo clarki clarki*). *Science, N.Y.* **142**, 486–488.

Hellawell, J. M. (1969). Age determination and growth of the grayling *Thymallus thymallus* (L.) of the River Lugg, Herefordshire. *J. Fish Biol.* **1**, 373–382.

Hellawell, J. M. (1971). The food of the grayling, *Thymallus thymallus* (L.) of the River Lugg, Herefordshire. *J. Fish Biol.* **3**, 187–197.

Hoar, W. S. (1956). The behaviour of migrating pink and chum salmon fry. *J. Fish. Res. Bd Can.* **13**, 309–325.

Hoar, W. S. (1965). The endocrine system as a chemical link between the organism and its environment. *Trans. R. Soc. Can.* **3**, 175–200.

Hoar, W. S. and Cottle, M. K. (1952). Dietary fat and temperature tolerance of goldfish. *Can J. Res., Zool.* **30**, 41–48.

Hoar, W. S. and Dorchester, J. E. C. (1949). The effect of dietary fat on the heat tolerance of goldfish (*Carassius auratus*). *Can. J. Res., D.* 27, 85–91.

Hoar, W. S. and Robinson, G. B. (1959). Temperature resistance of goldfish maintained under controlled photoperiods. *Can. J. Zool.* 37, 419–428.

Hochachka, P. W. and Somero, G. N. (1971). Biochemical adaptation to the environment. In *Fish Physiology, Vol. VI* (W. S. Hoar and D. J. Randall, eds), pp. 99–156. London and New York: Academic Press.

Hokanson, K. E. F. (1977). Temperature requirements of some percids and adaptations to the seasonal temperature cycle. *J. Fish Res. Bd Can.* 34, 1524–1550.

Hokanson, K. E. F., McCormick, J. H., Jones, B. R. and Tucker, J. H. (1973). Thermal requirements for maturation, spawning and embryo survival of the brook trout, *Salvelinus fontinalis*. *J. Fish. Res. Bd Can.* 30, 975–984.

Hughes, G. M. (1964). Fish respiratory homeostasis. In *Homeostasis and Feedback Mechanisms*, pp. 81–107. Symp. Soc. Exp. Biol, No. 18. Cambridge: Cambridge University Press.

Hughes, G. M. and Roberts, J. L. (1970). A study of the effect of temperature changes on the respiratory pumps of the rainbow trout. *J. exp. Biol.* 52, 177–192.

Hughes, G. M. and Shelton, G. (1962). Respiratory mechanisms and their nervous control in fish. In *Advances in Comparative Physiology and Biochemistry, Vol. 1* (O. Lowenstein, ed.), pp. 275–365. London and New York: Academic Press.

Hutchison, V. H. (1976). Factors influencing thermal tolerances of individual organisms. In *Thermal Ecology, Vol. II* (G. W. Esch and R. M. McFarlane, eds), pp. 10–26. ERDA Symp. Ser. CONF-750425 Natl. Inf. Serv., Springfield, Va.

Irvine, D. G., Newman, K. and Hoar, W. S. (1958). Effects of dietary phospholipid and cholesterol on temperature resistance of goldfish. *Can. J. Zool.* 35, 691–709.

Johansen, P. H. (1967). The role of the pituitary in the resistance of the goldfish (*Carassius auratus* L.) to a high temperature. *Can. J. Zool.* 45, 329–345.

Johnson, L. (1980). The arctic charr, *Salvelinus alpinus*. In *Charrs. Salmonid Fishes of the Genus Salvelinus* (E. K. Balon, ed.), pp. 15–98. The Hague: Junk.

Jones, J. W. (1959). *The Salmon*. London: Collins. 192pp.

Jordan, C. M. and Garside, E. T. (1972). Upper lethal temperatures of three-spine stickleback, *Gasterosteus aculeatus* (L.), in relation to thermal and osmotic acclimation, ambient salinity and size. *Can. J. Zool.* 50, 1405–1411.

Kaya, C. M. (1977). Reproductive biology of rainbow and brown trout in a geothermally heated stream: the Firehole River of Yellowstone National Park. *Trans. Am. Fish. Soc.* 106, 354–361.

Kaya, C. M. (1978). Thermal resistance of rainbow trout from a permanently heated stream, and of two hatchery strains. *Progve Fish Cult.* 40, 138–142.

Kennedy, M. (1969). Spawning and early development of the dace, *Leuciscus leuciscus* (L.). *J. Fish Biol.* 1, 249–259.

Kokurewicz, B., Kowelewski, M. and Witkowski, A. (1980). Influence of constant and variable temperatures on the embryonic development of European grayling, *Thymallus thymallus* (L.). *Zoologica Pol.* 27, 335–362.

Kubb, R. N., Spotila, J. R. and Pendergast, D. R. (1980). Mechanisms of heat transfer and time-dependent modeling of body temperatures in the largemouth bass (*Micropterus salmoides*). *Physiol. Zool.* 53, 222–239.

Kwain, W.-H. (1975). Effects of temperature on development and survival of rainbow trout, *Salmo gairdneri*, in acid waters. *J. Fish. Res. Bd Can.* 32, 493–497.

Leffler, J. W. (1978). Ecosystem responses to stress in aquatic microcosms. In *Energy and Environmental Stress in Aquatic Ecosystems* (J. H. Thorp and J. W. Gibbons, eds), pp. 102–119 Technical Information Center U.S. Department of Energy. CONF-771114.

Lillelund, K. (1966). Investigations into the hatching of pike (*Esox lucius* L.) eggs in relation to temperature and light. *Arch. FischWiss.* **17**, 95–113.

Love, R. M. (1970). *The Chemical Biology of Fishes*. London and New York: Academic Press. 547pp.

Lowe, C. H. and Heath, W. G. (1969). Behavioral and physiological responses to temperature in the desert pupfish (*Cyprinodon macularius*). *Physiol. Zool.* **42**, 53–59.

Lugo, A. E. (1978). Stress and ecosystems. In *Energy and Environmental Stress in Aquatic Ecosystems* (J. H. Thorp and J. W. Gibbons, eds), pp. 62–101. Technical Information Center U.S. Department of Energy. CONF-771114.

Macan, T. T. (1958). The temperature of a small stony stream. *Hydrobiologia* **12**, 89–106.

Maetz, J. (1974). Aspects of adaptation to hypo-osmotic and hyperosmotic environments. In *Biochemical and Biophysical Perspectives in Marine Biology*, Vol. 1 (D. C. Malins and J. R. Sargent, eds), pp. 1–167. London and New York: Academic Press.

Mann, R. H. K. (1971). The populations, growth and production of fish in four small streams in southern England. *J. Anim. Ecol.* **40**, 155–190.

Mathur, D. and Silver, C. A. (1980). Statistical problems in studies of temperature preference of fishes. *Can. J. Fish. Aquat. Sci.* **37**, 733–737.

May, R. M. (1973). Stability and Complexity in Model Ecosystems. Monographs in Population Biology 6. Princeton, New Jersey: Princeton University Press. 265pp.

May, R. M. (Ed.). (1976). *Theoretical Ecology : Principles and Applications*. Oxford: Blackwell. 317pp.

Mazeaud, M. M. and Mazeaud, F. (1981). Adrenergic responses to stress in fish. In *Stress and Fish* (A. D. Pickering, ed.), pp. 49–75. London and New York: Academic Press.

Mazeaud, M. M., Mazeaud, F. and Donaldson, E. M. (1977). Primary and secondary effects of stress in fish: Some new data with a general review. *Trans. Am. Fish. Soc.* **106**, 201–212.

McCauley, R. W. (1958). Thermal relations of geographic races of *Salvelinus*. *Can. J. Zool.* **36**, 655–662.

McCauley, R. W. (1977). Laboratory methods for determining temperature preference. *J. Fish. Res. Bd Can.* **34**, 749–752.

McCauley, R. W. and Huggins, N. (1976). Behavioral thermoregulation by rainbow trout in a temperature gradient. In *Thermal Ecology, Vol. II* (G. W. Esch and R. W. MacFarlane, eds), pp. 171–175. Proc. Symp. held at Augusta. Va., April 2–5, 1975. ERDA Symp. Ser. CONF-750425. Natl. Tech. Inf. Serv., Springfield, Va.

McCormick, J. H., Hokanson, K. E. F. and Jones, B. R. (1972). Effects of temperature on growth and survival of young brook trout, *Salvelinus fontinalis*. *J. Fish. Res. Bd Can.* **29**, 1107–1112.

Mortimer, C. H. and Moore, W. H. (1970). The use of thermistors for the measurement of lake temperatures. *Mitt. int. Verein. theor. angew. Limnol.* **No. 2**, 1–42. (revised).

Murray, R. W. (1971). Temperature receptors. In *Fish Physiology, Vol. V* (W. S. Hoar, and D. J. Randall, eds), pp. 121–133. London and New York: Academic Press.

Needham, P. R. (1961). Observations on the natural spawning of eastern brook trout. *Calif. Fish Game* **47**, 27–40.

Odum, H. T. (1967). Work circuits and systems stress. In *Symposium on Primary Productivity and Mineral Cycling in Natural Ecosystems.* (H. E. Young, ed.), pp. 81–138. Orano: University of Maine Press.

Odum, H. T. (1974). Energy cost-benefit models for evaluating thermal plumes. In *Thermal Ecology* (J. W. Gibbons and R. R. Sharitz, eds), pp. 628–649. AEC Symposium Series, 1973. CONF-730505, NTIS.

Otto, R. G. and Gerking, S. D. (1973). Heat tolerance of the Death Valley pupfish (Genus *Cyprinodon*). *Physiol. Zool.* **46**, 43–49.

Papadopol, M. and Weinberger, M. (1975). On the reproduction of *Phoxinus phoxinus* (Linnaeus, 1758) (Pisces: Cyprinidae) with notes on other aspects of its life history. *Vest. csl. zool. Spol.* **39**, 39–52.

Peterson, R. H., Spinney, H. C. E. and Sreedharan, A. (1977). Development of Atlantic salmon (*Salmo salar*) eggs and alevins under varied temperature regimes. *J. Fish. Res. Bd Can.* **34**, 31–43.

Pickering, A. D. (1981). Introduction. In *Stress and Fish* (A. D. Pickering, ed.), pp. 1–9. London and New York: Academic Press.

Pimm, S. L. and Lawton, J. H. (1980). Are food webs divided into compartments? *J. Anim. Ecol.* **49**, 879–898.

Randall, D. J. and Cameron, J. N. (1973). Respiratory control of arterial pH as temperature changes in rainbow trout *Salmo gairdneri*. *Am. J. Physiol.* **225**, 997–1002.

Randall, D. J. and Hoar, W. S. (1971). Special techniques. In *Fish Physiology, Vol. VI* (W. S. Hoar and D. J. Randall, eds), pp. 511–528. London and New York: Academic Press.

Reichenbach-Klinke, H. H. (Ed.). (1976). Die Gewässeraufheizung und ihre Auswirkung auf den Lebensraum Wasser. In *Fisch und Umwelt, Vol 2. Seminar 1975*, pp. 153–161. Stuttgart: Gustav Fischer Verlag.

Reynolds, W. W. (1977). Temperature as a proximate factor in orientation behavior. *J. Fish. Res. Bd Can.* **34**, 734–739.

Reynolds, W. W. and Casterlin, M. E. (1979). Thermoregulatory behavior of brown trout, *Salmo trutta*. *Hydrobiologia*, **62**, 79–80.

Reynolds, W. W., Casterlin, M. E., Matthey, J. K., Millington, S. T. and Ostrowski, A. C. (1978). Diel patterns of preferred temperature and locomotor activity in the goldfish *Carassius auratus*. *Comp. Biochem. Physiol.* **59A**, 225–227.

Richards, F. P., Reynolds, W. W. and McCauley, R. W. (1977). Temperature preference studies in environmental impact assessments: an overview with procedural recommendations. *J. Fish. Res. Bd Can.* **34**, 728–761.

Roberts, J. L. (1961). The influence of photoperiod upon thermal acclimation by the crucian carp *Carassius carassius*. *Zool. Anz.* (Suppl.) **24**, 73–78.

Rozin, P. and Mayer, J. (1961). Thermal reinforcement and thermo-regulatory behavior in the goldfish, *Carassius auratus*. *Science, N.Y.* **134**, 942–943.

Sadler, K. (1979). Effects of temperature on the growth and survival of the European eel, *Anguilla anguilla* L. *J. Fish Biol.* **15**, 499–507.

Scholander, P. F., van Dam, L., Kanwisher, J. W., Hammel, H. T. and Gordon, M. S. (1957). Supercooling and osmoregulation in Arctic fish. *J. cell. comp. Physiol.* **49**, 5–24.

Shelton, G. (1970). The regulation of breathing. In *Fish Physiology, Vol. IV. The nervous system, circulation and respiration* (W. S. Hoar and D. J. Randall, eds), pp. 293–359. London and New York: Academic Press.

Shrode, J. B. and Gerking, S. D. (1977). Effect of constant and fluctuating tempera-
    tures on reproductive performance of a desert pupfish, *Cyprinodon n. nevadensis*.
    Physiol. Zool. **50**, 1–10.
Sigler, W. F. (1958). The ecology and use of carp in Utah. *Utah Agric. Exp. Stn Bull.*
    405, 63pp.
Slobodkin, L. B. and Sanders, H. L. (1969). On the contribution of environmental
    predictability to species diversity. In *Diversity in Ecological Systems* (G. M.
    Woodwell and H. H. Smith, eds), pp. 82–95. Brookhaven Symposia in Biology,
    No. 22, 1969. USAEC Report BNL-50175.
Somero, G. N. and de Vries, A. L. (1967). Temperature tolerance of some Antarctic
    fishes. *Science. N.Y.* **156**, 257–258.
Spaas, J. T. (1960). Contribution to the comparative physiology and genetics of the
    European salmonidae. III. Temperature resistance at different ages. *Hydro-
    biologia* **15**, 78–88.
Spigarelli, S. A. and Thommes, M. M. (1979). Temperature selection and estimated
    thermal acclimation by rainbow trout (*Salmo gairdneri*) in a thermal plume.
    J. Fish. Res. Bd Can. **36**, 366–376.
Spigarelli, S. A., Romberg, G. P., Prepejchal, W. and Thommes, M. M. (1974). Body
    temperature characteristics of fish at a thermal discharge on Lake Michigan. In
    Thermal Ecology, Vol. 1 (J. W. Gibbons and R. R. Sharitz, eds), pp. 119–132.
    AEC(CONF 730505) Natl Tech. Inf. Serv., Springfield, Va.
Stevens, E. D. and Fry, F. E. G. (1970). The rate of thermal exchange in a teleost,
    Tilapia mossambica. Can. J. Zool. **48**, 221–226.
Stevens, E. D. and Fry, F. E. G. (1974). Heat transfer and body temperatures in
    non-thermoregulatory teleosts. *Can. J. Zool.* **52**, 1137–1143.
Stevens, E. D. and Neill, W. H. (1978). Body temperature relations of tunas,
    especially skipjack. In *Fish physiology, Vol. VII* (W. S. Hoar and D. J. Randall,
    eds), pp. 316–359. London and New York: Academic Press.
Stevens, E. D. and Sutterlin, A. M. (1976). Heat transfer between fish and ambient
    water. *J. exp. Biol.* **65**, 131–145.
Stott, B. (1977). On the question of the introduction of the grass carp (*Cteno-
    pharyngodon idella* Val.) into the United Kingdom. *Fish. Mgmt* **8**, 63–71.
Strange, R. J., Schreck, C. B. and Golden, J. T. (1977). Corticoid stress responses to
    handling and temperature in salmonids. *Trans. Am. Fish. Soc.* **106**, 213–218.
Swee, U. B. and McCrimmon, H. R. (1966). Reproductive biology of the carp,
    Cyprinus carpio L., in Lake St. Lawrence, Ontario. *Trans. Am. Fish. Soc.* **95**,
    372–380.
Swift, D. R. (1961). The annual growth-rate cycle in brown trout (*Salmo trutta* Linn.)
    and its cause. *J. exp. Biol.* **38**, 595–604.
Swift, D. R. (1964). The effect of temperature and oxygen on the growth rate of the
    Windermere char (*Salvelinus alpinus willughbii*). *Comp. Biochem. Physiol.* **12**,
    179–183.
Swift, D. R. (1965a). Effect of temperature on mortality and rate of development of
    the eggs of the Windermere char (*Salvelinus alpinus*). *J. Fish. Res. Bd Can.* **22**,
    913–917.
Swift, D. R. (1965b). Effect of temperature on mortality and rate of development of
    the eggs of the pike (*Essox lucius* L.) and the perch (*Perca fluviatilis* L.) *Nature,
    Lond.* **206**, No. 4983, 528.
Talmage, S. S. and Coutant, C. C. (1978). Thermal effects. *J. Wat. Pollut. Control
    Fed.* **50**, 1514–1553.

Talmage, S. S. and Coutant, C. C. (1979). Thermal effects. *J. Wat. Pollut. Control Fed.* **51**, 1517–1554.

Timmermans, J. A. (1978). De Graskarper (*Ctenopharyngodon idella*) Eerste ervaringen in België. *Trav. Stn Rech. Groenendaal, Ser. D*, **No. 47**, 24pp.

Tyler, A. V. (1966). Some temperature relations of two minnows of the genus *Chrosomus*. *Can. J. Zool.* **44**, 349–364.

Weatherley, A. H. (1959). Some features of the biology of the tench, *Tinca tinca* (Linnaeus) in Tasmania. *J. Anim. Ecol.* **28**, 73–87.

Webster, D. A. (1962). Artificial spawning facilities for brook trout, *Salvelinus fontinalis*. *Trans. Am. Fish. Soc.* **91**, 168–174.

Wedemeyer, G. (1973). Some physiological aspects of sublethal heat stress in the juvenile steelhead trout (*Salmo gairdneri*) and coho salmon (*Oncorhynchus kisutch*). *J. Fish. Res. Bd Can.* **30**, 831–834.

Wootton, R. J. (1976). *The biology of the Sticklebacks.* London and New York: Academic Press. 387pp.

Yamazaki, F. (1965). Endocrinological studies on the reproduction of the female goldfish, *Carassius auratus* L., with special reference to the function of the pituitary gland. *Mem. Fac. Fish. Hokkaido Univ.* **13**, 1–64.

11. Methods for Determining the Tolerance of Fishes to Environmental Stressors

G. A. WEDEMEYER[1] and D. J. McLEAY[2]

[1] *National Fisheries Research Center, Bld 204, Naval Support Activity, Seattle, Washington 98115, U.S.A.*
[2] *B.C. Research, 3650 Wesbrook Mall, Vancouver, B.C., Canada*

Abstract. Environmental stress is an inescapable part of the life of fish, particularly those in intensive culture. Stress may be well within physiological control system capabilities and be sublethal, or it may require a physiological response in excess of ability to accommodate and be lethal or result in disease. In the case of anadromous fishes, stress can affect the parr–smolt transformation, resulting in impaired migratory behavior, decreased osmoregulatory competence and reduced early marine survival.

This chapter discusses methods for measuring physiological effects of single and multiple stressors on fishes. Additionally, standardized challenge tests are described for determining tolerance limits to environmental stressors. Together with other appropriate measurements of fish condition and performance, these methods will assist in the assessments of fish health needed for quality control in intensive fish culture, and will permit the generation of standardized environmental requirements data needed for meaningful environmental impact assessments.

I INTRODUCTION

(a) The Aquatic Environment

In discussing methods for determining the tolerance of fishes to environmental stressors, a good starting place is a consideration of normal conditions in the aquatic environment itself. Fishes, even under the best of conditions, live under dynamic chemical and physical conditions, many of which have no analogue in the terrestrial environment. Although individual fishes, populations and ecosystems may be adapted to these conditions, this does not imply the absence of an energy drain (Lugo, 1978). For example, euryhaline and anadromous fishes must cope physiologically with the effects of salinity even though they are adapted to salinity *per se* (see Eddy, 1981, this volume).

Thus, the homeostatic control systems of fish are continually impacted by the normal demands of the aquatic environment itself. Superimposed on this may be the effects of adverse environmental conditions including pollutants, land or water project developments within the area, and, in the case of fish in intensive culture, the effects of operating procedures such as handling, crowding, transporting, and disease treatments. Examples of environmental alterations common to both aquaculture and development projects which can debilitate but are not necessarily lethal when they occur singly, include exposure to low concentrations of aquatic contaminants, unionized ammonia, nitrite, carbon dioxide (especially in recirculation systems—see Smart, 1981, this volume), unfavorable temperatures, hypoxia, atypical light levels, sediment loads, physical trauma (entrainment, impingement at power plants) and population densities in hatcheries dictated more by production goals than by biological considerations (Piper, 1980). All of these, singly or together, can impose a considerable load, or stress, on homeostatic mechanisms. At the individual fish level, stress that exceeds physiological tolerance limits will eventually be lethal. Less severe stress, which is more common, will load or limit physiological systems, reduce growth, predispose to infectious diseases if fish pathogens are present, and reduce ability to tolerate additional stressors. At the population level, the effects of stress may be manifested as reduced spawning success, increased larval mortality, reduced recruitment to succeeding life stages, and overall population declines (McFarlane and Franzin, 1978).

(b) Environmental Stress: a Definition and Overview

Unfortunately, the term "stress" is used inconsistently. It is sometimes taken to mean the environmental alteration (stressor) itself and sometimes the response of the fish, population, or ecosystem (see Pickering, 1981, this volume, for further discussion). Stress was defined by Selye (1950) as: "the sum of all the physiological responses by which an animal tries to maintain or re-establish a normal metabolism in the face of a physical or chemical force". This definition does not consider the fact that the outcome of stress may be negative for an individual but positive for the population. For example, mortality of individual fish due to exhaustion from crowding may actually enhance survival of the population when space or food supplies are limiting. Stress is better defined as the *effect* of any environmental alteration or force that extends homeostatic or stabilizing processes beyond their normal limits, at any level of biological organization (Esch and Hazen, 1978). For the purposes of this paper, "stressor" will be used to mean the environmental factor itself and we recommend that this terminology be adopted for fisheries biology in general. That is, a stress factor, or stressor, is an environmental change that is severe enough to require a "physiological" response on the part of a fish, population, or ecosystem. If the stress response can re-establish a satisfactory relationship between the changed environment and the fish, population, or ecosystem, adaptation to the stressor will occur. However, because of species' shifts and energy drains which may occur, the original conditions may never be restored.

At the organism level, a series of physiological changes occurs, following a stressful challenge, which Selye (1973) termed the general adaptation syndrome (GAS). It traditionally has been described as consisting of: (1) an alarm reaction in which catecholamine and corticosteroid "stress hormones" are released; (2) a stage of resistance during which adaptation occurs; (3) a stage of exhaustion if adaptation is lost because the stress was too severe or long lasting.

Although it is not universally agreed that the GAS occurs in fishes, it is widely accepted that the stress response as a whole is characterized by physiological changes which tend to be similar for stressors as varied as handling, disease treatments, fright, forced swimming, anesthesia, rapid temperature changes, or scale loss. Thus, the stress response of fishes is analogous in many ways to that occurring in the higher vertebrates (Peters, 1979).

Only a general understanding exists of the sequence of physiological, behavioral, and genetic alterations that occur as fishes (or fish populations) attempt to maintain themselves in the face of short or long-term stressful environmental changes. However, the following outline can be used for discussion (Chavin, 1973; Schreck *et al.*, 1976; Wedemeyer *et al.*, 1976; George, 1977; Mazeaud *et al.*, 1977).

(i) *Primary alterations.*
1. Release of adrenocorticotropic hormone (ACTH) from the adenohypophysis.
2. Release of "stress hormones" (catecholamines and corticosteroids) from the interrenal.

(ii) *Secondary alterations (physiological).*
1. Blood chemistry and hematological changes, such as hyperglycemia, hyperlacticemia, hypochloremia, leucopenia, and reduced blood clotting time.

2. Tissue changes, such as depletion of liver glycogen, and interrenal Vitamin C.
3. Metabolic changes, such as a negative nitrogen balance, and oxygen debt.
4. Diuresis, with resultant blood electrolyte loss.

(iii) *Tertiary effects.*
1. Whole-animal:
   (a) impaired growth, parr–smolt transformation, spawning success, migratory behavior;
   (b) increased disease incidence (infectious and non-infectious).
2. Population parameters:
   (a) reduced intrinsic growth rate, recruitment, compensatory reserve;
   (b) altered species abundance and diversity.

Thus, a fish's or fish population's tolerance to environmental alterations depends at least in part upon the individual fish's ability to regulate stabilizing processes so as to accomplish the required physiological or behavioral adaptation. Single or multiple stressors requiring an adjustment in excess of the fish's ability to accommodate will eventually be lethal; either directly, or indirectly as the result of secondary processes such as disease. An understanding of the physiology of the stress response, and the degree of environmental alteration to which fishes (both individuals and populations) can adapt through these mechanisms, is important when considering the limits of change in the aquatic environment which can be allowed when habitat alterations (including pollutant discharges) are proposed. Although fishes can frequently survive stressors for limited periods because of their homeostatic capabilities, these should not be used as an excuse for allowing marginal conditions to be created in the aquatic environment. Instead, these capabilities should be used to set priorities and tolerance limits that will protect fish, population, and ecosystem health and quality. This report will be concerned primarily with methods for determining the tolerance of fishes to single and multiple environmental stress factors.

II MEASURING THE PHYSIOLOGICAL EFFECTS OF STRESSORS ON FISHES

At the present time, sensitive, unequivocal measurements of either the severity of the stress caused by environmental alterations or the tolerance limits for adaptation, are not always possible. This is especially true of the present predictive methodology for assessing the potential effects of multiple stressors. Thus, death must still be used occasionally as an end point. Nevertheless, experience has shown that certain of the blood chemistry, tissue, whole animal, and population changes resulting from the primary, secondary, and tertiary aspects of the stress response can be quantified and have potential as indices. As would be expected, many of the physiological tests needed to measure these changes require complex laboratories and equipment. However, some, such as the occult hemoglobin test to detect acute stress, are available that use simple, prepackaged reagents easily available from biomedical supply houses, and thus can be performed in any modestly equipped fisheries facility (Smith and Ramos, 1976).

Certain of these physiological tests may also be employed to detect the early stages of disease processes or sublethal effects of environmental contaminants, and to evaluate nutritional status in diet formulation research. Good examples of tests having such potential are the recently developed C-reactive protein determination for the detection of incipient disease, and the ketone-mucus test as an index of nutritional status (Ramos and Smith, 1978a,b). An outline summary of the physiological tests for stress assessment which will be discussed in the following sections are summarized in Table I together with interpretive guidelines. Laboratory procedures for performing these tests are given in Wedemeyer and Yasutake (1977).

TABLE I   Summary Interpretation of Physiological Tests to Assess the Effects of Environmental Stressors on Fish.

| Clinical test | Possible significance if: | |
	Too low	Too high
1. Ammonia (water, unionized)	No recognized significance	Gill hyperplasia, predisposition to bacterial gill disease
2. Blood cell counts		
a. Erythrocytes	Anemia, hemodilution due to impaired osmoregulation	Stress polycythemia dehydration, hemoconcentration due to gill damage
b. Leucocytes	Leucopenia due to acute stress	Leucocytosis due to bacterial infection
c. Thrombocytes	Abnormal blood clotting time	Thrombocytosis due to acute or chronic stress
3. Chloride (plasma)	Gill chloride cell damage, compromised osmoregulation	Hemoconcentration, compromised osmoregulation
4. Cholesterol (plasma)	Impaired lipid metabolism	Fish under chronic stress, dietary lipid imbalance

TABLE I (*continued*)

Clinical test	Possible significance if:	
	Too low	Too high
5. Clotting time (blood)	Fish under acute stress, thrombocytopenia	Sulfonamides or antibiotic disease treatments affecting the intestinal microflora
6. Cortisol (plasma)	Interrenal exhaustion from severe stress	Fish under chronic or acute stress
7. Glucose (plasma)	Inanition	Acute or chronic stress
8. Glycogen (liver or muscle)	Chronic stress, inanition	Liver damage due to excessive vacuolation. Diet too high in carbohydrate
9. Hematocrit (blood)	Anemia, hemodilution	Hemoconcentration due to gill damage, dehydration; stress polycythemia
10. Hemoglobin (blood)	Anemia, hemodilution, nutritional disease	Hemoconcentration due to gill damage, dehydration; stress polycythemia
11. Lactic acid (blood)	No recognized significance	Acute or chronic stress, swimming fatigue
12. Methemoglobin (blood)	No recognized significance	Excessive NO_2^- in water or use of O_2 instead of air in fish hauling trucks
13. Nitrite (water)	No recognized significance	Methemoglobinemia in fish population
14. Osmolarity (plasma)	External parasite infestation, heavy metal exposure, hemodilution	Dehydration, salinity increases in excess of osmoregulatory capacity, stress-induced diuresis, lactic acidosis
15. Total protein (plasma)	Infectious disease, kidney damage, nutritional imbalance, inanition	Hemoconcentration, impaired water balance

The examples are based on salmonids but are applicable, with caution, to other fishes. See Wedemeyer and Yasutake (1977) for methodology and expected baseline values for comparison.

(a) Primary and Secondary Effects

As mentioned, much recent research has centred around certain of the primary and secondary aspects of the stress response that can be measured by means of biomedical test procedures. Examples of blood chemistry tests that appear to be practical include the measurement of circulating levels of the primary stress hormones themselves (catecholamines or corticosteroids), and such secondary blood chemistry changes as hyperlacticemia, hypochloremia or hyperglycemia (Hattingh, 1976; Mazeaud et al., 1977; McLeay, 1977; Wedemeyer and Yasutake, 1977). Hematological changes that are proving to be useful as indices include quantifying the decrease in blood clotting time and changes in the differential leucocyte count (McLeay, 1976b; Casillas and Smith, 1977). Leucocytosis and eosinophilia may both occur under certain conditions, but are probably of limited usefulness in quantifying the stress response in fishes because of low sensitivity and high variability. However, leucopenia has recently been found to be a significant part of the physiological response to acute stressors such as crowding and a new rapid method, termed leucocrit, has been developed for its measurement (McLeay and Gordon, 1977). Changes in erythrocyte counts (as approximated by the hematocrit) or in hemoglobin levels are probably most useful as indicators of hemodilution or hemoconcentration, although anemias or stress polycythemia may occasionally occur (Soivio and Oikari, 1976; see also Soivio and Nikinmaa, 1981, this volume).

Secondary tissue responses that reflect the effects of acute stressors include depletion of muscle and liver glycogen and interrenal Vitamin C (Wedemeyer, 1969; McLeay and Brown, 1975). For assessing the severity of chronic stress, the extent of any interrenal hypertrophy may be semiquantitated microscopically by estimating nuclear diameters and cell size (McLeay, 1975a). The duration of the stress has an important bearing on the severity of the tissue changes that occur. An acute stress results in a reversible depletion of Vitamin C, corticosteroids, cholesterol, and other lipids, in the interrenal tissue. Under chronic stress, hyperplasia and hypertrophy of the interrenal tissue and of the corticotropic tissue in the adenohypophysis may also occur. Eventually, the cells may degenerate and the animal is unable to synthesize additional corticosteroids (stage of exhaustion). However, if the stressor is removed, gradual recovery of interrenal and adenohypophyseal function may occur (Donaldson and McBride, 1974; McLeay, 1975a; Noakes and Leatherland, 1977; see also Donaldson, 1981, this volume; Schreck, 1981, this volume).

(b) Tertiary Effects

It has long been known from experience with hatchery fish that several whole-animal responses to environmental stressors occur that can be used as a form of biological monitoring. These include behavioral changes such as inhibited feeding or migratory activity; hatchery production traits such as decreased growth and food conversion, or increased morbidity and mortality rates due to increased susceptibility to fish diseases. At the population level, recent studies have shown that biological monitoring to assess the effects of environmental stressors can be carried out by measuring changes in parameters such as intrinsic growth rate, disease incidence, spawning success, longevity, egg size, or recruitment rates. Unfortunately, these are presently difficult to use, in a predictive sense, to assess the likely impacts of proposed land and water development projects that will result in multiple stressors (Snieszko, 1974; Hodgins et al., 1977; Ryan and Harvey, 1977; McFarlane and Franzin, 1978).

Of the tertiary effects which are receiving serious attention, fish disease incidence is potentially a very sensitive index of incipient stress. Experience has shown that the mere presence of many of the fish pathogens will result in epizootics only if unfavorable environmental conditions also exist and the host defense system has been compromised. It is well established that fish diseases are not necessarily single-caused events but are the end result of the relationship between the pathogen, the fish, and the environment. If this relationship is balanced, good health and growth will result. If it is marginal, chronic disease problems and reduced growth will occur. If it is unsatisfactory, poor growth and overt disease will result. Good examples of stress-mediated diseases which can be used as indicators include those due to facultative bacterial fish pathogens such as *Aeromonas, Pseudomonas* and myxobacteria which are continuously present in most natural waters. Epizootics will usually not occur unless environmental quality and the defense systems of the fish also deteriorate. A classic example is bacterial gill disease which, in aquaculture, will frequently respond to the simple treatment of reducing the fish population density in the ponds. Other stress-mediated infectious fish diseases that signal adverse conditions with a high degree of probability include vibriosis (*Vibrio anguillarum*), bacterial hemorrhagic septicemia (*Aeromonas* and *Pseudomonas* sp.) and protozoan parasite and fungus infestations such as costiasis (*Ichtyoboda* (≡ *Costia*) *necatrix*) and *Saprolegnia*. Based on recent case-history observations, viral erythrocytic necrosis (VEN) and vibriosis are also potentially useful indicator diseases for stress in marine aquacultural systems and estuaries. Of course, fish disease incidence can be used more easily as an index of environmental stress in aquacultural facilities than in natural waters. A summary list of diseases together with a description of the environmental conditions implicated in their occurrence is presented in Table II (see Ellis, 1981, this volume; Fletcher, 1981, this volume for the effects of stress on the defence mechanisms).

TABLE II   Environmental Stressors which are Debilitating to Warm and Cold Water Fishes and Increase Susceptibility to the Indicated Diseases.

Disease	Environmental stress factors predisposing to disease
Furunculosis (*Aeromonas salmonicida*)	Low oxygen ($\approx$4 mg l^{-1}); crowding; handling in the presence of *A. salmonicida*; handling for up to a month prior to an expected epizootic.
Bacterial gill disease (*Myxobacteria* spp)	Crowding; unfavorable environmental conditions such as chronic low oxygen (4 mg l^{-1}); elevated ammonia (0·02 mg l^{-1} unionized); particulate matter in water.
Columnaris (*Flexibacter columnaris*)	Crowding or handling during warm (15°C) water periods if carrier fish are present in the water supply; temperature increase to about 30°C, if the pathogen is present, even if not crowded or handled.
Kidney disease (*Renibacterium salmoninarum*)	Water hardness less than about 100 mg l^{-1} (as $CaCO_3$); diets containing corn gluten or of less than about 30% moisture.
Hemorrhagic septicemia (*Aeromonas* and *Pseudomonas* spp.)	Pre-existing protozoan infestations such as *Costia*, *Trichodina*; inadequate cleaning leading to increased bacterial load in water; particulate matter in water; handling; crowding; low oxygen; chronic sublethal exposure to heavy metals, pesticides or polychlorinated biphenyls (PCBs); for carp, handling after overwintering at low temperatures.
Vibriosis (*Vibrio anguillarum*)	Handling; dissolved oxygen lower than about 6 mg l^{-1}, especially at water temperatures of 10–15°C; brackish water, of 10–15‰ salinity.
Parasite infestations (*Costia, Trichodina, Hexamita*)	Overcrowding of fry and fingerlings; low oxygen; excessive size variation among fish in ponds.
Spring viremia of carp	Handling after overwintering at low temperatures.
Fin and tail rot	Crowding; improper temperatures; nutritional imbalances; chronic sublethal exposure to PCBs; or to suspended solids at 200–300 mg l^{-1}.
Coagulated yolk of eggs and fry	Rough handling; malachite green containing more than 0·08% zinc, gas supersaturation of 103% or more; mineral deficiency in incubation water.
"Hauling loss" (delayed mortality)	Hauling, stocking, handling in soft water (less than 100 mg l^{-1} total hardness); mineral additions not used; CO_2 above 20 mg l^{-1}.
Blue sac disease of eggs	Crowding; accumulation of nitrogenous metabolic wastes due to inadequate flow patterns.

III MEASURING THE TOLERANCE OF FISHES TO STRESSORS: CHALLENGE TESTS

Meaningful methods for determining the impact of stressors on fish health are essential for quality control in production fish hatcheries, fish farming/ranching operations, and in developing concepts, methods and standards for predicting the impact of proposed environmental alterations on fish and fish populations. An assessment of fish health should not be restricted to an examination of internal changes within the animal since "clinical" biochemical/physiological/histological profiles may not in themselves provide sufficient information with which to appraise the overall condition of fish, their predisposition to infections, and their ability to tolerate natural or man-made environmental alterations. A combination of appropriate blood and other tissue analyses with standardized stressor challenge tests will be needed to provide the most meaningful assessment of fish condition.

Implicit in the application of challenge tests for evaluating the condition and determining the tolerance of fish to adverse conditions is the concept that the impact of multiple stressors on the magnitude of the stress response elicited is largely additive or synergistic; and that this "stress load", if sufficient in magnitude and duration, is debilitating. Such debilitation is known to result in a reduction of zones of tolerance to environmental extremes (Fry, 1947; Brett, 1958) and an increase in susceptibility to disease (Wedemeyer et al., 1976) to the extent that the fish's and fish population's chances for survival are reduced.

Although the systematic development and standardization of a battery of challenge tests for determining the tolerance of fish to environmental stressors has received little attention to date, in the judgement of the authors, a number of approaches hold promise. Methodologies for conducting such challenge tests under standardized conditions are proposed here. In certain instances (i.e. freshwater challenge tests) we are unaware that such tests have been applied; and are proposing them for evaluation as to their utility for assessing fish condition in terms of ability to tolerate environmental stressors. The procedures cited for conducting each challenge test should be considered advisory. Some may require additional testing and modification to meet specific requirements. For example, one or more stressor challenges could be combined to enable a more comprehensive estimate of fish condition in terms of ability to tolerate environmental alterations.

(a) Temperature Tolerance Tests

Exposure of fishes to abrupt temperature increases or decreases, effects characteristic stress reactions (Allan, 1971; Wedemeyer, 1973; Strange *et al.*, 1977). Such thermal stress loadings can be controlled in order to determine if the fishes' zones for temperature tolerance have been reduced by prior exposure to other stressors.

The classical method for measuring temperature tolerance is to transfer groups of fish directly from a holding tank into tests tanks at the desired range of temperatures. The upper and lower tolerance limits are taken as the temperature at which 50% of the test fish survive for 24 h. An alternative method used for measuring the critical thermal maximum (CTM) is to acclimate groups of fish at the desired temperature and then warm the water at a constant rate (conventionally $1°C\,min^{-1}$) until permanent loss of equilibrium or death ensues (Hutchison, 1961; Mihursky and Kennedy, 1967; Paladino and Spotila, 1978). Regardless of the procedure employed, these tests use temperature as a challenge stressor in order to determine: (1) the fishes' zone(s) of thermal tolerance, and (2) if it has been reduced by the impact of other stressors. In making such comparisons, consideration must be given to the fish species tested as well as its history of thermal and photoperiodic acclimation, since these variables can alter zones of thermal tolerance appreciably (Hoar, 1956; McLeay and Gordon, 1978a).

A practical application of this is to determine the extent to which simultaneous exposure to contaminants change normal CTM values. In these tests, fish are exposed to a range of strengths of each contaminant throughout the period of increasing temperatures. The rate of temperature increase should be more gradual ($1°C\,h^{-1}$) than that prescribed previously in order to provide sufficient time for the contaminant to exert its toxic effect. For several industrial effluents and pure chemicals, the median effective concentrations that will reduce the CTM of fishes falls in the range of $0·1–0·5$ of the respective median lethal concentration (Howard, 1973; McLeay and Howard, 1977; McLeay and Gordon, 1978a, 1980); however some contaminants will cause a marked reduction in the upper thermal tolerance zone whereas others cause only a slight impairment (McLeay and Gordon, 1980). Such qualitative differences in the effect of toxicants on ability to withstand heat stress are thought to be due to their diverse influences on the causes of thermal death. Although our knowledge of the causes of thermal death is still very incomplete, tissue anoxia at upper lethal temperatures has been confirmed, at least for salmonid fish (Hughes and Roberts, 1970; Heath and Hughes, 1973). Thus, the effects of environmental factors that reduce oxygen exchange at the gills, impair tissue respiration, or increase metabolic demand, may be intensified by increased temperatures. Testing for ability to withstand a thermal challenge might, therefore, be especially useful if these effects are involved. For a more detailed consideration of thermal relationships in teleost fish the reader is referred to Elliott (1981, this volume).

(b) Tolerance to Hypoxia: Sealed Jar Tests

The use of sealed jar tests (also called residual oxygen bioassays) was originally proposed by Carter (1962) as a rapid, simple means for measuring effects of toxicants on ability of fish to withstand an oxygen depletion. In these tests, fish are placed in individual glass jars, containing water (controls) or toxicant solutions, which are initially oxygen-saturated and temperature adjusted. The jars are filled completely, sealed to exclude air exchange, and the residual dissolved oxygen at death and the time to death are measured for each fish. Provided that sufficient replicate jars (i.e. 10 or more) are tested for each treatment, and that fish loading (g fish l^{-1} solution) and test temperature are held constant, this test normally shows an elevation in residual oxygen levels at death, proportional to toxicant concentration. Threshold-effect concentrations are normally equivalent to, or slightly less than, those which are acutely lethal (sensitivity $\simeq$ 4-day LC50 value) (McLeay, 1976; Gordon and McLeay, 1977; Vigers and Maynard, 1977; Giles and Klaprat, 1979).

Elevation of residual oxygen levels due to effects of other stressors can be expected to occur if their mode of action interferes with O_2 uptake, CO_2 unloading at the gills, impaired oxygen transport to the brain and other vital organs, or blocked aerobic metabolic pathways. Although ability to withstand hypoxia has been shown to respond to a variety of pollutants known to affect fish respiration (McLeay, 1976; Vigers and Maynard, 1977), recent evidence suggests that this test is ineffective in detecting contaminants which exert their toxic action otherwise (McLeay and Gordon, 1980). Thus, this challenge test might prove useful for detecting the effects of other stressors on tolerance to hypoxia only in instances where respiratory efficiency has been impaired. Sealed jar tests have been applied successfully to toxicity studies with marine as well as freshwater fish species (Ballard and Oliff, 1969) and in field monitoring surveys of toxic zones of influence of industrial discharges within receiving waters (McLeay and Gordon, 1978b). Physiologically useful data may also be derived from this test by relating oxygen consumption to survival time.

The application of sealed jar tests to assess overall fish health has received little attention. Nevertheless, this approach may prove worthwhile for characterization of fish stocks including the evaluation of hatchery treatment effects. However, widespread use of sealed jar tests for assessing fish condition in terms of their tolerance to hypoxia challenge awaits further definition of the internal and external factors which impose an effect. The simplicity and rapidity (5–8 h for salmonid species with a fish loading of 4–5 g l^{-1}) of this procedure does support its application as a screening method for measuring the impact of single and multiple environmental stressors in terms of predicting effects on ability to withstand oxygen depletions. Hughes (1981, this volume) discusses the physiological responses of fish to low oxygen tensions and the effects of certain environmental pollutants on these responses.

(c) Swimming Stamina Tests

Swimming stamina has been measured by many investigators, generally as a means for assessing fish condition. The most common test devices in current use are tunnels and rotary-flow systems. Measurements of swimming endurance include determinations of critical swimming speed, fatigue time, index of performance and performance rating.

Reduction in dissolved oxygen concentrations impairs the swimming performance of salmonid and other fish species (Davis et al., 1963; Kutty, 1968; Kutty and Saunders, 1973). The process of smoltification also reduces the swimming ability of Pacific salmon relative to that of parr (Smith and Margolis, 1970; Glova and McInerney, 1977). Horak (1972), however, found no conclusive evidence that hatchery-reared rainbow trout, *Salmo gairdneri*, with a high stamina performance index survived better in lakes or streams than did fish with a low index. Additionally, McNeish and Hatch (1978) were unable to relate differences in performance ratings for juvenile Atlantic salmon, *Salmo salar*, to differing hatchery practices. Larmoyeux and Piper (1973) found an improved swimming performance for rainbow trout reared in recycled hatchery water for 230 days, compared with those reared in fresh water. Acute (up to 1 week) exposure of fish to sublethal concentrations of a number of contaminants impairs swimming performance (Waiwood and Beamish, 1978). More prolonged exposures, however, may result in unimpaired swimming stamina; even in instances where growth is inhibited and where histopathologies and other evidence for a state of chronic stress are apparent (Larmoyeux and Piper, 1973; Webb and Brett, 1973; McLeay and Brown, 1979).

The above findings indicate that the use of swimming stamina tests to evaluate fish health has a number of limitations. Although swimming stamina may be impaired by environmental conditions that are acutely stressful, chronic stress (particularly if due to hypoxia) may result in the compensatory development of a more efficient cardiorespiratory system resulting in stamina performance equal to or better than that of unstressed fish. Perhaps the determination of swimming efficiency based on tail-beat frequency versus swimming speed (body lengths s^{-1}) may prove to be a more relevant measure of fish condition (L. S. Smith, personal communication). In any event, the sophisticated apparatus required for conducting swimming stamina tests also prevents their use for routine monitoring of fish condition in field or hatchery operations.

(d) Scope for Activity

The difference between standard oxygen consumption rate (fish at rest and undisturbed) and active oxygen consumption rate (fish stimulated to swim at maximum sustained speed) is defined as "scope for activity" (Fry, 1947). Scope for activity has long been considered as a means for assessing the impact of environmental stressors on fish (Brett, 1958), and as an index of the energy available for swimming (Brett, 1964) or growth (Brett, 1976). Similarly, Sprague (1971) proposed effects on scope for activity as a sensitive procedure for determining sublethal effects of pollutants on respiration and performance. Because environmental stressors may raise the standard metabolic rate, or, alternatively, lower the active metabolic rate (for fishes adapted to expend such energy), the net effect would be to reduce the scope for activity of the fish (Fry, 1971). Dickson and Kramer (1971) used scope for activity as a means of comparison between responses of different strains or species of fish to temperature and photoperiod fluctuations, starvation, and the onset of sexual maturity. Mayer and Kramer (1973) reported a reduction in scope for activity of rainbow trout chronically exposed to recycled hatchery water; and concluded that this test was a far better index of fish fitness than other tests including swimming stamina. Wohlschlag and Wakeman (1978) used changes in scope for activity to evaluate the stress caused by salinity alterations (such as would be caused by freshwater inflow diversions) on the estuarine fish *Cynoscion nebulosus*. Active and standard metabolism, swimming speed and scope for activity were all a function of salinity, and the optima agreed with the zoogeographic salinity distribution for this species. Similar metabolic data for other environmental changes are needed to provide more complete information on the likely bioenergetic costs of proposed environmental alterations.

(e) Disease Challenge Tests

The increased susceptibility of stressed fish to disease has been discussed in an earlier section of this report. It is now well accepted that the stress loading affects the likelihood of contracting infectious diseases. The use of standardized disease challenge tests would therefore permit a comparison of the effects of stressors on fish stocks in terms of their influence on disease resistance. A quantifiable determination of the extent to which contaminants and other environmental stressors decrease this resistance would be useful in biological monitoring for environmental quality.

Inroads have been made towards the use of challenge tests with infectious disease agents in order to evaluate effects of stressors on fish. In controlled laboratory studies, Iwama (1977) found increased susceptibility of juvenile chinook salmon (*Oncorhynchus tshawytscha*) to bacterial kidney disease in fish exposed to sublethal concentrations of the biocide sodium penta-chlorophenate. Grobers *et al.* (1978) experimentally infected three salmonid fish species with *Aermonas salmonicida* and *A. hydrophila*, and determined the extent to which water temperature accelerated the progress of infection. Hetrick *et al.* (1979) challenged rainbow trout with infectious hematopoietic necrosis (IHN) virus under controlled conditions and provided evidence that prior exposure to sublethal concentrations of copper increased disease susceptibility.

The development and standardization of disease challenge tests requires controlled methods for experimentally reproducing the disease; with extensive knowledge concerning the route of administration, dosage and test duration required for clinical signs to be manifested. Michel (1980) recently reported the development of a standardized model for experimental furunculosis in rainbow trout. Gould *et al.* (1978) developed a reliable method for challenging sockeye salmon (*Oncorhynchus nerka*) with *Vibrio anguillarum* under standardized conditions. Similar models for viral, protozoan and other bacterial pathogens would greatly assist in applying infectious disease challenge tests to the assessment of fish quality and the determination of tolerance limits to environmental stressors.

In the case of non-infectious diseases, evidence is now accumulating which suggests that the development of standardized procedures for assessing susceptibility to carcinogenicity is feasible, which will also provide a means of comparing the influence of genetic strain and condition as well as the influence of environmental stressors (McLeay, 1979). The pioneering study of Sinnhuber and co-workers with rainbow trout and carcinogens (Sinnhuber *et al.*, 1977; Grieco *et al.*, 1978; Wales *et al.*, 1978) provide direction for future efforts in this regard.

(f) Reference Toxicants

Within fisheries research, reference toxicants have been used primarily by aquatic toxicologists endeavoring to establish inter- and/or intra-laboratory consistency in reproducibility of bioassay results. A number of chemicals have been proposed and examined as candidate reference toxicants, including DDT, dodecyl sodium sulphate, sodium pentachlorophenate, sodium chloride, sodium azide and phenol. The following criteria are considered prerequisites for effective reference toxicants: chemical able to distinguish fish condition; reproducible results for healthy fish under defined, standardized procedures; rapid detection of abnormal fish by a deviant response; chemical able to link the work of different investigators; chemical a general stressor, resulting in a non-specific integrated biological response (Alderdice, 1963); chemical highly soluble and stable in water, easily measured and toxic to fish at low concentrations; chemical sufficiently uncommon in nature that there is little risk that fish have been exposed to it. Based on these stringent criteria, no single chemical fits all the requirements. However sodium pentachlorophenate, sodium chloride and phenol can distinguish differences due to adverse fish condition or rearing procedures (Adelman and Smith, 1976; Alexander and Clarke, 1978) and presently appear as the best candidate reference toxicants.

Conventional tests with reference toxicants are conducted in order to determine the concentration of chemical which is acutely lethal to fish (24- or 96-h median lethal concentration; LC50) or the lethal time to 50% mortality (LT50) of fish exposed to one or more chemical concentrations. The chemical/physical characteristics (i.e. pH, hardness, temperature, dissolved oxygen content), of the dilution water used, together with those specific properties of the reference toxicant employed (i.e. solubility, ionization equilibrium, mode(s) of toxic action) can markedly affect the toxicity value obtained and should be monitored routinely during such tests.

Although reference toxicants are not used routinely by hatchery or other persons concerned with the measurement of tolerance to stressors, appropriate toxicant challenge tests may assist in distinguishing between healthy and diseased fish, or between tolerant versus less tolerant groups. Adelman and Smith (1976) reported that sodium chloride enabled the distinction between groups of goldfish (*Carassius auratus*) defined previously as healthy or unhealthy (infested with skin flukes, and a probable bacterial infection). Alexander and Clarke (1978) found that rainbow trout exposed previously to starvation, temperature changes and sublethal concentrations of chlorine were more susceptible to phenol than control fish reared under optimum conditions; however groups of rainbow trout which experienced high mortalities during holding, or which were subjected to crowding, tolerated a phenol challenge as well as controls. Sodium dodecyl sulphate proved to be of no value in distinguishing between control rainbow trout and those just transported from hatchery to laboratory or sampled from a stock tank with high mortalities (Pessah et al., 1976).

The foregoing studies indicate that it is unrealistic to expect that a single response (death) to a chemical stressor can reveal more than superficial information about the fitness and health of fish. However the use of appropriate reference toxicant challenges may prove of value for this purpose if combined with other challenge tests and physiological analyses.

The use of any reference toxicant for this purpose will require previous standardization for each fish species by many bioassays in order to establish a baseline from which comparisons can be made.

(g) Seawater Challenge Tests: for Fish in Fresh Water

The direct transfer of freshwater-acclimated fish to sea water elicits a stress response (Hirano, 1969; Singley and Chavin, 1975). The severity of the stress resulting from such an osmoregulatory challenge depends on a number of variables including species (stenohaline vs euryhaline), developmental stage (i.e. parr or smolt if salmonid fish), fish size, season, water temperature, and salinity. In addition, it is known that diseased fish or those stressed by pollutants, adverse hatchery conditions or natural environmental stressors, prior to seawater challenge, have a reduced chance for survival and display greater physiological imbalances during or subsequent to this challenge (Wedemeyer et al., 1980). Thus the exposure of freshwater-acclimated fish to standardized seawater challenges may assist in distinguishing between healthy, robust fish and those weakened by natural or man-made stressors.

Clarke and Blackburn (1977, 1978) have developed a standardized seawater challenge test for determining the progress of smoltification in juvenile salmon. In this test, fish are transferred directly from fresh water to sea water (28‰) at their acclimation temperature; and their plasma sodium concentration measured at 24 h post-transfer. Smolts are able to regulate their plasma sodium (and magnesium) levels at or near normal values within 24 h of transfer to sea water; whereas nonsmolts (or parr) suffer a substantial plasma sodium elevation which may persist for several days (Clarke and Blackburn, 1978). Ability to adapt to sea water, and other indicators of osmo-ionic imbalance during smoltification, together with observations of mortalities, can be applied effectively to assess anadromous fish condition and the impact of environmental stressors. Research will be required to determine the optimum salinity and test duration for other fish species and developmental stages, as well as the specific effects of disease and diverse stressors on the response(s) measured. For further information on the effects of seawater transfer the reader is referred to Eddy (1981, this volume).

(h) Freshwater Challenge Tests: for Fish in Sea Water

The development and application of freshwater challenge tests for assessing the condition of marine or seawater-acclimated fish and the impact of prior stressors on their ability to osmoregulate seems warranted. Although we are unaware of any studies related to the development of controlled freshwater challenge tests, such tests could prove of practical value in the neophyte salmonid fish farming/ranching industry. The pen rearing of salmon and trout in marine or estuarine waters often results in considerable stress which can manifest itself as decreased growth, disease resistance, and chance for survival (Allee, 1978). Other marine fish-cultural operations as well as estuarine/marine monitoring surveys concerned with the impact of pollutant discharges on the health of native or hatchery-reared fish populations need practical methodologies for measuring fish condition. These should include the effects of pollutants on tolerance to subsequent stressors. The availability of standardized challenge tests, including a freshwater challenge with attendant measurements of homeostatic imbalances, would assist fisheries biologists in assessing the condition of fish stocks and the probable impact of environmental alterations on their well-being.

(i) Crowding Stress Test

Crowding of fish occurs frequently in intensive fish-culture; both within holding ponds and during such practices as disease treatments, hauling and pond splitting. Recent studies have shown that population densities considered acceptable in normal hatchery practice can cause a significant stress response (Wedemeyer, 1976; Strange et al., 1978; Burton and Murray, 1979; Murray and Burton, 1979; Specker and Schreck, 1980). For salmonids, crowding stress tests can be conducted by holding groups of fish sampled from each fish population or sub-population in question at population densities of $1 \cdot 3$–$64 \, \mathrm{g \, m^{-3}}$ for a fixed period, usually 24 h, followed by physiological measurements of the extent of the stress response elicited. Conditions such as temperature and rate of water exchange within the test tanks are dependent upon the intent of the study. That is, the intent may be to assess the influence of particular fish-cultural practices, state of fish health, pollutants, or the influence of other stressors on the ability of fish to tolerate crowding. Standardized crowding challenges can also be employed in conjunction with other controlled stressor tests in order to assess tolerance to multiple stress factors under sub-optimum environmental conditions, such as those due to habitat alterations under overwintering conditions.

(j) Blood-sugar Stress Test

Although measurements of circulating levels of corticosteroids and catecholamines are used frequently to estimate the severity and duration of the stress response (see Donaldson, 1981; Mazeaud and Mazeaud, 1981, this volume) the analytical procedures required are expensive and not amenable to routine hatchery applications nor field monitoring surveys where test results are needed during the course of the studies. The measurement of blood-sugar levels (plasma glucose), on the other hand, is a simple yet effective method for evaluating the effects of a variety of stressors (McLeay and Brown, 1975; Silbergeld, 1975; Hattingh, 1976; Wedemeyer and Yasutake, 1977). Furthermore, the elevation of blood sugar levels in fish by both corticosteroids and catecholamines enables the measurement of this parameter, as a secondary stress response, to detect stress mediated through direct sympathetic (chromaffin tissue) as well as humoral (interrenal tissue) pathways.

Both manual and automated methods are now available for measuring plasma glucose quickly, accurately and at reasonable cost, with 5–10 µl of sample. This permits the examination of fish weighing only a few grams as well as repetitive sampling of larger fish. The technical skill and equipment required for manual determinations also allows measurements to be carried out under field conditions.

Blood-sugar stress evaluation tests can also be employed in conjunction with standardized stressor challenge tests in order to determine tolerance to challenge; and as a means for assessing fish health in terms of capacity to mount a stress reaction with subsequent recovery. In the case of pollutant stressors, for instance, a procedure has been standardized which enables determination of the threshold concentration of industrial effluent or chemical contaminant which elicits an acute stress response in salmonid fish within the laboratory or in field situations (McLeay, 1977; McLeay and Gordon, 1978b, 1980). To use this procedure, groups of fish are acclimated to running water in test tanks for 48 h, followed by exposure to a range of sublethal dilutions of contaminants for 24 h. A dose-dependent hyperglycemia normally results. The blood-sugar stress evaluation test can be similarly applied in order to ascertain the extent to which other challenges, such as hypoxia, temperature changes, crowding and salinity alterations, are acutely stressful. Diseased fish or strains genetically less able to tolerate environmental stressors might also be distinguished from healthy, robust individuals by monitoring not only their tolerance to standardized challenges in terms of treatment required to elicit an acute stress response (hyperglycemia), but also their ability to show homeostatic recovery (i.e. return of blood sugar levels to basal values) when the challenge is removed.

The known influence of diet, time since last feeding, state of liver glycogen stores, fish developmental stage and season on the magnitude of the hyperglycemia caused by the stressor necessitates consideration of these variables when monitoring the blood sugar level as an index of stress (Nakano and Tomlinson, 1967; McLeay, 1977; Gordon and McLeay, 1978).

(k) Leucocrit Stress Test

Acute exposure of salmonid and other species to diverse stressors results in moderate-to-severe leucopenia which is caused by increased pituitary–interrenal activity (Srivastava and Agrawal, 1977; McLeay and Gordon, 1977; Peters et al., 1980). More particularly, the administration of ACTH, corticosteroids or stressors to teleost fish causes a decline in the number of circulating lymphocytes; presumably due to the lymphocytolytic properties of corticosteroids as demonstrated in mammals (Dougherty, 1960; Burton et al., 1967). This action may serve to immediately increase the available antibody titer and provide a ready source of protein for gluconeogenesis; however the deleterious side-effects of this secondary stress response in terms of depression of the immunological system and loss of resistance to infectious diseases are also significant (Dougherty, 1960; McLeay, 1973a). For further details of the modulation of defence mechanisms by corticosteroids see Ellis (1981, this volume).

Examination of fish for leucopenia or leucocytosis has required differential blood cell counts; a tedious procedure which is not readily amenable to field studies of fish condition nor practical in fish cultural facilities. A rapid, approximate procedure termed "leucocrit" has been developed recently (McLeay and Gordon, 1977) which permits an estimation of the number of circulating white blood cells, without the need for specialized stains or a compound microscope, in the same manner that the hematocrit is used as a substitute for the more tedious red blood cell count. To determine the leucocrit, blood is collected in heparinized microhematocrit tubes, centrifuged, and the thickness of the buffy coat (i.e. the layer of white blood cells between the packed erythrocytes and the plasma) measured using a low-power microscope with an ocular micrometer. The leucocrit value, defined as the volume of packed leucocytes expressed as a percentage of the whole blood volume, is then calculated.

For salmonid and other fish species where lymphocytes comprise the majority of the circulating leucocytes, a leucocrit stress bioassay can be used as a simple, practical test for determining situations which are acutely stressful and the tolerance of fish to standardized stressor challenges. The applications available for this test are identical to those described for the blood-sugar stress test; albeit the significance of the secondary stress responses measured may differ. Furthermore, although hyperglycemia can be elicited by both catecholamines and adrenocorticosteroids; leucopenia appears not to be caused by catecholamines, at least for some fish species (Srivastava and Agrawal, 1977). Thus, leucocrit and plasma glucose values can be measured from the same centrifuged blood sample, which provides two secondary stress indices for each fish examined. As with blood glucose determinations, leucocrit values can be measured in salmonid fish as small as 1 g wet wt; however such young fish have low leucocrit values relative to more mature fingerlings and the use of fish 1·5–2 g or larger is desirable, particularly when both leucocrit and plasma glucose analyses are to be performed on the same blood sample (McLeay and Gordon, 1977).

Leucocrit stress tests have been used to determine the threshold concentrations of industrial effluent and of a number of chemical pollutants that are acutely stressful to salmonid fish species (McLeay and Gordon, 1977, 1979, 1980). This bioassay has also proved useful in assessing the toxic zone of influence to fish of waste discharges within receiving waters (McLeay and Gordon, 1978b). Although the application of this test with other stressor challenges is merited, consideration must be given to species as well as developmental stage and prior history of fish treatment. Subacute or chronic exposure of salmonid fish to stressors may increase rather than decrease total leucocyte counts (and leucocrit values) (McLeay, 1973b; McLeay and Brown, 1974). Furthermore, in species where lymphocytes do not comprise a preponderance of the total leucocyte volume, an acute stress response (lymphopenia) may not be detected by measurement of leucocrit values. In such instances, lymphopenia may occur while the leucocrit value may be unchanged or even elevated, due to a concomitant increase in the number of large granulocytes (Peters et al., 1980).

IV SUMMARY AND CONCLUSIONS

Our present, partial understanding of the mechanism of the stress response can be used to test the degree of stress which fishes can tolerate; primarily at the species level and to a lesser extent, at the population and ecosystem levels.

For tests of the severity of stress and of the time needed for recovery, measuring the "stress hormones" themselves, or the resulting blood and tissue chemistry changes are recommended. These would include catecholamines, cortisol, or blood glucose, lactate, and electrolytes (especially chloride). Specifically, the extent and duration of hyperglycemia and hypochloremia are particularly useful in monitoring how severe stress is and the recovery time needed. In addition to changes in mean values of these parameters, changes in their variability (standard deviation or variance) also furnishes useful information.

Of the tissue changes that can be measured, depletion of interrenal Vitamin C, and liver or muscle glycogen are quite readily quantitated. Interrenal hypertrophy can be semi-quantitated microscopically and provides useful information on chronic effects.

Challenge tests for measuring tolerance limits to stressors were also discussed. A good measure of the point at which a particular environmental alteration has become biologically significant is when it causes a decrease in ability to tolerate an additional stress factor. For example, decreased ability to tolerate an oxygen depletion, or decreased swimming performance, can serve to provide information on the salinity tolerance limits of estuarine fishes when the biological impact of proposed alterations in freshwater inflows are being assessed.

Challenge tests which are particularly straightforward to use are ability to withstand crowding (population density increases), temperature changes (heat or cold shock), and, for evaluating smolt functionality, the seawater tolerance test.

Together with other appropriate measures of fish health and quality, the use of the methods discussed should assist in increasing efficiency in artificial propagation through improved quality control, and in generating the standardized environmental requirements data needed for habitat-based predictive methodology for environmental impact assessment.

REFERENCES

Adelman, I. R. and Smith, L. L. Jr. (1976). Fathead minnows (*Pimephales promelas*) and goldfish (*Carassius auratus*) as standard fish in bioassays and their reaction to potential reference toxicants. *J. Fish. Res. Bd Can.* **33**, 209–214.

Alderdice, D. F. (1963). Some effects of simultaneous variation in salinity, temperature and dissolved oxygen on the resistance of juvenile coho salmon (*Oncorhynchus kisutch*) to a toxic substance. Ph.D. Thesis, University of Toronto, Toronto, Ont. 177pp.

Alexander, D. G. and Clarke, R. McV. (1978). The selection and limitations of phenol as a reference toxicant to detect differences in sensitivity among groups of rainbow trout (*Salmo gairdneri*). *Wat. Res.* **12**, 1085–1090.

Allan, G. D. (1971). Measurement of plasma cortisol and histometry of the interrenal gland of juvenile, presmolt coho salmon (*Oncorhynchus kisutch* Walbaum) during cold temperature acclimation. M.Sc. Thesis, University of British Columbia, Vancouver, B.C. 63pp.

Allee, B. J. (1978). Current status of ocean ranching of salmon. In *Drugs and Food from the Sea: Myth or Reality?* (P. N. Kaul and C. J. Sindermann, eds), pp. 377–381. Norman, Oklahoma: The University of Oklahoma.

Ballard, J. A. and Oliff, W. D. (1969). A rapid method for measuring the acute toxicity of dissolved materials to marine fishes. *Wat. Res.* **3**, 313–333.

Brett, J. R. (1958). Implications and assessments of environmental stress. In *The Investigations of Fish-Power Problems* (P. A. Larkin, ed.), pp. 69–83. Vancouver, B.C.: H. H. MacMillan Lectures in Fisheries, University of British Columbia.

Brett, J. R. (1964). The respiratory metabolism and swimming performance of young sockeye salmon. *J. Fish. Res. Bd Can.* **21**, 1183–1226.

Brett, J. R. (1976). Scope for metabolism and growth of sockeye salmon, *Oncor-hynchus nerka*, and some related energetics. *J. Fish. Res. Bd Can.* **33**, 307–313.

Burton, A. F., Storr, J. M. and Dunn, W. L. (1967). Cytolytic action of cortico-steroids on thymus and lymphoma cells *in vitro*. *Can. J. Biochem.* **45**, 289–297.

Burton, C. B. and Murray, S. A. (1979). Effects of density on goldfish blood—I. Hematology. *Comp. Biochem. Physiol.* **62A**, 555–558.

Carter, L. (1962). Bioassay of trade wastes. *Nature, Lond.* **196**, 1304.

Casillas, E. and Smith, L. S. (1977). Effect of stress on blood coagulation and haematology in rainbow trout (*Salmo gairdneri*). *J. Fish Biol.* **10**, 481–491.

Chavin, W. (1973). *Responses of Fish to Environmental Change*, pp. 1–459. New York: Charles C. Thomas Co.

Clarke, W. C. and Blackburn, J. (1977). A seawater challenge test to measure smolting of juvenile salmon. *Fish. Mar. Serv. Res. Dev. Tech. Rep.* **705**, 1–11.

Clarke, W. C. and Blackburn, J. (1978). Seawater challenge tests performed on hatchery stocks of chinook and coho salmon in 1977. *Fish. Mar. Serv. Res. Dev. Tech. Rep.* **76**, 1–19.

Davis, G. E., Foster, J., Warren, C. E. and Doudoroff, P. (1963). The influence of oxygen concentration on the swimming performance of juvenile Pacific salmon at various temperatures. *Trans. Am. Fish. Soc.* **92**, 111–124.

Dickson, I. W. and Kramer, R. H. (1971). Factors influencing scope for activity and active and standard metabolism of rainbow trout (*Salmo gairdneri*). *J. Fish. Res. Bd Can.* **28**, 587–596.

Donaldson, E. M. (1981). The pituitary–interrenal axis as an indicator of stress in fish. In *Stress and Fish* (A. D. Pickering, ed.), pp. 11–47. London and New York: Academic Press.

Donaldson, E. M. and McBride, J. R. (1974). Effect of ACTH and salmon gonado-tropin on interrenal and thyroid activity of gonadectomized adult sockeye salmon (*Oncorhynchus nerka*). *J. Fish. Res. Bd Can.* **31**, 1211–1214.

Dougherty, T. F. (1960). Lymphocytokaryorrhectic effects of adrenocortical steroids. In *The Lymphocyte and Lymphocytic Tissue* (J. W. Rebuck, ed.), pp. 112–124. New York: Haper (Hoeber).

Eddy, F. B. (1981). Effects of stress on osmotic and ionic regulation in fish. In *Stress and Fish* (A. D. Pickering, ed.), pp. 77–102. London and New York: Academic Press.

Elliott, J. M. (1981). Some aspects of thermal stress on freshwater teleosts. In *Stress and Fish* (A. D. Pickering, ed.). pp. 209–245. London and New York: Academic Press.

Ellis, A. E. (1981). Stress and the modulation of defence mechanisms in fish. In *Stress and Fish* (A. D. Pickering, ed.), pp. 147–169. London and New York: Academic Press.

Esch, G. W. and Hazen, T. C. (1978). Thermal ecology and stress: A case history for red-sore disease in largemouth bass. In *Energy and Environmental Stress in Aquatic Systems* (J. Thorp and J. Gibbons, eds), pp. 331–363. U.S. Department of Energy, Symposium Series 48, National Technical Information Service, Pub-lication CON-7711111 U.S. Dept. Commerce, Springfield, Virginia, U.S.A.

Fletcher, T. C. (1981). Non-antibody molecules and the defence mechanisms of fish. In *Stress and Fish* (A. D. Pickering, ed.), pp. 170–189. London and New York: Academic Press.

Fry, F. E. J. (1947). Effects of the environment on animal activity, *Univ. Toronto Stud. Biol. Ser.* **55**, *Publ. Ont. Fish. Res. Lab.* **68**, 5–62.

Fry, F. E. J. (1971). The effect of environmental factors on the physiology of fish. In *Fish Physiology, Vol. 6* (W. S. Hoar and D. J. Randall, eds), pp. 1–98. London and New York: Academic Press.

George, C. J. (1977). The implication of neuroendocrine mechanisms in the regulation of population character. *Fisheries* 2, 14–19.

Giles, M. A. and Klaprat, D. (1979). The residual oxygen test: a rapid method for estimating the acute lethal toxicity of aquatic contaminants. In *Toxicity Tests for Freshwater Organisms* (E. Scherer, ed.), pp. 37–45. Canad. Spec. Publ. Fish. Aquat. Sc. No. 44. Winnipeg: Dept. Fisheries and Oceans.

Glova, G. J. and McInerney, J. E. (1977). Critical swimming speeds of coho salmon (*Oncorhynchus kisutch*) fry to smolt stages in relation to salinity and temperature. *J. Fish. Res. Bd Can.* 34, 151–154.

Gordon, M. R. and McLeay, D. J. (1977). Sealed-jar bioassays for pulpmill effluent toxicity: effects of fish species and temperature. *J. Fish. Res. Bd Can.* 34, 1389–1396.

Gordon, M. R. and McLeay, D. J. (1978). Effect of photoperiod on seasonal variations in glycogen reserves of juvenile rainbow trout (*Salmo gairdneri*). *Comp. Biochem. Physiol.* 60, 349–351.

Gould, R. W., Antipa, R. and Amend, D. F. (1978). Immersion vaccination of sockeye salmon (*Oncorhynchus nerka*) with two pathogenic strains of *Vibrio anguillarum*. *J. Fish. Res. Bd Can.* 36, 222–225.

Grieco, M. P., Hendricks, J. D., Scanian, R. A., Sinnhuber, R. O. and Pierce, D. A. (1978). Carcinogenicity and acute toxicity of dimethyl nitrosamine in rainbow trout (*Salmo gairdneri*). *J. Natn. Cancer Inst.* 60, 1127–1130.

Groberg, W. J. Jr., McCoy, R. H., Pilcher, K. S. and Fryer, J. L. (1978). Relation of water temperature to infections of coho salmon (*Oncorhynchus kisutch*), chinook salmon (*O. tshawytscha*), and steelhead trout (*Salmo gairdneri*) with *Aeromonas salmonicida* and *A. hydrophila*. *J. Fish. Res. Bd Can.* 35, 1–7.

Hattingh, J. (1976). Blood sugar as an indicator of stress in the freshwater fish, *Labeo capensis* (Smith). *J. Fish Biol.* 10, 191–195.

Heath, A. G. and Hughes, G. M. (1973). Cardiovascular and respiratory changes during heat stress in rainbow trout (*Salmo gairdneri*). *J. exp. Biol.* 59, 323–338.

Hetrick, F. M., Knittel, M. D. and Fryer, J. L. (1979). Increased susceptibility of rainbow trout to infectious hematopoietic necrosis virus after exposure to copper. *Appl. Environm. Microbiol.* 37, 198–201.

Hirano, T. (1969). Effects of hypophysectomy and salinity change on plasma cortisol concentration in the Japanese eel, *Anguilla japonica. Endocr. jap.* 16, 557–560.

Hoar, W. S. (1956). Photoperiodism and thermal resistance of goldfish. *Nature, Lond.* 178, 364–365.

Hodgins, H. O., McCain, B. B. and Hawkes, J. (1977). Marine fish and invertebrate diseases, host disease resistance, and pathological effects of petroleum. In *Effects of Petroleum on Arctic and SubArctic Marine Environments and Organisms. II. Biological Effects* (D. Malins, ed.), pp. 95–148. London and New York: Academic Press.

Horak, D. L. (1972). Survival of hatchery-reared rainbow trout (*Salmo gairdneri*) in relation to stamina tunnel ratings. *J. Fish. Res. Bd Can.* 29, 1005–1009.

Howard, T. E. (1973). Effects of kraft pulp mill effluents on the stamina, temperature tolerance and respiration of some salmonid fish. Ph.D. Thesis, University of Strathclyde, Glasgow, 183pp.

Hughes, G. M. (1981). Effects of low oxygen and pollution on the respiratory systems of fish. In *Stress and Fish* (A. D. Pickering, ed.), pp. 121–146. London and New York: Academic Press.

Hughes, G. M. and Roberts, J. C. (1970). A study of the effect of temperature changes on the respiratory pumps of the rainbow trout. *J. exp. Biol.* **52**, 177–192.

Hutchison, V. (1961). Critical thermal maxima in salamanders. *Physiol. Zool.* **34**, 92–105.

Iwama, G. (1977). Some aspects of the interrelationship of bacterial kidney disease infection and sodium pentachlorophenate exposure in juvenile chinook salmon (*Oncorhynchus tshawytscha*). M.Sc. Thesis, University of British Columbia, Vancouver, B.C. 106pp.

Kutty, M. N. (1968). Influence of ambient oxygen on the swimming performance of goldfish and rainbow trout. *Can. J. Zool.* **46**, 647–653.

Kutty, M. N. and Saunders, R. L. (1973). Swimming performance of young Atlantic salmon (*Salmo salar*) as affected by reduced ambient oxygen concentration. *J. Fish. Res. Bd Can.* **30**, 223–227.

Larmoyeux, J. D. and Piper, R. G. (1973). Effects of water reuse on rainbow trout in hatcheries. *Progve Fish Cult.* **35**, 2–8.

Lugo, A. E. (1978). Stress and ecosystems. In *Energy and Environmental Stress in Aquatic Systems* (J. Thorp and J. Gibbons, eds), pp. 62–101. U.S. Department of Energy Symposium Series 48. National Technical Information Service, U.S. Dept. of Commerce, Springfield, Virginia, U.S.A.

Mayer, F. L. Jr. and Kramer, R. H. (1973). Effects of hatchery water reuse on rainbow trout metabolism. *Progve Fish Cult.* **35**, 9–10.

Mazeaud, M. M. and Mazeaud, F. (1981). Adrenergic responses to stress in fish. In *Stress and Fish* (A. D. Pickering, ed.), pp. 49–75. London and New York: Academic Press.

Mazeaud, M. M., Mazeaud, F. and Donaldson, E. M. (1977). Primary and secondary effects of stress in fish: some new data with a general review. *Trans. Am. Fish. Soc.* **106**, 201–212.

McFarlane, G. A. and Franzin, W. G. (1978). Elevated heavy metals: A stress on a population of white suckers, *Catostomus commersoni*, in Hammel Lake, Saskatchewan. *J. Fish. Res. Bd Can.* **35**, 963–970.

McLeay, D. J. (1973a). Effects of cortisol and dexamethasone on the pituitary–interrenal axis and abundance of white blood cell types in juvenile coho salmon, *Oncorhynchus kisutch*. *Gen. comp. Endocr.* **21**, 441–450.

McLeay, D. J. (1973b). Effects of a 12-hr and 25-day exposure to kraft pulp mill effluent on the blood and tissues of juvenile coho salmon (*Oncorhynchus kisutch*). *J. Fish. Res. Bd Can.* **30**, 395–400.

McLeay, D. J. (1975a). Variations in the pituitary–interrenal axis and the abundance of circulating blood-cell types in juvenile coho salmon (*Oncorhynchus kisutch*), during stream residence. *Can. J. Zool.* **53**, 1882–1891.

McLeay, D. J. (1975b). Sensitivity of blood cell counts in juvenile coho salmon (*Oncorhynchus kisutch*) to stressors including sublethal concentrations of pulp mill effluent and zinc. *J. Fish. Res. Bd Can.* **32**, 2357–2364.

McLeay, D. J. (1976). A rapid method for measuring the acute toxicity of pulpmill effluents and other toxicants to salmonid fish at ambient room temperature. *J. Fish. Res. Bd Can.* **33**, 1303–1311.

McLeay, D. J. (1977). Development of a blood sugar bioassay for rapidly measuring stressful levels of pulpmill effluent to salmonid fish. *J. Fish. Res. Bd Can.* **34**, 477–485.

McLeay, D. J. (1979). Potential impact of mutagenicity contained in aquatic discharges on Canadian fisheries. Summary document. B.C. Research Project Report No. 1-05-126. Prepared for Fisheries and Oceans, Ottawa, Ont.

McLeay, D. J. and Brown, D. A. (1974). Growth stimulation and biochemical changes in juvenile coho salmon (*Oncorhynchus kisutch*) exposed to bleached kraft pulpmill effluent for 200 days. *J. Fish. Res. Bd Can.* **31**, 1043–1049.

McLeay, D. J. and Brown, D. A. (1975). Effects of acute exposure to bleached kraft pulpmill effluent on carbohydrate metabolism of juvenile coho salmon *Oncorhynchus kisutch*) during rest and exercise. *J. Fish. Res. Bd Can.* **32**, 753–760.

McLeay, D. J. and Brown, D. A. (1979). Stress and chronic effects of untreated and treated bleached kraft pulpmill effluent on the biochemistry and stamina of juvenile coho salmon (*Oncorhynchus kisutch*). *J. Fish. Res. Bd Can.* **36**, 1049–1059.

McLeay, D. J. and Gordon, M. R. (1977). Leucocrit: a simple hematological technique for measuring acute stress in salmonid fish, including stressful concentrations of pulpmill effluent. *J. Fish. Res. Bd Can.* **34**, 2164–2175.

McLeay, D. J. and Gordon, M. R. (1978a). Effect of seasonal photoperiod on acute toxic responses of juvenile rainbow trout (*Salmo gairdneri*) to pulpmill effluent. *J. Fish. Res. Bd Can.* **35**, 1388–1392.

McLeay, D. J. and Gordon, M. R. (1978b). Field study of the effects to fish of treated, partially treated and untreated kraft pulp mill effluent. *B.C. Research Project Report* No. 1-05-902. Prepared for the Council of Forest Industries of British Columbia.

McLeay, D. J. and Gordon, M. R. (1979). Concentrations of Krenite causing acute lethal, avoidance and stress responses with salmon. *B.C. Research Project Report* No. 1-04-156. Prepared for Dupont Canada Inc.

McLeay, D. J. and Gordon, M. R. (1980). Short-term sublethal toxicity tests to assess safe levels of environmental contaminants. *B.C. Research Project Report* No. 1-11-299. Prepared for Environment Canada, Ottawa.

McLeay, D. J. and Howard, T. E. (1977). Comparison of rapid bioassay procedures for measuring toxic effects of bleached kraft mill effluent to fish. In *Proc. 3rd Aquatic Toxicity Workshop, Halifax, N.S., Nov. 2–3, 1976* (W. R. Parker et al., eds), pp. 141–155. Halifax: Environm. Prot. Serv. Tech. Rep. No. EPS-5-AR-77-1.

McNeish, J. D. and Hatch, R. W. (1978). Stamina tunnel tests on hatchery-reared Atlantic salmon. *Progve Fish Cult.* **40**, 116–117.

Michel, C. (1980). A standardized model of experimental furunculosis in rainbow trout (*Salmo gairdneri*). *Can. J. Fish. Aquat. Sci.* **37**, 746–750.

Mihursky, J. A. and Kennedy, V. S. (1967). Water temperature criteria to protect aquatic life. *Am. Fish. Soc. Spec. Publ.* **4**, 20–32.

Murray, S. A. and Burton, C. B. (1979). Effects of density on goldfish blood—II. Cell morphology. *Comp. Biochem. Physiol.* **62A**, 559–562.

Nakano, T. and Tomlinson, N. (1967). Catecholamine and carbohydrate concentrations in rainbow trout (*Salmo gairdneri*) in relation to physical disturbance. *J. Fish. Res. Bd Can.* **24**, 1701–1715.

Noakes, D. L. G. and Leatherland, J. (1977). Social dominance and interrenal cell activity in rainbow trout, *Salmo gairdneri* (Pisces, *Salmonidae*). *Env. Biol. Fish.* **2**, 131–136.

Paladino, F. V. and Spotila, J. R. (1978). The effect of arsenic on the thermal tolerance of newly hatched muskellunge fry (*Esox masguinongy*). *J. Thermal Biol.* **3**, 223–227.

Pessah, E., Wells, P. G. and Schneider, J. R. (1976). Dodecyl sodium sulphate (DSS) as an intralaboratory reference toxicant in fish bioassays. In *Proc. 2nd Aquatic Toxicity Workshop, Toronto, Ont., Nov. 4–5, 1975* (G. R. Craig, ed.), pp. 93–121. Spons. by Water Resources Br., Ont. Minist. Environm.

Peters, G. (1979). Zur interpretation des begriffs "stress" beim fisch. *Fisch und Tierschutz, Fisch und Umwelt* Heft. 7. Stuttgart, New York: Fischer-Verlag.

Peters, G., Delventhal, H. and Klinger, H. (1980). Physiological and morphological effects of social stress in the eel, (*Anguilla anguilla* L.). *Arch. FischWiss.* **30**, 157–180.

Pickering, A. D. (1981). Introduction: the concept of biological stress. In *Stress and Fish* (A. D. Pickering, ed.), pp. 1–9. London and New York: Academic Press.

Piper, R. (Ed.) (1980). *Fish Hatchery Management*, U.S. Fish and Wildlife Service, Wash., D.C. (In press).

Ramos, F. and Smith, A. C. (1978a). The C-reactive protein test for detection of early disease in fishes. *Aquaculture* **14**, 261–266.

Ramos, F. and Smith, A. C. (1978b). Ketone bodies in fish skin mucus as an indicator of starvation: a preliminary report. *J. Fish Biol.* **12**, 105–108.

Ryan, P. M. and Harvey, H. H. (1977). Growth of rock bass, *Ambloplites rupestris*, in relation to the morphoedaphic index as an indicator of an environmental stress. *J. Fish. Res. Bd Can.* **34**, 2079–2088.

Schreck, C. B. (1981). Stress and compensation in teleostean fishes: response to social and physical factors. In *Stress and Fish* (A. D. Pickering, ed.), pp. 295–321. London and New York: Academic Press.

Schreck, C. B., Whaley, R. A., Bass, M. L., Maughan, O. E. and Solazzi, M. (1976). Physiological responses of rainbow trout (*Salmo gairdneri*) to electroshock. *J. Fish. Res. Bd Can.* **33**, 76–84.

Selye, H. (1950). Stress and the general adaptation syndrome. *Brit. Med. J.* **1**, 1383–1392.

Selye, H. (1973). The evolution of the stress concept. *Am. Sci.* **61**, 692–699.

Silbergeld, E. K. (1975). Blood glucose: a sensitive indicator of environmental stress in fish. *Bull. Environm. Contam. Toxicol.* **11**, 20–25.

Singley, J. A. and Chavin, W. (1975). The adrenocortical-hypophyseal response to saline stress in the goldfish, *Carassius auratus* L. *Comp. Biochem. Physiol.* **51A**, 749–756.

Sinnhuber, R. O., Hendrix, J. D., Wales, J. H. and Putman, G. B. (1977). Neoplasms in rainbow trout, a sensitive animal model for environmental carcinogenesis. *Ann. N.Y. Acad. Sci.* **298**, 389–408.

Smart, G. R. (1981). Aspects of water quality producing stress in intensive fish culture. In *Stress and Fish* (A. D. Pickering, ed.), pp. 277–293. London and New York: Academic Press.

Smith, A. C. and Ramos, F. (1976). Occult hemoglobin in fish skin mucus as an indicator of early stress. *J. Fish Biol.* **9**, 537–541.

Smith, H. D. and Margolis, L. (1970). Some effects of *Eubothrium salvelini* on sockeye salmon, *Oncorhynchus nerka*, in Babine Lake, British Columbia. *J. Parasit.* **56**, 321–322.

Snieszko, S. F. (1974). The effects of environmental stress on outbreaks of infectious diseases of fishes. *J. Fish Biol.* **6**, 197–208.

Soivio, A. and Nikinmaa, M. (1981). The swelling of erythrocytes in relation to the oxygen affinity of the blood of the rainbow trout, *Salmo gairdneri* Richardson. In *Stress and Fish* (A. D. Pickering, ed.), pp. 103–119. London and New York: Academic Press.

Soivio, A. and Oikari, A. (1976). Haematological effects of stress on a teleost, *Esox lucius* L. *J. Fish Biol.* **8**, 397–411.

Specker, J. L. and Schreck, C. B. (1980). Stress responses to transportation and fitness for marine survival in coho salmon (*Oncorhynchus kisutch*) smolts. *Can. J. Fish. Aquat. Sci.* **37**, 765–769.

Sprague, J. B. (1971). Measurement of pollutant toxicity to fish—III Sublethal effects and "safe" concentrations. *Wat. Res.* **5**, 245–266.

Srivastava, A. K. and Agrawal, U. (1977). Involvement of pituitary–interrenal axis and cholinergic mechanisms during the cold-shock leucocyte sequence in a fresh water tropical teleost, *Colisa fasciatus*. *Archs Anat. microsc.* **66**, 97–108.

Strange, R. J., Schreck, C. B. and Golden, J. T. (1977). Corticoid stress responses to handling and temperature in salmonids. *Trans. Am. Fish. Soc.* **106**, 213–218.

Strange, R. J., Schreck, C. B. and Ewing, R. D. (1978). Cortisol concentrations in confined juvenile chinook salmon (*Oncorhynchus tshawytscha*). *Trans. Am. Fish. Soc.* **107**, 812–819.

Vigers, G. A. and Maynard, A. W. (1977). The residual oxygen bioassay: a rapid procedure to predict effluent toxicity to rainbow trout. *Wat. Res.* **11**, 343–346.

Waiwood, K. G. and Beamish, F. W. H. (1978). Effects of copper, pH and hardness on the critical swimming performance of rainbow trout (*Salmo gairdneri* Richardson). *Wat. Res.* **12**, 611–619.

Wales, J. H., Sinnhuber, R. O., Hendricks, J. D., Nixon, J. E. and Eisele, T. A. (1978). Aflatoxin B_1 induction of heptocellular carcinoma in the embryos of rainbow trout (*Salmo gairdneri*). *J. Natn. Cancer Inst.* **60**, 1133–1139.

Webb, P. W. and Brett, J. R. (1973). Effects of sublethal concentrations of sodium pentachlorophenate on growth rate, food conversion efficiency, and swimming performance in underyearling sockeye salmon (*Oncorhynchus nerka*). *J. Fish. Res. Bd Can.* **30**, 499–507.

Wedemeyer, G. (1969). Physiological response of juvenile coho salmon (*Oncorhynchus kisutch*) and rainbow trout (*Salmo gairdneri*) to handling and crowding stress in intensive fish culture. *J. Fish. Res. Bd Can.* **33**, 2699–2702.

Wedemeyer, G. (1973). Some physiological aspects of sublethal heat stress in the juvenile steelhead trout (*Salmo gairdneri*) and coho salmon (*Oncorhynchus kisutch*). *J. Fish. Res. Bd Can.* **30**, 831–834.

Wedemeyer, G. A. (1976). Physiological response of juvenile coho salmon (*Oncorhynchus kisutch*) and rainbow trout (*Salmo gairdneri*) to handling and crowding stress in intensive fish culture. *J. Fish. Res. Bd Can.* **33**, 2699–2702.

Wedemeyer, G. and Yasutake, W. T. (1977). Clinical methods for the assessment of the effects of environmental stress on fish health. *U.S. Tech. Pap. U.S. Fish Wildl. Serv.* **89**, 1–18. Wash., D.C., U.S.A.

Wedemeyer, G. A., Meyer, F. P. and Smith, L. (1976). Environmental stress and fish diseases, Book 5. In *Diseases of Fishes* (S. F. Snieszko and H. R. Axelrod, eds), pp. 1–192. New Jersey: T. H. F. Publ. Inc.

Wedemeyer, G. A., Saunders, R. L. and Clarke, C. C. (1980). Environmental factors affecting smoltification and yearly marine survival of anadromous salmonids. *Mar. Fish. Rev.* **42**, 1–14.

Wohlschlag, D. E. and Wakeman, J. M. (1978). Salinity stresses, metabolic responses, and distribution of the coastal spotted seatrout, *Cynoscion nebulosus. Contributions in Mar. Sci.* **21**, 172–185. Univ. Texas Marine Sci. Institute.

12. Aspects of Water Quality Producing Stress in Intensive Fish Culture

G. R. SMART

Shearwater Fish Farming Limited, Finnarts Bay, Ballantrae, Ayrshire, Scotland

Abstract. To the fish farmer, impaired food conversion efficiency can be a sensitive indicator of stress. Poor water quality, or even fluctuations in water quality may cause significant reductions in appetite, growth and food conversion efficiency. Data are presented to show the influence of environmental oxygen, ammonia and carbon dioxide concentrations on these aspects of fish performance.

Fluctuations of dissolved oxygen concentrations can occur as a result of changes in temperature, plant metabolism or water availability. Reduced oxygen concentrations may impair food intake and increase susceptibility to parasite infections and other water pollutants.

Under certain rearing conditions, ammonia (an end product of protein metabolism) may accumulate in the water. The influences of pH, temperature and salinity on the concentrations of ammonia which can be allowed to accumulate are discussed.

Elevated CO_2 concentrations may accompany the use of spring/borehole water or may occur when water is re-cycled. Data are presented which indicate that this can result in the deposition of calcium salts in the kidney and stomach, a condition known as nephrocalcinosis. Affected fish may show not only a depression of appetite, growth and food conversion, but a decreased ability to withstand husbandry procedures such as grading or transfer to salt water.

I INTRODUCTION

The fish farmer carries out many procedures (e.g. netting, grading, transporting, transfer to salt water) which are known to stress fish. Superimposed on these direct husbandry stresses are the stresses of poor water quality, protozoan or other parasitic infestations, bacterial, viral or fungal infections and even the presence of predatory birds such as gulls and herons. These stresses are all likely to disrupt the farmer's production plans. Thus, from the fish farmer's point of view, stress might be considered to be a state caused by some procedure, environmental or other factor which impairs the fish's ability to grow to market size at the expected rate.

Farmed fish show a wide range of responses to stressful stimuli. Many of these reactions are readily apparent; fish may die, lose appetite or show bizarre behavioural patterns. Alternatively, they may show no abnormal mortality rates, feed and behave normally, but convert their food less efficiently. The food conversion ratio (FCR = "dry" food fed/wet weight gain) for most commercial trout feeds will be in the region $1 \cdot 5$–$2 \cdot 0$: 1. For salmonids, food represents at least 60% of the production costs and consequently a poor FCR can be economically disastrous. Poor FCRs can be good monitors of the extent to which fish are, or have been, stressed because they indicate that an increased proportion of the ration may be expended in metabolic processes other than growth (perhaps due to the energy lost in compensatory, physiological stress responses).

This review examines the stresses produced by fluctuations of three important aspects of water quality—the concentrations of oxygen, ammonia and carbon dioxide. Much of the work refers to the rainbow trout, *Salmo gairdneri*, although reference is also given to other species of farmed fish.

II DISSOLVED OXYGEN

For extensive reviews of the dissolved oxygen (DO) requirements of fish the reader is referred to reviews by Doudoroff and Shumway (1970) and Alabaster and Lloyd (1980). The concentration of dissolved oxygen will normally be the primary aspect of water quality to be considered in the planning of a fish farm. Water availability must be accurately matched to the water requirements which can be calculated from a knowledge of the oxygen requirements of the species under culture conditions and the minimum DO required for successful culture. The oxygen requirements of farmed rainbow trout have been studied by Willoughby (1968), Liao (1971), Speece (1973) and Muller-Feuga *et al.* (1978). Jones *et al.* (1980) have presented data for the turbot, *Scophthalmus maximus*. For salmonids, the minimum DO required is 5–6 mg l^{-1} (Westers and Pratt, 1977) whereas for the channel catfish, *Ictalurus punctatus*, and Tilapia species the minimum is 3 mg l^{-1} (Carter and Allen, 1976; Balarin, 1978).

Table I gives an indication of the water requirements for rainbow trout culture at various temperatures. The requirements are very high and even in the best planned farms there may be occasions when the DO falls below the

TABLE I Water Requirements for Salmonid Culture.

Temperature °C	Oxygen requirement kg O$_2$ tonne fish^{-1} day^{-1}	[a] Daily water requirement (m^3 day^{-1}) for effluent oxygen concentration of	
		(a) 5 mg l^{-1}	(b) 6 mg l^{-1}
6	2·6	347	400
8	3·4	492	576
10	4·3	683	811
12	5·1	879	1063
14	6·0	1111	1364
16	6·8	1360	1700

[a] Represents minimum daily water requirement for one tonne of farmed rainbow trout, mean weight 200 g held at range of temperatures. Inflow water supply is assumed to be 100% saturated with oxygen in all cases. Fish fed "dry" diet at manufacturers recommended levels, (from Forster et al., 1977).

minimum level. The first indication the farmer has of low oxygen concentrations is that fish refuse food and congregate around the water inflow. There may be numerous causes of the reduced DO; the quantity of water available may be decreased (e.g. during drought), the oxygen content of the inflow water may have dropped (e.g. at elevated temperatures) or there may be large fluctuations in the metabolic activity of the fish. Figure 1 shows a typical daily variation in the oxygen consumption of rainbow trout on a fish farm and also shows the effect of a stressful husbandry procedure such as grading on oxygen consumption.

Two recent developments in salmonid farming have been aimed at overcoming some of these problems. The first of these involves culture in sea water in large sea cages or in land-based tanks. This largely overcomes the problem of water shortage or reduced oxygen concentrations in the incoming water, both common features of freshwater trout farming (Landless, 1976; Edwards, 1978). The second development concerns the use of water re-oxygenation techniques (Liao and Mayo, 1972, 1974; Forster et al., 1977) and gives the opportunity to operate at any desired DO concentration.

In view of the possibility that rainbow trout might grow more efficiently at oxygen concentrations much higher than the minimum level of 5 mg l^{-1}, a trial was set up by Shearwater Fish Farming Ltd in which groups of rainbow trout were reared at different oxygen concentrations maintained at 7, 10 and 14 mg l^{-1}. This corresponded to 60, 85 and 120% saturation respectively. Table II shows that growth and FCR of the three groups were very similar and indicates no direct advantage in the practice of growing fish at a DO well above the minimum. Carter and Allen (1976) reported similar data for

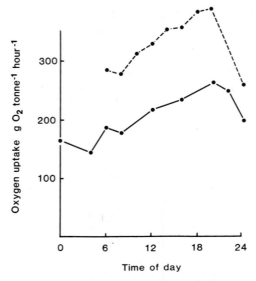

Fig. 1 Typical daily oxygen consumption of intensively reared rainbow trout. A total weight of 1·75 tonnes of fish (mean weight 80 g) were held in a 25 m³ rearing tank and fed a commercial trout diet according to the recommended feeding levels. Food was given at hourly intervals between 9·00 and 17·00 ●—● control fish, ●– – –● oxygen consumption of the same fish 1 day after they had been graded into the rearing tank. All measurements of oxygen consumption were made at 9°C.

TABLE II Effect of Oxygen Concentration on Growth and Food Conversion Ratio (FCR) of Rainbow Trout at 9°C.

| | I | | II |
| | Days 1–70 | | |
Oxygen conc. (mg l⁻¹)	% wt increase	FCR	Days 71–90 FCR
7	87	1·69:1	2·61:1
10	87	1·72:1	2·63:1
14	91	1·66:1	2·62:1

I—growth and FCR at constant oxygen concentration.
II—subsequent FCR of each group of fish at fluctuating oxygen concentrations.
Two hundred fish were kept at each oxygen concentration and fed by commercial trout pellets according to manufacturers recommendations.

channel catfish. They showed that as long as the oxygen concentration was above 3 mg l^{-1}, further increase in DO did not increase food consumption or improve growth and food conversion efficiency. The experiment shown in Table II was subsequently continued for a further 20 days during which time the DO concentrations in the rearing tanks were allowed to fluctuate randomly by altering the DO content of the inflow water. However, in no instance did the oxygen concentration drop below the minimum level. In all cases, conversion ratio was adversely affected during this period. Further research is required to determine how variations in DO might have an adverse effect on food conversion.

Finally, it is worth re-emphasizing that low environmental oxygen concentrations may enhance the stressful effects of other toxicants (Lloyd, 1961) or increase the probability of disease (Sniesko, 1974). It may also be worth examining whether high concentrations of DO may be beneficial in moderating the effects of other pollutants.

III AMMONIA

(a) Equilibriation of Ammonia in Aqueous Solutions

The total ammonia in aqueous solution exists in two forms; ionized ammonia (NH_4^+) and un-ionized ammonia (NH_3). The relative proportions of these two forms depends mainly on pH but is also influenced by temperature and ionic strength. It is well recorded that the un-ionized form of ammonia is far more toxic to fish than the ionized form (Wuhrman and Woker, 1948; Downing and Merkens, 1955). Thus, when comparing data on the toxicity of ammonia to fish, one should compare un-ionized ammonia (UIA) concentrations rather than total ammonia concentrations. UIA concentrations may be calculated by measuring the total ammonia (TA) concentration using, for example, the phenol-hypochlorite reaction (Harwood and Kuhn, 1970) or an ammonia probe (Barica, 1973; Bigg and Alexander, 1980), and then calculating the UIA concentration from the following formula:

$$\% \text{UIA} = \frac{100}{1 + \text{antilog (pKa} - \text{pH)}}$$

pKa is the negative logarithm of the ionization constant and its value will depend on temperature and ionic strength. pKa values for fresh water have been published by Trussel (1972) and Emerson et al. (1975) and for saline waters by Whitfield (1974) and Bower and Bidwell (1978).

The probable reason for the acute toxicity of UIA in fresh water is the fact that it will readily diffuse across the gill membrane into the circulation whereas the ionized form will not. Smart (1975) reported that increases in the blood ammonia concentration of rainbow trout could be correlated with increases in environmental UIA concentrations, although not necessarily with environmental TA concentrations. In this study the UIA concentrations in both water and blood were recalculated in terms of partial pressures of ammonia (pNH_3), and it was shown that under most conditions, water and blood pNH_3 were in equilibrium. This suggested that UIA readily diffused across the membrane. However, Fromm and Gillette (1968) reported that blood ammonia concentrations increased with both increasing environmental TA and UIA concentrations. They concluded that, because blood ammonia concentrations always exceeded the concentration in the water, the increase in blood ammonia resulted from inhibition of excretion rather than inward transfer. Fromm and Gillettes' interpretations were, however, based on blood ammonia concentrations of control fish which were ten times higher than those reported by other workers.

Interestingly in a study of the acute toxicity of ammonia to fish, Hillaby and Randall (1979) suggested that although in water the un-ionized form determined toxicity, in the blood it appeared that either the total or even the ionized form produced the toxic effects.

(b) Sources of Ammonia

It is possible that ammonia may be present in significant amounts in the incoming water supply if the farm is located downstream of a sewage disposal works, an industrial process or the unlawful discharge of silage or manure. Alternatively, in intensive fish-rearing units ammonia excreted by the fish as a result of protein metabolism may accumulate in the water. In conventional fish farms, the water flow will be sufficiently high to keep metabolically produced ammonia concentrations well below harmful levels. Thus, although elevated ammonia levels are often claimed to be major stresses, in reality they are rarely the cause of problems unless the farm is receiving ammonia-polluted water, there is considerable water re-cycling or because the water supply has a high pH.

(c) Biological Effects of Ammonia Pollution

(i) *Acute lethality*. Alabaster and Lloyd (1980) have extensively reviewed the toxicity data concerning ammonia. For adult rainbow trout, the lethal threshold concentration of UIA is approximately 0·45 mg NH_3–N l^{-1}. Table III shows the TA concentrations producing such an UIA at a range of pHs and temperatures in fresh water. The major observable symptoms are hyperventilation, hyperexcitability, coma and convulsions, but these are

TABLE III Total Ammonia Concentrations (mg NH_3–N l^{-1}) Producing Un-ionized Ammonia Concentrations of 0·45 mg NH_3–N l^{-1} (Lethal Threshold Concentration) at Different pHs and Temperatures in Fresh Water.

| pH | Temperature °C | | | |
	5	10	15	20
6·5	1139	750	500	346
7·0	360	241	167	113
7·5	114	76	53	36
7·8	57	38	27	18
8·0	37	25	17	12
8·2	23	15	11	8
8·5	12	8	5	4

Note: in full strength sea water (34‰) at pH 8·0, TA required to exceed lethal threshold concentration would be 31 and 22 mg NH_3–N l^{-1} at 10°C and 15°C respectively.

readily reversible if the fish are placed in ammonia-free water before 95% of the average survival time in the particular UIA concentration has elapsed (Smart, 1975).

There has been considerable research into the primary toxic action of ammonia in both human and veterinary medicine and it is generally agreed that the primary effect is on the nervous system (Visek, 1968) although the actual mechanism has not been resolved. Walker and Schenker (1970) and Breen and Schenker (1972) have suggested that ammonia may produce an impairment of cerebral energy metabolism, resulting in depletions of adenosine triphosphate (ATP) and phosphocreatine (PC) in the brain. Following the injection of rats with ammonium acetate, Schenker *et al.* (1967) reported significant decreases in the concentrations of ATP and PC in the basilar regions of the brain. Smart (1975) also found decreased medullary concentrations of these high energy phosphates in rainbow trout exposed to acutely lethal UIA concentrations. Other possible mechanisms have been suggested, however, such as an effect on neuronal membranes or an alteration of neurotransmitters and these possibilities are receiving further study.

(ii) *Chronically toxic concentrations.* A number of toxic effects have been reported for UIA concentrations below those which are acutely lethal.

Bullock (1972) and Smart (1976) have shown that prolonged exposure to ammonia causes gill damage characterized by a large number of aneurysms in the lamellae. Aneurysms were also reported by Larmoyeux and Piper (1973) but in addition they noted a hyperplasia of the gill epithelium. However, these authors did not claim that such damage was wholly attributable to ammonia.

Lloyd and Orr (1969) measured urine production rates in rainbow trout exposed to ammonia and found that at UIA concentrations above 12% of the lethal threshold concentration the rate of urine excretion increased. They suggested that this diuresis was caused by an ammonia-induced increased permeability to water. Prolonged exposure (13 days) of coho salmon, *Oncorhynchus kisutch*, to UIA concentrations ranging between $0 \cdot 05$ and $0 \cdot 18$ mg NH_3–N l^{-1} caused a progressive acidemia which subsequently led to a reduction in the blood oxygen carrying capacity (Sousa and Meade, 1977). It was suggested that the toxic effect was induced by an accumulation of acid metabolites following enzymatic stimulation of glycolysis by ammonium ions. All three of these toxic effects might be expected to significantly reduce a farmed fish's ability to survive. Even if fish were able to overcome these effects by some compensatory physiological mechanism, it may be at a metabolic cost and therefore the conversion of food to fish tissue may proceed less efficiently.

(iii) *"Safe" levels.* U.S. Environmental Protection Agency (1976) and EIFAC (1970) recommend UIA concentrations of $0 \cdot 016$ and $0 \cdot 021$ mg NH_3–N l^{-1} respectively as the maximum which can be tolerated by fish for long periods. However, Schulze-Wiehenbrauck (1976) concluded that UIA concentrations up to $0 \cdot 13$ mg NH_3–N l^{-1} were harmless to growth and conversion ratio of rainbow trout and that concentrations up to $0 \cdot 15$ mg NH_3–N l^{-1} only temporarily affected growth. Forster and Smart (1979) reported no adverse effects on growth or conversion ratio up to $0 \cdot 07$ mg NH_3–N l^{-1}; at $0 \cdot 10$ mg NH_3–N l^{-1} there was an initial lethargy, loss of appetite and poor growth during the first two weeks. Subsequently fish appeared to acclimate to this concentration and grow normally. Table IV shows the TA concentrations giving a "safe" UIA concentration of $0 \cdot 07$ mg NH_3–N l^{-1} at various pHs and temperatures in fresh water.

It is interesting at this point to consider under what conditions the accumulation of metabolically produced ammonia might produce adverse effects on fish. In teleosts, ammonia is the major end product of nitrogen metabolism; estimates of the percentage total nitrogen excreted as ammonia vary from $51 \cdot 7\%$ (Fromm and Gillette, 1968) to 90% (Forster and Goldstein, 1969). Maetz (1972) reported that 98% of the ammonia excreted is eliminated via the gills. The bulk of this ammonia is excreted passively in

TABLE IV Total Ammonia Concentrations (mg NH_3–$N\,l^{-1}$) Producing Un-ionized Ammonia Concentration of 0.07 mg NH_3–$N\,l^{-1}$ (Considered to be the "safe" Concentration for Intensive Rearing of Post-alevin Rainbow Trout) in Fresh Water.

| pH | Temperature °C | | | |
	5	10	15	20
6·5	188	125	83	58
7·0	62	39	28	19
7·5	19	13	9	6
7·8	9·6	6·5	4·4	3·1
8·0	6·1	4·1	2·8	1·9
8·5	3·0	1·4	0·9	0·7

Note: in sea water at 15°C, pH 8·0, TA required to exceed "safe" concentration would be 3·4 mg NH_3–$N\,l^{-1}$.

the un-ionized form (Kerstetter et al., 1970; de Vooys, 1968; Smart, 1975) although some ionized ammonia may be excreted in exchange for Na^+ ions.

Figure 2 shows a typical daily ammonia excretion pattern for farmed rainbow trout held at 10°C in an intensive rearing tank and fed a commercial trout diet. Taking the maximum total ammonia excretion rate of 700 mg NH_3–N kg $fish^{-1}$ day^{-1}, and the relevant minimum water requirement shown in Table I for a conventional fish farm, it can be calculated that a TA concentration in the region of 1 mg NH_3–$N\,l^{-1}$ will accumulate in the effluent. Under these conditions, a pH of 8·65 would be required in order for an UIA concentration of 0·07 mg NH_3–$N\,l^{-1}$ to be exceeded. These calculations indicate that metabolically produced ammonia is unlikely to be a problem to fish held in such a system. If, by using re-oxygenation techniques, water requirement was reduced ten-fold, then a TA concentration of 10 mg NH_3–$N\,l^{-1}$ might result and the "safe" level would be exceeded at a pH of 7·6.

Finally, this section will consider some of the factors which may modify the acceptance of a generalized "safe" concentration. Most of the data reported above originate from work on adult rainbow trout. There is some evidence from the work of Calamari (quoted in Alabaster and Lloyd, 1980) that rainbow trout alevins may be particularly sensitive to ammonia, but that their tolerance increases as they reach the fingerling stage. Burkhalter and Kaya (1977) found that elevated levels of ammonia produced a condition

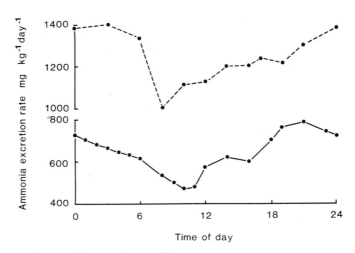

Fig. 2 Typical daily ammonia excretion of intensively reared rainbow trout. A total of 2·4 tonnes of fish (mean weight 82 g) were held in a 25 m³ rearing tank and fed a commercial trout diet according to the recommended feeding levels. Ammonia excretion rate was calculated from a knowledge of the effluent water ammonia concentration, water flow rate and total weight of fish on the assumption that no ammonia was lost to the atmosphere under test conditions (pH 6·7)—see Weiler (1979). ●——● control fish, ●– – –● ammonia excretion rate of the same fish 1 day after they had been graded into the rearing tank. All measurements of ammonia excretion rate were made at 9°C. Brett and Zala (1975) give data for the ammonia excretion rate of sockeye salmon fed a maintenance diet.

known as blue-sac disease in rainbow trout sac fry. According to Robinette (1976), growth of channel catfish is unaffected by UIA concentrations up to 0·06 mg NH_3–N l^{-1} but no growth occurs at concentrations of 0·12 and 0·13 mg NH_3–N l^{-1}. However, Colt and Tchobanoglous (1978) indicated that growth of this species was reduced at UIA concentrations as low as 0·048 mg NH_3–N l^{-1}. The growth of Dover sole, *Solea solea*, and turbot is unaffected by UIA levels of 0·066 and 0·10 mg NH_3–N l^{-1} respectively in sea water at 16°C (Alderson, 1979).

Salinity—as salinity increases there is a reduction in the percentage UIA in solution at any particular pH and temperature (see Bower and Bidwell, 1978). One interesting point is that in studies by Herbert and Shurben (1965) using rainbow trout and by Alabaster *et al.* (1979) using Atlantic salmon, *Salmo salar*, UIA appears to be considerably less toxic in 30% sea water than in either fresh water or 100% sea water. As 30% sea water is roughly iso-osmotic with fish blood it has been assumed that this observation results from decreased osmotic stress at the intermediate salinity. For further examples of the ameliorating effects of saline solutions on the performance of fish under stress see Schreck (1981, this volume).

Oxygen—low oxygen concentrations may considerably increase the toxicity of ammonia to fish (Lloyd, 1961). Larmoyeux and Piper (1973) reported that only 0.014 mg NH_3–$N\,l^{-1}$ was harmful to rainbow trout in a water re-use system, when the dissolved oxygen concentration was as low as 3.8 mg l^{-1}.

Temperature—Brown (1968) has suggested that a decrease in temperature below 3°C may result in increased susceptibility to un-ionized ammonia possibly because de-toxification processes occur at a reduced rate.

IV FREE CARBON DIOXIDE

Elevated concentrations of free CO_2 are of significance to fish culturists where spring or bore-hole water supplies are used. Such supplies may contain high concentrations of CO_2. Furthermore, in intensive rearing systems employing re-oxygenation, metabolically produced CO_2 will accumulate in the water.

The harmful effects of CO_2 on fish have usually been associated with reductions in oxygen affinity and oxygen capacity of the blood (Alabaster *et al.*, 1957; Basu, 1959; Saunders, 1962). The physiological responses to exposure have also been extensively studied and give some indication of how fish are able to acclimate to elevated levels of CO_2 (see Lloyd and Swift, 1976; Eddy *et al.*, 1977). Unfortunately there are few data on the concentrations of CO_2 which are detrimental to the growth and food conversion of farmed fish. Klontz (1973) has suggested that 12 mg l^{-1} may be detrimental to growth and 20 mg l^{-1} may be lethal. However, numerous hatcheries in the U.K. have been known to operate with free CO_2 concentrations in excess of these limits. Consequently, a chronic toxicity trial was set up and Table V shows the growth and food conversion ratios (FCR) of groups of fish held at CO_2 concentrations of 12, 24 and 55 mg l^{-1} for 275 days. Growth and FCR were similar at 12 and 24 mg l^{-1} but at 55 mg l^{-1} there was an initial loss of appetite and both growth and FCR were poor during the first 28 days. Subsequently there was a marked improvement, suggesting some degree of acclimation. Perhaps the most interesting observation in the study was that increases in CO_2 concentrations were correlated with increases in the incidence of a condition known as nephrocalcinosis (Smart *et al.*, 1979).

Nephrocalcinosis is a condition which is immediately recognizable at autopsy by the presence of white calcareous deposits in the kidney. No infective agent has been associated with the condition (see review by Landolt, 1975). In the study described above, histological examinations showed changes not only in the kidney but also in the stomach. At their most

TABLE V Summary of Growth, Food Conversion Ratio (FCR) and Incidence of Nephrocalcinosis in Rainbow Trout Reared at Different Free CO_2 Concentrations for 275 Days.

CO_2 concentration mg l^{-1}	Mean weight (g)		FCR	% fish showing gross nephrocalcinosis
	Start	Finish		
12	20	205	1·41 : 1	4·8
22	20	196	1·45 : 1	9·7
55	18	135	1·67 : 1	45·2

Note: A minimum of 400 fish were used for each treatment (see Smart et al., 1979 for experimental details).
The water temperature throughout the investigation was 9°C.

extensive, lesions in the kidney revealed widespread calcification, gross dilation and distortion of tubules and ducts, with cellular degeneration and chronic inflammatory change. Lesions in the stomach consisted of areas of calcification and granuloma formation. Details of the pathological changes are given by Smart et al. (1979) and by Harrison and Richards (1979). The calcareous particles were found to be composed mainly of calcium phosphate (Smart et al., 1979; Gillespie and Evans, 1979).

The mechanisms underlying the development of the condition are not known. It is possible that calcium hydrogen phosphate present in the urine (Hickman and Trump, 1969) could be precipitated if the urine pH became alkaline. Lloyd and Swift (1976) showed that rainbow trout held for two days at a CO_2 concentration of 21 mg l^{-1} exhibited increases in urine pH to 8·0 and marked increases in urinary phosphate concentrations. Eddy et al. (1979) reported alkaline urine in fish showing gross signs of nephrocalcinosis. However, this may be only a small part of the story; kidney stone formation in mammals is not a simple precipitation process and such observations do not explain the stomach changes.

Examination of fish from a number of fish farms with high CO_2 concentrations in the water supply have revealed the presence of nephrocalcinosis. The severity of the condition at a particular CO_2 concentration does appear to vary greatly according to diet and environmental factors such as ionic content. High mortalities are rarely reported in fresh water and Landolt (1975) has observed that, in the absence of undue stress, mortality was low. Recently there have been a number of reports from fish farms suggesting that nephrocalcinosis was responsible for mortalities of rainbow trout held in sea water. At first consideration this is puzzling because one would not expect to find high free CO_2 concentrations in the sea. However, further investigations have revealed that the fish had recently been transferred from freshwater farms with a high CO_2 water supply, where no mortality problem had been encountered. The indications are that, in fresh water, these fish are able to contend with extensively damaged kidneys whereas in sea water they are less able to cope and growth, food conversion and survival may be seriously impaired.

V CONCLUDING REMARKS

The stress imposed by poor water quality can result in reduced survival, growth and food conversion efficiency of fish held in intensive rearing systems. In the present review, oxygen, ammonia and carbon dioxide were considered crucial aspects of water quality since fluctuations in their concentrations are significantly influenced by fish metabolism as well as by the incoming water supply.

Finally, it should be emphasized that water quality control forms an essential part of fish health management. No single aspect of water quality however, should ever be considered in isolation from the influence of other water quality parameters. For example, the multiple effects of temperature and salinity on the toxicity of ammonia illustrates the possible range and complexity of interactions. The nutritional and disease status of the fish may also be important—feeds that are nutritionally deficient (e.g. due to error in manufacture or poor storage) and parasitic infections (with protozoans such as *Ichtyobodo* ($\equiv$*Costia*), *Trichodina* and *Hexamita*) are both capable of debilitating fish without necessarily causing high mortalities. This may further reduce the fish's ability to withstand any deterioration in water quality or may mean that a concentration previously considered "safe" may now be contributing to poor growth and food conversion.

REFERENCES

Alabaster, J. S., Herbert, D. W. M. and Hemens, J. (1957). The survival of rainbow trout (*Salmo gairdneri* Richardson) and perch (*Perca fluviatilis* L.) at various concentrations of dissolved oxygen and carbon dioxide. *Ann. appl. Biol.* **45**, 177–188.

Alabaster, J. S. and Lloyd, R. (1980). *Water Quality Criteria for Freshwater Fish.* London: Butterworths. 297pp.

Alabaster, J. S., Shurben, D. G. and Knowles, G. (1979). The effect of dissolved oxygen and salinity on the toxicity of ammonia to smolts of salmon, *Salmo salar* L. *J. Fish Biol.* **15**, 705–712.

Alderson, R. (1979). The effects of ammonia on the growth of juvenile Dover sole, *Solea solea* (L.) and turbot, *Scophthalmus maximus* (L.). *Aquaculture* **17**, 291–309.

Balarin, J. D. (1978). *Tilapia. A guide to their biology and culture in Africa*. Stirling: University of Stirling.

Barica, J. (1973). Reliability of an ammonia probe for electrometric determination of total ammonia nitrogen in fish tanks. *J. Fish. Res. Bd Can.* **30**, 1389–1392.

Basu, S. P. (1959). Active respiration of fish in relation to ambient concentrations of oxygen and carbon dioxide. *J. Fish. Res. Bd Can.* **16**, 175–212.

Bigg, W. L. and Alexander, I. J. (1980). Analysis of NO_3^- and NH_4^+ in dilute nutrient solutions using ion-sensing electrodes. *Lab. Pract.* **29**, 924–925.

Bower, C. E. and Bidwell, J. P. (1978). Ionization of ammonia in seawater: effects of temperature, pH and salinity. *J. Fish. Res. Bd Can.* **35**, 1012–1016.

Breen, K. J. and Schenker, S. (1972). Hepatic coma: present accounts of pathogenesis and therapy. In *Progress in Liver Diseases, Vol. IV* (H. Popper, and F. Schaffner, eds), pp. 301–302. New York and London: Grune and Stratton.

Brett, J. R. and Zala, C. A. (1975). Daily pattern of nitrogen excretion and oxygen consumption of sockeye salmon (*Oncorhynchus nerka*) under controlled conditions. *J. Fish. Res. Bd Can.* **32**, 2479–2486.

Brown, V. M. (1968). The calculation of the acute toxicity of mixtures of poisons to rainbow trout. *Wat. Res.* **2**, 723–733.

Bullock, G. L. (1972). Studies on selected myxobacteria pathogenic for fishes and on bacterial gill disease in hatchery-reared salmonids. *Tech. Pap. Bur. Sport Fish. Wildl.* **60**, 30pp.

Burkhalter, D. E. and Kaya, C. M. (1977). Effects of prolonged exposure to ammonia on fertilized eggs and sac fry of rainbow trout (*Salmo gairdneri*). *Trans. Am. Fish. Soc.* **106**, 470–475.

Carter, R. R. and Allen, K. O. (1976). Effects of flow rate and aeration on survival and growth of channel catfish in circular tanks. *Progve Fish Cult.* **38**, 204–206.

Colt, J. and Tchobanoglous, G. (1978). Chronic exposure of channel catfish, *Ictalurus punctatus*, to ammonia: effects on growth and survival. *Aquaculture* **15**, 353–372.

de Vooys, G. G. N. (1968). Formation and excretion of ammonia in Teleostei I. Excretion of ammonia through the gills. *Archs int. Physiol. Biochim.* **76**, 268–272.

Doudoroff, P. and Shumway, D. L. (1970). Dissolved oxygen requirements of freshwater fishes. *FAO Fish. Tech. Rep.* **86**, 1–291.

Downing, K. M. and Merkens, J. C. (1955). The influence of dissolved oxygen concentration on the toxicity of un-ionized ammonia to rainbow trout (*Salmo gairdneri* Richardson). *Ann. appl. Biol.* **43**, 243–246.

Eddy, F. B., Lomholt, J. P., Weber, R. E. and Johansen, K. (1977). Blood respiratory properties of rainbow trout (*Salmo gairdneri*) kept in water of high CO_2 tension. *J. exp. Biol.* **67**, 37–47.

Eddy, F. B., Smart, G. R. and Bath, R. N. (1979). Ionic content of muscle and urine in rainbow trout (*Salmo gairdneri* Richardson) kept in water of high CO_2 content. *J. Fish Dis.* **2**, 105–110.

Edwards, D. J. (1978). *Salmon and Trout Farming in Norway*. Farnham, Surrey: Fishing News (Books) Ltd. 195pp.

EIFAC (1970). Water quality criteria for European freshwater fish. Report on ammonia and inland fisheries *EIFAC Tech. Pap.* **11**, F.A.O. Rome.

Emerson, K., Russo, R. C., Lund, R. E. and Thurston, R. V. (1975). Aqueous ammonia equilibrium calculations: effect of pH and temperature. *J. Fish. Res. Bd Can.* **32**, 2379–2383.

Forster, J. R. M. and Smart, G. R. (1979). Water economy in aquaculture. In *Power Plant Waste Heat Utilization in Aquaculture* (B. L. Godfriaux, A. S. Able, A. Farmanarmaian, C. R. Greene and C. A. Stevens, eds), pp. 3–11. New Jersey, U.S.A.: Allanheld, Osman and Co.

Forster, J. R. M., Harman, J. P. and Smart, G. R. (1977). Water economy—its effect on trout farm production. *Fish Farm. Internat.* **4**, 10–13.

Forster, R. P. and Goldstein, L. (1969). Formation of excretory products. In *Fish Physiology, Vol. I* (W. S. Hoar and D. J. Randall, eds), pp. 313–350. London and New York: Academic Press.

Fromm, P. O. and Gillette, J. R. (1968). Effect of ambient ammonia on blood ammonia and nitrogen excretion of rainbow trout (*Salmo gairdneri*). *Comp. Biochem. Physiol.* **26**, 887–896.

Gillespie, D. C. and Evans, R. E. (1979). Composition of granules from kidneys of rainbow trout (*Salmo gairdneri*) with nephrocalcinosis. *J. Fish. Res. Bd Can.* **36**, 683–685.

Harrison, J. G. and Richards, R. H. (1979). The pathology and histopathology of nephrocalcinosis in rainbow trout (*Salmo gairdneri* Richardson) in fresh water. *J. Fish. Dis.* **2**, 1–12.

Harwood, J. E. and Kühn, A. L. (1970). A colorimetric method for ammonia in natural waters. *Wat. Res.* **4**, 805–811.

Herbert, D. W. M. and Shurben, D. S. (1965). The susceptibility of salmonid fish to poisons under estuarine conditions. II Ammonium chloride. *Int. J. Air Water Pollut.* **9**, 89–91.

Hickman, C. P. and Trump, B. J. (1969). The kidney. In *Fish Physiology, Vol. I* (W. S. Hoar and D. J. Randall, eds), pp. 91–239. London and New York: Academic Press.

Hillaby, B. A. and Randall, D. J. (1979). Acute ammonia toxicity and ammonia excretion in rainbow trout (*Salmo gairdneri*). *J. Fish. Res. Bd Can.* **36**, 621–629.

Jones, A., Brown, J. A. G., Douglas, M. T., Thompson, S. J. and Whitfield, R. J. (1980). Progress towards developing methods for the intensive farming of turbot (*Scophthalmus maximus* L.) in cooling water from a nuclear power station. In *New Developments in the Utilization of Heated Effluents and of Recirculation Systems for Intensive Aquaculture*. EIFAC/80/Symp. E/B, Stavanger, Norway. 14 + VIII pp.

Kerstetter, T. H., Kirschner, L. B. and Rafuse, D. D. (1970). On the mechanisms of sodium ion transport by the irrigated gills of rainbow trout (*Salmo gairdneri*). *J. gen. Physiol.* **56**, 342–359.

Klontz, G. W. (1973). *Syllabus of Fish Health Management. Part I. Fish Culture Methods*. Texas, U.S.A.: Texas A & M University Sea Grant Program.

Landless, P. J. (1976). Acclimation of rainbow trout to sea water. *Aquaculture* **7**, 173–179.

Landolt, M. L. (1975). Visceral granuloma and nephrocalcinosis of trout. In *The Pathology of Fishes* (W. E. Ribelin and G. Migaki, eds), pp. 793–799. Madison, Wisconsin: The University of Wisconsin Press.

Larmoyeux, J. D. and Piper, R. G. (1973). Effects of water re-use on rainbow trout in hatcheries. *Progve Fish Cult.* **35**, 2–8.

Liao, P. B. (1971). Water requirements of salmonids. *Progve Fish Cult.* **33**, 210–215.

Liao, P. B. and Mayo, R. D. (1972). Salmonid hatchery water re-use systems. *Aquaculture* **1**, 317–335.

Liao, P. B. and Mayo, R. D. (1974). Intensified fish culture combining water re-conditioning with pollution abatement. *Aquaculture* **3**, 61–85.

Lloyd, R. (1961). Effect of dissolved oxygen concentrations on the toxicity of several poisons to rainbow trout (*Salmo gairdneri*). *J. exp. Biol.* **38**, 447–455.

Lloyd, R. and Orr, L. (1969). The diuretic response by rainbow trout to sub-lethal concentrations of ammonia. *Wat. Res.* **3**, 335–344.

Lloyd, R. and Swift, D. J. (1976). Some physiological responses by freshwater fish to low dissolved oxygen, high carbon dioxide, ammonia and phenol with particular reference to water balance. In *Effects of Pollutants on Aquatic Organisms* (A. P. M. Lockwood, ed.), pp. 47–71. Cambridge: Cambridge University Press.

Maetz, J. (1972). Interaction of salt and ammonia transport in aquatic organisms. In *Nitrogen Metabolism and the Environment* (J. W. Campbell and L. Goldstein, eds), pp. 105–154. London and New York: Academic Press.

Muller-Feuga, A., Petit, J. and Sabaut, J. J. (1978). The influence of temperature and wet weight on the oxygen demand of rainbow trout (*Salmo gairdneri*) in freshwater. *Aquaculture* **14**, 355–363.

Robinette, H. R. (1976). Effect of selected sublethal levels of ammonia on the growth of channel catfish (*Ictalurus punctatus*). *Progve Fish Cult.* **38**, 26–29.

Saunders, R. L. (1962). The irrigation of the gills in fishes. II. Efficiency of oxygen uptake in relation to respiratory flow, activity and concentrations of oxygen and carbon dioxide. *Can. J. Zool.* **40**, 817–862.

Schenker, S., McCandless, D. W., Brophy, E. and Lewis, M. S. (1967). Studies on the intracerebral toxicity of ammonia. *J. clin. Invest.* **46**, 838–848.

Schreck, C. B. (1981). Stress and compensation in teleostean fishes: response to social and physical factors. In *Stress and Fish* (A. D. Pickering, ed.), pp. 295–321. London and New York: Academic Press.

Schulze-Wiehenbrauck, H. (1976). Effects of sublethal ammonia concentrations on metabolism in juvenile rainbow trout (*Salmo gairdneri* Richardson). *Ber. dt. wiss. Kommn. Meeresforsch.* **24**, 234–250.

Smart, G. R. (1975). The acute toxic mechanisms of ammonia to rainbow trout (*Salmo gairdneri*). Ph.D. thesis, University of Bristol. U.K.

Smart, G. R. (1976). The effect of ammonia exposure on gill structure of the rainbow trout (*Salmo gairdneri*). *J. Fish Biol.* **8**, 471–475.

Smart, G. R., Knox, D., Harrison, J. G., Ralph, J. A., Richards, R. H. and Cowey, C. B. (1979). Nephrocalcinosis in rainbow trout *Salmo gairdneri* Richardson; the effect of exposure to elevated CO_2 concentrations. *J. Fish Dis.* **2**, 279–289.

Sniesko, S. F. (1974). The effects of environmental stress on outbreaks of infectious diseases of fishes. *J. Fish Biol.* **6**, 197–208.

Sousa, R. J. and Meade, T. L. (1977). The influence of ammonia on the oxygen delivery system of coho salmon hemoglobin. *Comp. Biochem. Physiol.* **58A**, 23–28.

Speece, R. E. (1973). Trout metabolism characteristics and the rational design of nitrification facilities for water re-use in hatcheries. *Trans. Am. Fish. Soc.* **102**, 323–334.

Trussel, R. P. (1972). The percent un-ionized ammonia in aqueous ammonia solutions at different pH levels and temperatures. *J. Fish. Res. Bd Can.* **29**, 1505–1507.

U.S. Environmental Protection Agency (1976). *Quality Criteria for Water.* Washington, D.C.: U.S. Government Printing Office. 256pp.

Visek, W. J. (1968). Some aspects of ammonia toxicity in animal cells. *J. Dairy Sci.* **51**, 286–295.

Walker, C. O. and Schenker, S. (1970). Pathogenesis of hepatic encephalopathy— with special reference to the rôle of ammonia. *Am. J. clin. Nutr.* **23**, 619–632.

Weiler, R. R. (1979). Rate of loss of ammonia from water to the atmosphere. *J. Fish. Res. Bd Can.* **36**, 685–689.

Westers, H. and Pratt, K. M. (1977). Rational design of hatcheries for intensive salmonid culture, based on metabolic characteristics. *Progve Fish Cult.* **39**, 157–165.

Whitfield, M. (1974). The hydrolysis of ammonium ions in sea water—a theoretical study. *J. mar. Biol. Assoc., U.K.* **54**, 565–580.

Willoughby, H. (1968). A method for calculating carrying capacities of hatchery troughs and ponds. *Progve Fish Cult.* **30**, 173–174.

Wuhrmann, K. and Woker, H. (1948). Experimentelle Untersuchungen über die Ammoniak- und Blausäurevergiftung. *Schweiz. Z. Hydrol.* **11**, 210–244.

13. Stress and Compensation in Teleostean Fishes: Response to Social and Physical Factors

C. B. SCHRECK

Oregon Cooperative Fishery Research Unit, Oregon State University, Oregon 97331, USA

Abstract. Stress in teleostean fishes induces elaboration of catecholamines and corticosteroid hormones (primary response), which affect energy mobilization and hydromineral balance. This stress response is extremely polymorphic. Review of the responses of fish, primarily salmonids, to physical disturbances such as handling and severe crowding indicates that the response is immediate and that almost ideal or perfect compensation is achieved in corticosteroids and other factors related to the General Adaptation Syndrome even if the imposition of stress is chronic. However, in the interim between alarm and compensation, the performance capacity of the fish is reduced.

There may be a psychological component to stress in fish populations. Social status is apparently associated with a particular state of stress. For example, a direct relation has been demonstrated between clinical indicators of stress and dominance rank in coho salmon (*Oncorhynchus kisutch*), with subordinates appearing to be the most stressed. However, a clear relation between population density and stress has not been demonstrated.

The initial moments of a stressful encounter may be the major contributors in terms of eliciting a clinical stress response and affecting performance capacity of a fish. This contention is based on studies of the effects of transportation on salmon and the use of anesthetics in moderating the stress response. It appears that a stress response is invoked when the fish experiences fright, discomfort, or pain.

It logically follows that stresses reduce the performance capacity of the individual due to the costs associated with trying to maintain homeostasis. Because of the polymorphic nature of the stress response, bioassays of performance should be coupled with clinical assessments of stress. Such bioassays indicate that the osmotic costs associated with stress may be extremely important in terms of the ability of the fish to resist the imposition of stress.

I propose that the performance capacity of a fish is limited by its genotype. This "fundamental" capacity is further restricted by the fish's environment, creating a "realized" performance capacity that defines the true performance capability of the individual. Both potential and realized performance capacities can be different for various ontogenetic stages. Stress further restricts at least certain aspects of the realized capacity. Performance capacity of a fish or population of fish can thus be viewed as an N-dimensional geometric volume pulsating through time. A number of management or culture practices can be adapted to help prevent reduction of the realized performance capacity by stress.

I INTRODUCTION

The stress response of teleostean fishes is considered to be similar in nature to the General Adaptation Syndrome (GAS) proposed for mammalian vertebrates (Gronow, 1974a, b; Selye, 1976; Delventhal, 1978; Peters, 1979; Wedemeyer, 1980). In theory, the GAS-type response should be elicited by any stressful situation (Selye, 1936, 1950a, b, 1971, 1973a, b, 1974). Implicit in this concept is the probability that the health or well-being of fish may be impaired by stress, at least momentarily. One might thus alternately view stress not directly in physiological terms but rather functionally as defined by Brett (1958) (for further discussion of the concept of stress see Pickering, 1981, this volume). If stress reduces the ability or capacity of fish to maintain homeostasis or do, physiologically or behaviorally, those things they must do to persist, grow, and reproduce, then an understanding of the stress response is of value from husbandry and management perspectives.

It is of interest to know how a healthy individual differs from an unhealthy one and the factors, intrinsic and extrinsic to the fish, that affect a stress response. Health is a state of optimal physical and mental well-being and is not just the mere absence of disease and infirmity. The physiological responses to a variety of stresses have been outlined for fishes by Gronow (1974a, b), Mazeaud et al. (1977) and Peters (1979) and by several papers in this volume (see e.g. Billard et al., 1981; Donaldson, 1981; Eddy, 1981; Hughes, 1981; Mazeaud and Mazeaud, 1981). My objectives are to evaluate the dynamics of this stress reaction in terms of compensation versus exhaustion, to review the nature of the factors that cause stress responses and to consider a conceptual framework of stress applicable to fishery management and culture problems. I use information from the literature and from my own laboratory to support the following contentions: (1) Deleterious consequences of a chronic stress are manifested immediately. If resistance does not lead to exhaustion, the primary stress reactions achieve nearly perfect or ideal compensation, although not necessarily the same performance capacity. (2) A GAS-type stress response is evoked by those factors that cause fright, discomfort, or pain. (3) The psychological aspects of stress are extremely important in determining the severity of the imposition on the fish. (4) The osmotic imbalance consequent to stress is a significant cost in terms of expenditures needed to achieve resistance and compensation.

I center this discussion on handling and crowding types of stress. The GAS is polymorphic and can be modified by the specific effects of various stressful stimuli. For example, rearing temperature can modify the corticoid stress response in cutthroat trout, *Salmo clarki* (Strange *et al.*, 1977), some secondary stress responses in goldfish, *Carassius auratus* (Umminger and Gist, 1973) and plasma cortisol and glucose dynamics in channel catfish, *Ictalurus punctatus* (Strange, 1980). Response to water quality factors can be unpredictable, as seen by intoxication of coho salmon, *Oncorhynchus kisutch*, by certain heavy metals some of which, e.g. copper, produce a GAS-type reaction whereas others, such as cadmium, do not, even though they may be present at lethal concentrations (Schreck and Lorz, 1978). It thus appears warranted to avoid consideration of the stress of toxicological factors, temperature, or disease for this context, since specific effects of such stimuli could only confound an attempt to elucidate the general nature of the stress response. Inasmuch as my own work has been concentrated on the corticoid hormones as primary stress factors, I will focus on these steroids in support of my arguments. Catecholamines have received considerably less attention than the interrenal hormones (see Mazeaud and Mazeaud, 1981, this volume). The secondary stress effects—those primarily involved with energy stores and water–electrolyte balance—are probably the direct result of the endocrine-stress axis, and covary in one way or another with the hormones. Corticoids may thus provide a reasonable basis for depicting the stress reaction as reviewed by Barton and Toth, 1980 (see also Donaldson, 1981, this volume). I do not mean to imply, however, that the corticosteroids are necessarily better indicators of stress than the catecholamines or the large number of secondary stress factors.

II NATURE OF THE STRESS RESPONSE

Characterization of the stress response and interpretation of its physiological significance requires determination of basal, resting conditions and establishment of dose–response curves (Schreck, 1976). Two questions are salient: (1) Does the physiological response to stress in fish subjected to acute stress differ from those experiencing chronic stress? (2) What are the physiological stress responses to sublethal versus lethal stressful conditions?

Depending on the severity of the stress, corticoid levels in the circulation peak in 1 to 24 h in salmonids (Simpson, 1975/76; Strange et al., 1978; Barton et al., 1980). An acute stress reaction is experienced when the stress is removed before compensation has been achieved. In such situations, as when fish are transferred from one tank to another or in transportation via truck, plasma levels of corticoids return to resting levels in about 2 to 24 h for salmon of the genus Oncorhynchus (Strange and Schreck, 1978; Strange et al., 1978; Barton et al., 1980; Specker and Schreck, 1980). Plasma catecholamine patterns, which also respond rapidly to stress, follow a somewhat similar trend (Mazeaud et al., 1977; Mazeaud and Mazeaud, 1981, this volume), although circulating glucose concentration remains elevated longer in salmonids (Nakano and Tomlinson, 1967). Secondary stress responses require a few days to recover in rainbow trout, Salmo gairdneri, after being hooked (Wydoski et al., 1976). No significant increase in plasma cortisol was noted in goldfish suspended in a net in the air for 60 s (Fryer, 1975). During prolonged exposure to a stressful situation, such as severe crowding and confinement, compensation in cortisol levels occurs in about 1 to 2 weeks in juvenile salmonids (Fig. 1). This form of stress also steadily increases corticoids in adult chinook salmon, O. tshawytscha, for at least 3 days (Hane et al., 1966), and cortisol was elevated by confining powan, Coregonus lavaretus, for this period of time (Fuller et al., 1974). After the alarm and resistance phase during chronic, sublethal stress, "ideal" or "perfect" compensation as described by Precht (1958) is achieved. That is, corticoid titers return to prestress levels even though the imposition is still present. Wedemeyer (1972) demonstrated that a number of secondary stress responses followed similar trends after coho salmon and steelhead trout were stressed by handling. In severely confined channel catfish, glucose concentrations initially rose more slowly and continued to increase longer than did those of cortisol (Strange, 1980). Rates of excretion of corticoids also increase in rainbow trout during exposure to sublethal stress (McKim, 1967).

Little is known about the stress response at death. Although physiological changes during senescence in salmon have been described (Robertson and Wexler, 1957; Hane and Robertson, 1959; Robertson et al., 1961a, b; Schmidt and Idler, 1962; Hane et al., 1966; Idler et al., 1963, 1966; Berdyshev, 1967; Fagerlund, 1967, 1970; Van Overbeeke and McBride, 1967; Donaldson and Fagerlund, 1968, 1972), it is not possible to separate the effects of ageing and death from those of maturation and reproduction in these species. Comfort (1964) reviewed senescence in fish, and Gerking (1959) discussed the physiological changes occurring during ageing, but both investigators considered this topic from the standpoint of reproduction and growth. Death in sexually immature Atlantic cod, Gadus morhua, is

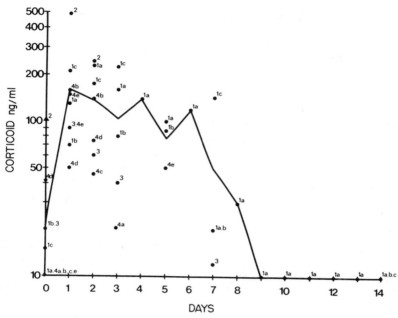

Fig. 1 Plasma corticosteroid concentration in juvenile salmonids during chronic exposure to stress (handling, crowding, confinement). The data were obtained from a number of sources; the points represent means reported in individual studies, for each respective day. The line represents the mean of the data from all studies. The data for day 0 were taken immediately before the fish were stressed. I have subjectively interpreted the degree of stress used in each case. 1 = Strange *et al.* (1978)—chinook salmon, 1a is from Fig. 3—moderate stress, 1b is from Fig. 4—moderate stress, 1c is from Fig. 5—moderate stress. 2 = Strange *et al.* (1977)—chinook salmon—severe stress. 3 = Simpson (1975/76)—rainbow trout—mild stress. 4 = J. M. Redding and C. B. Schreck (unpublished data), 4a = steelhead trout—mild stress, 4b = steelhead trout—severe stress, 4c = steelhead trout—severe stress, 4d = coho salmon—severe stress, 4e = coho salmon—mild stress.

apparently accompanied by impaired cortisol metabolism (Idler and Freeman, 1965). More definitive work is needed to clarify the stress responses that precede or accompany death. Moribund fish can have the capacity to further elevate their cortisol levels, as evidenced by the response of coho salmon to handling after they had already been fatally stressed by copper intoxication (Schreck and Lorz, 1978). That fish can also die without increases in corticoid titers was demonstrated by Strange and Schreck (1978), who subjected chinook salmon to a lethal dose of the anesthetic ethyl m-amino-benzoate methanesulfonate (MS222). Severely crowded, moribund juvenile chinook salmon exhibited extremely high plasma cortisol levels (Strange *et al.*, 1978); the same effect occurred in catfish, except that glucose returned to near basal levels in the dying fish (Strange, 1980).

III COMPONENTS OF STRESS

(a) Psychological Considerations

It appears that a GAS-type stress response is evoked in teleosts by situations which cause fright, discomfort, or pain (Schreck and Lorz, 1978). Circumstances such as netting and severe close confinement (e.g. Strange et al., 1978), struggling out of water (Mazeaud et al., 1977), or capture by hook and line (Wydoski et al., 1976) must certainly be disturbing to the fish in terms of fright and possibly in terms of pain or discomfort. These stresses produce a physiological stress response. As I mentioned, Strange and Schreck (1978) killed fish without inducing a stress response by using an anesthetic; presumably anesthetics do not induce fright or discomfort.

The psychological aspects of stress appear to be important in terms of physiological responses to stressful situations and perhaps the ability of the fish to resist exhaustion or achieve compensation. Salmonids subjected to stress such as transportation, a routine management practice, display an immediate GAS-like stress response. The initial moments of the capture and loading process may be the most important in effecting the stress response and are perhaps the most significant in terms of establishing the condition of the fish with respect to survival during transportation or ability to perform after liberation (Specker and Schreck, 1980). In an anthropomorphic sense, the fright and anxiety, and perhaps immediate trauma, associated with being chased and netted may be more important in reducing survival than confinement at high density for long periods of time. This is apparent in the study of Specker and Schreck (1980) in which all *en route* mortality of juvenile coho salmon occurred within the first few hours of a 12 h transport. Barton et al. (1980) also concluded from this physiological assessment of transportation stress in rainbow trout that "the most traumatic event of the stocking operation was "capture" at the hatchery, evoking the highest stress response." Mortality encountered in transporting and handling American shad, *Alosa sapidissima*, was also attributed to stress arising from "excitement" (Chittenden, 1971). The importance of fright was further exemplified in the stress response, shown by elevation in plasma cortisol levels, of adult sockeye salmon, *O. nerka*, that were aware of the presence of a dip net (Fagerlund, 1967). Fright also appeared to steadily increase cortisol for up to 25 min in carp, *Cyprinus carpio*, exposed for a few seconds to the thrashing of another fish (Redgate, 1974).

The importance of the psychological component of stress has received little attention in fishes although it is the basis of a large literature in human medicine (see Selye, 1974). To provide an understanding of the fright or psychological well-being aspect of stress in teleosts, recent investigations have followed three avenues of research: (1) anesthetics, (2) elimination of visual awareness, and (3) conditioning or training.

Conceptually, the first two approaches attempted to eliminate "awareness" of a stressful situation. Strange and Schreck (1980) showed that the fright aspects of capture and severe confinement of chinook salmon were eliminated by the use of an anesthetic. Both the cortisol stress response and exhaustion were moderated, even in fish that were "awake" during the confinement for up to 10 h. Hyperglycemia induced by handling was also reduced by anesthesia in brook trout, *Salvelinus fontinalis* (Houston *et al.*, 1971). Leloup-Hatey (1961) also found that anesthetics prevented hypercorticoidism in carp transferred to sea water.

The psychological aspects of stress thus appear important in determining the severity of a stress. Elimination of the visual assessment of the severity of a stressful situation could potentially have a calming effect, much like that induced by blindfolding of a horse that is led out of a fire. The importance of visual perception is apparent in that visual isolation of fish in a population is important to territorial behavior (Kalleberg, 1958; Yamagishi, 1962). To further evaluate this possibility, preliminary studies on the effects of visual awareness of the stress have been conducted (J. M. Redding and C. B. Schreck, unpublished data). Juvenile steelhead trout were severely stressed by close confinement in small live-cages in either the light or in the dark, after the fish had been acclimated in holding tanks either in the light or in complete darkness. From these initial experiments it was found that the cortisol titers immediately following capture peaked at the same time in fish acclimated to light or dark. However, fish from either acclimation condition which were then confined in the darkness appeared to be less stressed than those confined in the light. During the 2 day test, cortisol levels began a steady decrease within 7 h in fish held in the dark but remained elevated in fish held in the light.

The eventuality that the loss of visual contact *per se* of a fish's surroundings could be stressful was also investigated (J. M. Redding and C. B. Schreck, unpublished data). Dye that absorbed light matching as closely as possible the visual pigments and not transmitting light below 550 nm was perfused into well-lit tanks or into tanks maintained in the dark. No corticoid stress response was evident among fish in either group of tanks. Thus, the loss of visual contact apparently was not stressful in this situation. However, chronic exposure to darkness has been reported to be stressful to other fish; for example, it caused hypertrophy and hyperplasia of interrenal tissue with subsequent atrophy in the Mexican tetra, *Astyanax mexicanus* (Rasquin and Rosenbloom, 1954).

Conditioning-type training experiments can be of value in elucidating the importance of the psychological aspects of stress. Positive conditioning may be potentially useful in changing the perception by fish of an apparently stressful situation as a positive, or even desirable one. Physical training can also influence the physical condition of fish. For example, physical training shortened the recovery time in terms of energy metabolism during exertion in rainbow trout (Hochachka, 1961) and reduction in blood lactate following exercise in Atlantic salmon, *Salmo salar*. Training also prevented the reduction in white cell count and increase in osmolality that usually accompany capture-stress in the mummichog, *Fundulus heteroclitus* (Slicher *et al.*, 1966). Positive conditioning may likewise improve the psychological condition of fish. Stress-induced changes in carbohydrate metabolism of goldfish were eliminated by a conditioning procedure that associated handling stress with feeding (Rush and Umminger, 1978). However, habituation did not reduce the elevated breathing rate induced by handling in the bluegill, *Lepomis machrochirus* (Chiszar *et al.*, 1972). In the light of this information an experiment was initiated to determine if positive conditioning could be used to reduce the stress of netting juvenile coho and chinook salmon (C. Ejike and C. B. Schreck, unpublished data). Duplicate groups of seven coho salmon were each netted and suspended in the air for 10 s twice a day for 5, 10, 15 or 20 days and fed immediately after they were returned to the water. Triplicate groups of eight chinook salmon were similarly captured and held in the air for 20 s twice a day for 5, 10, or 15 days and fed after release. Escape (avoidance of capture) and feeding behavior of both species were compared with the responses in coho or chinook salmon that had been subjected to only one training session and to unhandled controls. The day after the last conditioning trial for each species the fish were again captured, suspended, fed, and were sampled 1 h after they were returned to their tanks. The results indicate that both the coho and chinook salmon became conditioned to the capture stress in about a week. After this number of training sessions the fish no longer actively tried to avoid capture, and fed vigorously after they were returned to the water. Plasma levels of cortisol in the chinook salmon were indicative of the conditioning, averaging 76 ± 18 ng ml^{-1} (mean $\pm SEM$) in the fish with only one experience in the net and 52 ± 26, 8 ± 4, and 22 ± 9 ng ml^{-1} in the groups after 5, 10, and 15 days conditioning, respectively. The plasma levels were 4 ± 3 ng ml^{-1} in the unhandled control group whereas severe crowding in a barely submerged dip net for 30 min resulted in an elevation to 159 ± 38 ng ml^{-1}. The cortisol titers in the coho salmon were extremely low, possibly indicating that the netting procedure was only slightly stressful. Plasma cortisol levels in "stressed" unexperienced coho salmon averaged 25 ± 7 ng ml^{-1}, whereas in those conditioned for 5, 10, 15 or 20 days it was 7 ± 2, 7 ± 3, 9 ± 4, and 17 ± 7 ng ml^{-1}, respectively. In unhandled control fish the mean was 18 ± 6 ng ml^{-1}. These experiments suggest that fish can be conditioned to avoid a stress response and help to demonstrate the importance of fright compared to pain and discomfort as an element necessary for a physiological stress reaction.

The physiological reactions that follow acute, sublethal stressful encounters are rapid and rather transient. However, there may be a psychological element responsive to stress that is more persistent. Using behavioral conditioning trials to demonstrate recognition of odorants by juvenile coho salmon, Sandoval (1979) found that an "acclimation" period of between 5 and 7 weeks was necessary after transportation before the fish could be conditioned. This period contrasts strikingly with a non-transported group of salmon that responded to conditioning within only a few days. Further, coho salmon that were conditioned to behaviorally respond to the presence of an odorant required 2 days to regain their level of performance after a brief transportation stress.

(b) Social Considerations

The psychological and behavioral aspects of stress may be extremely important in natural waters in helping to establish the relative fitness of individual fish. Social dominance hierarchies are well established in fish populations. Dominance behavior is the analog of territorial behavior (Wilson, 1975). Submissive individuals appear to be in a less favorable situation than dominant ones for obtaining necessary resources. King (1973) proposed the following verbal model for agonistic behavior.

> Winners gain social status, access to commodities, freedom of movement, and reproductive success. Frequent agonistic encounters affect the physiology of the population through the pituitary–adrenal–gonadal axis. These physiologically stressed individuals readily succumb to shortages of necessary resources, or they become exposed to predation and severe weather, or they fail to mature and reproduce.

King (1973) also indicated that empirical evidence supporting all aspects of this model are frequently wanting. Wilson (1975) noted that "In general, aggressive–submissive exhanges increase sharply when food is clumped instead of scattered and domination of one piece of food or of a small area of ground on which food is concentrated become profitable". Dominant rainbow trout have more body fat than do subordinates, and social status also appears to be positively correlated with hepatic glycogen content in coho salmon (Ejike and Schreck, 1980). There may also be a positive relationship between growth and dominance rank (Yamagishi, 1962; Li, 1973; Li and Brocksen, 1977).

Social rank appears to correlate to chronic imposition of psychological stress, subordinate individuals being the more stressed. Interrenal cell dimensions were greater in subordinate pumpkinseeds, *Lepomis gibbosus* (Erickson, 1967), rainbow trout (Noakes and Leatherland, 1977), and coho salmon (Ejike and Schreck, 1980). Relative freedom from stress in dominant individuals is reflected in their lower plasma cortisol levels than in subordinates, as seen in European eels, *Anguilla anguilla* (Delventhal, 1978; Klinger *et al.*, 1979; Peters *et al.*, 1980a, b; see also abstract by Peters *et al.*, 1981, this volume) and coho salmon (Ejike and Schreck, 1980) (Fig. 2). It thus appears that dominant individuals may be free of the stress that is

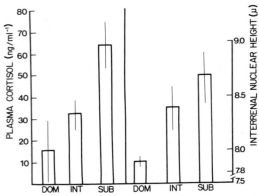

Fig. 2   Plasma cortisol levels and interrenal nuclear height in relation to the social hierarchy of coho salmon (DOM—dominant fish, INT—intermediate fish, SUB—submissive fish). Values are expressed as mean ±S.E.M. n = 3, 7 and 8 for DOM, INT and SUB, respectively. (Modified from Ejike and Schreck, 1980).

concomitant with being harassed whereas subordinates constantly exist in a state of mild fright of aggressive threat from more dominant fish. Thines and Heuts (1968) proposed that "perception of fear in congeners . . . itself elicits aggressive behavior [in fishes]". The endocrine events characteristic of aggression may not necessarily be the same as those of social dominance, for agonistic behavior involves excitation whereas dominance reflects security and freedom from threat. In reaction to psychological stress, fishes appear to have responses similar to those of mammals in the pituitary–adrenal axis.

As indicated by the review of mammalian systems provided by Leshner (1978) adrenocortical activity is elevated in subordinates, and the mere threat of defeat is sufficient to increase corticoid titers. Chronic exposure to adrenocorticotropin may depress aggressive activity and the consequent elevation in adrenal hormones may stimulate behavior associated with avoidance of attack. Aggressive animals tend to have elevated androgen levels that also play a role in maintaining dominance. Fighting in the Siamese fighting fish, *Betta splendens*, causes secondary stress responses (Gronow,

1974b). The finding by Noakes and Leatherland (1977) that dominant rainbow trout, like those at the bottom of a hierarchy, also appeared to be stressed (as judged by interrenal cell height) may reflect aggressive tendencies of their fish, or differences in densities or other experimental conditions used in their study. However, using the same criterion of interrenal cell height, dominant pumpkinseed (Erickson, 1967), European eels (Delventhal, 1978; Klinger et al., 1979; Peters et al., 1980a, b), coho salmon (Ejike and Schreck, 1980), and swordtails, Xiphophorus helleri (Scott and Currie, 1980) would appear to be less stressed than the other fish in their hierarchies. Prior experience may also be important in determining dominance behavior and reactions in fish (McDonald et al., 1968).

Population density may influence performance of fish in a hierarchy (Li and Brocksen, 1977). Andrews (1979) stated that

> Sensitivities to chronic social challenge intensity differ between social ranks of animals [mammals] from species populations so that adverse effects of crowding are differentially distributed to members of the population. Moreover, the degree of tolerance to crowding (density) appears to depend upon the type of social organization, behavioral conditioning and genetic background of each population.

In this respect, it would be interesting to know the physiological consequences of social interactions between hatchery and wild fish. Kalleberg (1958) suggested that hatchery fish are less aggressive than wild fish in a stream situation. However, other recent studies have indicated that hatchery salmonids are more aggressive than wild stocks, particularly at the higher densities (Moyle, 1969; Fenderson and Carpenter, 1971; Bieber, 1977).

Fish may react to increases in population density by a generalized stress response (George, 1977). However, neuro-endocrine modulated control of populations due to crowding, as proposed for mammalian vertebrates by Christian (1975) has not been demonstrated in fishes. As I have shown, fish respond to severe crowding by a transient stress achieving ideal compensation in these stress factors. I am not implying that performance capacity of crowded fish is the same as that of fish reared at lower densities. In an attempt to determine if density (numbers of fish l^{-1} min^{-1} water inflow) or loading (weight of fish l^{-1} min^{-1} water inflow—see Westers, 1970) contribute to stress, an experiment with yearling coho salmon was conducted (C. B. Schreck and A. Hemmingsen, unpublished data). We reared duplicate groups of fish in hatchery troughs at four different densities and under four different loading regimes, representing culture conditions ranging from sparsely populated to severely crowded with minimal water flow to abundant water flow. Although substantial differences in treatment-related growth were apparent, no indication of stress responses in the fish could be inferred from levels of plasma cortisol (Fig. 3).

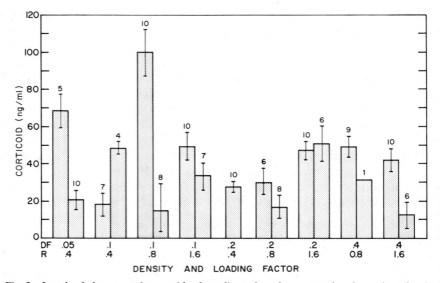

Fig. 3   Levels of plasma corticosteroids of yearling coho salmon reared under various density (*DF*) and loading (*R*) factors. The two bars for each treatment represent duplicates. The first bars for the *DF* 0·1–R.8 and *DF* 0·05–R.4 treatments were probably artificially elevated, because of sampling difficulties. Density and loading factors calculated according to Westers (1970). Corticosteroid levels presented as mean ±S.E.M., number of fish used for each sample is indicated on the figure.

In coho salmon, however, aggressive distance is rather closely defined and varies with the size of the fish (Dill, 1978). Wedemeyer (1976) found that moving juvenile coho salmon into fairly dense conditions resulted in a significant physiological stress response that required at least 1 week for recovery.

Crowding is obviously important to the well-being of fish, and apparently induces liberation of a water-borne factor from some species that affects the immune system of conspecifics, as in blue gourami, *Trichogaster trichopterus* (Perlmutter *et al.*, 1973) and tilapia, *Sarotherodon mossambica* (Henderson-Arzapalo *et al.*, 1980). For further discussion of the immuno-suppressive effects of stress the reader is referred to Ellis, 1981, this volume. In view of the possibility of stress-induced, water-borne factors, a preliminary study was conducted to determine if coho salmon liberate a substance into the water in response to stress that could elicit a stress response in other individuals (C. B. Schreck, unpublished data). Duplicate tanks were set up in series so that water from two of the tanks flowed out through two other tanks. The fish in one of the "upstream" tanks were stressed by being suspended in a dip net in that tank; the fish in the tank receiving the effluent from the stressed group were left unhandled. For comparison, fish in the downstream tank in the other series were similarly stressed and the group upstream remained untouched. Fish in two other tanks served as unstressed controls. After 75 min of confinement, all fish were sampled for cortisol determination. Because the fish in the effluent from the stressed fish did not exhibit elevated cortisol levels but both groups in the dip net had high concentrations of the steroid (Table I), it is concluded that either no water borne stress factor was liberated or that the fish did not respond to it.

TABLE I Plasma Cortisol Levels in Coho Salmon Severely Confined (Stressed), Exposed to Effluent from Stressed Fish, or Unstressed Controls.

	Tank	
	A flowing into B	
Treatment	stressed	unstressed
Cortisol	179 ± 16 (11)	17 ± 5 (12)
	C flowing into D	
Treatment	unstressed	stressed
Cortisol	12 ± 5 (12)	188 ± 13 (12)
	E flowing into F	
Treatment	unstressed	unstressed
Cortisol	31 ± 6 (12)	7 ± 2 (12)

Water from Tank A flowed into Tank B, water from Tank C flowed into Tank D. Tanks E and F are separate, control tanks. Cortisol levels are expressed as ng ml^{-1} (Mean ±S.E.M.).

(c) Bioenergetic and Osmoregulatory Considerations

As indicated in most of the reviews on the physiological reaction to stress in fish, the factors responding are generally related in some way to energy mobilization and water-mineral balance. It is probably safe to assume that the energetic aspects of the stress response are adaptive. The depletion of liver glycogen, hyperglycemia, and change in protein and fatty acid composition must reflect the need for energy necessary to combat or resist the stress (catatoxic or syntoxic responses, respectively, in the terms of Selye (1971, 1973a, b)). Stress also appears to be accompanied by a breakdown of barriers to water and electrolyte flux, stressed fish becoming hydrated in fresh water and dehydrated in sea water (Stevens, 1972; Mazeaud et al., 1977). During the alarm phase of stress responses, water may follow an osmotic gradient. It is thus likely that some of the energy stores mobilized during the stress response are necessary to restore osmotic equilibrium. For further details of the effects of stress on the osmoregulatory systems of fish the reader is referred to Eddy, 1981, this volume.

The osmotic disturbances in fish subsequent to stress may be viewed as a potential secondary, stressful situation. Rapid change in the ambient salinity may cause a physiological stress response in its own right. For example, mild challenge of goldfish with saline produced rapid increases in plasma ACTH and cortisol and a hyperglycemia (Chavin and Young, 1970; Chavin, 1973; Singley and Chavin, 1975a). Exposure of chinook salmon smolts to sea water caused a transient, small increase in circulating cortisol that peaked in 1 h (Strange and Schreck, 1980). However, cortisol levels remained constant when American eels, *A. rostrata*, adapted to sea water were subjected to fresh water (Nishimura *et al.*, 1976).

The osmotic costs associated with stress may be significant in terms of the ability of a fish to cope with the situation. The severity of a stress can sometimes be reduced if the water balance problem is alleviated. Addition of salt (NaCl) to the ambient medium in freshwater-adapted euryhaline species appears to help fish overcome various types of handling stress. For example, the addition of approximately 5 g l^{-1} NaCl reduces the physiological stress responses to handling in salmonids (Wedemeyer, 1972; Wedemeyer and Wood, 1974), their resistance to fungal infection (Long *et al.*, 1977) and survival (Hattingh *et al.*, 1975). Furthermore, Atlantic salmon smolts showed a more rapid recovery from elevated plasma glucose and lactate following exercise in salt water compared with fresh water (Wendt and Saunders, 1973).

The beneficial effects of the addition of salt on survival were also evident in freshwater-adapted, yearling chinook salmon stressed by severe confinement. Fish confined in dilute saline solutions (5 g l^{-1} NaCl) experienced a lower mortality than those confined in fresh water, although the cortisol stress response was not moderated by the salt (Strange and Schreck, 1978). Mortality was not only reduced when smolt-sized chinook salmon adapted to fresh water were severely confined in about $3 \cdot 0 \text{ g l}^{-1}$ sea water (Instant Ocean®), but the increase in plasma cortisol level was markedly lower than in fish stressed in fresh water (Strange and Schreck, 1980). Mild saline (6 mg l^{-1} sea water) clearly lessened the severity of stress by severe confinement in coho salmon smolts in which elevation of plasma cortisol and reduction in hepatic glycogen were not apparent. This contrasts markedly to fish stressed in fresh water (C. B. Schreck and C. Ejike, unpublished data). These findings could also be explained by an increase in clearance of cortisol in fish in saline water. Leloup-Hatey (1974), for example, found that the metabolic clearance rate of cortisol in seawater-adapted European eels was twice as fast as in freshwater-adapted fish.

Stress-induced reduction in total calcium or sodium in the salmon were not moderated by the saline, but osmotic pressure was maintained. However, recovery of electrolytes of the more stenohaline northern pike, *Esox lucius*, were not consistent between fish handled in brackish water or fresh water, and hemoglobin concentration decreased back to normal more rapidly in the group in fresh water (Soivio and Oikari, 1976).

The sparing effects of salt on stress in freshwater-adapted fish may be efficaceous only under circumstances when the fish are in good physical conditions. Preliminary data on effects of transportation of chinook salmon smolts in 5 g l^{-1} NaCl indicated that survival was increased in apparently healthy fish whereas it appeared to be unaffected in another group with a bacterial kidney infection (*Renibacterium salmoninarum*) (S. E. Jacobs and C. B. Schreck, unpublished data).

IV PERFORMANCE CAPACITY AND THE CONCEPTUALIZATION OF STRESS

Fry (1947) used an autecological approach to view performance through the concept that the environment influences activity by acting on metabolism and that activities are the result of organized metabolism. The Fry paradigm of viewing performances as a metabolic scope provides a means of conceptualizing the reserve capacity of fish to perform under various environmental states (Brett, 1976; Kerr and Ryder, 1977). In this approach, emergent behaviors of systems, observed at several hierarchical levels of ecological organization, are used (Kerr, 1976). Warren *et al.* (1979) presented a framework for considering potential and realized capacities of organismic systems within an environmental system. The physiologic system of fish can be viewed through a construct somewhat analogous to the geometric metaphor of niche by Hutchinson (1957) (see also review by Haefner, 1980). Magnuson *et al.* (1979) adapted a similar approach in construction of a "thermal niche" for fish. An examination of the response of ecosystems, positively and negatively, to stress (Lugo, 1978) and models of environmental stress (Ulanowicz, 1978) are heuristic from a physiological perspective.

I believe that the concept of stress and physiological performance can be viewed as an N-dimensional geometric physiological capacity, delimited ultimately by the organism's genotype and proximately by environmental influences and stress. Performance capacity is the totality of all possible individual, discrete performances. Individual performances can be represented as vectors (Fig. 4). Each performance vector describes the capacity or the potential ability of the fish to perform a necessary activity,

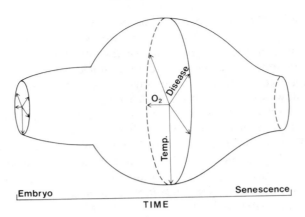

Fig. 4   Conceptualization of the performance capacity of a fish (or stock) and some representative performance vectors. The shape of the performance capacity through time is not meant to reflect the exact change through ontogeny of any given species.

such as resisting a pathogen, metabolizing at various temperatures, obtaining oxygen, swimming, psychologically resisting social interactions, and performing all other activities necessary for the fish to persist and ultimately reproduce. At any given time, the performance capacity describes the organismic potential for conducting these activities.

This potential performance capacity is delimited by the fish's genotype. There is a genetic component for the physiological mechanisms for each individual performance vector. For example, resistance to certain bacterial pathogens is correlated with transferrin genotypes in some salmonids (Suzumoto *et al.*, 1977; Pratschner, 1978; Winter *et al.*, 1980). Tolerance or performance in terms of such parameters as swimming, growth, and survival under such environmental variables as oxygen level and temperature also have a genetic basis in clinids (Johnson, 1971), catostomids (Koehn, 1970), salmonids (Tsuyuki and Williscroft, 1977; Redding and Schreck, 1979; Klar *et al.*, 1979), and cyprinids (Powers, 1980). There are also differences in such components of stress responses as glucose level, blood cell counts, and coagulation rates between hatchery-reared and wild trout (Casillas and Smith, 1977), although these effects may not necessarily be genetic. There are even genetically based differences in the response to psychic stress, as demonstrated in rats by Friedman and Iwai (1976).

Performance capacity also changes with ontogeny. A large body of literature has been directed toward this prospect, particularly with regard to tolerance of such factors as adverse non-optimum temperature and low dissolved oxygen. This topic is not reviewed here; I merely note that basal levels of various factors associated with the GAS of stress, such as plasma corticoid levels, can vary with developmental stage in some fish (McLeay, 1975; Singley and Chavin, 1975b; J. L. Specker and C. B. Schreck, unpublished data). Thus, the potential performance capacity of an organism can fluctuate through time (Fig. 4). The composition of the performance vectors can also change through time and their relative contribution to the well-being of the organism can vary.

> The environments in which organisms live are not stable throughout time. Animals live in environments where physical, chemical and biological parameters are continually changing (Powers, 1980).
> Perturbations in the spatial, social and temporal features of niches elicit physiological responses to these perturbations by individual members of . . . species populations which occupy the hypervolume of niche space. Such responses include adjustments in the amplitude and timing of rhythms in metabolism, neuroendocrine function, reproductive dynamics and animal activities. Amplitudes and capacities of responses appear to be differentially distributed to members of . . . populations according to behavioral type. (Andrews, 1979)

Changes in time course of physiological systems responding to fluctuating environmental states vary with the system and the duration and severity of the change, ranging from fractions of seconds to several generations (Prosser, 1958). A number of papers have documented the natural seasonal changes in physiological factors such as blood constituents of fish (see e.g. Bridges et al., 1976).

The environment further constrains the performance capacity, creating a realized performance capacity (Fig. 5). This can be most easily appreciated by consideration of the concept of genetotrophism which states that nutrition regulates the expression of the genotype. That is, the environment

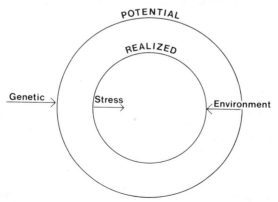

Fig. 5   The relationship between the potential and realized performance capacities and the influence of the ultimate (genetic) and proximate (environment and stress) limiting factors on the geometric configuration of the capacities.

provides the raw materials necessary to construct the phenotype (Williams, 1963). Nutrition is known to affect the performance of fish. For example, Mehrle *et al.* (1977) reviewed the effects of diet quality on toxicological research, and Wydoski and Wedemeyer (1976) stated that nutrition is important to blood chemistries and the stress response of fish. In concert with the determination of diurnal rhythms of some factors associated with the GAS of goldfish, Delahunty *et al.* (1978) found that feeding schedule markedly affected the diel periodicity of plasma cortisol. In addition, other elements of the habitat affect performance capacity, restricting performance vectors to a realized state. The importance of environmental quality and disease resistance is a salient example (see e.g. Wedemeyer and Wood, 1974). Because the variability in the phenotype is modified by the environment, the actual realized performance capacity is a somewhat reduced version of the potential capacity.

The realized performance capacity can be further modified by stress. Stress can reduce performance vectors (such as reduced ability to resist crowding or disease, as shown previously), thereby contracting further the geometric space of the realized capacity (Fig. 5). That is, stress can place a load on the physiologic system that impairs to some degree the ability of the organism to perform certain activities.

A conceptual model of stress can be envisioned as an N-dimensional geometric configuration described by individual performance capabilities. This geometric configuration is delimited by the genotype (potential capacity) and further by the conditions of the environment and stress (realized capacity, Fig. 6). Because different ontogenetic stages have different potential capacities and because the environment changes temporally, this N-dimensional construct pulsates through time.

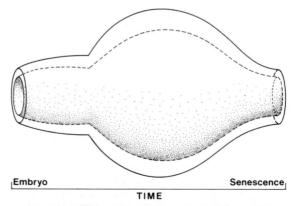

Fig. 6 Pulsation of the potential performance capacity due to genetic constraints and the realized performance capacity due to genetic factors, environmental constraints and stress through development.

V STRESS CONTROL IN MANAGEMENT AND CULTURE

Fishery managers should be concerned with optimizing the space of the realized performance capacity of their stocks. Since the importance of the various performance activities relative to each other are not known, it would be premature to manage for maximization of all vectors. Some activities of the fish are undoubtedly more important than others, and one would need to consider the contribution of each performance factor under various management options.

Tentative conclusions from this conceptual construct, supported by data reviewed in earlier sections of this paper, are applicable in a fishery management concept. During any form of handling practice, the marked importance of the initial, early encounters of a stressful situation should be borne in mind. To the extent practical, treatment of fish should be directed toward the avoidance of frightening them. If more than one imposition of stress is to be made on the fish, adequate time for recovery from the first stress should be made available whenever possible. A stress places a physiologic load on the fish, thereby reducing its capacity to perform with regard to subsequent stresses. The appropriate recovery time depends upon the severity and duration of the initial stress and on habitat conditions—such as temperature. As judged by physiological indicators of stress, about 10 to 14 days may be the maximum time necessary. However, adjustment to psychological-behavioral factors may require longer time.

In management programs involving habitat alterations, effects on social systems of populations should be considered. Changes affecting habitat availability or fish density could impose low-level, chronic stress on segments of a population, thereby affecting their performance in resisting other stresses. Introducing hatchery-reared fish into waters containing a wild population could conceivably result in reduced performance by both stocks because of the increased psychological stress attributable to artificial, elevated densities and social pressures.

Physiological indicators of stress must be validated before they can be used as the basis for management decisions. If a goal of management is to ensure optimum performance capacity of fish, these physiological responses should be indicative of a change in one or more of the performance vectors.

ACKNOWLEDGEMENTS

The following colleagues or students contributed significantly to the information and thoughts presented in this paper. I am extremely pleased to acknowledge their efforts in elucidating the stress concept for fish and their role in guiding my thinking and formulation of conceptual frameworks:

Charles R. Berry, Chiweyite Ejike, James T. Golden, Steven E. Jacobs, Hiram W. Li, J. Michael Redding, Jennifer L. Specker, Richard J. Strange, and Lavern J. Weber. I am also grateful to my wife, Jacquelyn, for her thorough help with the literature in this review.

Cooperators are Oregon State University, Oregon Department of Fish and Wildlife, and the United States Fish and Wildlife Service.

REFERENCES

Andrews, R. V. (1979). The physiology of crowding. *Comp. Biochem. Physiol.* **63A**, 1–6.

Barton, B. A., Peter, R. E. and Paulencu, C. R. (1980). Plasma cortisol levels of fingerling rainbow trout (*Salmo gairdneri*) at rest, and subjected to handling, confinement, transport, and stocking. *J. Fish. Res. Bd Can.* **37**, 805–811.

Barton, B. A. and Toth, L. T. (1980). Physiological stress in fish: A literature review with emphasis on blood cortisol dynamics. *Fish. Res. Sec., Fish and Wildlife Div., Alberta Dept. Energy Natural Resources, Fish. Research Pap.* No. **21**, 18pp.

Berdyshev, G. D. (1967). Mechanisms of the genetically caused death of Far-Eastern salmon after spawning. In *Metabolism and Biochemistry of Fishes* (G. S. Karzinkin, ed.). Transl. 1977 by Indian National Sci. Doc. Ctr, New Delhi. U.S. Dept. Comm. NTIS.

Billard, R., Bry, C. and Gillet, C. (1981). Stress, environment and reproduction in teleost fish. In *Stress and Fish* (A. D. Pickering, ed.), pp. 185–208. London and New York: Academic Press.

Bieber, G. F. (1977). Comparative behavior of the progeny of hatchery and wild steelhead trout (*Salmo gairdneri*). Master's Thesis, Oregon State University, Corvallis, Oregon. 32pp.

Brett, J. R. (1958). Implications and assessments of environmental stress. In *Investigations of Fish-power Problems* (P. A. Larkin, ed.), pp. 69–83. H. R. MacMillan Lectures in Fisheries, University of British Columbia, Vancouver.

Brett, J. R. (1976). Scope for metabolism and growth of sockeye salmon, *Oncorhynchus nerka*, and some related energetics. *J. Fish. Res. Bd Can.* **33**, 307–313.

Bridges, D. W., Chech, J. J. and Pedro, D. N. (1976). Seasonal hematological changes in winter flounder, *Pseudopleuronectes americanus*. *Trans. Am. Fish. Soc.* **105**, 596–600.

Casillas, E. and Smith, L. S. (1977). Effect of stress on blood coagulation and haematology in rainbow trout (*Salmo gairdneri*). *J. Fish Biol.* **10**, 481–491.

Chavin, W. (1973). Teleostean endocrine and paraendocrine alterations of utility in environmental studies. In *Responses of Fish to Environmental Changes* (W. Chavin, ed.), pp. 199–238. Springfield, Illinois: Charles C. Thomas, Publisher.

Chavin, W. and Young, J. E. (1970). Effects of alloxan upon goldfish (*Carassius auratus* L.). *Gen. comp. Endocr.* **14**, 438–460.

Chiszar, D., Moody, M. and Windell, J. T. (1972). Failure of bluegill sunfish, *Lepomis macrochirus*, to habituate to handling. *J. Fish. Res. Bd Can.* **29**, 576–578.

Chittenden, M. E. Jnr (1971). Transporting and handling young American shad. *N.Y. Fish Game J.* **18**, 123–128.

Christian, J. J. (1975). Hormonal control of population growth. In *Hormonal Correlates of Behavior, Vol. I* (B. E. Eleftheriou and R. Sprott, eds), pp. 205–274. New York: Plenum Press.

Comfort, A. (1964). *The Biology of Senescence.* New York: Elsevier. 414pp.

Delahunty, G., Olcese, J., Prack, M., Vodicnik, M. J., Schreck, C. B. and de Vlaming, V. (1978). Biurnal variations in the physiology of the goldfish, *Carassius auratus. J. Interdiscpl. Cycle Res.* **9**, 73–88.

Delventhal, H. (1978). Experimentelle Stressuntersuchungen am europaischen Aal, *Anguilla anguilla* (Linne, 1758)—physiologische und ethologische Aspekte. Diplomarbeit, Univ. Hamburg, Hamburg, West Germany. 147pp.

Dill, L. M. (1978). Aggressive distance in juvenile coho salmon (*Oncorhynchus kisutch*). *Can. J. Zool.* **56**, 1441–1446.

Donaldson, E. M. (1980). Pituitary–interrenal axis as an indicator of stress in fish. In *Stress and Fish* (A. D. Pickering, ed.), pp. 11–47. London and New York: Academic Press.

Donaldson, E. M. and Fagerlund, U. H. M. (1968). Changes in the cortisol dynamics of sockeye salmon (*Oncorhynchus nerka*) resulting from sexual maturation. *Gen. comp. Endocr.* **11**, 552–561.

Donaldson, E. M. and Fagerlund, U. H. M. (1972). Corticosteroid dynamics in Pacific salmon. *Gen. comp. Endocr.* Suppl. **3**, 254–265.

Eddy, F. B. (1981). Effects of stress on osmotic and ionic regulation in fish. In *Stress and Fish* (A. D. Pickering, ed.), 77–102. London and New York: Academic Press.

Ejike, C. and Schreck, C. B. (1980). Stress and social hierarchy rank in coho salmon. *Trans. Am. Fish. Soc.* **109**, 423–426.

Ellis, A. E. (1981). Stress and the modulation of defence mechanisms in fish. In *Stress and Fish* (A. D. Pickering, ed.), pp. 147–169. London and New York: Academic Press.

Erickson, J. G. (1967). Social hierarchy, territoriality, and stress reactions in sunfish. *Physiol. Zool.* **40**, 40–48.

Fagerlund, U. H. M. (1967). Plasma cortisol concentration in relation to stress in adult sockeye salmon during the freshwater stage of their life cycle. *Gen. comp. Endocr.* **8**, 197–207.

Fagerlund, U. H. M. (1970). Dynamics of cortisone secretion in sockeye salmon (*Oncorhynchus nerka*) during sexual maturation and after gonadectomy. *J. Fish. Res. Bd Can.* **27**, 2323–2331.

Fenderson, O. C. and Carpenter, M. R. (1971). Effects of crowding on the behavior of juvenile hatchery and wild landlocked Atlantic salmon (*Salmo salar* L.). *Anim. Behav.* **19**, 439–447.

Friedman, R. and Iwai, J. (1976). Genetic predisposition and stress-induced hypertension. *Science, N.Y.* **193**, 161–162.

Fry, F. E. J. (1947). Effects of the environment on animal activity. Univ. Toronto Studies. *Biol. Ser. No. 55. Publs Ont. Fish. Res. Lab.* No. 68. Toronto University: Toronto Press. 62pp.

Fryer, J. N. (1975). Stress and adrenocorticosteroid dynamics in the goldfish, *Carassius auratus. Can. J. Zool.* **53**, 1012–1020.

Fuller, J. D., Scott, D. B. C. and Fraser, R. (1974). Effects of catching techniques, captivity and reproductive cycle on plasma cortisol concentration in the powan (*Coregonus lavaretus*), a freshwater teleost from Loch Lomond. *J. Endocr.* **63**, 24.

316   C. B. SCHRECK

George, C. J. (1977). The implication of neuroendocrine mechanisms in the regulation of population character. *Fisheries* **2**, 14–19 and 30.

Gerking, S. D. (1959). Physiological changes accompanying ageing of fishes. *Ciba Foundation. Coloquia on Ageing* **5**, 181–207.

Gronow, G. (1974a). Stresseffekete bei teleosteern. Ph.D. Thesis, Christian–Albrechts–Universität zu Kiel, Kiel. 144pp.

Gronow, G. (1974b). Über die Anwendung des an Säugetieren erarbeiteten Begriffes "Stresz" auf Knochenfische. *Zool. Anz.* **192**, 316–331.

Haefner, J. W. (1980). Two metaphors of the niche. *Synthesis* **43**, 123–153.

Hane, S. and Robertson, O. H. (1959). Changes in plasma 17-hydroxy-corticosteroids accompanying sexual maturation and spawning of the Pacific salmon (*Oncorhynchus tshawytscha*) and rainbow trout (*Salmo gairdneri*). *Proc. Nat. Acad. Sci. U.S.A.* **45**, 886–893.

Hane, S., Robertson, O. H., Wexler, R. C. and Krupp, A. (1966). Adrenocortical response to stress and ACTH in Pacific salmon (*Oncorhynchus tshawytscha*) and steelhead trout (*Salmo gairdneri*) at successive stages in the sexual cycle. *Endocrinology* **78**, 791–800.

Hattingh, J., Fourie, F. and Van Vuren, J. (1975). The transport of freshwater fish. *J. Fish Biol.* **7**, 447–449.

Henderson-Arzapalo, A., Stickney, R. R. and Lewis, D. H. (1980). Immune hypersensitivity in intensively cultured *Tilapia* species. *Trans. Am. Fish. Soc.* **109**, 244–247.

Hochachka, P. W. (1961). The effect of physical training on oxygen debt and glycogen reserves in trout. *Can. J. Zool.* **39**, 767–776.

Houston, A. H., Madden, J. A., Woods, R. J. and Miles, H. M. (1971). Some physiological effects of handling and tricaine methanesulfonate anesthetization upon brook trout, *Salvelinus fontinalis*. *J. Fish. Res. Bd Can.* **28**, 625–633.

Hughes, G. M. (1981). Effect of low oxygen and pollution on the respiratory systems of fish. In *Stress and Fish* (A. D. Pickering, ed.), pp. 121–146. London and New York: Academic Press.

Hutchinson, G. E. (1957). Concluding remarks. *Cold Spring Harb. Symp. quant. Biol.* **22**, 415–427.

Idler, D. R. and Freeman, H. C. (1965). A demonstration of an impaired hormone metabolism in moribund Atlantic cod (*Gadus morhua* L.). *Can. J. Biochem.* **43**, 620–623.

Idler, D. R. and Truscott, B. in collaboration with H. C. Freeman, G. Chang, P. J. Schmidt, and A. P. Ronald. (1963). *In vivo* metabolism of steroid hormones by sockeye salmon. A. impaired hormone clearance in mature and spawned Pacific salmon (*Oncorhynchus nerka*). B. Precursors of 11-ketotestosterone. *Can. J. Biochem. Physiol.* **41**, 875–887.

Idler, D. R., Schmidt, P. J., Truscott, B. and Freeman, H. C. (1966). Impaired hormone metabolism in relation to spawning and death of salmon. *Food Sci.* **2**, 211–218.

Johnson, M. S. (1971). Adaptive lactate dehydrogenase variation in the crested blenny, *Anoplareus*. *Heredity* **27**, 205–226.

Kalleberg, H. (1958). Observations in a stream tank of territoriality and competition in juvenile salmon and trout (*Salmo salar* L. and *S. trutta* L.) *Rep. Inst. Freshwat. Res. Drottningholm* **39**, 55–98.

Kerr, S. R. (1976). Ecological analysis and the Fry paradigm. *J. Fish. Res. Bd Can.* **33**, 329–332.

Kerr, S. R. and Ryder, R. A. (1977). Niche theory and percid community structure. *J. Fish. Res. Bd Can.* **34**, 1952-1958.

King, J. A. (1973). The ecology of aggressive behavior. *A. Rev. Ecol. Syst.* **4**, 117-138.

Klar, G. T., Stalnaker, C. B. and Farley, T. M. (1979). Comparative physical and physiological performances of rainbow trout, *Salmo gairdneri*, of distinct lactate dehydrogenase B[2] phenotypes. *Comp. Biochem. Physiol.* **63A**, 229-235.

Klinger, H., Peters, G. and Delventhal, H. (1979). Physiologische und morphologische Effects von sozialem Stress beim Aal, *Anguilla anguilla* L. *Verh. dt. zool. Ges.* **1979**, 246.

Koehn, R. K. (1970). Functional and evolutionary dynamics of polymorphic esterases in catostomid fishes. *Trans. Am. Fish. Soc.* **99**, 219-223.

Leloup-Hatey, J. (1961). Rôle de l'agitation musculaire dans le determinisme de l'hypercorticosteroidemie observée chez la carpe (*Cyprinuus carpio* L.) après un passage direct de l'eau douce à une solution saline équilibrée isotonique a l'eau de mer. *Compt. Rend. Sci. Soc. Biol.* **155**, 241-245.

Leloup-Hatey, J. (1974). Influence de l'adaptation a l'eau de mer sur la fonction interrenalienne de l'Anguille (*Anguilla anguilla* L.). *Gen. comp. Endocr.* **24**, 28-37.

Leshner, A. I. (1978). *An Introduction to Behavioral Endocrinology.* New York: Oxford University Press. 361pp.

Li, H. W. (1973). A bioenergetic analysis of intraspecific and interspecific competition in two teleost fishes. Ph.D. Thesis, University of California, Davis, California. 87pp.

Li, H. W. and Brocksen, R. W. (1977). Approaches to the analysis of energetic costs of intraspecific competition for space by rainbow trout (*Salmo gairdneri*). *J. Fish Biol.* **11**, 329-341.

Long, C. W., McComas, J. R. and Monk, B. H. (1977). Use of salt (NaCl) water to reduce mortality of chinook smolts, *Oncorhynchus tshawytscha*, during handling and hauling. *U.S. Natl. Mar. Fish. Ser., Mar. Fish. Rev.* **39**, 6-9.

Lugo, A. E. (1978). Stress and ecosystems. In *Energy and Environmental Stress in Aquatic Systems* (J. H. Thorp and J. W. Gibbons, eds), pp. 62-101. Springfield, Virginia: Technical Information Center, U.S. Department of Energy.

Magnuson, J. J., Crowder, L. B. and Medvick, P. A. (1979). Temperature as an ecological resource. *Am. Zool.* **19**, 331-343.

Mazeaud, M. M. and Mazeaud, F. (1981). The role of catecholamines in the stress response of fish. In *Stress and Fish* (A. D. Pickering, ed.), pp. 49-75. London and New York: Academic Press.

Mazeaud, M. M., Mazeaud, F. and Donaldson, E. M. (1977). Primary and secondary effects of stress in fish: Some new data with a general review. *Trans. Am. Fish. Soc.* **106**, 201-212.

McDonald, A. L., Heimstra, N. W. and Damkot, D. K. (1968). Social modification of agonistic behavior in fish. *Anim. Behav.* **16**, 437-441.

McKim, J. M. (1967). Stress hormone metabolites and their fluctuations in the urine of rainbow trout (*Salmo gairdneri*) under the influence of various sublethal stressors. Ph.D. Thesis, University of Michigan, Ann Arbor, Michigan.

McLeay, D. J. (1975). Variations in the pituitary-interrenal axis and the abundance of circulating blood-cell types in juvenile coho salmon, *Oncorhynchus kisutch*, during stream residence. *Can. J. Zool.* **53**, 1882-1891.

Mehrle, P. M., Mayer, F. L. and Johnson, W. W. (1977). Diet quality in fish toxicology: Effects on acute and chronic toxicity. In: F. L. Mayer and J. L. Hemelink (eds), pp. 269–280. Am. Soc. Test. Mater., Spec. Tech. Publ. 634. Philadelphia: American Society for Testing and Materials.

Moyle, P. B. (1969). Comparative behavior of young brook trout of domestic and wild origin. *Progve Fish Cult.* **31**, 51–56.

Nakano, T. and Tomlinson, N. (1967). Catecholamine and carbohydrate concentrations in rainbow trout (*Salmo gairdneri*) in relation to physical disturbance. *J. Fish. Res. Bd Can.* **24**, 1701–1715.

Nishimura, H., Sawyer, W. H. and Nigrelli, R. F. (1976). Renin, cortisol and plasma volume in marine teleost fishes adapted to dilute media. *J. Endocr.* **70**, 47–59.

Noakes, D. L. and Leatherland, J. F. (1977). Social dominance and interrenal cell activity in rainbow trout, *Salmo gairdneri* (Pisces, Salmonidae). *Env. Biol. Fish.* **2**, 131–136.

Perlmutter, A., Sarot, D. A., Yu, M., Filazzola, R. J. and Seeley, R. J. (1973).The effects of crowding on the immune response of the blue gourami, *Trichogaster trichopterus*, to infectious pancreatic necrosis (IPN) virus. *Life Sci.* **13**, 363–375.

Peters, G. (1979). Zur Interpretation des Begriffs "Stress" beim Fisch. *Fisch und Tiershutz* **7**, 25–32.

Peters, G., Delventhal, H. and Klinger, H. (1980a). Stress diagnosis for fish in intensive culture system. *FAO, United Nations EIFAC/80/Symp.*: E/37, 12pp.

Peters, G., Delventhal, H. and Klinger, H. (1980b). Physiological and morphological effects of social stress on the eel (*Anguilla anguilla* L.). *Arch. FischWiss.* **30**, 157–180.

Peters, G., Klinger, H. and Delventhal, H. (1981). Stress diagnosis of eels. (Abstract). In *Stress and Fish* (A. D. Pickering, ed.), pp. 333–334. London and New York: Academic Press.

Pickering, A. D. (1981). Introduction: the concept of biological stress. In *Stress and Fish* (A. D. Pickering, ed.), pp. 1–7. London and New York: Academic Press.

Powers, D. A. (1980). Molecular ecology of teleost fish hemoglobins: Strategies for adapting to changing environments. *Am. Zool.* **20**, 139–162.

Pratschner, G. A. (1978). The relative resistance of six transferrin phenotypes of coho salmon (*Oncorhynchus kisutch*) to cytophagosis, furunculosis, and vibriosis. Masters Thesis, University of Washington, Seattle, Washington. 71pp.

Precht, H. (1958). Concepts of the temperature adaptation of unchanging reaction systems of cold-blooded animals. In *Physiological Adaptations* (C. L. Prosser, ed.), pp. 50–78. Baltimore, Maryland: Lord Baltimore Press, Inc.

Prosser, C. L. (1958). General summary: The nature of physiological adaptation. In *Physiological Adaptations* (C. L. Prosser, ed.), pp. 167–180. Baltimore, Maryland: Lord Baltimore Press, Inc.

Rasquin, P. and Rosenbloom, L. (1954). Endocrine imbalance and tissue hyperplasia in teleosts maintained in total darkness. *Bull. Am. Mus. Nat. Hist.* 104 Art. **4**, 359–426.

Redding, J. M. and Schreck, C. B. (1979). Possible adaptive significance of certain enzyme polymorphisms in steelhead trout (*Salmo gairdneri*). *J. Fish. Res. Bd Can.* **36**, 544–551.

Redgate, E. S. (1974). Neural control of pituitary–adrenal activity in *Cyprinus carpio*. *Gen. comp. Endocr.* **22**, 35–41.

Robertson, O. H., Krupp, M. A., Favour, C. B., Hane, S. and Thomas, S. F. (1961a). Physiological changes occurring in the blood of the Pacific salmon (*Oncorhynchus tshawytscha*) accompanying sexual maturation and spawning. *Endocrinology* **68**, 733–746.

Robertson, O. H., Krupp, M. A., Thomas, S. F., Favour, C. B., Hane, S. and Wexler, B. C. (1961b). Hyperadrenocorticism in spawning, migratory, and nonmigratory rainbow trout (*Salmo gairdneri*); comparison with Pacific salmon (Genus *Oncorhynchus*). *Gen. comp. Endocr.* **1**, 473–484.

Robertson, O. H. and Wexler, B. C. (1957). Pituitary degeneration and adrenal tissue hyperplasia in spawning Pacific salmon. *Science, N.Y.* **125**, 1295–1296.

Rush, S. B. and Umminger, B. L. (1978). Elimination of stress-induced changes in carbohydrate metabolism of goldfish (*Carassius auratus*) by training. *Comp. Biochem. Physiol.* **60A**, 69–73.

Sandoval, W. A. (1979). Odor detection by coho salmon (*Oncorhynchus kisutch*): A laboratory bioassay and genetic basis. Master's Thesis, Oregon State University, Corvallis, Oregon. 43pp.

Schimdt, P. J. and Idler, D. R. (1962). Steroid hormones in the plasma of salmon at various stages of maturation. *Gen. comp. Endocr.* **2**, 204–214.

Schreck, C. B. (1976). The stress concept in fisheries: Implications in environmental monitoring. *Proc. West. Assoc. State Game Fish Comm.* **56**, 186–188.

Schreck, C. B. and Lorz, H. W. (1978). Stress response of coho salmon (*Oncorhynchus kisutch*) elicited by cadmium and copper and potential use of cortisol as an indicator of stress. *J. Fish. Res. Bd Can.* **35**, 1124–1129.

Scott, D. B. and Currie, C. E. (1980). Social hierarchy in relation to adrenocortical activity in *Xiphophorus helleri* Heckel. *J. Fish Biol.* **16**, 265–277.

Selye, H. (1936). A syndrome produced by diverse nocuous agents. *Nature, Lond.* **138**, 32.

Selye, H. (1950a). Stress and the general adaptation syndrome. *Br. Med. J.* **1**, 1383–1392.

Selye, H. (1950b). *The Physiology and Pathology of Exposure to Stress.* Montreal: Acta, Inc. 822pp.

Selye, H. (1971). *Hormones and Resistance, Parts 1 and 2.* New York: Springer-Verlag. 1140pp.

Selye, H. (1973a). Homeostasis and heterostasis. *Perspect. Biol. Med.* **1973**, 441–445.

Selye, H. (1973b). The evolution of the stress concept. *Am. Scient.* **61**, 692–699.

Selye, H. (1974). *Stress without Distress.* Philadelphia, Pennsylvania: J. B. Lippincott Co. 171pp.

Selye, H. (1976). *Stress in Health and Disease.* Boston, Massachusetts: Butterworth. 1256pp.

Simpson, T. H. (1975/76). Endocrine aspects of salmonid culture. *Proc. R. Soc. Edinb.* (B) **75**, 17, 241–252.

Singley, J. A. and Chavin, W. (1975a). The adrenocortical-hypophyseal response to saline stress in the goldfish, *Carassius auratus* L. *Comp. Biochem. Physiol.* **51A**, 749–756.

Singley, J. A. and Chavin, W. (1975b). Serum cortisol in normal goldfish (*Carassius auratus* L.). *Comp. Biochem. Physiol.* **50A**, 77–82.

Slicher, A. M., Pickford, G. E. and Pang, P. K. T. (1966). Effects of "training" and of volume and composition of the injection fluid on stress-induced leukopenia in the mummichog. *Progve Fish Cult.* **28**, 216–219.

Soivo, A. and Oikari, A. (1976). Haematological effects of stress on a teleost, *Esox lucius* L. *J. Fish Biol.* **8**, 397–411.

Specker, J. L. and Schreck, C. B. (1980). Stress responses to transportation and fitness for marine survival in coho salmon (*Oncorhynchus kisutch*) smolts. *J. Fish. Res. Bd Can.* **37**, 765–769.

Stevens, E. D. (1972). Change in body weight caused by handling and exercise in fish. *J. Fish. Res. Bd Can.* **29**, 202–203.

Strange, R. J. (1980). Acclimation temperature influences cortisol and glucose concentrations in stressed channel catfish. *Trans. Am. Fish. Soc.* **109**, 298–303.

Strange, R. J. and Schreck, C. B. (1978). Anesthetic and handling stress on survival and cortisol concentration in yearling chinook salmon (*Oncorhynchus tshawytscha*). *J. Fish. Res. Bd Can.* **35**, 345–349.

Strange, R. J. and Schreck, C. B. (1980). Seawater and confinement alters survival and cortisol concentration in juvenile chinook salmon. *Copeia* **1980**, 351–353.

Strange, R. J., Schreck, C. B. and Golden, J. T. (1977). Corticoid stress response to handling and temperature in salmonids. *Trans. Am. Fish. Soc.* **106**, 213–218.

Strange, R. J., Schreck, C. B. and Ewing, R. D. (1978). Cortisol concentrations in confined juvenile chinook salmon (*Oncorhynchus tshawytscha*). *Trans. Am. Fish. Soc.* **107**, 812–819.

Suzumoto, B. K., Schreck, C. B. and McIntyre, J. D. (1977). Relative resistance of three transferrin genotypes of coho salmon (*Oncorhynchus kisutch*) and their hematological responses to bacterial kidney disease. *J. Fish. Res. Bd Can.* **34**, 1–8.

Thines, G. and Heuts, B. (1968). The effect of submissive experiences on dominance and aggressive behavior of *Xiphophorus* (Pisces, Poeciliidae). *Z. Tierpsychol.* **25**, 139–154.

Tsuyuki, H. and Williscroft, S. N. (1977). Swimming stamina differences between genotypically distinct forms of rainbow (*Salmo gairdneri*) and steelhead trout. *J. Fish. Res. Bd Can.* **34**, 996–1003.

Ulanowicz, R. E. (1978). Modeling environmental stress. In *Energy and Environmental Stress in Aquatic Systems* (J. H. Thorp and J. W. Gibbons, eds). pp. 1–18. Springfield, Virginia: Technical Information Center, U.S. Department of Energy.

Umminger, B. L. and Gist, D. H. (1973). Effects of thermal acclimation on physiological responses to handling stress, cortisol and aldosterone injections in the goldfish, *Carassius auratus*. *Comp. Biochem. Physiol.* **44A**, 967–977.

Van Overbeeke, A. P. and McBride, J. R. (1967). The pituitary gland of the sockeye (*Oncorhynchus nerka*) during sexual maturation and spawning. *J. Fish. Res. Bd Can.* **24**, 1791–1810.

Warren, C. E., Allen, M. and Haefner, J. W. (1979). Conceptual framework and the philosophical foundations of general living systems theory. *Behav. Sci.* **24**, 296–310.

Wedemeyer, G. (1972). Some physiological consequences of handling stress in the juvenile coho salmon (*Oncorhynchus kisutch*) and steelhead trout (*Salmo gairdneri*). *J. Fish. Res. Bd Can.* **29**, 1780–1783.

Wedemeyer, G. (1976). Physiological response of juvenile coho salmon (*Oncorhynchus kisutch*) and rainbow trout (*Salmo gairdneri*) to handling and crowding stress in intensive fish culture. *J. Fish. Res. Bd Can.* **33**, 2699–2702.

Wedemeyer, G. (1980). Environmental stress as a cause of fish disease. Aquamed, Tavolek, Redmond, Washington. 3pp.

Wedemeyer, G. and Wood, J. (1974). Stress as a predisposing factor in fish diseases. *U.S. Fish Wildlife Serv., Fish Dis. Leafl.* **38**, 8pp.

Wendt, C. A. G. and Saunders, R. L. (1973). Changes in carbohydrate metabolism in young Atlantic salmon in response to various forms of stress. *Spec. Publs. int. Atlant. Salm. Found.* **4**, 1, 55–83.

Westers, H. (1970). Carrying capacity of salmonid hatcheries. *Progve Fish Cult.* **22**, 43–46.

Williams, R. J. (1963). *Biochemical Individuality.* New York: John Wiley and Sons, Inc. 214pp.

Wilson, E. O. (1975). *Sociobiology: The New Synthesis.* Cambridge, Massachusetts: The Belknap Press of Harvard University Press. 697pp.

Winter, G. W., Schreck, C. B. and McIntyre, J. D. (1980). Resistance of different stocks and transferrin genotypes of coho salmon, *Oncorhynchus kisutch*, and steelhead trout, *Salmo gairdneri*, to bacterial kidney disease and vibriosis. *Fishery Bull. Fish Wildl. Serv. U.S.* **77**, 795–802.

Wydoski, R. S. and Wedemeyer, G. A. (1976). Problems associated with the physiological monitoring of fish populations using field sampling techniques. *Proc. West. Assoc. State Game Fish Comm.* **56**, 24.

Wydoski, R. S., Wedemeyer, G. A. and Nelson, N. C. (1976). Physiological response to hooking stress in hatchery and wild rainbow trout (*Salmo gairdneri*). *Trans. Am. Fish. Soc.* **105**, 601–606.

Yamagishi, H. (1962). Growth relation in some small experimental populations of rainbow trout fry, *Salmo gairdneri* Richardson, with special reference to social relations among individuals. *Jpn. J. Ecol.* **12**, 43–53.

14. A Brief Summing Up

A. S. GRIMM

Department of Zoology, University College of North Wales, Bangor, Wales

All the delegates at the FSBI International Symposium on "Stress in Fish" participated in an impressively wholehearted and friendly manner. I believe that, in spite of our diverse backgrounds, there was a willingness to consider the other man's point of view in our common concern for a better understanding of stress in fish.

In a collection of papers with such a broad canvas stretching from pesticide pollution to pituitary peptides to pathology, one should resist the temptation to select highlights. However it is difficult to refrain from singling out Dr Schreck's conceptual model of stress impinging on and reducing the life-time performance capacity of fish. If the collection needed a unifying concept then I believe his model provides one in which ecologist, physiologist, fisheries scientist and farmer can find common ground. The success of the model will be measured by the research which it stimulates and I look forward eagerly to the development of the model and its application to lifetime, seasonal and diurnal performance.

The need for reliable quantitative measurements of performance and of the stress-induced reduction in performance was emphasized by Drs Wedemeyer and McLeay. They discussed the value of a variety of "stress bioassays" and of predictive tests for assessing the impact of environmental and man-made stressors on the performance of salmonids in particular. While many of the current bioassays deal with single stressors Dr Wedemeyer emphasized the need to examine the additive or synergistic effects of multiple agents on fish performance. In the natural environment stressors seldom act singly, nor do fish live singly—a point made by Dr Elliott who drew attention to the lack of information on the effects of thermal stresses on populations of fish and on communities.

As a physiologist I am conscious of several lacunae in our understanding of the primary and secondary responses to stressors. Firstly a point of endocrine methodology. The measurement of catecholamines in biological fluids is still not something undertaken lightly. What is needed is a quantum jump in the reliability, specificity and simplicity of assay techniques, such as radio-immunoassay has given to peptide and steroid endocrinologists. Secondly, much more work is needed on the mechanism of action of corticosteroids in conditions of stress. Undoubtedly cortisol has a pronounced catabolic action but how often is this action demonstrable at physiological levels of hormone rather than at pharmacological doses? Perhaps more emphasis should be given to the permissive role of cortisol in which the hormone, rather than exerting any independent action, is necessary for the maintenance of tissue responsiveness to other hormonal and neural agents. Thirdly, there is a great lack of knowledge of the neural pathways from the stage of stressor detection by receptors to the stage of primary endocrine response by pituitary–interrenal and sympathetic systems.

For many years the hormones of these systems have occupied a pre-eminent position in endocrine studies on stress. No doubt this is partly historical and due to the fact that it was in the adrenals that Selye found the earliest detectable changes following trauma. The time is right for a de-emphasizing of the role of the traditional pituitary–interrenal and adrenomedullary systems. Other endocrine systems deserve closer attention. In this respect it is encouraging to see Dr Simpson's work on plaice thyroid and also recent unpublished work by Jenkins and Dodd which suggests that the stress response of marine fish to trawl capture may involve a massive stimulation of the anterior pituitary and the release of many if not all adenohypophyseal hormones.

What of the future? Dr Donaldson referred to the family of adreno-corticotrophic-related peptides in the adenohypophysis. I can envisage a most exciting area of research on the behaviour and function of the endor-phins, encephalins and other peptides derived from the adenohypophyseal megapeptide. But a word of caution. The administration of non-piscine hormones to intact fish might produce a plethora of effects which would be difficult to interpret and of limited value. It is essential that such work be done with piscine material which has been rigorously purified and adminis-tered to simple systems. Only then will it be possible to determine the role of these natural opiates and stimulants on the state of psychological awareness which is such a fundamental requirement for the stress response. In the second symposium on stress in fish I look forward to a paper on "The use of natural fish opiates for the suppression of the stress response to handling and transport".

Abstracts of the Oral Papers Presented at the F.S.B.I. International Symposium, "Stress in Fish", University of East Anglia, Norwich, September 9–12, 1980

Daily Variations in Plasma Cortisol Levels of Individual, Female Rainbow Trout (*Salmo gairdneri* Richardson): Differences Between Normal and Non-adapted Fish

C. Bry

Laboratoire de Physiologie des Poissons, I.N.R.A., 78350 Jouy en Josas, France

The daily fluctuations in plasma cortisol levels, measured by a protein-binding assay with a chromatographic step, were examined in individual, female rainbow trout a few months after ovulation. Each fish was transferred into an individual tank and acclimated to environmental conditions of 14 h light–10 h dark, 13°C and a fixed feeding time. Dorsal aorta catheterization was performed, and six blood samples were taken from each trout at 28 h intervals between day 5 and day 11 after the operation. In some fish, a second series of six samples was taken under the same conditions between day 15 and day 21. Most normal, steadily feeding individuals exhibited significant variations in plasma cortisol concentrations: peaks averaged 20–40 ng ml^{-1} and occurred shortly after feeding as well as at the end of the light period or at night. Baseline levels were less than 10 g ml^{-1}. When two sampling series were carried out, the peak associated with feeding recurred, suggesting a daily periodicity. Clear-cut differences with the above patterns were found in non-adapted animals, i.e. in fish distressed by the presence of the cannula or by a change of environment shortly before cannulation: cortisol fluctuated, but in an erratic manner, showing no indication of periodicity. Peak concentrations were very high $(80-150 \text{ ng ml}^{-1})$ and minimum levels were seldom less than 20 ng ml^{-1}. It is concluded that plasma cortisol may vary widely in both normal and disturbed rainbow trout. Rhythmic fluctuations, however, can only be found in well-adapted fish and the periodicity of medium-term variations in plasma cortisol might be an in-depth indicator for adaptation in trout.

Effects of Exercise at Different Swimming Speeds on Blood Cortisol Levels in the Rainbow Trout, *Salmo gairdneri* Richardson

P. R. Zelnik and G. Goldspink

Dept. Zoology, University of Hull, Hull, England

Preliminary experiments were performed to determine the diurnal variation in cortisol, using trout which had been cannulated three days previously. These results indicated that cortisol levels were relatively stable between 10.00 h and 18.00 h, thus permitting experimentation during this period without diurnal fluctuations masking the cortisol response. Uncannulated fish were exercised in a flume for 2 h at 1, 2·6 and 5 bl s^{-1} and plasma samples taken from groups of 5 animals at 15, 30, 60 and 120 min after the start of exercise and at $1\frac{1}{2}$ h, 12 h and 24 h after the exercise ceased. The cortisol levels in all cases were elevated after 15 min, but the magnitude of the elevation increased with swimming speed. At 1 bl s^{-1} the cortisol levels increased from 76·4 ($\pm$20·4) to 129·2 ($\pm$20·4) ng ml^{-1} [Mean ($\pm$S.D.)]. At 2·6 bl s^{-1} the increase was from 72·4 ($\pm$17·1) to 254·4 ($\pm$34·4) ng ml^{-1} and at 5 bl s^{-1} the increase was from 69·5 ($\pm$27·5) to 326·4 ($\pm$39·0) ng ml^{-1}.

The cortisol levels were relatively stable over the exercise period and all groups recovered to baseline levels after 24 h, though the sample taken 12 h after the termination of exercise was elevated due to regular nocturnal increases in cortisol levels. There were no significant changes in blood sugar levels during and after exercise at 1 and 3·2 bl sec^{-1}.

Physiological Effects of Sublethal Acid Exposure in the Brown Trout, *Salmo trutta* L.

P. G. McWilliams

Dept. Biological Sciences, University of Lancaster, Lancaster, Lancashire, England

Low pH is known to markedly affect several important physiological processes in freshwater teleosts, including O_2 transport by the blood and salt regulation, so that survival of fish in acid waters is invariably reduced. Transfer to low pH media retards the rate of sodium uptake but accelerates the rate of sodium loss. An hypothesis is proposed, based on measurements on the transepithelial potential across the gills, which largely accounts for the increased loss of sodium from fish in acid conditions and calcium is shown to be an important factor with respect to changes in the permeability of the gill to certain ions. Acclimation of brown trout to sublethal acid water is demonstrated and discussed in terms of changes in sodium fluxes and gill permeability.

Some Diseases of Fingerling Rainbow Trout, *Salmo gairdneri* Richardson, and their Relation to Water Quality

D. Bucke

MAFF, Directorate of Fisheries Research, Fish Diseases Laboratory, Weymouth, Dorset, England

Histopathological changes in 0+ rainbow trout have been investigated. These changes can often be related to some toxic or irritant action on the fish resulting from variables in water quality. The levels of infectious diseases which may occur as the fish grow on can invariably be related to the condition of the water in which they are raised. Examples of these diseases are bacterial gill disease, infectious pancreatic necrosis, proliferative kidney disease and bacterial kidney disease. Attempts at inducing these diseases within the laboratory have been made and the histopathology is compared to that of the naturally occurring diseases.

Ontogenetic Development of the Immune System in Fish

M. J. Manning, M. Ruglys, M. F. Grace and J. W. Botham

Dept. Zoology, University of Hull, Hull, England

The paper described the histogenesis of the lymphoid organs and the functional differentiation of the immune system in rainbow trout *Salmo gairdneri* Richardson (at 14°C) and in mirror carp *Cyprinus carpio* L. (at 22°C). In these fish, as in all vertebrates, the thymus is the first lymphoid organ to develop. It appears in the rainbow trout at 5 days pre-hatch and in the carp at day 2 post-hatch. The kidney becomes lymphocytic at day 5 post-hatch in the trout and at day 6–8 post-hatch in the carp. The thymus and kidney are the major lymphoid organs in young carp and trout, the spleen being slow to develop in these fish. Alloimmune reactivity was demonstrable at day 26 in trout and day 16 in carp. Overcrowding and/or underfeeding influenced the timing, but not the sequence, of histogenesis. Cortisol phosphate failed to affect the development of the lymphoid organs of the trout when applied at doses of 1 mg l^{-1} to the tankwater during the first months of histogenesis.

The fish (particularly the young carp) are free-living and vulnerable to encounters with potential pathogens in their environment at a stage when their lymphoid organs are still very immature. Possibly non-specific mechanisms such as phagocytosis form a first line of defence since uptake of carbon by macrophages can be demonstrated before the differentiation of the immune system. The paper discussed problems associated with immunizing fish against disease, particularly with reference to questions of immunity versus tolerance in situations where young fish are exposed to antigen at an early stage in development.

Heavy Metals and the Humoral Immune Response of Freshwater Teleosts

J. G. O'Neill

Department of Life Sciences, Trent Polytechnic, Nottingham, England

The teleosts *Salmo trutta* and *Cyprinus carpio* were exposed to levels of waterborne heavy metals, $0.75 \text{ mg Ni l}^{-1}$, $1.06 \text{ mg Zn l}^{-1}$, $0.29 \text{ mg Cu l}^{-1}$ and $1.01 \text{ mg Cr l}^{-1}$. These mean levels were estimated to be non-toxic, at pH 7·8, water hardness $207 \text{ mg l}^{-1} \text{ CaCO}_3$ and water temperature 15·5°C, over the 38 weeks exposure period required to examine the primary and secondary immune responses of the fish. The humoral neutralization antibody response to single intraperitoneal inoculations of *MS2* bacteriophage, in Freund's incomplete adjuvant, was followed using a 50% bacteriophage neutralization titre (SD_{50}) method.

A suppression of the immune response was observed in fish exposed to the four heavy metals. The humoral antibody response was suppressed totally only in *C. carpio* exposed to Cu or Cr, and these fish subsequently died of heavy metal toxicosis. A suppression of the primary blood clearance of live *MS2* bacteriophage was observed in *S. trutta* exposed to the heavy metals, with the exception of the Zn-exposed fish, and in *C. carpio* exposed to Cu. Following the suppressed primary responses the Ni-exposed *S. trutta* and Zn-exposed *C. carpio* exhibited elevated antibody titres in response to the second *MS2* bacteriophage challenge.

Many modes of heavy metal action have been implicated in immune suppression. Heavy metals are known to block the active sites of antibody molecules and disturb the metabolism, ionic balance and cellular division of immunocompetent cells. Although, after continued exposure to Ni and Zn, an adjuvant-like action on these mechanisms was also implicated. A cortico-steroid-mediated stress reaction may have been responsible for the suppression of *MS2* bacteriophage blood clearance.

Biotelemetry and Assessment of Environmental Stress In Fish

I. G. Priede

Department of Zoology, University of Aberdeen, Tillydrone Avenue, Aberdeen, Scotland

A fish may be thought to have been designed by natural selection to live in a certain optimum environment. Any change in the environment in terms of temperature, P_{O_2}, salinity etc. may be regarded as a stress applied to the animal. If the change reaches the limits of tolerance then the probability of mortality rapidly increases. The physiological response of the animal, change in heart rate, ventilation rate, blood pH etc. can be regarded as strain which also may vary within a scope of tolerance.

By means of small telemetry transmitters attached to individual fish it is now possible to continuously monitor either the external microenvironment or the internal physiology of a fish free-living in its natural habitat.

Most fish spend most of their time living well within the bounds of any tolerance limits. Relatively little time is spent near the lethal limits but small changes in this time would be reflected in large changes in the mortality rate of the population. Only with continuous monitoring such as biotelemetry allows is sufficient resolution attained on the time scale to detect such changes in the distribution of time spent at different levels of stress or strain.

Biotelemetry is necessarily confined to the measurement of electrical potentials (e.g. electrocardiograms, electromyograms) or variables which are readily converted to electrical potentials by means of suitable trans-ducers. It is therefore unlikely that direct measurement of endocrine changes as associated with the stress general adaptation syndrome will ever be possible. The interpretation of biotelemetry records in the field must be based on a thorough understanding of the fishes physiology and behaviour derived from laboratory studies.

Physiological and Ecological Assessments of the Effects of Stress in Fish and their Application to Pesticide Pollution Monitoring

P. Fox, P. Matthiessen and R. Douthwaite

COPR, 56, Grays Inn Road, London, England

When assessing the long term dangers of environmental pollutants, physiological parameters which act as indicators of stress may have predictive value if they can be related to factors that influence survival. This paper outlines techniques used in an integrated investigation in which physiological stress and ecological abnormalities were monitored simultaneously in an attempt to establish links between the two.

As a result of measures to control tsetse fly in the Okavango Delta in Botswana, fish in Okavango waters are frequently subjected to sublethal concentrations of the insecticide endosulfan. Physiological studies indicated that there were changes in haematological parameters and histopathological defects in the brain and liver. Ecological studies showed that these changes accompanied behavioural disturbances which impaired reproduction and caused fish to become more vulnerable to predation by fish-eating birds.

Appropriate techniques were developed for monitoring these parameters in remote and difficult tropical conditions and these are discussed in the light of practical problems.

Douthwaite, R. J., Fox, P. J., Matthiesen, P. and Russell-Smith, A. (1980). *Endosulfan Monitoring Project: Final Report to the Botswana Government*, Overseas Development Administration, mimeo. report (available from COPR, London).
Matthiessen, P. (1981). Haematological changes in fish following aerial spraying with endosulfan insecticide for tsetse fly control in Botswana. *J. Fish Biol.* **18**, 461–469.
Matthiessen, P. and Roberts, R. J. (1981). Histopathological changes in the liver and brain of fish exposed to endosulfan insecticide during tsetse fly control operations in Botswana. *J. Fish Dis.* (in press).

Effects of Dissolved Zinc on the Stickleback *Gasterosteus aculeatus* L.

A. E. Brafield and C. Wilshaw

Queen Elizabeth College, University of London, Campden Hill Road, London, England

Toxicity trials indicate a 48-h LC50 of about 12 mg Zn^{2+} l^{-1} and a threshold LC50 of about 7 mg Zn^{2+} l^{-1} in hard water (total hardness, as $CaCO_3$, 280 mg l^{-1}). Reducing the hardness of the water increases the susceptibility of the fish to dissolved zinc (the 48-h LC50 in water of 50 mg $CaCO_3$ l^{-1} is about $7 \, \text{mg} \, Zn^{2+} \, l^{-1}$, for example) but prior exposure to low zinc levels decreases susceptibility.

Fish have been exposed to radioactive zinc and the activity in subcellular fractions of the gills measured. Those containing nuclei (and cell debris) showed higher activity than the microsomal ones. The mitochondrial fractions gave very low radioactive counts.

Electron-dense granules have been found in the gill filaments and gill arches of both normal and zinc-exposed fish, sometimes within cells but more often in extracellular tracts in the filaments. Electron probe X-ray micro-analysis shows zinc to occur in these granules, but granules in control tissue invariably contain less than those from fish previously exposed to zinc.

Exposure of fish to stable and radioactive zinc in different salinities showed the lowest uptake of zinc by all organs to be in water of similar osmotic concentration to that of the blood of the fish. The gills and kidneys accumulated more zinc than the liver, gonads and carcase, but less than the gut.

Interference of the Organochlorine o,p'DDD With Interrenal Function and Cortisol Metabolism in *Sarotherodon aureus*

Z. Ilan and Z. Yaron

Dept. Zoology, George S. Wise Faculty of Life Sciences, Tel Aviv University, Tel Aviv, Israel

The combined stress of netting, handling and bleeding in *S. aureus* is followed by a twofold increase, within 60 min, in the level of circulating cortisol as compared with that of resting fish, undisturbed for 4 h. The level of cortisol in resting fish after treatment with o,p'DDD ($50 \, \text{mg} \, \text{kg}^{-1}$) was higher than that measured in the same fish before treatment ($155 \cdot 8 \pm 12 \cdot 7$ vs $86 \cdot 9 \pm 11 \, \text{ng ml}^{-1}$; $n = 16$). The stress of handling and bleeding did not induce, however, any increase in the cortisol level in the treated fish ($147 \cdot 2 \pm 12 \cdot 2 \, \text{ng ml}^{-1}$; $n = 16$). The absence of any increase in cortisol level in response to stress lasted more than 4 months after a single treatment with o,p'DDD.

The level of cortisol in the plasma reflects an equilibrium between the input (cortisol secretion rate) and the output (cortisol metabolism). Therefore, the effects of the organochlorine on cortisol in *S. aureus* was investigated directly at the input and output sites. o,p'DDD was found to suppress the response of the isolated interrenal tissue to ACTH in superfusion. This suppression was found to result from interference of the organochlorine with the generation of cyclic AMP in the interrenal cells (Ilan and Yaron, 1980. *J. Endocrinol.* **86**, 269–277).

In the present study the metabolic clearance rate of cortisol was estimated from the total radioactivity of plasma samples taken at intervals after an intracardiac injection of ^{3}H-cortisol. The half-life of the steroid in the circulation of o,p'DDD-treated fish was about four times longer than that of control fish ($t\frac{1}{2} = 216$ and 58 min, respectively). The hepatic metabolism of cortisol was studied directly by incubations of liver slices with ^{3}H-cortisol. The disappearance of the labelled cortisol from the medium was considerably slower in incubations of liver from o,p'DDD-treated fish; $t\frac{1}{2} = 155$ min, as compared with $t\frac{1}{2} = 85$ min in the controls.

The high resting level of cortisol in plasma of fish treated with o,p'DDD is attributed to the retarded metabolism of the steroid by the liver. The lack of increased cortisol level in treated fish stressed by handling and bleeding is attributed to the unresponsiveness of the interrenal tissue to endogenous ACTH.

The Effects of Pollutants on Steroid Hormone Metabolism in Fish

H. C. Freeman, G. B. Sangalang and J. F. Uthe

Government of Canada Fisheries and Oceans, P.O. Box 550, Halifax, Nova Scotia, Canada

It is suggested that blood cortisol levels, by themselves, are poor indicators of stress in fish. A determination of the capacities of the interrenals and gonads in fish to biosynthesize steroid hormones *in vitro* under the stress of pollutants (administered *in vivo* or *in vitro*) indicate the potential of the pollutant to affect the overall physiology of the fish. Examples are given of the *in vitro* effects of cadmium and PCB (Aroclor 1254) on steroid hormone metabolism and reproduction in the common brook trout (*Salvelinus fontinalis* (Mitchill)) and the effects of PCB (Aroclor 1254) on the Atlantic cod (*Gadus morhua* L.) following *in vivo* exposure.

The biosynthetic capacities of organs (interrenals and gonads) are determined after *in vitro* incubation of tissues with radioactive steroid precursors. The steroids and their metabolites are extracted with organic solvents and are separated by thin layer chromatography (TLC). Autoradiograms of steroids and metabolites are prepared from the TLC plates giving a picture of the effects of the pollutant(s) on steroidogenesis.

Chronic sublethal levels of cadmium and PCB are shown to alter steroid hormone metabolism and interfere with the reproductive process. It is thought that this method has a great potential for determining the toxicity and stress of sublethal levels of pollutants on fish.

Selected Blood Component Value Changes in Rainbow Trout (*Salmo gairdneri* Richardson) Exposed to Single Pollutants and Following Endogenous Cortisol Suppression with Betamethasone Injections

D. J. Swift

MAFF, Directorate of Fisheries Research, Fisheries Laboratory, Lowestoft, Suffolk, England

Rainbow trout were exposed to sublethal phenol or unionized ammonia concentrations or to hypoxia. Blood samples were taken after various exposure periods and the packed cell volume (PCV) value, the whole blood glucose concentration, and the plasma cortisol and chloride concentrations measured. At low pollutant concentrations there were no significant changes in the blood component values compared to those for control fish. At higher concentrations the general response to the stressors was significant increases in the PCV value and the glucose and cortisol concentrations during the first few hours of exposure, followed by a gradual return to normal values in the subsequent exposure time. The increases in glucose and cortisol were approximately proportional to the pollutant concentrations; no such correlation was found for the PCV values. No clear pattern of plasma chloride ion changes was found in any experiment. Levels of no acute effect in terms of toxic units (TU) based on the pollutants' 48 h LC50 values, were estimated for phenol as 0·3 TU and for unionized ammonia as 0·1 TU, using the plasma cortisol concentration measurements.

Betamethasone-injected fish had undetectable plasma cortisol concentrations 24 h after injection. When exposed to hypoxia or phenol these fish showed a similar pattern of changes in blood component values to that found in exposed sham-injected fish; there was no cortisol stress response in betamethasone treated fish. Suppression of rainbow trout plasma cortisol levels with betamethasone apparently has no effect on the fish's short term blood component responses to the pollutants tested.

Stress Diagnosis of Eels

G. Peters, H. Klinger and H. Delventhal

Institut für Hydrobiologie und Fischereiwissenschaft, Institut für Biochemie der Universität Hamburg, 2 Hamburg 50, Olbersweg 24, W. Germany

Under natural conditions, stress plays the role of a regulatory mechanism important for the survival of the individual and the species. In captivity, this regulatory mechanism loses its biological purpose and because the animals cannot escape, stress becomes a physiological burden. We analyzed the burden placed by stress on healthy eels, using a warm-water circulation-system. Pairs of experimental eels and controls were kept in 50 litre tanks. Fights between the members of each pair always occurred, which led to one becoming dominant within a few hours. In order to judge the burden placed on the fish, more than 20 physiological and morphological parameters were measured after 5–10 days. These values were then compared with corresponding data obtained from fish afflicted with ulcer disease.

Intraspecific aggression, in this case battles for rank, produces great stress in the subordinate animal which can lead to death within a few days in extreme situations. Social subdominance is negatively related to obtainable blood volume, spleen weight, lymphocyte count, liver glycogen content, stomach diameter, and thickness of the gastric mucosa and positively related to leucocrit, granulocyte count, concentration of glucose, lactate and cortisol in the blood, epidermal permeability, and interrenal cell diameter. Fish under stress show an increased variability in most of the stress parameters. In contrast to the stressed fishes, those with diseases show a different set of changes in the parameters mentioned above, although some of them are alike. Thus, long term stress should be diagnosed by the simultaneous appearance of numerous physiological and haematological symptoms or by the occurrence of morphological or morphometric alterations of the organs.

Some Effects of Therapeutic Treatments with Copper Sulphate and Formalin in Rainbow Trout (*Salmo gairdneri* Richardson)

R. Wootten and H. A. Williams

DAFS, Marine Laboratory, P.O. Box 101, Victoria Rd., Torry, Aberdeen, Scotland

Formalin and copper sulphate ($CuSO_4$) are commonly used in aquaculture for the treatment of ectoparasites and other diseases. Little is known of the effects of these chemicals on fish when used at therapeutic concentrations. In our experiments rainbow trout were exposed to single and repeated doses of formalin (200 p.p.m. for 1 h) and $CuSO_4$ (0·5 p.p.m. for 1 h). Changes in haematological parameters (haematocrit, haemoglobin concentration and blood glucose) and serum enzyme levels were observed.

Haematocrit and haemoglobin concentrations were raised significantly immediately after $CuSO_4$ treatment and the former was still elevated after 24 h. Haematocrit alone was elevated after formalin treatment. Blood glucose was raised after a single $CuSO_4$ treatment and remained so for at least 24 h but with formalin a significant increase was observed only after repeated treatments. Increases in the serum levels of lactate dehydrogenase

(LDH), and hydroxybutyric dehydrogenase (HBDH), glutamic oxaloacetic transaminase (GOT) and glutamic pyruvate transaminase (GPT) were observed after formalin and $CuSO_4$ treatments. Histological studies indicated that both formalin and $CuSO_4$ treatments affect liver histology. Damage is more severe after $CuSO_4$ treatment. It is suggested that increased serum enzyme activity reflects the liver damage.

The experiments suggest that both types of treatment cause stress in rainbow trout but that $CuSO_4$ is more harmful than formalin. The implications of the results obtained are briefly discussed in relation to the use of formalin and $CuSO_4$ as therapeutants.

The Influence of Hatchery Conditions on the Haemoglobin System of *Salmo salar* (L.)

H. J. Koch

Zoological Institute of the University, B-3000 Louvain, Belgium

When prevented from migrating into sea water, sea-going *Salmo salar* show unusual proportions in their multiple haemoglobin system. The haemoglobins of several hundred specimens, kindly provided by Swedish and Norwegian Authorities and Research Institutions, were studied. Analysed as carboxyhaemoglobins, they were separated by means of electrophoresis on starch gel. The electropherograms show the existence of two groups which have been called HbA and HbC. The haemoglobins were eluted from the starch gel, transformed into cyanomethaemoglobins and quantified at 542 Å.

In hatchery-reared fishes from Lule älv stock kept permanently in fresh water under the best possible conditions at the Swedish Salmon Research Institute, the HbA : HbC ratio is significantly higher (95% confidence level or better) than in animals of the same size and of the same origin after growing up in the Baltic and migrating back into the fresh water of their native river, where they were released as smolts.

The high proportion of HbA observed in artificially land-locked salmon is mainly due to the relative abundance of the A_3 component in the HbA group. It is not correlated with sex or the degree of sexual maturity.

A high proportion of HbA is also observed in fishes reared in net cages in sea water in Norway and fed on dry pellets. The reverse prevails in fishes kept in a fjord and receiving at least partially wet food. Dry food (Bergström and Koch, 1969) shifts the anodic component A_3 to a higher value in young salmon.

It seems justified to consider a high HbA proportion as a measure of a lasting stress situation caused either by crowding, dry food or both.

Damage, Disease, and Repair in Intensive Fish Culture

E. A. Needham

Home Farm, Maryculter, Aberdeen, Scotland

Damage in fish is analogous to burns in humans. When scales are lost or fins damaged there is a breach in the integument which can pose immense problems of osmotic control and microbial infection. In humans with severe burns the treatment is to maintain salt and water balance and prevent infection. Although the physical processes of repair in fish are well understood and are best described as a battleground between the renewing tissue and invading microorganisms, the physiological processes are not. At high temperatures, when fish are maturing and when fish are in a low nutritional plane, the microorganisms can win.

Abstracts of the Poster Papers Presented at the F.S.B.I. International Symposium "Stress in Fish", University of East Anglia, Norwich, September 9–12, 1980

Recent Fish Mortalities Attributable to *Prymnesium parvum* **Carter, (Chrysophyta, Haptophyceae) in the Norfolk Broads**

J. S. Wortley

Anglian Water Authority, Norfolk and Suffolk River Division, P.O. Box 50, Norwich, Norfolk, England

Prymnesium parvum Carter was first implicated in the death of fish in the Norfolk Broads in 1969 when more than 250 000 common bream (*Abramis brama* L.), pike (*Esox lucius* L.) and other species died in the River Thurne broads. Frequent, smaller fish mortalities associated with mass development of the phytoflagellate occurred subsequently and ichthyotoxin production by the alga was first identified by specific bioassay in 1974. Other unexplained fish mortalities occurring infrequently in these waters prior to 1969 are also now thought to have been caused by *P. parvum* ichthyotoxin.

The apparent increased frequency in the occurrence of *P. parvum* and associated fish mortalities have been attributed to recent nutrient enrichment of the waterways by natural enlargement of a winter gull roost. Chloride concentration of the water varies between 500–3000 mg l^{-1} and originates mostly from saline ground water entering the system via land drainage pumps. Sublethal levels of ichthyotoxin detected by bioassay allow prediction of fish mortalities although the size of the area (220 ha.) and the interests of its National and Local Nature Reserves preclude the use of algicides. Observations show that fish subjected to sublethal levels of ichthyotoxin move away from areas of high toxicity and form dense aggregations in areas where there is an inflow of toxin-free water.

In 1975, the Anglian Water Authority installed a well-point system adjacent to Hickling Broad capable of pumping 2000 m³ d⁻¹ of toxin-free ground water into a 400 m dyke leading to the broad. This fish "refuge" has been operated on three occasions. Observations show that large numbers of fish aggregate in the dyke during times of high ichthyotoxin concentration.

Most fish which escape are thought to move away from the broads into the River Thurne. Maximum mortalities occur when fish are trapped in areas offering no access to toxin-free water.

Sublethal Effects of the Insecticide Endosulfan on
Tilapia rendalli (Boulenger)

P. Matthiessen[1] and P. Fox[2]

[1] C.O.P.R., 56, Grays Inn Road, London, England
[2] C.O.P.R., College House, Wright's Lane, London, England

The investigation examined some of the effects of pesticide-induced stress at both the histological and ecological levels. These effects were observed during repeated applications of endosulfan at ultra-low volume doses for tsetse fly control in the Okavango Delta, Botswana. The applications caused a very small amount of acute mortality in fish populations, but the survivors developed abnormalities in brain histology which may have been responsible for behavioural disturbances and for the inhibition of nest-building.

A microscopical examination of brain sections of *T. rendalli* revealed meningeal and sub-ependymal oedema, encephalitis, gliosis and an extensive infiltrate of inflammatory eosinophilic cells that sometimes persisted for many months after spraying. Infra-red aerial photographs of the breeding areas of *T. rendalli* clearly revealed the circular nests from which mud and debris are cleared by the fish prior to spawning. The technique was therefore used to census such areas and this indicated significant reductions in nest density in pesticide-contaminated areas.

Effects of Treated, Municipal Waste Water on the Hepatic Metabolism of 4-Androstene-3,17-Dione in Rainbow Trout, *Salmo gairdneri* Richardson

T. Hansson

Dept. Zoophysiology, University of Göteborg, Box 250 59, Göteborg, Sweden

Many aquatic pollutants, such as chlorinated hydrocarbons and petroleum products, have the potential to interact with the cytochrome P-450-mediated drug and steroid metabolism in fish liver. It has been suggested that many environmental pollutants may interfere with the normal animal function by disturbing the hormonal system. Since it is known that municipal waste water contains a variety of potential pollutants it was considered of interest to study the effects of treated municipal waste water on the hepatic metabolism of 4-androstene-3,17-dione in rainbow trout, *Salmo gairdneri*.

Two groups of rainbow trout (wt 15–20 g) were exposed for 14 days to waste water (from the sewage treatment plant, Ryaverket, in Gothenburg) diluted with dechlorinated tap water to final concentration of 17 and 50% respectively. The control group was exposed to dechlorinated tap water. Whereas waste water treatment had no effect on the total amount of liver microsomal cytochrome P-450 the effects on the steroid metabolism were marked. Exposure of trout to 50% waste water caused a significant decrease in the 6β-hydroxylase activity whilst 17-hydroxysteroid oxidoreductase activity was significantly increased in trout exposed to 17% or 50% waste water. In addition, 50% waste water treatment significantly increased the liver somatic index values. The complexity of waste water composition, however, precludes any identification of the possible agents responsible for the observed effects.

Since there is evidence that exposure of fish to environmental contaminants, such as heavy metals, may induce a stress response in the fish resulting in elevated plasma cortisol levels, the effects of cortisol on the hepatic metabolism of androstenedione were studied. Intra-peritoneal implantation of cortisol-containing cholesterol pellets (20 mg cortisol) in juvenile rainbow trout (wt 60–80 g) mimicked the effects of waste water on the hepatic metabolism of androstenedione which indicates that the observed effects in waste water exposed fish may be due to elevated cortisol levels induced by environmental stress, e.g. chemical pollution, and/or direct effects of some agents on the liver. It is possible that stress-induced alterations in the hepatic metabolism of steroid hormones may have physiological consequences for the fish, e.g. during certain stages of the reproductive cycle.

Sublethal Physiological Effects on Fish Exposed to Effluent from a Titanium Dioxide Industry

A. Larsson[1], K.-J. Lehtinen[2] and C. Haux[3]

[1] Swedish Environment Protection Board, Brackish Water Toxicology Laboratory, Studsvik, Nyköping, Sweden
[2] Swedish Water and Air Pollution Research Institute, Studsvik, Nyköping, Sweden
[3] Dept. Zoophysiology, University of Göteborg, Box 250 59, Göteborg, Sweden

Some physiological effects of an effluent from a titanium dioxide industry, located on the southwest coast of Finland, were studied in a laboratory experiment on flounders, Platichthys flesus L. The effluent was highly acid (pH ~1) and contained iron sulphate (4%), sulphuric acid (3%) and various amounts of heavy metals, such as zinc, lead, cadmium and copper.

The experiment was performed in aquaria with a continuous flow of brackish water (salinity: 7‰). The effluent was distributed to the test aquaria by means of a peristaltic pump and the dosage maintained for 14 days. The experiment consisted of a control group, a low dose group (370 μl effluent l^{-1} brackish water), and a high dose group (685 μl l^{-1} brackish water).

A brown precipitate of effluent products was found on the gill lamellae of the exposed fish. This precipitate consisted mainly of an iron-titanium complex, but a co-precipitation of other heavy metals also occurred. The titanium dioxide industrial effluent caused dose-dependent reductions of the sodium chloride concentrations, as well as the osmolarity of the blood plasma. Furthermore, significantly enhanced levels of blood glucose and blood lactate, and a slightly decreased number of lymphocytes were found in the exposed fish.

The observed disturbances in fish exposed to the effluent are probably results of a mechanical action of the precipitate on the gill tissue and/or a disturbed gill function caused by biochemical action of heavy metals present in the precipitate. Some of the noted responses (hyperglycemia, hyperlactemia, and polycythemia) may also be attributed to a general stress syndrome caused by the exposure.

Some Toxic Effects of Lead on Fish

C. Haux[1], M.-J. Sjöbeck[1] and A. Larsson[2]

[1] Dept. Zoophysiology, University of Göteborg, Box 250 59, Göteborg, Sweden
[2] Swedish Environment Protection Board, Brackish Water Toxicology Laboratory, Studsvik, Nyköping, Sweden

This report describes some physiological effects of inorganic lead on rainbow trout, Salmo gairdneri Richardson, after 1, 4, 8 and 16 weeks of exposure to sublethal levels of lead (5, 25 and 125 $\mu g\ Pb^{2+}\ l^{-1}$) in the water, and after a subsequent recovery period for 16 weeks in lead-free water.

The lead-exposed fish showed a dose-dependent inhibition of the erythrocyte ALA-D activity. At the end of the exposure period (16 weeks), the erythrocyte ALA-D activity was inhibited by about 60% in the lowest (5 $\mu g\ l^{-1}$) and by more than 95% in the highest (125 $\mu g\ l^{-1}$) lead concentration. After 16 weeks of recovery the ALA-D activity still showed high degree of inhibition (by 44–80%). This slow recovery of the ALA-D activity makes this enzyme useful as a valuable diagnostic indicator for detecting lead exposure of fish, even several weeks after the exposure has ceased.

Despite the persistent, pronounced inhibition of ALA-D activity in the lead-exposed fish, no significant effects could be detected on the haemoglobin content, haematocrit value or red blood cell (RBC) number. Thus, the consequence of the observed lead-induced enzyme inhibition, in terms of disturbed erythrocyte function is still an unanswered question.

The lead exposure also caused a disturbed ion balance, indicated by slightly reduced blood plasma chloride levels. Furthermore, the carbohydrate metabolism was affected by lead. A significant and persistent hypoglycemia and an initial slight increase in blood lactate were found after lead exposure. The hypoglycemic response might be a result of lead-induced morphological and functional changes in renal tubular cells. Such a renal effect is common in lead-exposed mammals and is accompanied by a glucosuria.

During the recovery period, a few individuals, previously exposed to the highest lead concentration, showed black tails and spinal deformities.

Effects of Cadmium on Carbohydrate Metabolism in Fish

A. Larsson[1] and C. Haux[2]

[1] Swedish Environment Protection Board, Brackish Water Toxicology Laboratory, Studsvik, Nyköping, Sweden
[2] Dept. Zoophysiology, University of Göteborg, Box 250 59, Göteborg, Sweden

The influence of cadmium on carbohydrate metabolism was studied in the flounder, (Platichthys flesus L.), and in the rainbow trout, (Salmo gairdneri Richardson). The fish were exposed to sublethal levels of cadmium (25 and 250 $\mu g\ Cd^{2+}\ l^{-1}$) for 80 days in a continuous flow experiment in brackish water (salinity 7‰).

Both test concentrations of cadmium caused significantly increased blood glucose levels. This hyperglycemia was more pronounced in the rainbow trout (increased by 20 and 122% respectively) than in the flounder (increased by 23 and 71% respectively). The blood lactate was unaffected in the flounder, but showed a 4-fold increase in the rainbow trout exposed to the high cadmium concentration.

A species difference was also noted in the effects on the glycogen reserves in the liver. Thus, in the rainbow trout exposed to the high cadmium concentration, the liver glycogen content was reduced by 35%, whereas in the flounder in the same test concentration liver glycogen was elevated by 80%. In muscle tissue, the glycogen content was reduced in both fish species, the reduction being more pronounced in the rainbow trout.

The strong hyperglycemic response as well as the decrease in glycogen reserves in muscle tissue suggest a reduced insulin secretion in cadmium-exposed fish. This assumption is in line with other reports showing that cadmium inhibits the insulin production in the pancreatic islets. An involvement of other hormones, e.g. catecholamines and corticosteroids, in the cadmium-induced effects on the carbohydrate metabolism is also probable. One possible explanation for the more pronounced response to cadmium in rainbow trout may be a higher metabolic activity in this species.

The Effects of Copper on Osmotic and Ionic Regulation by the Gills of the Flounder, *Platichthys flesus* L.

R. M. Stagg and T. J. Shuttleworth

Dept. Biological Sciences, University of Exeter, Hatherly Laboratories, Prince of Wales Rd., Exeter, England

The effect of copper (Cu^{2+}) on osmotic and ionic regulation in the flounder has been studied using both *in vivo* and *in vitro* techniques on seawater- and freshwater-adapted fish. Fish maintained in "polluted aquaria" containing 0.01 mg l^{-1} Cu^{2+} in fresh water and 0.167 mg l^{-1} Cu^{2+} in sea water showed changes in plasma sodium, chloride and potassium concentrations suggestive of induced ionic imbalance. Alterations to plasma electrolyte status could be caused by a variety of factors affecting different target organs. Effects on the gills using a variety of experimental approaches were studied.

Potential measurements were carried out on isolated, perfused gills bathed inside and outside with an identical saline to determine the activity of the electrogenic ionic pump. A reduction of the potential with copper in the perfusate at 10 μM l^{-1} suggests that ion pumps are directly affected by the metal. Na-K-ATPase has been widely implicated in ionic and osmo-regulatory mechanisms. Alterations to Na-K-ATPase activity measured in control fish and in fish kept in "polluted aquaria" suggest that this enzyme is affected by copper at low concentrations. *In vitro* application of copper to gill homogenates caused a marked reduction in Na-K-ATPase activity. The

binding of ^{3}H ouabain (a specific inhibitor of Na-K-ATPase) was determined in control and copper-treated fish, and the results support the data
obtained from ATPase measurements. Making certain assumptions
concerning the nature of the gill epithelium and the potential measured
across the gills in the whole fish, the relative permeabilities of sodium and
chloride can be measured using the Goldman equation. Results indicate that
there is little difference in the relative permeability of the two ions in control
and copper-treated fish. It is suggested that copper has a specific, inhibitory
action on a Na-K-ATPase-mediated pump in the gills of the flounder and
that this effect may reach significant levels at low ambient concentrations of
the metal.

Surface Permeability in Fish: Effects of External Calcium and Toxicant Action

P. Gregory and N. A. A. Macfarlane

Dept. Life Sciences, Trent Polytechnic, Burton St., Nottingham, England

Water quality variations may modify the toxicity of pollutants to fish. For
example, heavy metals are generally less toxic in hard than in soft waters.
Large surface area and high permeability make the fish gill a major site for
the entry and toxic effects of pollutants. Branchial permeability to water and
ions is strongly influenced by external $[Ca^{2+}]$. Hence an attempt has been
made to link Ca^{2+} mediated alterations in branchial permeability to changes
in uptake of copper.

Branchial water permeability in mirror carp, *Cyprinus carpio*, was
measured as tritiated water turnover in artificial fresh waters (15°C, pH 6·1)
in relation to varied external $[Ca^{2+}]$. Turnover rates in fish adapted to
0·1 mM and 10 mM external $[Ca^{2+}]$ were $60·5 \pm 2·6$ ($n = 20$) and $36·0 \pm 1·4\%$ h^{-1} ($n = 20$) respectively ($p < 0·001$). The effect of Ca^{2+} in reducing
water permeability, which is also observed in other species, may be due to
the ion's role in cell membrane stabilization.

Groups of fish ($n = 5$) in low (0·1 mM) and high (5 mM) calcium were
exposed to Cu^{2+} (0, 0·01 and 0·1 mg l^{-1}) for 14 days under static test
conditions. Plasma and tissue samples (gill, gut, skin, skeletal muscle and
residue) were analysed for Cu^{2+} by atomic absorption spectrophotometry.

Plasma $[Na^+]$ and $[Cl^-]$ were depressed ($p < 0·01$) and plasma $[Cu^{2+}]$
elevated ($p < 0·05$) at the high toxicant concentration, but varied external
$[Ca^{2+}]$ was without effect. Highest tissue Cu^{2+} levels were found in the gut
(20 and 70 μg g^{-1} dry weight for 0 and 0·1 mg l^{-1} Cu^{2+} respectively, $p < 0·001$). Levels in the range 10–20 μg g^{-1} dry weight were found in gill and

skin. Lowest levels (<5 μg g^{-1} dry weight) were found in skeletal muscle and the fish residue. In general, tissue copper levels were increased in fish exposed to the higher level of the toxicant but apparently, high external $[Ca^{2+}]$ did not significantly depress Cu^{2+} uptake, though the sample size was small. The protective effect of water hardness, therefore, may not be wholly explained by reduced toxicant uptake, although ideally the turnover of Cu^{2+} in the fish should be determined.

Sublethal Effects of Acid Water

D. J. A. Brown[1], R. Morris[2] and S. A. Goldthorpe[2]

[1] *C.E.G.B. Research Division, Freshwater Biology Unit, Scientific Services Centre, Ratcliffe-on-Soar, Nottingham, England*
[2] *Dept. Zoology, University of Nottingham, University Park, Nottingham, England*

A great deal of research is currently directed to the effects of acid water on fish, mainly in connection with the problem of acid rainfall draining into poorly buffered waters in Scandinavia, U.S.A. and Canada. Survival times of fish are undoubtedly related to pH over a certain range, but the precise lethal value will vary markedly depending upon various biological factors (e.g. species, size and strain), physical factors (e.g. temperature and season) and chemical factors (e.g concentrations of other ions). One of the suggested causes of death of fish in acid waters is failure to regulate their internal ion content. It might be expected that the concentration of ions in the external medium would affect the ability of the fish to ion-regulate and indeed, addition of salts to acid waters has been shown to lead to improved survival of brown trout.

Isotopic experiments (Na^{22}) have been conducted to investigate the rates of uptake and loss of sodium under a range of conditions of pH and external sodium concentration. Sodium influx rates appear to be largely independent of pH, whereas sodium loss rates differ in various pHs. In higher external sodium concentrations the efflux rates increase with decreasing pH. Sodium loss via the kidney at different pHs has also been measured. With relatively slow rates of change of pH (1 unit every 2 days) the rate of renal loss is reduced relative to the control rate at pH 7·0. Alternatively, immediate transfer from pH 7·0 to pH 5·0 or 4·0 results in a significant increase in the rate of sodium lost via the kidney. In contrast with the total loss rate described above, the renal loss of sodium appears to be independent of external sodium concentration. It is likely, therefore, that the heavy ion loss at high external sodium concentrations is via the gills. Experiments have shown that blood and muscle parameters are altered by pH and vary with season. Exposure to pH 4·0 causes a significant decrease in the sodium concentration of blood and muscle compared to values at pH 7·0, whereas haematocrit values showed a non-significant increase at pH 4·0. Blood sodium concentration and haematocrit are significantly higher, and muscle sodium concentration is significantly lower, when measured in July compared with values in January.

The effect of low pH on the heart and opercular rate of trout is also being studied, using a fish monitor developed by the Water Research Centre. Preliminary results suggest that a rapid drop in pH does not alter the heart rate, but causes an elevation of the opercular rate. A much larger increase is apparent in the "cough" rate, probably as a reaction to excessive mucous production.

The Effect of Ultraviolet Radiation on Teleost Epidermis

A. M. Bullock

S.M.B.A., Dunstaffnage Marine Research Laboratory, P.O. Box 3, Oban, Argyll, Scotland

The skin of fish, as in all vertebrates, is comprised of three distinct cellular layers—the epidermis, the dermis and the hypodermis. The dermis contains the scales and various pigment cells and provides the main structural limiting layer. External to the dermis, the epidermis is a considerably more delicate structure than that of the higher animals and is readily divisible into three layers, the cuticle, the epidermis proper and the basement membrane complex.

Experiments using plaice (*Pleuronectes platessa* L.) have demonstrated that the skin of this species is susceptible to moderate doses of short wavelength ultraviolet (UV-B) with a cumulative dose of 63 mJ cm^{-2} causing complete destruction of the epidermis, often within 48 h post-irradiation. Experiments presently underway suggest that irreversible changes in epidermal morphology may be induced at very much lower levels of irradiation.

In conjunction with the oral administration of phenothiazine, a compound used in fish culture for the eradication of intestinal parasites, irradiation with long wavelength ultraviolet (UV-A) has resulted in specific morphological changes in the skin of rainbow trout (*Salmo gairdneri* Richardson) and Atlantic salmon (*Salmo salar* L.). It is of particular interest that these changes are morphologically identical to those seen in the skin condition of salmonids known as ulcerative dermal necrosis (UDN). This costly disease has long been of interest to fishery biologists yet despite extensive research no causative agent has been found. It now seem possible that this condition may be due to a dietary photosensitizer which, in conjunction with exposure to significant levels of UV-A, culminates in this particular dermatopathy.

The Responses of the Brown Trout, *Salmo trutta* L. to Physical Handling

A. D. Pickering and T. G. Pottinger

Freshwater Biological Association, Ferry House, Far Sawrey, Nr. Ambleside, Cumbria, England

Handling is a common feature of intensive fish cultivation and an undesirable, but often unavoidable, factor in many experimental investigations. Some of the immediate effects of this type of stress, for example the pronounced elevation of plasma corticosteroids and changes in carbohydrate metabolism, are well documented. However, less attention has been given to the recovery times of such responses or to some of the slower, tissue reactions which may result from physical disturbance. The present investigation examines the time course of several such responses elicited by a single incidence of handling. The fish were removed by hand net from a fibreglass tank, confined in a small volume of water for 2 min and then returned to the tank. It is shown that the sampling of brown trout from any group of fish is sufficiently disturbing to the remaining fish to produce an elevation of blood cortisol and lactate levels. This is an important consideration in the design and statistical analysis of such experimental investigations.

Plasma cortisol levels were significantly elevated 2 h after handling ($p < 0.01$) but returned to basal levels within 8 h. Plasma lactate levels also showed a maximal elevation 2 h after the handling stress ($p < 0.001$) but in this case a fully stable recovery was not reached until 72 h post-handling. A peak of blood glucose occurred after 4 h ($p < 0.005$) followed by a significant depression after 30 h ($p < 0.005$) and a recovery to normal levels by 72 h.

Differential blood cell counts revealed a significant ($p < 0.05$) reduction in the concentration of circulating leucocytes at both 8 h and 30 h post-handling. This reduction in white blood cells, which returned to normal levels by 72 h, appeared to be caused by a decrease in the concentration of lymphocytes. The concentration of superficial, epidermal goblet cells increased significantly ($p < 0.01$) 1 week after the handling stress and returned to control levels after 2 weeks.

These results illustrate the dangers inherent in the use of single indices when monitoring the stress responses of teleost fish. In the present investigation, the recovery times varied between 8 h for plasma cortisol and approximately 2 weeks for epidermal mucous cells.

Aspects of Stress in Mackerel

S. J. Lockwood[1], D. J. Swift[1], M. G. Pawson[1], D. R. Eaton[1], R. G. Boutilier[2] and P. Aughton[2]

[1] *M.A.F.F., Directorate of Fisheries Research, Fisheries Laboratory, Lowestoft, Suffolk, England*
[2] *School of Biological Sciences, University of East Anglia, Norwich, England*

Stress induced in mackerel (*Scomber scombrus* L.) by capture and handling was investigated by field experiments off Mevagissey, Cornwall, in 1976 and 1979. This work had three parts: (i) determination of mortality rates associated with crowding and tagging, (ii) investigation of the mackerel's respiratory system at different swimming speeds and (iii) biochemical measurements on blood and muscle tissue to determine the physiological changes induced by crowding and handling.

Mackerel, caught on barbless hooks, were kept in large volume floating nets anchored in Mevagissey Bay. The mortality rates associated with different stocking densities was measured. Fish were stressed by crowding at densities of up to 1000 fish m^{-3} for 15 to 45 min followed by release into a large volume net. Twenty-four-hour mortality rates ranged from below 40% at the lowest density to 100% at the highest. Ninety-three fish were tagged with internal metal tags and were placed with 92 untagged but handled fish in an empty keep net. Seventeen tagged and four untagged fish died within the 16 days of the experiment (18·3% mortality).

The possibility that death during crowding was due to asphyxiation was examined. The opercular-buccal pump mechanism for gill irrigation was investigated in mackerel swimming at controlled rates in a flume. The results showed that mackerel can pump water over their gills in a rhythmic fashion and do not have to be moving at high speed to maintain adequate blood oxygenation and acid–base balance. This suggested that physical damage was a more likely cause of mortality than asphyxia. Crowding caused skin damage and a change in the overall body colour from green to blue. Blue fish were found to have high blood lactate, cortisol, and sodium ion concentrations but high concentrations were not statistically correlated with body colour. The mechanism of the colour change is unknown.

It was concluded: (1) crowding and "slipping" from commercial nets can result in mortality rates approaching 100%, (2) skin damage, not asphyxia, is the most probable cause of death, and (3) fish colour is not a 100% reliable indicator of subsequent survival, although avoidance of "blue" fish for tagging should increase the subsequent survival rate.

Plasma Corticosteroid Dynamics in Channel Catfish, *Ictalurus punctatus* (Rafinesque), Due to Handling and Water Quality

K. B. Davis, B. A. Simco and J. R. Tomasso

Dept. Biology, Memphis State University, Memphis, Tennessee, U.S.A.

Secretion of corticosteroid hormones is one component of the response to environmental stressors that occurs in fish. High biological loading in fish culture results in increased oxygen demand and waste product accumulation. This paper presents plasma corticosteroid hormone levels in channel catfish, *Ictalurus punctatus* (Rafinesque), under a variety of experimental conditions, including the effects of time of day, handling, fish density, acclimation temperature, increased environmental ammonia and nitrite, and decreased oxygen.

Resting plasma corticosteroid levels at 5 and 10°C were significantly higher than in fish held at 15 to 35°C. Fish confined in a net at these warmer temperatures had elevated steroid levels for up to 6 h. Recovery to resting levels was complete within 3 h after release from confinement.

Plasma steroid concentrations in fish held at 20°C were approximately 10 ng ml^{-1} and exhibited a slight diurnal change. Concentrations were unaffected by fish densities of 6, 12, 24 and 48 fish per 100 litres. Agonistic behaviour, indicated by bite marks, was more evident at the lowest density, and fish with bite marks had corticosteroid levels significantly higher than unmarked fish.

Exposure of fish to 0–5 mg l^{-1} nitrite and 0–200 mg l^{-1} total ammonia nitrogen for 24 h demonstrated increasing plasma corticosteroid concentrations to each metabolite. Water conditions that are thought to reduce the entry of these substances into the fish resulted in a suppression of the steroid response.

Plasma corticosteroid concentrations increased in response to oxygen depletion, but returned to control levels within 30 min after oxygen levels were elevated. The rapid recovery after induced elevation of plasma corticosteroid concentrations may help to explain why channel catfish readily tolerate stressful conditions frequently encountered in fish culture.

Natural Changes in Serum Cortisol in Atlantic Salmon (*Salmo salar* L.) During Parr–Smolt Transformation

P. Langhorne and T. H. Simpson

D.A.F.S., Marine Laboratory, P.O. Box 101, Victoria Rd., Aberdeen, Scotland

Serum samples were collected from wild and farmed juvenile salmon and cortisol levels measured by radio-immunoassay. Cultured salmon parr (one year old) were compared with fish undergoing parr–smolt transformation at two years of age (denoted S2's) between January and June. Fish expected to smoltify at one and three years of age (denoted S1's and S3's respectively) were also sampled; the S3 group in April and May and the S1 group in May and June. Mean cortisol levels in the parr population were low (<1 μg 100 ml^{-1}) throughout the experimental period. Cortisol titres in the S2 population began rising in April, becoming significantly higher than parr by May ($9 \cdot 8 \pm 2 \cdot 5$ μg 100 ml^{-1}), then dropped significantly to $4 \cdot 0 \pm 0 \cdot 6$ μg 100 ml^{-1} after three weeks in sea water. In early June, the S1 group had significantly higher cortisol titres ($6 \cdot 8 \pm 2 \cdot 8$ μg 100 ml^{-1}) than parr. The S3 population did not show a significant elevation of serum cortisol before transfer to sea water in mid May. Wild smolts, caught as downstream migrants in early April and held in a restricted section of a natural stream, had high serum cortisol levels in mid April ($18 \cdot 4 \pm 3 \cdot 5$ μg 100 ml^{-1}) and mid May ($12 \cdot 2 \pm 2 \cdot 7$ μg 100 ml^{-1}). The farmed smolt populations were transferred to sea water in mid May (S2's and S3's) and early July (S1's). Survival after one week in sea water was low in the S3 population ($25 \cdot 3\%$) and high in the S1 and S2 populations ($94 \cdot 4\%$ and $88 \cdot 4\%$ respectively). Fish from the S1 and S2 populations showing parr-like colouration at the last freshwater sampling (i.e. May for S3's and June for S1's) had significantly lower cortisol levels ($2 \cdot 1 \pm 0 \cdot 7$ μg 100 ml^{-1}) than fish showing smolt colouration ($9 \cdot 8 \pm 2 \cdot 1$ μg 100 ml^{-1}). Both groups were significantly different from parr sampled over the same period. All the fish sampled from the S3 population displayed parr colouration.

These data suggest that serum cortisol is elevated in fish undergoing parr–smolt transformation, but only to a large degree (>5 μg 100 ml^{-1}) in fish displaying full smolt colouration. Survival after seawater transfer was low in the population showing low, pre-transfer serum cortisol levels.

(This work was carried out during the tenure of a N.E.R.C. Research Studentship awarded to P.L.).

The Influence of Crowding Stress on the Growth Rate and Feeding of *Cyprinus carpio* L.

W. T. Jackson and A. I. Payne

Dept. Biological Sciences, Lanchester Polytechnic, Priory St., Coventry, England

Although fish grown at high density produce high yields, their growth period appears to be shortened. The factors leading to this may be social/behavioural and/or chemical in nature. In pilot work, a non-significant trend was observed relating increased ammonia concentration to decreased food intake. Subsequently, a series of investigations was carried out designed to separate other crowding effects from the effects of ammonia.

Fed fish which were kept at different densities (0.085–5.45 g l^{-1}) with low ammonia concentrations (mean 0.003 mg NH_3–N l^{-1}) had reduced growth rates (wet weight) as density increased ($r = -0.695$, $p < 0.02$). In addition, there was a trend (not significant) towards reduced food consumption with increased density. Starved fish kept at different densities (1.25–5.84 g l^{-1}) showed no significant differences in the rate of weight loss. Varying the ammonia concentrations (mean concentration 0.2–0.47 mg l^{-1}) whilst retaining similar stocking densities led to some clarification. Increased ammonia concentration led to a reduction in specific growth rate ($r = -0.7733$, $p < 0.005$) but feeding rate showed no relationship or trend with ammonia. Feeding was, however, negatively correlated with density ($r = -0.8955$, $p < 0.001$).

The levels of ammonia tested were not excessive and are representative of values likely to be encountered in pond culture. With much higher concentrations, increasing physiological damage would probably affect growth by imposition of limiting factors on metabolism. The starved fish investigation demonstrated that any effects of density on growth were likely to have been caused by either reduced appetite, reduced assimilation efficiency or reduced metabolic efficiency.

Feeding rate, which was reduced by increasing stocking density, is likely to have been the major inhibitory factor within the present series of experiments, but the inhibitory effect of ammonia on specific growth rate (but not on feeding rate) indicates that metabolic or assimilatory efficiences were also involved. Later analyses will determine the separate and combined effects of density and ammonia on conversion efficiency.

Effects of Disturbance, and Adrenergic and Cholinergic Drugs on the Heart of the Eel (*Anguilla anguilla* L.), *in vivo* and *in vitro*

C. G. M. Rowing and A. Suitters

Dept. Zoology, University College of North Wales, Bangor, Gwynedd, LL57 2UW, Wales

In an isolated, perfused, eel heart preparation, acetylcholine caused a bradycardia and finally cessation of heart beat. This effect was potentiated by the anticholinesterase agent eserine and blocked by the muscarinic antagonist atropine. Administration of the muscarinic antagonist scopolamine *in vivo* caused an increase in both heart rate and dorsal aortic blood pressure (DAP) suggesting the removal of a cholinergic inhibition. This treatment also abolished the normal instantaneous bradycardia seen as a response to disturbance *in vivo* confirming that a cholinergic axis is dominant in this response.

The effect of catecholamines on the isolated, perfused, eel heart varied depending on the drug used. The beta-adrenergic agonist isoprenaline caused an increase in both heart rate and beat amplitude as did noradrenaline. Adrenaline however caused an increase in beat amplitude but a decrease in heart rate. The alpha-adrenergic agonist phenylephrine caused a decrease in both heart rate and beat amplitude. It is suggested from the pharmacological data that there are both alpha and beta-adrenergic receptors in the heart and that there are separate receptor groups for the inotropic and chronotropic responses. *In vivo* adrenergic responses to disturbance are seen only after cholinergic blockade when the bradycardia was replaced by an instantaneous tachycardia and rise in DAP. This response could be blocked by the alpha-adrenergic antagonist yohimbine to reveal a smaller and slower rise in the DAP which occurred without any change in heart rate. These secondary responses are discussed in relation to the responses of the heart and vasculature to catecholamines.

Effects of Stress Induced by Short Term Hypoxia on Blood Pressure and Heart Rate in the Atlantic Cod, *Gadus morhua* L.

A.-L. Ungell and I. Wahlqvist

Dept. Zoophysiology, University of Göteborg, Box 250 59, Göteborg, Sweden

Stress induced by short term hypoxia, has been found to increase the amount of circulating catecholamines in the dogfish, *Scyliorhinus canicula* L., without any effects on blood pressure (Butler *et al.*, 1978). Stevens and

Randall (1967) found that increased swimming activity caused a higher blood pressure in the ventral aorta initially and a corresponding small increase in the dorsal aorta of rainbow trout. Similar effects were seen in the cod, where stress, induced by lowering the water level, was found to have marked effects on blood pressure, heart rate and plasma levels of catecholamines (Wahlqvist and Nilsson, 1980). In the present, preliminary work the effects of short term hypoxia on blood pressure were studied in free-swimming Atlantic cod.

The afferent and efferent branchial arteries of the third gill arch were cannulated for ventral and dorsal aortic blood pressure recording respectively. The animals were left overnight to recover in the experimental aquarium at 10°C and a P_{O_2} of ca 155 mmHg.

A marked increase in ventral aortic blood pressure was seen within 5 min after exposure to hypoxic water (P_{O_2} 70–75 mmHg), and a transient increase in the dorsal aortic pressure was also seen. The ventral aortic pressure remained at a high level during hypoxia, and the heart rate decreased and remained at a lower level during the same period. After 3 h, the oxygen level of the water was restored to normal, and an immediate increase in heart rate and a decrease in ventral aortic pressure was seen. Transbranchial pressure drop was larger during hypoxia in spite of the bradycardia, which could indicate an increase in branchial vascular resistance. An increased vascular resistance has been found both in isolated gill preparations (Pettersson and Johansen, 1980) and in free-swimming fish (Holeton and Randall, 1967) during hypoxia. The general increase in blood pressure is probably due to an increased sympathetic activity, including a release of catecholamines from chromaffin tissue as found in the dogfish (Butler et $al.$, 1978).

Butler, P. J., Taylor, E. W., Capra, M. F. and Davison, W. (1978). *J. comp. Physiol.* **127**, 325–330.
Holeton, G. F. and Randall, D. J. (1967). *J. exp. Biol.* **46**, 297–305.
Pettersson, K. and Johansen, K. (1980). In preparation.
Stevens, E. D. and Randall, D. J. (1967). *J. exp. Biol.* **46**, 307–315.
Wahlqvist, I. and Nilsson, S. (1980). *J. comp. Physiol.* **137**, 145–150.

Circulatory Effects of Catecholamines in the Eel, Anguilla anguilla L.

J. C. Rankin[1] and M. M. Babiker[2]

[1] *Dept. Zoology, University College of North Wales, Bangor, Gwynedd, Wales.*
[2] *Dept. Zoology, University of Khartoum, Khartoum, Sudan*

Adrenaline and noradrenaline are released into the circulation when fish are stressed. These hormones affect cardiac function and blood flow through all organs of the body. Two organs will be considered; the gill and the kidney.

In vitro perfusion experiments using isolated gill arches or whole heads show that β-adrenergic receptors mediate vasodilation in the arterio–arterial pathway (afferent to efferent branchial arteries) and that α-adrenergic receptors mediate vasoconstriction in the arterior–venous pathway (afferent branchial arteries to branchial veno–lymphatic system). *In vivo* measurement of ventral and dorsal aortic blood pressures in chronically catheterised free-swimming eels gives the following information about the nature of the catecholamine action: (1) The transbranchial pressure drop is reduced by adrenaline and noradrenaline injection, in spite of an increased cardiac output, demonstrating the vasodilatory action. (2) The attenuation of the pulse pressure wave in the dorsal aorta is greatly reduced following adrenaline or noradrenaline injection, showing that the compliance of the branchial vasculature is reduced.

Catecholamines produce vasoconstriction in the *in situ* perfused kidney of the eel. This effect is more than compensated for *in vivo* by their pre- and post-branchial pressor actions, resulting from an increased cardiac output and peripheral vasoconstriction, and they produce large diuretic responses. These compensate for the increased branchial influx of water produced by the action of the hormones on the gills of freshwater adapted eels but are quite inappropriate in the seawater-adapted eels. It is possible that in other marine teleosts, such as the cod, *Gadus morhua* L., the renal vasoconstriction predominates over the increase in dorsal aortic blood pressure and catecholamines exert antidiuretic effects (Björnsson and Rankin, unpublished observations).

Effects of Catecholamines and β-endorphin on Perfused Brown Trout Gills in the Presence and Absence of Detergent

L. Bolis[1] and J. C. Rankin[2]

[1] *Instituto di Fisiologia Generale, Universita di Messina, Messina, Italy*
[2] *Dept. Zoology, University College of North Wales, Bangor, Gwynedd, Wales*

Low concentrations of detergent affect the vasodilatory responses to catecholamines in both trout and eel gills (Bolis and Rankin, 1980; Stagg, Rankin and Bolis, 1980). Experiments were carried out on the gills of the brown trout, *Salmo trutta*, L. using the perfusion technique of Rankin and Maetz (1971). Responses were quantified by taking the maximum increase in perfusion flow produced by a high concentration (10^{-7} or 10^{-6} mol l^{-1}) of noradrenaline. In control gills this was $100 \cdot 2 \pm 7 \cdot 1\%$ (mean $\pm$ SEM). In gills of trout kept for 24 h in water containing 1 mg l^{-1} of LAS (linear alkylate sulphonate, 12C chain length) the maximum noradrenaline effect was reduced to $49\cdot4\pm3\cdot5\%$. When these gills were perfused with Ringer containing β-endorphin (10^{-6} mol l^{-1}) the maximum noradrenaline effect was only reduced to $78\cdot8\pm4\cdot7\%$. In gills of trout kept in 1 mg l^{-1} LAS for 48 h, the maximum flow increase observed with noradrenaline was $27\cdot6\pm5\cdot3\%$ in the absence of β-endorphin but was $65\cdot0\pm3\cdot8\%$ in the presence of 10^{-6} mol l^{-1} β-endorphin. Pre-treatment with endorphin therefore appeared to partly prevent the detergent-induced inhibition of the noradrenaline response.

Pre-treatment of control trout gills with 10^{-6} mol l^{-1} β-endorphin appeared to increase their sensitivity to the vasodilatory action of noradrenaline, shifting the concentration-response curve to the left by about one order of magnitude. This effect was abolished by pre-treatment with 10^{-5} mol l^{-1} naloxone. These results raise the question of whether β-endorphin is involved in the adaptation responses to stress in trout by modulating the responsiveness of the tissues to catecholamines.

Bolis, L. and Rankin, J. C. (1980). *J. Fish Biol.* **16**, 61–73.
Rankin, J. C. and Maetz, J. (1971). *J. Endocr.* **51**, 621–635.
Stagg, R. M., Rankin, J. C. and Bolis, L. (1980). *Envir. Pollut.* **24**, 31–37.

The Influence of Stress on the Microflora of the Digestive Tract in the Rainbow Trout, *Salmo gairdneri* Richardson

R. Lesel

INRA, Centre de Recherches Hydrobiologiques, Laboratoire des Microorganismes, B.P.3, Saint-Pée-sur-Nivelle, Ascain, France

In aquaculture the frequent manipulation of fish causes a wide variety of stress responses. Studies were made on the effects of handling stress on the gut microflora of rainbow trout, *Salmo gairdneri* Richardson. The levels of bacterial microflora and the transit speed of bacterial spores used as tracer were measured. Within 5 to 7 h of handling there is a decrease in the total aerobic and facultative anaerobic microflora in the three digestive compartments (stomach, pyloric caeca, intestine), whilst the speed of transit of the tracer through the whole tract is accelerated, this increase being directly linked to the stomachal transit speed. It seems, therefore, that a stress factor may alter the bacterial population which is characteristically low in comparison with that of homoiothermic vertebrates. In addition, stress may affect the development of exogeneous bacteria in the digestive tract of fish.

Fish Species Index

Subject Index

A

Acclimation temperature, 219–221
Acetaminophen, 178
Acetylcholine, 60–61,
    effect on gill circulation, 83
    effect on heart rate, 351
Acid–base balance, effect of hypoxia,
    131–135
Acid glycoprotein, in mucous cells, 175
Acid stress, 27
    osmotic and ionic regulation, 89,
    326–327, 344–345
    reproduction, 189
ACTH, see Adrenocorticotropin
Active metabolic rate, 229–231, 260
Active oxygen consumption, 124–131,
    260
Acute phase protein, 150, 159, 176,
    179
Adenosine triphosphate
    ammonia toxicity and cerebral
    concentration, 283
    in erythrocytes, 103–119
Adrenaline
    distribution space, 55
    gill circulation, 83
    gill mucification, 174–175
    half life, 55
    osmotic and ionic regulation, 82–83
    tissue concentration, 51–52
Adrenergic responses to stress, 49–75
Adrenocorticotropin, 12–27, 157, 249
    biosynthesis and structure, 20–22
    extraction and bioassay, 18–20
Aeromonas, 176, 254–255
Aeromonas hydrophila, 178, 261
Aeromonas salmonicida, 162, 255, 261

Ageing, 298
Alkalosis, 134
Allergic responses, 148
Allograft rejection, 157, 164
Aminobenzoate methane sulphonate,
    30, 92–94, 104, 299
Aminoglutethimide phosphate, 154
Ammocoete, 60
Ammonia, 251, 333, 348
    biological effects, 282–283
    effect on growth rate, 350
    effect on plasma cortisol, 31–32, 37
    equilibration in aqueous solutions,
    281–282
    excretion, 284–286
    osmotic and ionic regulation, 88–89
    primary toxic action, 283
    "safe" levels, 284–285
    sources of, 282
    toxicity, effects of salinity, oxygen and
    temperature, 286–287
Anadromous fish, 85
Anaemia, 115, 122, 251–253
Anaerobiosis, 128, 130, 142
Anaesthesia
    adrenergic response to, 56, 57, 60, 68
    erythrocyte swelling, 104
    osmotic and ionic regulation, 92–94
    plasma cortisol, 29, 30, 32, 301
Androgens, 150–151, 199, 304
Androstenedione, 339
Anoxia, 56–57, 65
Antibiotics, 34, 252
    effects on immune response, 164
Antibody, 160–164
Antifreeze, 91
Antigen, 161
Appetite, 229–231, 278